From Jesus to the Internet

From Jesus to the Internet

A History of Christianity and Media

Peter Horsfield

WILEY Blackwell

This edition first published 2015
© 2015 John Wiley & Sons Ltd

Registered Office
John Wiley & Sons Ltd, The Atrium, Southern Gate, Chichester, West Sussex, PO19 8SQ, UK

Editorial Offices
350 Main Street, Malden, MA 02148-5020, USA
9600 Garsington Road, Oxford, OX4 2DQ, UK
The Atrium, Southern Gate, Chichester, West Sussex, PO19 8SQ, UK

For details of our global editorial offices, for customer services, and for information about how to apply for permission to reuse the copyright material in this book please see our website at www.wiley.com/wiley-blackwell.

The right of Peter Horsfield to be identified as the author of this work has been asserted in accordance with the UK Copyright, Designs and Patents Act 1988.

Library of Congress Cataloging-in-Publication Data is available for this title
Hardback: 9781118447376
Paperback: 9781118447383

A catalogue record for this book is available from the British Library.

Cover image: © Eddie Gerald / Alamy

Set in 10/12 of Sabon LT Std by Aptara
Printed and bound in Malaysia by Vivar Printing Sdn Bhd

1   2015

For Noah and Audrey

Contents

Acknowledgements

A work that covers more than two decades cannot help but be indebted to many people, not just for distinctive contributions but also for helpful conversations, numerous insights, and "things I should read" gained along the way. As Tennyson has astutely noted, "I am a part of all that I have met." But there are a number of people who played key roles at key times I wish to acknowledge. Tom Boomershine kickstarted my thinking on the topic again in three days of stimulating conversation in the early 1990s. The women of Shivers gave me new insights and understanding into a side of the church and Christianity I had not fully appreciated before. John Rickard gave me a space to begin to flesh out some of the wider historical issues. I have been very fortunate to be involved in a distinctive international community of supportive scholarly colleagues working in, or building, the emerging field of media, religion, and culture. In particular, thanks to the small group of colleagues I worked with over nine years on the International Study Commission on Media Religion and Culture. A better group of colleagues one could not find, thanks to the individuals, the leadership of Adan Medrano and Stewart Hoover, and the visionary support of the Porticus Foundation in the Netherlands. When I moved to my current university position, Lauren Murray as my Head of School was very supportive of my research in what was then an unusual field for a university school of communication. Grant Roff helped immensely over a lunch one day by clarifying my audience at a key time of the writing. The three anonymous reviewers of the draft, organized by Wiley-Blackwell, provided very useful feedback that informed this final version – as did a number of friends and colleagues who graciously took the time to read the draft and provide valuable feedback and suggestions: Philip Lee, Vanessa Born, Lynn Schofield Clark, Noel Turnbull, and Marilyn Born. Thanks also to Rachael Horsfield for her work in compiling the index.

Sections of chapters 3 and 4 were used in a chapter in Knut Lundby (ed.), *Religion across media: from Early Antiquity to Late Modernity* (New York: Peter Lang, 2013).

Sections of chapter 6 were used in a chapter in Kennet Granholm, Marcus Moberg, and Sofia Sjö (eds.), *Religion, media and social change* (New York: Routledge, 2014).

Introduction

The documents and other survivals of the past are dead to us until we ask them a question, until we want to know something from them. (Benedetto Croce, 1917)

What's this book about?

Interest has grown in recent decades in how media and religion interact and are connected. This interest has been stimulated by two current phenomena: the global spread and rapid take-up of new media on the one hand, and the reemergence of religion into the public domain as a significant global and cultural force on the other. The concurrence of these two phenomena has prompted people to wonder about whether and how the two are connected.

The interactions between media and religion were studied to some extent through the twentieth century. These studies tended to use a narrow view of media as primarily instruments for carrying messages or information. They also tended to view religion primarily as what was happening in religious institutions. The primary focus therefore was on how religious leaders and institutions used media to communicate their messages.

More recent studies of media and religion have taken a different approach. Working from a more cultural perspective, they view media not as individual instruments of communication but as part of a conglomerate of technological and nontechnological social mediation by which people access and contribute to processes of making meaning in their lives.

This approach also sees religion in broader terms. Rather than focusing on religious institutions, this view sees religion as something that occurs as people work with symbolic resources provided by their culture to create meaning for their daily lives, to share experiences of awe and mystery, to explore new alternative realities, and to manage the anxieties and unfilled possibilities of life.

From Jesus to the Internet, Peter Horsfield © 2015 John Wiley & Sons, Ltd. Published 2015 by John Wiley & Sons, Ltd.

While significant work has been performed in recent years in studying media and religion from this more cultural perspective, most of the work has lacked a historical dimension as a way of relating what is happening now to what has happened in the past. As a result, a lot of thinking about media and religion sees what is happening today as a distinctly modern issue.

This book provides some of that historical perspective through a focused study of one of the world's major religions, Christianity, examining the ways in which the processes of communication and technologies of media have conditioned how Christianity has developed historically. The intent is not to provide an encyclopedic description of all the ways in which Christianity has been mediated. It is, rather, to provide a historical survey, setting a framework within which specific instances may be examined in greater detail.

Doing so requires first clarifying some perspectives.

What do we mean by Christianity?

Christianity has its origins in the activities of Jesus, a Middle Eastern Jewish peasant who emerged as a charismatic religious reformer, preacher, teacher, faith healer, and miracle worker in the turbulent eastern Roman region of Galilee and Judea around the period 27–30 CE.

Today that Jewish peasant is revered as the founder and central figure of the global religion of Christianity, an immensely diverse religion whose adherents and followers make up around a third of the current world's population. Its members include Nobel laureates and uneducated peasants, high-income urban professionals living in the richest cities of the world and poor rural workers in the poorest countries of the world, the literate and illiterate, lawmakers and lawbreakers. The name "Christian" has been applied equally to people living within the feudalism of the Dark Ages and people living in today's globalized, technological world. Being Christian has been claimed by soldiers and pacifists, dominators and dominated, leaders who have sacrificed their lives for the defenseless and leaders who have slaughtered the defenseless.

Ask Christians what Christianity is, and you will get a multitude of definitions and opinions: someone who belongs to a church; someone who believes in particular doctrines such as the Trinity or salvation; someone who participates in Christian rites; someone who is kind, forgiving, or loving in nature; someone who has particular moral standards or behaviors, such as being honest or sexually "pure"; someone who lives in a Christian country; or someone who has had a particular emotional, spiritual, or psychic experience such as being born again or speaking in tongues. How do we chart our way through such a complex forest of opinion?

In a similar way, ask followers of Christianity for a coherent picture of who Jesus was, and you will find not one single historical account but an infinite mélange of opinions, based not only on the Bible but also on impressions gained through Christmas carols, cultural festivals, hymns, prayers, children's storybooks, Sunday School lessons, sermons, theological books, popular devotional guides, statues, paintings, and the movies. While Jesus has been the inspiration for many to live self-sacrificial lives in service of others, he has also been the justification for others to commit mass murder or extensive sexual abuse of children. While he's been the motivation for many to give away their wealth and possessions and live exemplary lives of voluntary poverty, he has also been the justification for Christians to take money from the poor to pay for excessive lifestyles or build opulent buildings. In my lifetime, Jesus has been presented variously as a first-century countercultural simple-living hippie, a radical social justice iconoclast, a gentle and caring religious teacher, a spiritual healer, a champion of the poor and outcast, an avenging and punishing lord of the universe, a self-sacrificing savior of the world, and the transcendent facilitator of modern capitalist prosperity and the urban lifestyle.

As if that wasn't enough confusion, within and between each of these standpoints is immense diversity. Bitter arguments have broken out, and tens if not hundreds of thousands of Christians have been killed, in the process of Christian groups fighting with other Christian groups to have their views accepted as "the" exclusive truth about Christianity. The history of Christianity is a history of someone or some group using force and their power to draw a line on who is included in Christianity and who isn't.

This diversity of opinions and perspectives points to the fact that Christianity is far more than just a repetition or reproduction of the message of Jesus. It has been a complex and expanding mediated phenomenon, a constant creative reproduction and rhetorical reworking of Jesus to match the conditions of an ever-expanding set of constantly changing circumstances. In the process, as Marianne Sawicki has noted also of the first century, the figure of Jesus has been conscripted to say and do things that likely would have astounded the Jew from Nazareth.[1]

In the religion of Christianity, Jesus the Middle Eastern peasant has been transformed into the most powerful and fecund reservoir of media resources the world has seen: snippets of history, biographies, stories, heroes, heroines, villains, personal testimony, libraries, cultural interpretations, philosophical speculations, artifacts, ritual practices, visual imagery, sensory experiences, nations, rule books, ethical systems, architectural constructions, and traditions of organizational structure and process. That reservoir of media resources makes Christianity capable of immense adaptability. Drawing from these historical media resources gives the appearance of continuity with the past while at the same time an immense capacity for regeneration and invention. It's left to your judgment and your personal view to decide whether Jesus himself would have been happy with what has been done to him.

Because of this immense complexity in the concept of Christianity, in this study I take a deliberately broad view of what Christianity is. My working definition is:

> Christianity is those activities, practices, ideas, artifacts, groups, and institutions that identify themselves, or may be identified with, the broad historical movement associated with the figure of Jesus.

I take such a broad view for a number of reasons that are important. One is that there have been continual struggles and conflicts to reduce the existing diversity to suit the needs and reinforce the power of particular groups over others. Understanding why such conflicts occurred and the factors that influenced them is more likely to be achieved by working with as broad a view of Christianity as possible.

A second is that media have often played an important part in these conflicts. Many of the fights in Christianity have either involved different uses of media or been about whether particular media are Christian or not. These sorts of media conflicts will be more identifiable if we follow as broad a view of Christianity as possible, rather than be restricted by a narrower definition established by the winners.

What do we mean by media?

The second critical issue to address is what is meant by "media." How one thinks about media can prejudge our conclusions by forcing thinking in one direction and missing others. Two common preconceptions about media need to be discussed to undertake a historical study such as this.

One is the assumption that media are primarily modern technological forms of communication, such as radio, television, the internet, mobile phones, social media, and so on. Thinking about media in this way suggests that questions about the interaction of media and Christianity are recent questions only. From a historical perspective, however, what is happening today with "new media" is consistent with the way in which Christianity through the centuries has continually defined and redefined itself within the demands and opportunities of available cultural processes and technologies of mediation.

The second dominant preconception is that media are to be understood just as technological instruments for carrying information or messages. This modern view, commonly called the "instrumental view" of media, has a strong focus on studying how media technologies and techniques could be used to produce particular outcomes, particularly in areas like advertising and marketing, corporate communications, politics, and even evangelism. But it is too restricted a concept for understanding the interaction of personal, social, cultural, political, and technological factors that come into play when people interact with each other and with their environments to survive, progress, and make life meaningful.

The wider view being taken in this study is that social reality itself is a mediated phenomenon, a communication ecology in which individual and social exchanges take place within a social matrix that is already rich in communicative materials such as traditions, material practices, symbols, artifacts, technologies and techniques, institutional structures, and patterns of relationship. To understand media, then, one needs to look not simply at individual media technologies but also at the cultural contexts in which these have emerged and to which they contribute. This includes nontechnological and bodily aspects of communication and their cultural significance.

For that reason, this book addresses a wide variety of mediated communication: the numerous styles and uses of oral communication; written text such as scriptures, different genres of religious writing, correspondence, signage, and archival libraries; visual media such as painted images, statues, decorations, symbols, illustrations, photographs, and moving pictures; material forms of communication such as prayer beads, bread and wine, buildings, and landscapes; tactile forms of communication such as physical greetings, kissing, the use of water or smell, and the feel of artifacts; sounds such as chanting, singing, intoning, and bell ringing; as well as technologically based media such as print, television, radio, telephone, and computer-based digital technologies of communication.

To chart a course through this complexity, in this study I will draw on a number of perspectives on media to give some focus to the analysis.

1. Although all media are different, in practice they draw on and interact with each other. On the one hand, each medium has particular ways of operating, sometimes called "affordances" or "liberties of action," that give them relative advantages for enabling or doing particular things more effectively than other media. It is these affordances and their relevance to the needs of a particular society that give a medium its social power and capital. On the other hand, both historically and today, people generally live in and move quite freely around layered media environments, integrating a variety of media and communication practices as they go about their daily lives. Media can also create their own layered environments within a marketplace, with different media performing particular functions that integrate in a complementary but continually changing way with others.

2. Along with the particular uses that are made of them, the technological and social characteristics of different media can be influential in shaping wider social perceptions, practices, and values. Walter Ong[2] proposes three particular characteristics of media that can be effective in this way. One is the different physical senses that are addressed and activated by a particular medium and the consequences these have for social perception and bodily participation. A second is how a medium facilitates the storage, retrieval, and reproduction of information, which has important consequences for how cultures form thought, analyze, and build systems of meaning. The third is how a particular medium sets people in relation to each other, and the influence that has on how relationships and patterns of authority are formed. The influences exerted by these technological, social, or sensory characteristics of a medium are generally subtle and subconscious, but they can also be profound and extensive. These will be explored further throughout the book.

3. Media exist as part of a wider structure of social, economic, and political orders, and these orders influence the shape that a medium takes and the social functions it performs. This is particularly noticeable in relation to media industries. Any medium of communication generally requires a range of supporting social structures and practices in order to function. These include shared language or literacy skills appropriate to the medium, educational systems to teach those language skills, the development of technical skills to use the medium to produce and receive content, social and economic infrastructure to supply the materials necessary for the medium to work, and legal regulations and policy structures to manage it. Even a simple medium like a written letter can't be used if there are no pen, ink, and paper to write with, no way for the letter to be carried, and no people with the literacy skills to write the letter and read it when it gets there. Having the resources to access all of these requirements is a crucial factor in accessing the advantages and power that a medium brings. As will become apparent in this study, the abilities of particular Christian institutions or leaders to adapt their message or practices to available media industries and to establish their own media industries have been important factors in some of the major shifts that have taken place within Christianity since its earliest days.

4. Media are intimately connected with language, and a study of the interaction of media and Christianity cannot take place without also considering language. Because one of the only ways we can understand the world is through its representation to us in verbal or visual language, the constructs of language are important elements in the production of religious meaning. From this perspective, language is more than just an agreed, functional arrangement of grammar and vocabulary by which people talk to each other; it is a crucial arena in which struggles for power take

place over such things as whose reality is represented in language and whose isn't, how different languages construct reality differently, whose language practices are recognized as competent and authoritative and whose aren't, who has the competency and legitimacy to speak and under what circumstances and who doesn't, what hierarchies of communication and language practice and power exist and what practices reinforce those hierarchies, who has the ability to command attention and who doesn't, and in what ways particular language practices reflect and constitute the patterns of social power within the wider culture.[3] Different media may contribute to this by giving preference to particular forms and uses of language and their language groups over others.

It is apparent, then, that media need to be approached and analyzed, not just from an atomistic way that looks at individual situations of communication but also as a holistic cultural matrix that forms around patterns of mediation, including groups and traditions of practice, patterns of production and consumption, protocols of power and authority, political associations, sources of identity, hierarchies of technical competencies, shared sensory expectations, and protocols of performance, experimentation, and change.[4]

Studying Christianity through the lens of cultural practices of media opens up a number of avenues for rethinking Christianity. Rather than accepting the hegemonic or so-called orthodox view that Christianity is a relatively coherent, structured, harmonious singular phenomenon, it suggests that Christianity needs to be looked at as a diversity of different cultural groups that are continually contending with each other in the process of making sense of and living out their particular religious identity. It also opens the scope to investigate how the different ways in which Christian groups communicate have shaped their Christian identity and informed their sense of difference.

Media and the historical development of Christianity

In line with the perspectives outlined in this Introduction, in this book Christianity will be looked at not just as an institution or religion that uses media, but also as a mediated phenomenon in itself: a phenomenon that has developed and been constructed in the processes of being communicated.

The following questions will be explored: How have all the mediational practices from within and outside Christianity interacted with each other and shaped what Christianity has become? How have the different practices of mediation used within Christianity supported, subverted, or negotiated with each other? In what ways have other traditions of communication been taken up and used to form different traditions within the religion? How have the groups associated with those different traditions and cultures co-operated or competed with each other?

As this book pursues these questions, a number of emphases will become apparent:

1. Media and Christianity will be studied not as separate domains but as symbiotic cultural phenomena that inform and are integral to each other. Christianity is a mediated phenomenon; there is no aspect of Christianity that can exist except as it is being communicated. At every step of the way, how it communicates itself becomes an indistinguishable part of what Christianity is, whether that communication be through oral speech and physical performance, silence, smells, writing, physical phenomena, visual artifacts, song and dance, printing, architecture, or electronic media.
2. The meanings of Christianity are to be found not just in what is presented in official texts and by official representatives or institutions, but also in the ideas and practices of common people, whether they agree or disagree with the official versions. The extent to which these common opinions can be accessed is precarious, as most of the resources that have been preserved reflect the viewpoints of those who had power to preserve their records and destroy others. But attempting to do so is important.
3. The truths of Christianity are not unconditioned revelations or disinterested receptions from God. Christian views of reality and concepts of truth and meaning, including statements about a transcendent God, are human constructions. They commonly emerge from the desire or need to build meaning into materialistic experiences and then identify those constructed meanings as being inherent in the experience. When the element of vested power is introduced into the analysis of Christianity, it challenges claims by particular groups that they alone represent or are concerned for the integrity of the religion.
4. This book seeks to take seriously the diversity of positions, practices, and phenomena that has characterized Christianity and media through the centuries, although not all of these, of course, can be dealt with. It is only by considering the widest diversity of phenomena possible that one can get a better idea of the forces and factors that have narrowed it down to particular emphases or orthodoxies, and the part that media have played in that narrowing (or broadening) process.
5. This book questions the idea that Christianity has a single defining essence. The diversity of Christianity, and the inescapable contradictions within it, means that coming to a conclusion about a core essence can only be done by one group of Christians denying legitimacy to the sincerely held beliefs of others. As noted in this Introduction, Christianity is perhaps best understood as a repository of beliefs, practices, and media

resources accumulated through its history that living people and groups constantly draw on to remake their view of Christianity in a way that is relevant for constantly changing circumstances.

The risk in a study such as this is that it is attempting something so broad that it could founder on the discrepancies of particulars. Any study of media and Christianity is investigating two huge phenomena that in themselves encompass most of life and human experience. It is likely to be open at every page to criticism by specialists who know the specifics of particular areas more than I ever will, although if it stimulates such an exchange it would have achieved a good purpose.

Questions also may be raised about the appropriateness of applying a modern concept such as media retrospectively to historical events and phenomena that occurred when people didn't even know the term. Can judgments be made about past phenomena on the basis of perspectives that are principally relevant today? I think they can. In fact, most historical studies choose specific topics, periods, or issues to investigate, not only because they are interesting in their own historical terms but also because looking back through the lens of the present can give us insights by which to better understand our own situations.

But the study has a particular context that justifies these risks. It arises at a historical point when, at the same time that there are major changes taking place in the global structures of media, there are also major changes taking place in the global structures and practices of Christianity. This book reflects a growing view that these significant changes in Christianity today are closely connected to changes taking place in new technologies, cultures, and global structures of media. However, it takes that connection further by proposing not only that media and Christianity are connected today, but also that they have always been connected. What we are seeing today is not just a late modern phenomenon, but another instance of a restructuring of Christianity on macro and micro levels, stimulated by and related significantly to major changes in the fundamental structures of socially mediated communication.

NOTES

1 Sawicki, 1994, pp. 85–86.
2 Ong, 1967, 1982.
3 For further insights on this, see Bourdieu, 1977; Lewis, 2005.
4 Couldry proposes a practice approach to the study of media that starts "not with media texts or media institutions but from media-related practice in all its looseness and openness. It asks quite simply: *what are people* (individuals, groups, institutions) *doing in relation to media* across a whole range of situations and contexts" (Couldry, 2012, p. 37).

1

In the Beginning

Investigating who Jesus was and how Christianity began is a media phenomenon in itself. It is difficult now to distill the original figure of Jesus from the memories, recollections, accumulations, inventions, myths, and interpretations that have become part of the Christian mediation of him, even in its earliest documents.[1] For some, getting a reasonable historical picture of Jesus is either not possible, not important, or not a question. But there's value in attempting to do so, in order to get at least an approximation of what was there in the beginning, as a basis for understanding how and why it's changed and which factors influenced the changes.

What has commonly been known about the history of Jesus and the beginning of Christianity comes from copies of copies of a relatively small number of written documents reproduced in what is now called the New Testament, comprising four Gospels, the Acts of the Apostles, and a number of letters. But these texts have particular characteristics that need to be considered in building an accurate picture.

One is that they did not begin to be written or compiled until at least twenty years after Jesus had been killed and a post-Jesus movement was underway. Although significant weight is given by many scholars to the dependability of the preservation of the events of Jesus in a Christian oral tradition,[2] much had happened in those intervening decades and there is evidence that some of those later events and the ideas that came out of them were taken up and included in the writing about Jesus as if they were part of Jesus' own story.

A second is that these key documents in the New Testament are just a few of a much larger number of documents also written about the same events. This larger corpus of documents were culled over a period of several hundred years in an ideological process of selection to create an authorized version of the history (a canon) that reflected the interests of those in power at the time. Many of those other documents, which offered alternative

From Jesus to the Internet, Peter Horsfield © 2015 John Wiley & Sons, Ltd. Published 2015 by John Wiley & Sons, Ltd.

viewpoints, were destroyed in what we would now call a process of media censorship and control.

A further consideration is that these few select documents are nothing like what we would call objective or balanced historical recording. They are partisan, creative, retrospective, interpreted reconstructions of something that happened several decades earlier by a passionate social minority group with a vested interest. Borg identifies them as testimony rather than what we understand as history, and they should be read therefore for their meaning and not primarily for their factuality.[3]

A final consideration is that the texts are a specific medium – writing. Although almost all of the earliest Christians were illiterate, the perspectives we have today on who Jesus was and what he did are the views of an unrepresentative group of literate Christians who made up less than 5% of the Christian community at the time.

There has been a significant scholarly interest from the start of the twentieth century to apply modern historical critical methods to these writings to try to separate out the more historical aspects of Jesus from later inventions and accumulations, in order to locate Jesus more accurately within the social, cultural, and religious milieus of his time. Some of the findings of this research have been controversial and in many cases contradict orthodox Christian beliefs. Many are still being debated.[4] Rather than one conclusion, at best what has been reached are a number of possible options, with Jesus being portrayed variously as a peasant sage, a social revolutionary, a religious mystic, a prophet of the end time, a marginal Jew, or the true Messiah.[5]

It is beyond the scope of this work to try to resolve issues that are unresolved by highly qualified biblical scholars. However, this body of research offers valuable insights that can be useful in getting a clearer picture of what Jesus may have thought and what he was doing. As Borg notes, Jesus ceases to be a credible figure and loses his humanness if attributes properly belonging to his followers after his death are ascribed to him before his death – it is "neither good history nor good theology."[6] Since the field is still a hotly contested one, what follows is my educated reading of that recent thinking compiled to give us a framework for understanding Jesus' thought and practice, and for reconsidering the development of thought and practice that followed him and the place of media in those developments.

The social and media context

Jesus was born and spent much of his life in the ancient Roman Middle Eastern region of Galilee. Because of its position on the trade routes between Asia Minor and Egypt, for more than a thousand years, the wider area of Palestine had negotiated its religious and political identity amid constant imperial occupations and cultural colonization. At the time of Jesus it was part of the Roman Empire, governed by rulers appointed by Rome according to Roman policy.

The Jewish society into which Jesus was born was diverse and highly stratified socially, economically, and religiously. Communication patterns and practices reflected and reinforced these class distinctions. The languages one spoke, the circumstances in which they were spoken, how they were spoken, whether one was literate in a particular language or another, and the extent of one's literacy were all markers of a person's or group's identity and place within the local and imperial cultural hierarchies. Three languages in particular were important in social positioning and stratification. Greek was the dominant language used in urban areas in business, international politics, and secular culture. Hebrew was the language of Jewish scriptures, and it was used primarily in the Temple and Jewish religious literature and practice. Its restricted use and literacy had led to the development of a religious leadership class based primarily on their capacity and resources to read and speak Hebrew. Aramaic, which had a number of dialects, was the common and most widely used language in general discourse and village life.

Levels of literacy were low and generally restricted to the upper classes. While there is a variety of opinions about levels of literacy, the estimation is that from 95 to 97 percent of the population were illiterate,[7] meaning that interactions of social and religious life, particularly in the towns and rural areas, were almost wholly oral in character.

Despite the general low levels of literacy, the religion of Jesus was a blended oral and literate religious culture. For hundreds of years, the Jews in Exile, in Israel, and in the Diaspora had been assembling and reproducing written scriptures and other texts. Protocols had been developed for how these written documents were to be integrated into worship, teaching, and wider oral practices of the religion. Different Jewish religious groups were marked not only by differences in their religious and cultural views, but also by different traditions of the integration of text into oral practice. These included the Sadducees, the hereditary priestly families and landholding aristocrats of Jerusalem; the Pharisees, a religious group marked by their piety born of struggles against secularizing trends a century earlier; the Scribes, a literate group who played a powerful role interpreting the written texts of the religion; and the Essenes, an apocalyptic sect and monastic community of Judaism.

For those living outside Jerusalem or without access to the Temple, the center of religious community was the local synagogue, a primarily lay-oriented community that stressed reading or recitation of the Hebrew scriptures, exposition of the scriptures when there was a person present who could do it, singing of hymns, and offering of prayers. Although illiterate, most heard the scriptures spoken sufficiently frequently to be able to recite significant portions of them from memory. Since most village people spoke Aramaic, a practice developed of providing oral Aramaic interpretations and applications of the Hebrew scripture readings, known as *targums*. When the Jerusalem Temple was destroyed in 70 CE, the synagogue form of worship with its combination of reading or reciting scriptures with oral commentary and debate became the common form of worship in reformed Rabbinic Judaism. In its early development, Christian communities drew significantly on this media model in the development of Christian worship practice.

A major issue in people's daily lives was making enough not only to provide the basic necessities of life but also to meet the financial burden of taxation. The Romans imposed heavy taxes, tolls, and tributes on occupied populations to support their imperial activities, the military, and the ruling elite. Depending on occupation and location, these imperial tax obligations could range from 12% to 50%.[8] Collection of taxes was leased out by the Romans to the local upper stratum, including religious leaders, who added to the imperial tax obligation their own costs and profits. These were ruthlessly collected, with military support provided to local tax collectors if needed. Jews were also obligated to pay religious tithes and taxes, specified in the Torah as part of the Covenant, for the support of the temple, its priests, and the poor. For farmers, the combined Jewish and Roman taxes were around 35 percent.[9]

For those living already at a marginal or subsistence level, meeting these obligatory taxes was crippling. In an empire that was dominantly agricultural, income and wealth were tied significantly to ownership of land. Those whose traditional or inherited land was not large or fruitful enough to support their family and meet their tax obligations eventually were driven into debt, were forced to sell their land to the upper classes, and became either a worker for others or even a slave in what Stegemann and Stegemann describe as "a regular process of pauperization."[10] Increasingly, the ownership of land and therefore wealth became concentrated and restricted to the upper classes.

Many coped by paying the Roman taxes, which were ruthlessly enforced, but not the religious ones, which lacked the same power of enforcement. In this situation, the only sanction the religious leaders could impose in the face of this loss of their income was to declare those who did not pay their religious dues to be ritually unclean and therefore excluded from religious participation until the taxes were paid.

This economic impact was felt particularly in the subsistence economy of the rural towns and small villages, and it led to a significant underclass – "a growing number of landless laborers, widespread emigration, and a social class of robbers and beggars."[11] The social disruption it caused produced numerous apocalyptic figures and movements – prophets, preachers, and messiahs – who traversed first-century Palestine proclaiming the day of God's judgment and the end of the world.[12]

This was the world Jesus grew up in.

Jesus in his media context

According to the Christian written tradition, Jesus grew up in Nazareth, a village in Galilee less than four miles away from a large urban center, Sepphoris. Prior to his religious ministry, he is identified as a carpenter (*tektōn*) and son of a carpenter.

These rural roots and manual occupation are indicators of Jesus' cultural and economic position. Geographically, coming from Nazareth associated him with an inconsequential part of the country. When it was recommended to the cultured and Greek-speaking Nathanael that he meet Jesus, Nathanael's response was "Can anything good come out of Nazareth?"[13]

Jesus' spoken language was a Galilean dialect of Aramaic, an identifiable accent and manner of speech that likewise were disdained by the religious elite and urban dwellers.[14] As a carpenter servicing different customers, including possibly in the nearby city of Sepphoris, Jesus may have had some knowledge also of Greek, Latin, and Hebrew words.

His identified occupation as a carpenter also locates Jesus socially. Although some modern interpretations romanticize him as a skilled specialist tradesman, the term was an occupational designation of a construction worker who could be a "mason, carpenter, cartwright, and joiner all in one."[15] The term "carpenter" was also a derogatory cultural signifier for the illiterate lower classes.

His birthplace and occupation therefore locate Jesus within the lowest, most vulnerable stratum of society, associated with small farmers, tenants, traders, day laborers, fishermen, shepherds, widows, orphans, prostitutes, beggars, and bandits. His people and family were people who were relatively poor if not absolutely poor, living at a subsistence level and constantly struggling for the basic necessities needed for survival.[16] This class stigmatization explains the reported response from people when Jesus began speaking publicly in his hometown: "'Where did this man get this wisdom and these deeds of power? Is not this the carpenter's son?' … And they took offense at him."[17]

Based on this background, it is also likely that, like others of his class, Jesus was illiterate. This likelihood goes against the largely unquestioned traditional Christian view that Jesus was naturally able to read and write. Unpacking this contradiction is important from a media perspective.

One of the grounds for the assumption that Jesus was able to read and write is a number of places in the Gospels where Jesus is referred to as reading and writing.[18] Some scholars argue that a Jewish boy of Jesus' time would have learned to read and write as part of his religious participation,[19] or that Jesus could not have expressed many of the sayings he did without a detailed knowledge of the texts of "The Law and the Prophets."[20] Later theological construction of Jesus as the Son of God also cast him as capable of superior human qualities and therefore at least equal to the abilities of the social elite.

However, Crossan argues a strong case that in a situation where 95 to 97 percent of the Jewish state was illiterate and where Jesus was a member of the lowest class in the society, it must be presumed that Jesus was illiterate.[21] Dunn likewise contends, "We have to assume, therefore, that the great majority of Jesus' first disciples would have been functionally illiterate. That Jesus himself was literate cannot simply be assumed."[22] The reason why Jesus' lower-class illiteracy was downplayed or changed in later writings about him has media relevance. Crossan suggests that Jesus' illiteracy posed a problem to later educated and literate Gentile Christians who wanted to commend the Christian faith to the cultured members of their own class, and they did so by writing it out in the writing of their stories. The later written accounts of Jesus as a young man debating the learned teachers in the temple and personally reading and interpreting a passage from Isaiah in the Nazareth synagogue both come from Luke's Gospel, the author of which was an educated physician living in Rome. Crossan sees them as later textual reworkings of Jesus to make him more culturally acceptable to the media culture of a different class. Accounts of Jesus reading and writing, he advocates, are "Lukan propaganda rephrasing Jesus' oral challenge and charisma in terms of scribal literacy and exegesis."[23]

Recognizing Jesus as illiterate does not contradict his frequent quoting of Jewish sayings and excerpts from scripture in his teachings, but locates them rather within the oral cultural practice of his time. It was a common and a significant skill of illiterate people to be able to recite significant passages of scripture from memory as a result of hearing them read frequently or being taught them. Through these oral practices, Jesus and most of his Jewish contemporaries would have known the foundational narratives, basic stories, and general expectations of his tradition and be able to use and quote them in communication and argument. How this was done, however, was distinctly oral in character and quite different from "the exact texts, precise citations, or intricate arguments of its scribal elites."[24]

While not a critical issue, considering the likelihood that Jesus was probably illiterate is important for a number of reasons. It recovers significant class and political dimensions in his religious message that were subsequently written out. It embeds his highly skilled oral charisma in his lower-class background rather than as a developed skill of a cultural elite. It also gives an insight into one of the early transformations of Jesus by followers who inhabited a differently mediated culture and wanted to make Jesus relevant to that culture. In this process, however, the distinctive claim of the lower classes for Jesus to have been one of them was taken away by a minority group of Christian writers. This concern would reemerge later in challenges to Christian writing. Because of the permanence of writing and the censorship of alternative views, however, the Lukan view that Jesus was literate would become unquestionably embedded in the Christian tradition.

As an adult, Jesus became a follower of the itinerant prophet, John the Baptist, before becoming a charismatic teacher himself. He gathered around him an inner band of disciples and other men and women who joined him in his travels and supported and helped him in his healing and miracle work. It was to this group primarily that Jesus passed on verbally his religious and social vision and teachings. It is noteworthy that the people he chose as his inner band were primarily members of his own class and subject to the same bitter poverty to which Jesus' religious message was addressed. Understanding this class reality gives a more realist insight into a number of incidents reported in the New Testament Gospels that are frequently spiritualized or allegorized. Jesus' many references to the poor and hungry and promises that in the coming Kingdom of God they will be fed are frequently interpreted as spiritual hunger, rather than seen for what they literally are: a political manifesto to the poor and starving that, in the coming Kingdom of God, they will have food to eat.

The activities of Jesus as they are recorded reflect two identifiable religious communication genres from within the Jewish tradition that carried cultural meaning for his audiences. His effectiveness as a communicator lies in his skill in activating and challenging the nuances of these cultural literacies.

One was that of the oral prophet, a recognized figure combining oral traditions of speech as charismatic, dramatic, and demonstrative performance. The identification of Jesus with this cultural genre is indicated in questions asked of Jesus' disciples on occasion if he was one of the revered Jewish prophets come back. Jewish prophets were largely rural-based critics that forthrightly addressed current public issues of political, social, and religious importance, particularly the oppressive effects of the urban religious government on the rural poor. Within the prophet's message was an emphasis on God's defense and vindication of the oppressed, a critique of the dominant systems of power and the power-holders causing the oppression, and the vision of a new age to come in which the present system of injustice is overcome, all of which can be seen in Jesus' message. [25]

The other communication genre reflected in Jesus' communication was that of the sage or wise teacher within the rabbinic tradition. Like most rabbis, Jesus gathered around him a group of identified disciples who travelled with him and assisted him in his work, and to whom he directed and entrusted his teaching.[26] On one occasion, Jesus sent out his disciples in pairs to proclaim more widely the good news he was bringing, something that Thiessen sees as an innovation among rabbis, and a means of mass communication of his message in an oral society, comparable to the coins and inscriptions of rulers.[27] This sending out of his disciples became an important signifier in later Christianity and was an important element in concepts of Christian mission.

One of the enduring characteristics of Jesus from a media or communication perspective is his outstanding skill and reputation as an oral communicator and charismatic performer. As Crossan describes him, he was "an illiterate peasant, but with an oral brilliance that few of those trained in literate and scribal disciplines can ever attain."[28] The oral characteristics of his communication had political significance for his audiences. They affirmed the dispossessed, disenfranchised, and illiterate rural and peasant classes and the value of their religious experience and culture in ways they could readily identify with, feel enfranchised by, and respond to. The popular appeal of Jesus can be understood within this context: his identification with his audience, his audience's identification of his shared cultural rootedness, and his outstanding skill in performing his message within the recognizable genres, relationships, responses, codes, tropes, and expectations of the highly developed oral culture from which he came and to which he spoke. Two genres of oral proclamation are particularly notable and have become emblematic of Jesus' teaching style: his short sayings or aphorisms, and his parabolic stories.

Numerous examples can be given of the terseness, parallelism, and rhythm of his teaching sayings, characteristics that facilitate memory and oral repetition even to the present time:

> Do not worry about tomorrow, for tomorrow will bring worries of its own.
> Do unto others as you would have them do unto you.
> Ask, and it will be given you; search, and you will find; knock, and the door will be opened for you.[29]

The skillfully constructed, memorable, cryptic, and often subversive character of Jesus' parabolic stories similarly explains their durability and generative power. Well-known parables such as The Lost Sheep, The Good Samaritan, and The Prodigal Son have a strong realism, are concise and economic in their narrative, have memorable and at times subversive characters, are dramatic in their reversals, and frequently have either a twist in the tail that upends audience expectations or a lack of closure that requires hearers to construct their own meaning. Bailey notes that they reflect characteristics still found in "Oriental storytelling":

> I discovered that the Oriental storyteller has a 'grand piano' on which he plays. The piano is built of the attitudes, relationships, responses and value judgments that are known and stylized in Middle Eastern peasant society. Everybody knows how everybody is expected to act in any given situation.

The storyteller interrupts the established pattern of behavior to introduce his irony, his surprises, his humor, and his climaxes. If we are not attuned to those same attitudes, relationships, responses, and value judgments, we do not hear the music of the piano.[30]

These multiple layers, nuances, resonances, sharp provocations, and controversial advocacy that mark Jesus' parables are largely lost to the modern audience, but would have engaged the minds and emotions of his audiences and stimulated discussion among hearers for days.[31] Christian leaders, theologians, and preachers frequently try to shut down this polysemy of the parables by giving "definitive" interpretations of their meaning within their own constructed theological systems. Freed from that constraining orthodoxy, however, the parables of Jesus remain even today as questions inviting an answer, and as an encouragement to audiences to participate by generating their own new meaning in the story.

The ordered nature of the documentary records of Jesus' teachings and stories does not give the full picture of how they were produced or received. Each of the Gospels tells the sayings and parables only once. The Gospel of Matthew, for example, groups together a large number of sayings in what is now a well-known section commonly called The Sermon on the Mount,[32] as if all were given on the one occasion. Other Gospels reproduce the sayings in different narrative settings. Dunn suggests that this ordering may reflect the practices of the early Christian oral tradition of preserving the tradition in blocks and series to facilitate memory.[33] In practice, though, as with other itinerant teachers, the sayings and stories would have been part of a repertoire of themes and topics that Jesus creatively retold in different settings in response to specific situations or questions.

In addition to his spoken words, he also performed his key messages. He gained some notoriety by assembling a questionable group of people into a new "kingdom community" that travelled with him. Against convention, he mixed with and shared hospitality with women and others designated as social outcasts, and included social nobodies and outcasts as protagonists and exemplars in his teachings and parabolic stories.

In a social context that saw the world of the spirit as a reality that continually intervened and influenced events in the material world, Jesus also communicated through actions that embodied prophetic meaning: casting out demons, healing the sick, and miraculously producing food to feed the hungry – performing the new reality he was speaking about. His chosen followers were given authority to do the same.

Although Jesus was rooted in the Jewish tradition of the teacher and the prophet, the biblical scholar Birger Gerhardsson notes that he does not fit into any Jewish category. He was not a common traditionist, a link in a chain of tradition presenting wisdom from others, but had original features – a

Jewish teacher with prophetic and messianic traits who impressed his hearers with the authority with which he spoke.[34]

In difference from most subsequent Christian theology, Jesus' theology was expressed in concrete, practical, and accessible terms. God was spoken of not as an abstract concept, but as a concrete presence interested in the practicalities of people's everyday lives and able to act on human needs. This religious language and theology relocated God away from the preserve of religious institutions into the everyday world of the home and marketplace. His teachings on the nature of God were commonly in narrative stories about everyday activities: a shepherd losing a sheep, a woman losing a coin, a farmer sowing a field. In place of his audience's religious positioning as unclean and excluded from official religious access to God, Jesus spoke of a direct and personal human relationship to a God who was gracious, compassionate, and forgiving.

The charismatic way in which Jesus was able to engage directly with people, and the enthusiasm with which common people responded to his presence, his speech, and his actions, is recorded in a number of places in the Gospel records, with large crowds not only coming to hear him but also following him from place to place. Memory and impact of this charismatic presence were significant factors in the response to the disciples preaching about him after his death.

There was also a political dimension to his religious message, a challenge to the religious authorities whose religious policies and interpretations were oppressing the poor and disenfranchised. Crossan identifies the political character of Jesus' message as different from that of the many other movements or acts of resistance that were active at the time, such as unarmed protestors, armed bandits, apocalyptic or millennial prophets, and royal or messianic claimants. He sees what Jesus was doing as "on the borderline between the covert and the overt arts of resistance ... (not) as open as the acts of protestors, prophets, bandits or messiahs ... (but) more open than playing dumb, imagining revenge, or simply recalling Mosaic or Davidic ideals."[35] Many of his stories invoked the oral strategies used by subordinated groups to resist or subvert the imposition of authority in situations where to resist more overtly would be fatal. The subversive use of double meanings, cultural codes and nuances, and exaggerations or particular attributes given to characters in many of Jesus' stories are largely lost to us today but would have been understood and talked about by his hearers. The parable of The Good Samaritan is a good example, where respected Jewish religious leaders pass callously by a person in need without helping, but the one who stopped to help was a Samaritan, a race that was culturally and religiously despised. The cutting nature of his challenge, however, was perceived by those in positions of power, making his arrest and crucifixion political as much as religious in motivation.

One of the significant issues or consequences of Jesus' oral communicative style is that he never, at least that we are aware of, gave a systematic summary or key points of his theological thinking that could be referred to as a yardstick for later interpretations of his key messages. He appears to have presumed the religious structure of Judaism, and in places in the recorded accounts of his message he explicitly states that he was not interested in developing an alternative to Jewish religious law and criticizes those who did not respect it.[36] His desire was not to destroy or replace Judaism, but to rekindle its heart. His focus as an oral communicator was not in developing a better philosophical or religious system to be taught to people, but in interactively engaging with people about rethinking the nature of faith and their ethical behavior in relation to issues they were concerned about. The intent of his proverbs, parables, lessons from nature, and prophetic performances was to kindle people's imaginations to be born afresh and see and live differently. His concerns were local not universal, concrete not abstract, provocative not systematized. The foundation for his work was not a philosophy, but a vision of God as an ever-present, gracious, and compassionate father whose nearby (in both space and time) spiritual kingdom opened new possibilities and challenged the values and false security of earthly powers and concerns.

This lack of closure and system in Jesus' sayings, stories, and actions has made them a fecund source of inspiration, renewal, interpretation, and provocation for people seeking to understand their meaning and relevance for new concrete situations. But their lack of system and definition has also made them problematic for reproducing them out of their oral context into different media of communication, or for making them the basis for religious organizations where order and predictability of meaning are essential for maintaining stability and power.

This difference in media systems – the oral charismatic and the written, philosophical, and organizational – underlies the immense amount of effort that has been put throughout Christian history into trying to build and connect the fixed structures of the new religion of Christianity on the fluid teachings and stories of Jesus. Jesus' intention appears to have been that his stories and teachings be engaged with and lived – not systematized into abstract philosophical doctrines and creeds.

This difference of media systems is also a consideration in the titles that have been ascribed to Jesus. A number of reputable scholars today are of the opinion that Jesus didn't see himself as the founder of a new religion, nor that he claimed for himself many of the exalted claims made about him in the later Christian tradition.[37] It is helpful to be reminded that Jesus wasn't Christian, but was Jewish – he was born a Jew, lived as a Jew, and died a Jew. The purpose of his mission in its context was distinctly Jewish: the renewal of Israel's relationship to God and calling Israel back to its divine calling to be an inclusive people of God in the face of practices of exploitation and sacrilege that belied that high destiny.

The most common title Jesus used of himself was the term "the son of man" or "a son of man." This was a Hebrew or Aramaic term from the Jewish tradition that was used to describe all of humanity or one's participation in humanity – similar to our English use of the term "humankind" or "I am one of you." The title "Son of Man" that is ascribed to Jesus in the later Greek-language Gospels is subtly different. It is a developed Greek translation of the Hebrew term, but refers to a transcendental apocalyptic figure that is the agent of God's judgment. From his textual research, Crossan considers it very unlikely that Jesus used the title "The Son of Man" to describe himself, but did use the term "son of man" in its generic native Hebrew and Aramaic sense to identify himself with those he was addressing. His use of it was "to emphasize that he shared with them a common destiny as *we* poor or destitute human beings."[38]

There are a number of references in the writings of Paul and the Gospels that give Jesus the title "the Son of God," and there is a similar significant debate among scholars about whether Jesus referred to himself individually in this way, and what exactly was meant when the term was used.[39] Certainly Jesus spoke of God in very intimate familial ways, such as in his use of the Aramaic term *Abba,* a term used on occasion by adults in referring to their natural fathers or an honored teacher.[40] Jesus' use of the term was part of his message to all: to see God as a close parent rather than a distant ruler. It does not necessarily indicate that Jesus saw himself as having a unique relationship with God that was unlike any other person's.

Jesus addressed God personally as a member of a monotheistic religious community. The term "Son of God" occurs in a number of places in Jewish scriptures, but where it does it refers to the nation of Israel as God's chosen son or as an honorific title given to the king of Israel. As a monotheistic Jew, the idea of seeing himself or any other human being as a preexistent divine "Son of God" would have been anathema to Jesus. It is instructive that most of Jesus' chosen disciples, after his death, retained a strongly monotheistic Christian theology, in which they recognized and affirmed Jesus as the Messiah sent by God, but never saw him in this role as divine or as the preexistent Son of God. It is noteworthy that because they refused to recognize Jesus as God or the Son of God, they were later branded as heretical and excommunicated by Gentile Christians.

On the other hand, the concept of a "Son of God" was a quite familiar one in Hellenistic culture, which was more polytheistic in its outlook and quite accepting of the existence of such intermediate spiritual beings. As we will explore further in the following chapter, the identification of Jesus as the "Son of God" appears not to have been part of Jesus' self-understanding or original message, but an innovation in Hellenistic Christianity made to facilitate Christianity's transition from its original Jewish context into the wider Greco-Roman world, where the main competitor for religious loyalty was Roman imperial theology, which declared that the great emperor, Caesar Augustus, was divine and was referred to variously as "Son of God," "Lord," "savior of the world," "bringer of peace," and divinely conceived.[41]

Remaking Jesus in speech and performance

The small inner circle of followers chosen by Jesus expected that he was inaugurating an imminent new kingdom of God on earth and that they would be part of it. That hope and expectation came to a sudden halt when he was arrested and quickly executed in Jerusalem by the Roman authorities. His death shocked and traumatized them, compounded by the fear that they could easily be identified, arrested, and suffer the same fate themselves. In the period following his death, they shared memories, discussed what had happened, and drew on their cultural media of written or memorized texts of scriptures for comfort and to gain an understanding of the meaning of what had happened.

Although there are different opinions about the particulars, sometime after his death[42] Jesus' followers appeared in public again, declaring Jesus as God's Messiah as promised in Jewish scriptures, and declaring that the last days were at hand and that Jesus would be returning imminently to establish God's Kingdom on earth. People were urged to put their faith in Jesus and prepare themselves for the coming end of the world.

There is a diversity of views within Christianity about what caused this transformation. Many Christians accept literally the narrative accounts in the Gospels and the Book of Acts, written 40–70 years after the events: that, after being dead and placed in a tomb for forty or more hours, the processes of natural decay in Jesus' body and brain were reversed, although the wounds of his crucifixion remained, and his heartbeat and breathing recommenced. He walked out of the tomb; interacted with and gave new instructions to his followers – a group of 500 on one occasion;[43] and then, in his body, he rose up through the clouds and disappeared, with two men in white robes saying that his body would return down through the clouds again one day. Some Christians see this narrative as a mythological construction, grounding what was primarily an experience of new insight and spiritual regeneration and redirection of the group. The Dutch Catholic theologian Edward Schillebeeckx, for example, describes it in terms that "the new orientation of living which this Jesus has brought about in their lives has not been rendered meaningless by his death – quite the opposite."[44] Some Christians see it in allegorical terms, with the impact of Jesus pointing to the unquenchable transformative power of God within life. There are numerous others – some psychological in nature, some theological, some mystical, some fantastic. Some of the media issues in these narratives will be explored in the following two chapters.

However it happened, following his death there was a significant transformation in the immediate followers of Jesus that in its transmission has had remarkable durability and motivating power. Conceptualizing Jesus as the promised Messiah, and themselves as participants in a divine action predicted in their holy scriptures, transformed the charisma of the person of Jesus into a charisma of his ongoing presence embodied in the people he had chosen to be his followers.

Inherent in this first experience for these first followers was a passion to communicate this new reality in a way that gripped others the way they themselves had been gripped by it, a task made more urgent because it involved a perception that these events were a precursor to the end of the world. From the very beginning, the character of the communication of Christianity hasn't been just a descriptive recital of information about facts or events. Much of Christianity through the centuries has been characterized by this rhetorical drive to communicate to and convince audiences of the crucial importance and urgency of what was being spoken about, and to win them over to their cause. In a way that would be followed by subsequent generations, the first followers utilized a full range of mediational actions of interpretation, rhetoric, and persuasion.

They looked back to their tradition, taking passages and verses from the Jewish scriptures, at times out of context, to remake Jesus into a historical prediction and thus give historical credibility to what they were saying. They borrowed concepts and practices from their Jewish culture and made those concepts also part of the message. With the push of new conviction and the pull of the urgency of the expected imminent end of the world, accuracy was less important than relevance and persuasion.

What becomes apparent from these beginnings is that while Jesus was the founding impulse, the dynamism and shaping of Christianity have come from this continually creative process of people making and remaking Jesus to be relevant to new circumstances and to win people over. Christianity spread and grew not just because it contained a message of spiritual power. It spread and grew because its adherents felt energized and at liberty to continually adapt and reinvent its meaning and practices to be relevant to the demands, opportunities, and communication systems of new contexts.

At first, with the expectation that time was short, and with the memory of Jesus sending them out in pairs specifically to Jews,[45] the primary focus of activity was on spreading the message to Jews living in Jerusalem and the near districts. This evangelizing activity was carried out by the disciples or itinerant prophets, who "continued Jesus' Galilean practice of travelling among the villages, casting out demons, working cures, maintaining an open table fellowship in thanksgiving, and speaking 'in Jesus name'."[46] Renouncing home, family, and belongings, they were supported in this by the hospitality of home gatherings of new followers, who provided the itinerant preachers with room, board, a supportive community for their missionary work, and often funding for the next stage of their journey.

People joined the group by confessing Jesus as the predicted Jewish Messiah, repenting of their sins, and, after the model of John the Baptist, being baptized in the name of Jesus. As the group grew, it functioned as an apocalyptic revitalization sect within the Jewish religion, one of many such sects.[47] They continued to see themselves as faithful Jews and followed the requirements of the Torah as followers of the Rabbi Jesus: "They observed the Sabbath, kosher laws, the great festivals of Judaism; they practised circumcision and kept all the other commandments required of faithful Jews everywhere."[48] In a way similar to that of Pharisaic home fellowships and study groups, they also met separately on a regular basis as groups in people's homes, where their identity as followers of Jesus was reinforced and expressed by confessing and praising Jesus as the Jewish Messiah, singing hymns, reading and reinterpreting their Jewish scriptures, recounting things that Jesus had said and done, baptizing new believers, and sharing in a communal meal that re-enacted the last meal Jesus had with his disciples. These Jewish Jesus communities were associated with synagogues across the region, including as far as Rome.

Coordination of the movement fell significantly to the inner circle who had been with Jesus throughout his ministry, particularly James (the brother of Jesus), Peter, John, and possibly Mary Magdalene and Mary, the mother of Jesus and James.[49] The major leadership role was taken by James, who was known as James the Righteous or James the Just, an ascription given only to those who followed the Torah strictly, and in recognition of his personal poverty and compassionate concern and work for the poor. This focus on service to the poor continued the emphasis of Jesus and would remain a strong emphasis of the Jewish Jesus Movement.[50]

Of particular focus in this early retelling of the Jesus story were his stories and sayings, accounts of his miracles and exorcisms, the telling of his death and resurrection, and his radical ethic, "an ethic of homelessness, detachment from the family, criticism of possessions and nonviolence."[51] In Thiessen's analysis, Jesus' death was regarded not "as a saving death which frees people from sins" but rather "as one of the prophets who died a martyr's death for their cause."[52] There was immediacy in this oral prophetic speech that blurred boundaries between what had happened in the past and what was happening now. Jesus was spoken of not as a past figure who was dead and gone but as a continuing presence alive in those who were now speaking and performing.

The nuance of this fluid boundary and movement between past and present realities that is possible and natural in oral performance is easily lost when the same experience is fixed in time via writing. The factual and theological problems that arose later when the resurrection of Jesus was written down as a separate, physical event that happened in the past did not arise in the same way in these early stages of oral proclamation. As Sawicki notes,

> The prophets proclaimed resurrection as a real-time experience. That is they were able to evoke the presence, power and life of the once-crucified Jesus, and to validate this experience, by wonderworks done through the mention of Jesus' name. In the heyday of the Christian prophets, there was as yet no story of resurrection as an event in someone else's past. Teachers later would narratize resurrection, but the prophetic way was simply to proclaim that one now lives and works among the people who is Jesus, who died.[53]

In this enthusiastic rhetorical telling and proclamation, there was significant adaptation of the sayings and events of Jesus' life in the process of bringing them to life for the audience. While greater constraints were followed in the oral transmission of a fixed tradition, in the process of retelling the apocalyptically charged message, the message gained new material and new meaning as the original Jesus was imaginatively recreated in the process of telling in new settings. The rabbinic and prophetic traditions within Judaism provided models for this process of change through adaptation and application of a master's sayings to different contexts and circumstances.

The events, stories, and meanings of Jesus' life in the earliest stages, then, were preserved through oral repetition and rehearsal and formed into a number of oral traditions, perhaps connected to specific Christian prophets or regions and preserved by rehearsal in activities of recruitment, instruction, and worship.[54] While there were common themes and practices across these different traditions, there was also diversity.

Küng names this early stage of communication and community formation of the Jesus Movement as the Jewish Apocalyptic Paradigm, which he associates with a number of distinctive characteristics.[55] It was apocalyptic and eschatological. The followers expected that Jesus would be returning very soon, and the focus of their proclamation and action was on preparing for an end that was about to come. It was strongly Jewish in character and Aramaic in its language, culture, and social location. It was deeply connected with the historical person of Jesus: his charismatic presence, his stories and teachings, his miracles and activities, his interactions with people, and his passion and death. It was subversive in its gender structures. Women, some of whom had travelled with Jesus during his itinerant ministry, were actively involved in it from the beginning, including as leaders. It was diverse and fluid in its communication forms. In addition to practical discourses of communication, prophecies, testaments, dreams, and visions were accepted as legitimate means of knowledge about the mysteries of the divine. It was practical in its orientation. It showed little concern for metaphysical abstractions or speculation. Its core beliefs centered on the historical person of Jesus and the practical and ethical implications of their new perspectives on faith: what did one need to do to live in accordance with the divine plan God had revealed to them and in anticipation of God's coming kingdom? In its earliest stages, it was a lower-class movement.

> It was not on the history of an upper class that historiography was usually ori-
> ented, but on the history of the lower classes: fishermen, peasants, craftsmen,
> little people who normally have no chronicler. The first generation of Chris-
> tians did not have the least political power and did not strive for positions in
> the religious and political establishments. They formed a small, weak, margin-
> al group of the society of their time, under attack and discredited.[56]

The transformation of this distinctive, lower-class, Aramaic Jesus Movement into the religion of Christianity is the focus of the following chapters.

NOTES

 1 See, for example, Allison, 2010, particularly Chapter 6, "How much history?"
 2 See, for example, J. D. G. Dunn, 2003.
 3 Borg, 2012, loc. 387.
 4 For good summaries of the major stages and approaches of this research, see Levine, 2006; Powell, 1998.
 5 Powell, 1998.
 6 Borg, 1994.
 7 See, for example, Crossan, 1994, p. 25; J. D. G. Dunn, 2003, p. 148.
 8 Stegemann & Stegemann, 1995, p. 119.
 9 Borg, 1987, p. 85.
10 Stegemann & Stegemann, 1995, pp. 110–123.
11 Borg, 1987, p. 85.
12 Aslan, 2013, loc. 139.
13 John 1:46.
14 While standing in a crowd in Jerusalem after Jesus was arrested, the disciple Peter was identified by a bystander as a Galilean and therefore likely associated with Jesus (Mark 14:70). It is not explained whether he was recognizable by his distinctive speech or dress or by some other factor.
15 Stegemann & Stegemann, 1995, p. 199.
16 Stegemann & Stegemann, 1995, p. 199.
17 Matthew 13:54–57.
18 Jesus is reported as astonishing the learned teachers in the temple (Luke 2:41–53), reading the scriptures in the synagogue in Nazareth (Luke 4:17), and writing on the ground (John 8:6).
19 See, for example, Borg, 1987.
20 See, for example, Gerhardsson, 2005.
21 Crossan, 1994, pp. 25–26.

22 J. D. G. Dunn, 2003, p. 148.
23 Crossan, 1994, p. 26.
24 Crossan, 1994, pp. 25–26.
25 Reuther, 1993, p. 24.
26 Byrskog, 1994.
27 Theissen, 2012, p. 74.
28 Crossan, 1994, p. 58.
29 Matthew 6:34, 7:12, 7:7–8.
30 Bailey, 1976, p. 35.
31 Linnemann, 1966, pp. 20–21.
32 Matthew 5:1–7:29.
33 J. D. G. Dunn, 2003.
34 Gerhardsson, 2005.
35 Crossan, 1994, p. 105, citing Scott, 1990.
36 For example, Matthew 5; Luke 10:25–28.
37 See, for example, Borg, 1987, pp. 10–11.
38 Crossan, 1994, p. 51.
39 For those arguing that Jesus didn't refer to himself as "Son of God," see Aslan, 2013; Borg, 1987; Crossan, 1994; Wilson, 2008. For a nuanced discussion between this and the orthodox position, see Borg & Wright, 1999.
40 D'Angelo, 2006, p. 64.
41 Borg, 2012, loc. 293.
42 The four New Testament Gospel narratives say this happened in three literal days. Some scholars suggest the three days were figurative to link retrospectively to references in the Jewish scriptures, and it could have been weeks, months, or perhaps years.
43 Paul, in I Corinthians 15:1–11.
44 Schillebeeckx, 1989, p. 333.
45 Three of the Gospels describe Jesus as sending out his disciples to spread his message. For example, "Go nowhere among the Gentiles, and enter no town of the Samaritans, but go rather to the lost sheep of the house of Israel" (Matthew 10:5).
46 Sawicki, 1994, p. 53.
47 White, 2004, pp. 128–132.
48 Wilson, 2008, p. 96.
49 Moltmann-Wendel, 1982.
50 Aslan, 2013, loc. 3128. The term "Jesus Movement" is used to describe this early stage of the movement that emerged following Jesus' death; it was largely Jewish in character. It is used also to distinguish it from the movement that was later called "Christian," which, although connected, had significant differences, as will be explained.
51 Theissen, 2003, p. 37.
52 Theissen, 2003, p. 38.
53 Sawicki, 1994, pp. 85–86.
54 Borg, 2012, loc. 347.
55 Küng, 1994, pp. 65–70.
56 Küng, 1994, p. 66.

2

Making Jesus Gentile

Context: the media world of the Roman Empire

The religious movement that emerged after Jesus' death entered an imperial world that was highly interconnected, with well-developed and effective communication systems, industries, and cultural practices. Those wider communication systems were crucial to the spread of the Jesus Movement and the way it developed.

The dominant forms of communication and social interaction for most of the population of the Roman Empire were oral and visual, in all their diversity and richness. The languages spoken varied widely, and they located people in terms of their locality, region, social position, and function. Latin and Greek as the shared languages of political administration made communication possible across these different language and cultural groups.

Levels of general literacy throughout the empire were low, although the boundaries between literacy and illiteracy were fluid. People considered to be functionally illiterate could be familiar with the meaning of some written signs or particular words for practical or business purposes. Some could read to a limited extent but not write. Someone who couldn't read or write could memorize extensive passages of writing and quote them from memory in discussions or negotiations with those who could read. Many letters were written with the expectation that they would be read aloud to a group where most would be illiterate, thus including the illiterate in literate activities. Important letters could be reread to such an extent that their content would be widely memorized, often verbatim. Written texts, even when read in private, would commonly be mouthed or read aloud while reading to facilitate hearing the writer's voice and

From Jesus to the Internet, Peter Horsfield © 2015 John Wiley & Sons, Ltd. Published 2015 by John Wiley & Sons, Ltd.

understanding the writer's meaning. Social activities catered to this diversity:

> Recitations of poetry and prose works, dramatic performances in theaters and at festivals, declamations in high rhetorical style, street corner philosophical diatribes, commemorative inscriptions, the posting and reading of official decrees, the routine traffic of legal and commercial documents all brought the fruits of literacy before the general population, educating the public in its uses and popularizing its conventions.[1]

Fluency in literacy, however, was a restricted skill. The effort and time associated with learning to read and write and the costs associated with writing and manuscript production meant that fluent literacy was restricted largely to trained officials and the upper classes, where the ability to read, write, and discuss the classics was a sign of an educated and cultured person. The Greco-Roman education system supported this elite culture, developing in its privileged students the skills needed "to read with precision, to determine the authenticity of texts, and to compile the most reliable readings and interpretations."[2] Students learned also the skills of integrating written texts into the oral disciplines of rhetoric and oratory.

Although levels of literacy across the Roman Empire were low, writing was crucial to the functioning of the empire, and an extensive communication and social infrastructure had developed to facilitate trade and cultural exchange and maintain political order across the empire.[3] There were industries to supply the materials and services for production and circulation of the extensive amount of written exchange that took place for personal, official. and cultural purposes. This included a network of secretaries, some of whom staffed the central offices of the Roman bureaucracy, and others who sold their services to personal, public, or business clients right down to the village level.[4]

Processes and facilities were also in place for storing and preserving the vast amount of documentation, manuscripts, and books that the empire produced. One imperial office in the mid-first century CE listed 247 documents received in a four-month period. A Roman prefect in Alexandria in the following century reported receiving 1804 petitions in a three-day period, all of which had to be publicly displayed.[5] There were an estimated 26–28 public libraries in Rome alone and a commercial book trade where copies were held or deposited and reproduced for sale.[6] The library in Alexandria, the most renowned library in the empire, held a reported 700,000 books in its collections.[7]

In their thinking and systems the Romans were pragmatic and eclectic, and for more than 400 years they had provided a structure of intellectual and practical universalism across the known world of the time. An overarching framework of adopted Greek universalistic philosophical thought was implemented in shared ideas of providence, moral freedom, responsibility, and immortality. Practical systems of law, governance, communication, administration, military enforcement, and religious tolerance were implemented across regional cultures.

This was the global context within which the movement that grew out of the activity of Jesus was born and developed. Although originating in a small region in the eastern fringe of the empire, it grew in an environment where there was a definite consciousness of world history embodied practically in the institutions, laws, political structures, and symbols of the empire. Once it took the first steps, imbibing this ambience of universal destiny would change the character of the Jesus Movement from a small local religious sect into a worldwide imperial religion that coopted that destiny.

Early Christian writing

Although the membership of the earliest Jesus Movement was predominantly illiterate, from the earliest times, possibly even while Jesus was still alive, people with the ability to write wrote down things he said and snippets of what had happened. These were the beginnings of later written works that integrated different oral and written accounts into longer documentary form.

The development of the Jesus Movement has been hidden to a certain extent within Christianity, by the way in which the documents in the Christian New Testament have been represented and by the way they are organized within the book. What has been largely hidden throughout Christian history is that the documents selected for inclusion in the New Testament represent only a portion of the writings and perspectives that were in circulation at the time. In addition, the documents aren't organized in the order in which they were written. While there are a range of literary options for the organization of material in any book, the way material is organized can have an influence on how the topic is perceived and understood. Furthermore, the authorship of many of the writings is uncertain or wrongly attributed. For example, there is now wide scholarly recognition that a number of the letters said to be written by Paul weren't written by him at all.

When the correct authors of the documents in the New Testament are properly ascribed, and they are reorganized in the chronological order of when they were written, a quite different picture appears.[8] The structure then becomes as follows.

The New Testament order and authors	*Historical dates and authors*
• The four Gospels (not in chronological order) • The Acts of the Apostles • Thirteen letters attributed to Paul: Romans, 1 and 2 Corinthians, Galatians, Ephesians, Philippians, Colossians, 1 and 2 Thessalonians, 1 and 2 Timothy, Titus, and Philemon • Eight "general" letters: Hebrews, James, 1 and 2 Peter, 1, 2, and 3 John, and Jude • The Revelation to John	50s CE: The seven authentic letters of Paul: 1 Thessalonians, Galatians, 1 Corinthians, Philemon, Philippians, 2 Corinthians, and Romans 70s: The Gospel of Mark 80s: Letters: James, Colossians, and Hebrews The Gospel of Matthew 90s: Letters: Ephesians and Revelation The Gospel of John 100s: Letters: Jude, and 1, 2, and 3 John 110s: The Gospel of Luke, Acts of the Apostles Letters: 2 Thessalonians, 1 Peter, 1 and 2 Timothy, and Titus 120s: Letter: 2 Peter

When considered in this way, some of the effects of the structural editing of the canonical New Testament become more apparent. For one, it hides the developmental nature of the early movement. For example, in the New Testament, the Gospels that purportedly tell the factual story of Jesus are presented first, followed by the Acts of the Apostles that purportedly tell the story of the origins of Christianity, beginning with the disciples and moving on to the ministry of Paul, whose letters follow. This creates a narrative sequence that constructs the life of the church as following on seamlessly from the life of Jesus, and the mission of Paul to the Gentiles following on seamlessly from the work of the disciples among the Jews. Then follow a series of letters that elaborate some of the specific issues arising within this sequential framework.

When seen chronologically and in terms of their correct authorship, however, a different picture emerges with a number of interesting aspects. One of those interesting aspects is that the earliest Christian writings for which we have a permanent record are not the Gospels telling the life of Jesus, but the seven letters written by Paul. If we are to get an idea of the contribution that written media made in the transition of the Jesus Movement into the Christian movement, we need to begin our consideration with the earliest Christian documents, the written letters of Paul.

Paul and letter writing

Although seen universally as a seminal figure in the historical development of Christianity, there is significant disagreement on the role played by Paul in the continuation of the mission of the person Jesus.

At one end of the spectrum is the orthodox Christian view that Paul faithfully extended what Jesus was seeking to do by translating it out of the confines of its specific Jewish setting into a gospel for all people, regardless of their race or culture. The early twentieth-century theologian Adolf Harnack reflected this view when he wrote,

> It was Paul who delivered the Christian religion from Judaism.... Without doing violence to the inner and essential features of the Gospel.... Paul transformed it into a universal religion and laid the ground for the great church.... In the course (of the apostolic age) the Gospel was detached from the mothersoil of Judaism and placed upon the broad field of the Graeco-Roman empire. The apostle Paul was the chief agent accomplishing this work, and in thereby giving Christianity its place in the history of the world.[9]

The New Testament scholar N.T. Wright notes the innovations of Paul, but similarly justifies them as a reasonable and valid extension of Jesus' thinking and activities:

> [So for] Paul, struggling to find ways of thinking the unthinkable and saying the unsayable ... it became natural for him to speak of Jesus as 'God's son' with the meaning, not just of God's messianic agent for Israel and the world, but of God's second self, God's ultimate self-expression as a human being.[10]

Contrary to this view are those who see Paul not simply as translating the Jewish message of Jesus into a Hellenistic context, but as founding a quite different religion, taking some aspects of Jesus' life but adapting them in a way that was not at all in line with how Jesus, or the disciples he personally chose to continue his work, saw it. The scholar Barrie Wilson, for example, sees in Paul's ideas a radical switch of the historical human being Jesus from someone who saw himself obliquely as the anticipated Messiah foretelling a coming Kingdom of God, to a divine Son of God or "Christ" figure that echoes the mythologies of Hellenistic mystery religions. Rather than extend the teachings and mission of Jesus into the Gentile world, Wilson advocates, Paul displaced the teachings of Jesus with his own invented religion that was anathema to Jesus' own disciples and would have been anathema to Jesus himself.[11]

It is beyond the scope of this particular work to attempt to resolve a debate that is historically and theologically complex, nuanced, and frequently contentious. However, given Paul's pivotal role in the development of Christianity, the media dimensions of the debate are important to explore.

Saul, or Paul as he came to be known, was from the cosmopolitan city of Tarsus, the capital of the Roman province of Cilicia in modern-day Turkey. Jewish by birth, he was for a time a member of the Jewish Pharisee or holiness sect within the Jewish Diaspora. He was also a Roman citizen (possibly from his parents), had received a Hellenistic education, and wrote in Greek.

Paul claims for himself early in his letters the role of Apostle to the Gentiles, a claim that is written into the mainstream of the Christian tradition by later Gentile Christian writers. The credit Paul gives to himself as being Apostle to the Gentiles hides the fact that before Paul, the Jewish Jesus Movement had already been spreading into the Greek-speaking Jewish Diaspora, had already been attracting Greek-speaking converts, and had already been dealing with issues raised by this cross-cultural engagement.[12] There was a substantial Jesus community in Alexandria from an early time and Greek-speaking followers of Jesus in Antioch well before Paul arrived. There was also significant diversity in how these Greek-speaking followers of Jesus in the wider empire were thinking about the implications of being a follower of Jesus in a different linguistic and geographic context.[13]

Paul describes himself in one of his earliest letters as violently persecuting and seeking to destroy the "church of God" before having a personal mystical experience in which God, who had "set me apart … even before I was born … was pleased to reveal his Son to me so that I might proclaim him among the Gentiles."[14]

After this personal vision, Paul showed little concern to align or reconcile his experience or what he was thinking with that of Jesus' disciples, the ones who had been entrusted personally by Jesus with the continuation of his message. Writing about what he did immediately after his mystical experience, Paul was quite adamant: "I did not confer with any human being nor did I go up to Jerusalem to those who were already apostles before me."[15] Paul also showed little concern for reconciling his understanding of his experience with what Jesus had actually said or done when he was alive. As Aslan, along with others, has noted, "There is almost no trace of Jesus of Nazareth in his letters. With the exception of the crucifixion and the Last Supper, which he transforms from a narrative to a liturgical formula, Paul does not narrate a single event from Jesus' life."[16]

Instead, Paul went off on his own to Arabia for an unspecified period before starting on his own itinerant mission promoting his own interpretation of the events of Jesus.[17] He travelled extensively throughout the Asia Minor region, supporting himself as a tentmaker while spreading his version of Jesus through conversation and public speaking.

The target audience for Paul, and the group among which he had most success, was Gentiles associated with Jewish synagogues in the urban areas of the Eastern Mediterranean. Known as "God-fearers," these were non-Jewish people who for various reasons were attracted to Judaism, but were not willing or ready to undergo the requirements or take on the obligations of fully converting to the religion.[18] Paul's gospel to this Hellenistic group was therefore a blend of both Jewish and Hellenistic religious culture. In his gospel, Paul transformed the concept of the human Jewish Messiah into Jesus the divine Christ or the divine Son of God, a spiritual being, spiritual person, or aspect of God sent by (his father) God to be incarnated as a human being. As a male human being, this preexistent Son of God was killed, but brought back to life by God and honored by God by being restored to the highest position of exultation, that of "the Lord Jesus Christ." These Greek terms and concepts were central to Paul's theology, and he used and promoted them extensively – he opened each of his letters with the greeting "Grace to you and peace from God our Father and the Lord Jesus Christ."

In a way reminiscent of Hellenistic mystery religion, Paul asserted that in the incarnation, death, resurrection, and exultation of Jesus, the power of evil was decisively overcome in this world and the otherworld, and a spiritual power was released onto the earth to free people from the bondage and death of sin and the flesh, and open to them a new spiritual life of freedom and eternal life.

Paul's interpretation of the meaning of Jesus was contentious and brought him into conflict with Jesus' disciples and other evangelists of the Jesus Movement – so he basically stayed away from them. Paul says it was three years after his conversion before he went to Jerusalem to speak with the key disciples James and Peter, and fourteen years before he met them a second time.[19] His account of what he did was obviously disputed, as he writes in parentheses, "In what I am writing to you, before God, I do not lie!" Paul justified this lack of consultation with those who had actually been with Jesus on the basis that his gospel came as a direct revelation from God and not from human conversation, including with the human being Jesus: "I did not receive it from any man, nor was I taught it, but I received it through a revelation of Jesus Christ."[20]

Luke, in his documentary account of the Acts of the Apostles, written around sixty years later, sought to reduce the extent of this conflict between Paul and the disciples by creating a narrative of Paul's mission as continuous with that of the Jewish disciples. Luke's later version, contrary to Paul's own account, says that Paul made contact with Jewish Christians within three days of his personal revelation,[21] and that though having disagreements with the disciples, Paul was supportive of them and on his travels raised funds to send to the Jerusalem church.

Of particular contention between Paul and Jesus' disciples was Paul's attitude toward the Jewish religious law. Paul saw the Jewish law as a major obstacle that prevented Greek God-fearers from becoming fully involved in what Paul saw as the universal message of the Jewish Jesus, and was critical of the disciples' requirement that Gentile followers of Jesus respect and keep the requirements of Jewish religious law. He was scathing in his denunciation of members of the Jesus Movement who were insisting that Paul's Gentile converts be circumcised and follow proper dietary laws, accusing them of bewitching people and suggesting that rather than remove other men's foreskins they should go and castrate themselves.[22] Paul's argument was that Jewish religious law was of no value and was unnecessary in establishing a relationship with God or receiving God's gift of salvation. The law may be of value in making people aware of their sinfulness, but it provided no remedy for it. That remedy is to be found in accepting the gift of saving grace given by God through the death and resurrection of Jesus Christ. For Paul, Jesus as the Christ had fulfilled what Judaism was meant to be and therefore rendered the requirements of Jewish religious practice as unnecessary. Paul makes no mention of the teaching ascribed to Jesus in the later document, the Gospel of Matthew, that the full requirements of the Jewish law were to be adhered to.[23]

With his critical views of Judaism and the Jewish law, and the increasing number of Gentiles converting to Paul's gospel, it became difficult for Paul and his converts to remain connected with Jewish synagogues in the way that Jewish Christians under the leadership of James and Peter had been able to do. In time, Paul's work resulted in the formation and growth of separate Gentile communities in the key regional cities of Asia Minor. They were first nicknamed "Christian" in Antioch around the year 60, and the label has become synonymous with the Pauline movement since then.

The odds against the success of Paul's enterprise were high. He was an individual justifying himself on the basis of a personal revelation, one that disagreed significantly with the insights and interpretation of the group chosen by Jesus to carry his message. Paul's slant was just one of a number of other interpretations of the Jesus message being made in the wider Hellenistic cultural setting.[24] He had not met or spent any time with Jesus personally, and in his letters he showed little knowledge of Jesus' teachings and activities and little concern for the issues that were central to Jesus' mission and message. Not only did he not quote Jesus as an authority, but also some of the things he was advocating would have been problematic, if not anathema, to the Jewish Jesus.

The lack of recognition that Paul was given is demonstrated by the number of times in his letters he self-justifies his position as a legitimate Apostle of Jesus. Yet as the first century progressed, the movement begun by Paul continued to spread and grow and acquired the name "Christian," while the Jesus Movement under the leadership of Jesus' disciples steadily diminished in size and influence.

A number of reasons can be noted for this shift. The authority and influence of the Jerusalem leadership of the Jesus Movement were destabilized by a number of crises in Jerusalem during the seventh and eighth decades of the first century: the Jewish civil wars; the execution of their revered leader, James, in 62 (most likely for his resistance to government exploitation of the poor); a shortage of funds; the Roman destruction of Jerusalem, and the forced relocation of the movement away from Jerusalem into the Jewish territories of the Decapolis. Once James and the Jerusalem community were gone, there was no equivalent authority to counter the personal revelations of Paul.

For the Christ movement of Paul, on the other hand, the audience was potentially all members of the empire. It offered a religious message that made available many of the benefits of the antiquity of Judaism without the restrictions of ethnic particularity. The mythology of Paul's message evoked the familiar mythologies of the Hellenistic mystery religions. The communal structure he fostered offered significant benefits and security, particularly to those whose social networks had been disrupted through migration from rural areas to urban centers.

It is here that media become a critical influence. One of the decisive factors in the durability and spread of Paul's reinterpreted religion was his effective use of the medium of letter writing in support of his personal travels, preaching, and community formation. Paul's writing placed his particular reinterpretation of Jesus and the work Paul was doing into the wider currents of circulation of what was the elite medium of his time. This circulation included not only Paul's own letters, but also Paul's written ideas being taken up and incorporated into later writings by other authors.

As noted in this chapter, letter writing was an important literary form in the Greco-Roman world. It was an important tool in a range of social functions, including the political and bureaucratic administrative needs of the far-flung empire, commerce and trade, and social, political, and cultural networking. Christian letters such as Paul's fall within this wider culture of letter writing and were one of the earliest genres of Christian writing. Eighty percent of the documents in the New Testament (twenty-two out of twenty-seven) are wholly or partly letters in form. Later Christians would use letters to such an extent that the apostolic letter, as it is called, became one of the most important genres in Christian literature.

The letters that Paul wrote were personal letters to the young Christ communities that he either founded personally or spent time with during the course of three missionary journeys around the Mediterranean. In distinction from literary letters of the time, Paul's letters were written primarily in response to practical situations, to address issues being faced by those churches with which he felt a personal bond and responsibility, or to provide them with support, advice, admonishment, exhortation, and encouragement in his absence. Along with the pastoral issues he addressed, in the letters he also elaborated his developing theological ideas, ideas that became formative to the subsequent Christian movement.

The power of Paul's letters was carried not only by their content but also by the aura and impact of the media form itself, as described by Roetzel:

> Since the literacy rate was a small fraction of the whole population, and since the expense of writing materials was considerable and the prospects for letter delivery uncertain, for the average person the arrival of a letter was momentous ... most letter recipients in the ancient world also shared the mood of the writer and read or circulated the letter in a broader circle. It is no wonder, then, that not only the underclass but also the privileged treasured these precious letters. The importance of letters qua letters was at least one important factor accounting for the preservation of the Pauline letters we possess. While their theological profundity and relevance doubtless were major factors in the letters' preservation, copying, and ultimate canonization, it is a mistake to ignore the impact of the medium itself on the early church.[25]

The letter form is crucial in understanding Paul's influence in shaping the Jesus Movement into the religion of Christianity. Through his letters, Paul was able to align himself with influential supporters who were similarly educated and culturally connected. The adoption of a medium that has such cultural associations does more than just utilize another instrument of communication; it associates a movement culturally. Paul follows a structure and protocols in his letters that invoke this cultural knowledge and facility.[26] They show characteristics of oral patterns of speech and rhetoric that evoked his personal presence, particularly where there were contentious issues being addressed.[27] Expounding his ideas in a medium that was associated with the exclusive elite classes of society was a further factor in Paul's transformation of the lower-class Jewish peasant into a persona of the literate culture of Hellenism.

In the nascent stage of the Christ movement, Paul's letters were widely copied and passed around, often carried by Christians in their travels to share with others, to be copied again and passed on. Collections of his letters were made and bound into codex form for easier reference and circulation. This circulation of Paul's letters is illustrated by an incident in 180 in which seven men and five women, otherwise insignificant villagers from a small North African village of Scillium (in what is now Tunisia), were brought before the Roman proconsul of the region and charged with participating in an illicit religion. Their leader, Speratus, brought with him to the hearing a bag containing a Latin translation of the Greek letters of Paul, "in case, perhaps, they might need to refer to them." Despite the pleading of the consul for them to reconsider their position, they refused to acknowledge the supreme lordship of the emperor and were beheaded.[28] Accounts of incidents like this added to the growing perception of Paul's letters as scripture.

Another indicator of the influence of Paul's letters is the large number of letters written by other authors but attributed to Paul's authorship. Seven of these are included in the Christian New Testament. There are different views on the legitimacy of this. One view is that it was a common practice of the time, done to extend the honor of a respected figure. The Jewish Apocrypha or Pseudepigrapha, for example, includes writings that claimed a scriptural legacy by being written in the name of an ancient or respected figure such as Enoch, Daniel, or Isaiah.[29] But there are views that see the practice as deception. Ehrman, for instance, names the pseudo-Pauline letters in the New Testament outright as forgeries, deliberately pretending to be from Paul in order to either undermine what Paul was doing or increase the authority of changes that the writer was seeking.[30] The pseudo-Pauline First Letter to Timothy, which advocates the primacy of the patriarchal household and male control of women's behavior, is a good example of this.

The other impact of Paul's letters was in the use made of them and their ideas by other writers. The incorporation of Paul's ideas into other Christian writings not only spread Paul's ideas more widely but also built their authority. Tabor goes so far as to describe Paul's success in the reshaping of the Jesus Movement as "almost wholly a *literary* victory." He identifies three key media documents that took up Paul's ideas and consolidated his influence: (1) the Gospel of Mark, which reworked a lot of Paul's ideas into his narrative of the career and death of Jesus; (2) the six later letters attributed to Paul, which domesticated Paul's message; and (3) the two later documents written by Luke, particularly the Acts of the Apostles, which constructed the history of Christian origins in a way that promoted Paul's significance, downplayed the differences between Paul and the disciples, and reframed Paul's work and ideas as a seamless continuation of those of Jesus' disciples. Almost half of Luke's version of how the movement spread, written from his location in Rome, are about Paul's activities in the West. The spread of Aramaic Christianity to the East is not included in Luke's history. Following the account of Paul's conversion in the Acts, almost the whole history of the church is about Paul, as if the Jerusalem church ceased to be active or of importance.[31]

Paul's letters steadily developed an official status as Christian teachings and gave Paul and his innovative ideas a permanent status and influence within Christianity long after his death. Through their repeated copying, circulation, and incorporation, his ideas about the new faith became influential in understandings of the faith in other regions and to future generations. In-fluential figures in Christianity such as Augustine in the fifth century, Luther in the sixteenth, and John Wesley in the eighteenth all attribute their Chris-tian conversions to reading the Letter of Paul to the Romans.

Paul's cultural translation of Jesus, however, had a number of major and permanent consequences. In his translation of Jesus into Hellenistic culture, Paul also relocated him into a different class and cultural position, changing the metaphor and cultural meaning of Jesus and his teaching away from that of a rural Jewish peasant to that of a Gentile aristocrat, the Lord Jesus Christ, whose lordship status is enhanced by his humble beginnings. Paul in one of his letters has a hymnal passage in which he portrays and celebrates his cul-tural relocation of Jesus as a cosmic ceremony presided over by God.[32] This aristocratic metaphor of Jesus as the Lord has had a major influence on how Christianity developed. While it provided the motivation for some Christians to resist or challenge political powers on the basis that they had a different Lord, it also impelled and justified the development of the Christian Church away from the inclusive community focus of Jesus into a domineering impe-rial organization ruled over by male lord bishops. This development and its media bases are explored in later chapters of this volume.

Paul's critique of the Jewish law also had profound consequences. Al-though many see Paul as not antagonistic toward Judaism,[33] others see Paul's depiction of the Jewish law as polemical and markedly different from what Jesus said about it.[34] Many see Paul's theological views and strong attacks on Judaism as laying the ground for historically constant Christian pogroms against the Jewish people.[35] That discussion linking Paul as a fol-lower of Jesus with anti-Semitism continues today.[36]

The end of the beginning

With the passing of time and the realization that the anticipated end of the world was not going to happen, the apocalyptic temporariness of the move-ment began to give way to establishing foundations for more permanence. What could now be called the Christian movement came to be identified with its loosely connected, scattered house churches throughout the Medi-terranean region, particularly in the coastal cities.

The first generation of Jesus' followers passed away around the seventh decade of that first century. James, the brother of Jesus, was murdered for opposing political exploitation in Jerusalem around 62. The destruction of Jerusalem by the Romans in 70 and the growth of the Gentile Christian movement significantly eroded the authority of the Jewish stream of Chris-tianity, which would later be declared heretical for their failure to accept the Hellenistic view that Jesus was God.

Tradition has Peter being martyred in Rome during the reign of Nero after the great fire in 64. Legends place Paul's death under house arrest somewhere between 60 and 62.

By the end of this first generation, the character of Christianity had changed markedly from being primarily a Jewish apocalyptic sect to a largely Gentile religious movement. The center of the movement had shifted practically and symbolically away from Palestine, the home of Jesus, to urban centers within the empire, such as Alexandria, Ephesus, Antioch, and Rome. The focus of the movement had shifted away from preparing for the imminent Kingdom of God toward reinterpreting the narratives and significance of Paul's Lord Jesus Christ and the Son of God into the language, interests, and values of Hellenistic culture and the political situation of the empire.

NOTES

1   Gamble, 1995, p. 8.
2   Mitchell, 2006, p. 191.
3   Innis, 1950.
4   Richards, 2004, p. 60.
5   Millard, 2000, p. 37.
6   Ward, 2000.
7   Barnes, 2000.
8   Borg, 2012, loc. 709–747.
9   Harnack, 1902, quoted in White, 2004, pp. 143–144.
10   Wright, 2005, p. 95.
11   Wilson, 2008. See also Tabor, 2012.
12   The Acts of the Apostles 6:1–6, 10:34–48.
13   White, 2004, p. 144.
14   Galatians 1:15–16.
15   Galatians 1:16.
16   Aslan, 2013, p. loc 2875. Different explanations are given for this. Borg advocates that the ubiquity of the oral tradition meant that Paul's audience would already have known this information and it wasn't necessary for Paul to repeat it (Borg, 2012, loc 535–536). Wilson argues to the contrary: that the reason why Paul made little reference to the historical Jesus and his teachings or didn't quote Jesus as an authority was because, in his theological outlook, the historical Jesus wasn't important. The major point of reference for Paul and his theology wasn't the real Jesus but "his mystical experience and 'the Christ' who spoke through him." (Wilson, 2008, p. 115).
17   Galatians, 1:13–17.
18   Borg, 2012, loc. 593.
19   Galatians 1:18–19, 2:1
20   Galatians 1:12.
21   Acts 9:10–22.

22 Galatians 5:7, 12.

23 Matthew 5:17–20.

24 Paul mentions other evangelists' interpretations of the meaning of Jesus that differ from his in a number of places in his letters.

25 Roetzel, 1997, p. 76.

26 See Roetzel, 1997, pp. 69–93; Watson, 1994.

27 Harvey, 1998.

28 Hastings, 1999.

29 White, 2004, p. 21.

30 Ehrman, 2006, pp. 45–69.

31 Tabor, 2012, p. 7.

32 Philippians 2.

33 See for example Borg, 2012, loc. 536: "Paul regarded himself as Jewish all of his life, not as a member of a new and different religion. His conversion was not from Judaism to Christianity, but from Pharisaic Judaism to Christian Judaism."

34 Paul, for example, spoke of the Jewish law as "the ministry of death, chiselled in letters on stone tablets" (2 Corinthians 3:7). Far from rejecting it, according to Matthew's Gospel, Jesus sought to enhance and intensify it, saying he had come not to dispense with it but to fulfill it (Matthew 5:25, 28).

35 See for example Wilson, 2008, pp. 234–235: "Supercessionalism was invented by Paul in his *Letter to the Galatians* ... now that Christ has come, Torah is obsolete. Hence there is no reason to follow Jewish law or, for that matter, to be Jewish."

36 See for example Bieringer & Pollefeyt, 2012.

3

The Gentile Christian Communities

The appeal of Christianity

When the disciples who had personally been with Jesus died and the Romans destroyed the city of Jerusalem in 70 CE, the Jewish Jerusalem church lost its leadership authority within the new movement. When the expected end of the world didn't happen, the intense missionary activity decreased and the Gentile Christian communities that were scattered but growing around the Mediterranean began adjusting to living their faith as a minority religious sect within the Roman Empire.

At this stage there was no united or homogenous Christian church, but what Harnack has called "confederated congregations of Christian believers who for the most part were gentile-born."[1] This confederation of largely urban congregations was the beginning of what was to become an empire-wide new religion. Building coherence and handling differences between these communities would be significant issues in the ensuing decades and centuries of development.

Stark, from his research, advocates that the growth in early Christianity occurred principally through the steady attraction of those who were either uprooted from their traditional communities through migration or disaffected by the lack of vitality and relevance of traditional religion and looking for something new.[2] Sawicki proposes similarly that the growth of Christianity occurred in the cracks of Hellenistic culture, not within its central stable structures.[3]

There were many things about Christianity that recommended it to the societies of the time. It had obvious vitality and passion and a compelling sense of universal destiny under its own lord in a political environment that was imperial in its outlook. This shared destiny was continually renewed and rehearsed in dynamic multimediated rituals. It had a strong community structure, gathering new believers into small and intimate gatherings

From Jesus to the Internet, Peter Horsfield © 2015 John Wiley & Sons, Ltd. Published 2015 by John Wiley & Sons, Ltd.

meeting in people's homes. Christian communities offered practical mutual help, including hospitality for strangers and care for those who were worse off, which provided important social structures of support, particularly for those who had left their rural family and village relationships and relocated to the cities as a consequence of imperial economic policies.[4]

Attention was given to moral education and a practical ethic addressed to issues of daily living, a resocialization process based on the tenets of the new faith. Characteristic among these was an idealization of asceticism, abstinence and virginity, and opposition to practices such as extramarital sexual relations, divorce, infanticide, abortion, and Christians participating in cultural religious festivals and games. Membership could include people from across the classes but without the class stratification. Slaves could be members without their masters, and wives could be members without their husbands.

These communities also offered opportunities for social leadership denied people in other places. While it is unlikely that Christianity attracted the upper orders of the Roman ranking system, it is wrong to see the early Gentile Christian movement as a solely or principally lower-class movement. It is now more widely accepted that the growth in early Gentile Christianity was largely from the middle and upper classes, with household leaders bringing with them into the faith their household dependents, including children, employees, and slaves.[5]

The class least represented in early Gentile Christianity was that of the rural peasantry and slaves – the most underprivileged classes.[6] The absence of this demographic in Gentile Christianity is a significant departure from the priorities of Jesus and his brother James, for whom the underprivileged rural and village workers were the major focus of concern.

Among those of status and influence attracted to Gentile Christianity were educated women, who made their homes available for community gatherings and played a leadership role similar to that of patrons of other clubs, guilds, or voluntary societies of the time. In his letters Paul addresses a number of women as church leaders and one of them at least, Junia, as an apostle. These women found in the Christian communities opportunity for leadership that was denied or problematic for them in the wider culture. Given a woman's responsibility in Roman society to manage the household, Osiek and Macdonald go so far as to say that "to step into a Christian house church was to step into a woman's world. This was true even when the leader of the assembly was male."[7]

Multimedia communities

From their earliest times, communal Christian gatherings were diversely mediated events, with the multisensory engagement concretizing the ideas of faith in bodily experience.

Central to community gatherings was worship, which incorporated performances of written, oral, and physical communication. The adopted day of Christian worship was Sunday, the recognized day of Jesus' resurrection but also adopted to distinguish Christian practice from the Jewish Sabbath. Sunday was a workday, so it's likely there were two worship gatherings on the day, similar to patterns of the Jewish synagogues. One was before work in the morning, incorporating prayers, readings of scriptures and sacred writings, and preaching. The other was after work around a ritual common meal. The intimacy and home setting of the gatherings led to the naming of the community as "the household of God."

Psalms from the Jewish scriptures were sung, from memory for most, and there were recitations or readings of Jewish scripture, with commentary, similar to practices in synagogues. There were readings also of Christian writings or letters, although access to circulating Christian writings varied extensively from place to place.

Two rituals are mentioned early as central in Christian material practice. One was baptism, a ceremony of initiation centering on a water bath in which the initiate was either fully immersed or washed, associating the person physically and metaphorically with burial and rebirth into a new life. The other was a community meal, first known as the Lord's Supper and later as "Eucharist" or thanksgiving, which reenacted in words and actions Jesus' last meal with his disciples.

The worship in the intimate spaces also included times of oral prophecy, including ecstatic phenomena such as trances or oral glossolalia (speaking in different tongues or esoteric languages). These ritualized practices retained contact with the strong prophetic tradition of the movement and its emphasis on signs and wonders. Prayers included both free-form and formulaic prayers, with people physically involved by kneeling, bowing, prostrating themselves, or standing with their arms raised and their palms forward, a Hellenistic signifier of piety but also reproducing the cruciform position. From the earliest times, there was opportunity in the ritual for members to exchange a "holy kiss," a Roman practice of greeting between close relatives and in this new context signifying belonging to an alternative family. Other practices, such as making the sign of the cross, would develop in later centuries.

Each of the practices adopted by the Christians had existing cultural associations that were redefined by their Christian use. As Meeks notes, "[T] hey combined features of household, cult, club, and philosophical school, without being altogether like any of them."[8] This intertextual signification gave members a sense of continuity with practices in the wider culture while also instilling difference.

The importance placed early in the movement on public reading indicates there were people in most Christian communities who had the skills of reading. Reading a written text was not just a technical exercise but also an interpretive one. Because of the lack of punctuation and spaces between words in the written script of the time (known as *scriptio continua*), a text was frequently capable of a variety of meanings. Meaning was constructed by the reader interpreting what possible meaning was intended or most suitable, and communicating this to hearers through their use of pace, space, inflexion, and grammatical construction. Most texts were written with this performance of the text in mind. In comparison with our present time, also, there was not the same distinction made between speech and singing, so that reading could be done in a combination of speech, chanting, singing, or a performance style suitable to the occasion of worship.

In time, the oral performance of the written text came to be formalized and its meaning more standardized through the use of written devices such as spacing and written accent marks, but until these devices were adopted, the reader in the community was an important figure in creating the meaning of the text as it was being read. Irenaeus, writing in the second half of the second century, highlights these issues in relation to the proper reading of a section of one of the letters to the Thessalonians:

> If then one does not attend to the [proper] reading [of the text] and if he does not exhibit the intervals of breathing as they occur, there will be not only incongruities but he will utter blasphemy when reading, as if the advent of the Lord could take place according to the working of Satan. So, therefore, in such passages the transposition [hyperbaton] must be exhibited by the reading and the apostle's meaning preserved accordingly.[9]

This skill in not just mouthing words but also reading interpretatively led to recognition of the ability to read as one of the gifts of the spirit, with the role of reader (*lector*) becoming defined as a specific role and placed under the auspices of the officeholders in the community. By the fourth century, as the canon of Christian scriptures became more defined and literacy within the community became more widespread, the reading of the Gospels in particular came to be seen as a privileged role and taken by the senior officeholder.

Christian writings

Although educated Christians included both men and women, it was men who carried the social capital and authority to write. As they did, they exercised a profound influence in the reframing of Gentile Christianity within the culture and philosophical traditions of Hellenism. As Gamble notes,

> It was from their ranks that there emerged the Christian literati who produced the great part of the literature of the early church ... they did not disavow their

intellectual capacities when they converted to Christianity. They turned their talents to the Christian cause.[10]

The influence of writing in the development of Christianity is connected with the particular characteristics or affordances of writing and the cultural capital and prestige associated with it.

One of those is the shaping of language, vocabulary, and grammar that needs to take place so that people beyond the immediate context of verbal exchange can understand the meaning. Writing also changes the nature of the audience, away from those physically present whom the speaker can see, to a person or group in the future, many of whom may be unknown to the writer. Writing operates by the writer imagining an audience. Writing also creates a shift in the nature of ideas and thinking, away from something that happens in a person toward something that exists outside a person, on paper, validated by its own logic as much as by the person saying it. In taking a form outside a person, writing makes transient ideas permanent. Something that may be simply a stage of a changing process of a person's thinking becomes fixed at what it was when it was written. Ideas and thinking are also changed by writing's storage capacity. Being able to write something down replaces the need to hold it in the mind. This frees space in the mind to invent new ideas and information rather than try to remember the old ones, and to focus therefore on the future rather than the past. These characteristics that were brought into Christianity by the increased use of writing played an influential part in how the original oral form of Jesus' message and the Jesus Movement developed.

In the early stages, most Christian writings were practical in their purpose. Their style and literary quality varied significantly, from a rough grammatical style in some of the gospels and apocalyptic writings, to more carefully composed works that reflect the writer's competence in Greek rhetoric and letter composition.[11] More cultured members of the wider society held a lot of Christian writing in scorn because of its roughness compared to the more elevated style of Greek literary writings.

As Christianity attracted more people from the educated classes, however, Christian writing developed into the beginnings of what could be called a Christian literature, with a number of identifiable genres. *Letters*, such as those of Paul, were probably the most extensive and influential, widely used in the development of Christian identity and the building of networks across the scattered Christian communities. *Apocalyptic writings* such as The Revelation to John (c. 90) and The Shepherd of Hermas (c. 100) adapted the cultural genre of apocalypticism for its own purposes. *Apologies or defences of the faith*, such as The First Apology of Justin Martyr (c. 150) and Ireneaus' Against Heresies (c. 180), were written to explain the new faith or defend it against attack. *Manuals of practice*, such as the early Didache, were compilations of teachings or instructions for church organization, rituals, or Christian living. There was also *Christian fiction*, works that appear to have imitated fictional work of the wider culture. The apocryphal Acts of Andrew and the Acts of the Apostles appear to fall in this category.

Along with these, two other genres were formative: written gospels and martyr stories.

The written gospels

Written gospels are probably the most widely recognized genre of Christian writing because of their prominent place in the Christian New Testament. However, the four Gospels in the Christian canon – Mark (written in the 70s), Matthew (80s), John (90s), and Luke (110s) – are only part of a much larger group of Christian gospels in circulation in the first century of Christianity. Burns suggests there may have been as many as 560 gospels ascribed to various apostles.[12] Crossan[13] groups all the gospels into four categories: Sayings Gospels, such as the document Sayings Q and The Gospel of Thomas; Biography Gospels, such as the four New Testament Gospels; Discourse Gospels, such as The Apocryphon of James and The Sophia of Jesus Christ; and Biography-Discourse Gospels, such as Epistle of the Apostles or John's Preaching of the Gospel. Some of these, such as the document called Sayings Q and The Gospel of Thomas, were written earlier than those in the New Testament and were the sources of some of the material used in the later New Testament Gospels.

The Gospels had a number of significant effects in the development of Christianity. One was in positioning Christianity within the Greco-Roman culture of the empire. The four New Testament Gospels utilized a media genre from Hellenistic culture, the "Lives" of important people. These ancient "Lives" were not so much historical accounts as tributes written for particular purposes such as funerals or anniversary celebrations. They included not just actual events from the person's life, but also "oral traditions, legends, and exaggerations that grew up to fit the fame or *persona* of the character in later times."[14] Recreating Jesus in such a cultural genre form furthered the transformation of the Jewish Jesus into a Hellenistic "celebrity" with associated traditions, legends, and exaggerations incorporated into his story.

A second effect of the written Gospels was in fixing the circulation of faith ideas to a specific time, context, and medium. Sawicki sees this transition of the oral telling of the story of Jesus into a fixed and permanent text as a new media development for the Christian movement and a significant departure from the practices of Jesus and his immediate followers:

> There was a time when a textual, written Gospel was an oddity, a curious innovation among the Jesus movements. Sayings of and about Jesus ordinarily

were recited to the accompaniment of certain distinctive practices, which could not be replicated in texts. The textual practice of writing itself does not come from Jesus; writing Gospels was an innovation introduced in several early churches.... The "old" way, the way that arguably came from Jesus, was to vary the sayings about God's kingdom and to improvise.[15]

Some defend the writing of the Gospels on the grounds that it was necessary to place some controls on the variations, improvisations, and inventions that were being made by the oral prophets and evangelists. What is frequently overlooked, however, is that the Gospel writers themselves engaged in the same invention as part of their writing process. While they drew on and used existing oral traditions and written material, they fashioned that material into their own version of the tradition by selecting particular materials over others, structuring and integrating the material in their own particular way, and introducing new material that they or others had more recently written. The fixed and permanent nature of the written text in the Gospels established their particular written accounts as more authoritative. They also concretized what may have been more fluid analogies or thoughts used in oral speech into objective realities. Sawicki cites The Gospel of Mark as an example of this:

> The author of Mark was no ordinary villager. He belonged to the Hellenized cultural élite and had the advantage of advanced training in rhetorical composition. From Mark's vantage point – within the polis, astride the divergence of several contrasting Jesus movements, amid violent insurrection and the brutal reaction of the Roman administration, and in the aftermath of significant failures to get Jews and Greeks to swallow Gospel teaching – it was clear that there had to be a better way. Mark chose the way of text. Mark's text is one continuous, creative makeover of Jesus into a disciple-gathering teacher.[16]

The differences that exist between the different Gospels, even those in the New Testament, give an indication of a number of the literary strategies used by the Gospel writers in their own creative reworking of Jesus.[17]

One was the invention of narratives of Jesus' birth in the Gospels of Matthew and Luke. The two accounts are different and reflect the different audiences for which the Gospels were written. The narrative of Jesus' birth in the Gospel According to Luke, which was written to recommend Jesus to people of the wider Roman Empire, has striking resemblances to a mythical account, in circulation at the time, of the birth of Caesar Augustus, the great Roman emperor who after his death was declared divine and the Son of God. Similar to the earlier account of Augustus, Jesus' conception is described as miraculously virginal and Mary is told by an angel that her child would be called the Son of God. In the Gospel According to Matthew, written for a largely Jewish audience, the birth narrative of Jesus evokes the birth narratives of Moses, the highly revered liberator and lawgiving figure of Judaism. Both Gospels also provide a genealogy of Jesus to establish his credentials to their respective audiences, but the Gospel According to Matthew with its focus toward a Jewish audience begins its genealogy with Abraham, the father of Judaism, whereas the Gospel According to Luke, with its focus on a wider Gentile audience, traces Jesus' genealogy back to Adam, the first human. Although both genealogies disagree in a number of interesting ways, they are alike in tracing Jesus through the line of Joseph, even though both record that Joseph wasn't involved in Mary's impregnation.

A second means of remaking Jesus in the Gospel writing was through a process of retrospective textual exegesis, in which present meanings are read back onto earlier passages to enhance their credibility. So in Matthew's birth narrative, for example, the author has Jesus' parents fleeing to Egypt to escape his being murdered by King Herod. With echoes of Moses again, Matthew's account reads,

> Then Joseph got up, took the child and his mother by night, and went to Egypt, and remained there until the death of Herod. This was to fulfill what had been spoken by the Lord through the prophet, "Out of Egypt I have called my son."[18]

A similar example of retrospective exegesis is Matthew's use of a quotation from the book of the Hebrew prophet Hosea to support the view that Jesus is the Son of God. The passage he uses, however, is referring not to Jesus but to the nation of Israel, and their escape from bondage in Egypt:

> When Israel was a child I loved him, and out of Egypt I called my son.[19]

The Gospel of John takes this recreation further, identifying the person Jesus with the Hellenistic philosophical concept of the Logos (Word), the intellectual structure of the universe. Through this analogy, the human being Jesus is literalized as being with God from the beginning of time and the agent by which all of creation was brought into being, before becoming flesh and living as a human being.[20]

While these theological innovations facilitated Christianity's transition from its specific Jewish context into a context of mythologies of the wider Greco-Roman world, their ramifications were immense. Not least were how to resolve the philosophical conundrums of both a Father God and a Son God, and an integrated human being who was both fully human and fully divine. As we will see, these conundrums took hundreds of years to work out, in the process of which tens of thousands of Christians were murdered or ostracized by other Christians for getting the answer slightly wrong or adhering to a wrong position.

The "fixing" of the faith in writing rather than oral speech posed another problem: how to activate an experience of faith in their audiences when presented in such a depersonalized textual form. Reading a written text did not instigate the same sensory experiences as the dynamic oral communication of a person's presence. To address this, Christians adopted Jewish rabbinic traditions of integrating written text with oral speech, with a personally present teacher or preacher reading or citing the text, and then orally applying it to everyday situations or ethical questions.

Although communicating what may be seen as the same reality, the oral and written communication of faith began to create quite different ways of conceptualizing and reproducing that reality in the minds and lives of their audiences. As a consequence, quite different structures of social and religious power based on those different styles of mediation and hermeneutics also developed: one based on textual authority, and one based on oral, prophetic, or charismatic authority. These media-based hermeneutical systems became competing systems of authority, and contests between traditional text-based Christian authority and charismatic Christian authority have continued to recur throughout Christianity's history.[21]

A final way in which the written Gospels have been influential in the shaping of Christianity has been in establishing the importance of the physical world in Christian thought and spirituality. Crossan[22] advocates that the Gospels finally chosen for inclusion in the New Testament reflect the outcome of an extended debate within Christianity about the nature and relationship of the physical and spiritual worlds. Within the Hellenistic world, there were two main positions on how the physical world was related to the spiritual world (albeit with a range of intermediate positions): the *sarcophobic* position (i.e., flesh-fearful), a view that saw the flesh and physical world as being unimportant or even inimical to the spirit and was often associated with more Gnostic expressions of Christianity; and the *sarcophilic* position (i.e., flesh-loving), which affirmed the material body and physical world as being important. Interestingly, within the context of this debate, one of the key points of contention about Jesus being the Son of God was not whether God could become a human being – that was largely taken for granted within the culture. The point of contention was: when Jesus as the Son of God became a human being, was he an actual physical human being or was he a spiritual being appearing in a human form but not really physical? Both of these views were reflected in the large number of gospels that were in circulation.[23]

At the end of a long process of theological discussion and practice, the four Gospels chosen to be in the authorized canon of Christian writings are all biography gospels. They present Jesus as an actual, historical, embodied person – he is physically born of a woman, he becomes hungry, he gets tired, his body is hurt. For Crossan, the choice of these four "biography" Gospels to be in the Christian scriptures reflects a victory not only of those four particular Gospels but also of that particular cosmological viewpoint that the physical aspects of life are important. It is argued that this dominant Christian approach of taking materialism seriously provided the foundation for the growth of western science.

The other perspective – denying that the material body had any importance – didn't necessarily go away but continued to appear in mystical, ascetic, and Gnostic movements and in conflicted or repressive Christian attitudes toward the body, sex, and women that have persisted to the present time.

The Acts of the Apostles

The Acts of the Apostles is the second document in the New Testament written by the author known as Luke. The date of authorship is estimated as the first decade of the second century. In the form of a history, its presence in the Christian canon has given it a significant influence as the "canonical" account of the origins of Christianity. Luke's Acts, along with his gospel, shows a particular purpose in his writing: to legitimize culturally the new religion of Paul and to gain acceptance of the legal freedom given to Jews for Christians as well.[24] His strategy in his writings is well outlined by Wilson:

> In both his gospel and the Book of Acts, Luke was writing for a Roman audience, trying to impress upon them that the movement was a religion fit for the Roman Empire. But he had a problem. This was a new religion on the scene, bereft of noble ancestry. But noble ancestry is precisely what the religion needed if it were to succeed on the Roman stage. In linking the Gentile Christ Movement through the Jesus Movement back to Jesus and biblical Judaism, he was creating an impeccable heritage for this new religion.... He was also grounding the Christ of Paul in an actual historical being, Jesus, through the Jesus Movement.... Romans, not knowing the history, would be impressed with such an ancient movement that had entered their world. It was also successful in that this account shapes our perceptions and authorizes us to see The New Testament through the eyes of Paul.[25]

Luke achieved this outcome in a number of ways. One was by downplaying Paul's independence, even to the point of contradicting Paul's own writings. For example, although Paul writes that after having his mystical revelation he spoke to no one about it,[26] Luke records Paul immediately going to the house of Ananias, a member of the Jewish Jesus Movement, who healed and baptized him.[27] A second was by inventing, or misconstruing, a meeting of Paul with Jesus' disciples in Jerusalem. The Acts reports that at this meeting the disciples endorsed Paul's ideas. Paul's letters reflect a different view, and he continued to attack quite stridently Jews who tried to have his Gentile converts circumcised. A third was construction of a different reading on Paul's relationship to Judaism. Whereas Paul throughout his letters was adamant that Jesus Christ and the law of love had superseded the necessity of the Jewish religious law, Luke has Paul defending himself before Roman authorities by saying, "I worship the God of our ancestors, believing everything laid down according to the law or written in the prophets."[28] Luke's desire to recommend Paul's Christianity to the people of the Roman Empire explains his failure to report on the extensive spread of Christianity beyond the Roman Empire to the East.

The strategy sustained in writing was an effective one. Luke's portrayal of the continuities between the historical Jewish Jesus of the disciples and the Gentile Son of God of Paul and the Gospel writers became the dominant one in Christian historical perception. The politically expedient view that Gentile Christianity had fulfilled or superseded Judaism was reproduced by many later Christian writers. It laid the basis for the later ostracism of Jewish Christians as being heretical and for the constantly recurring persecution of Jews by Christians throughout history.

The lives of the martyrs

The other major genre of Christian writing was martyrologies, or accounts of martyrdom. As a minority social group, with a number of suspect social practices and a potentially politically subversive theology of the lordship of Jesus rather than the emperor, Christians were occasionally subject to derision, scapegoating, and political persecution. The extent of this persecution of Christians is the subject of debate, as the historical facts of the number of actual martyrs and the events of their martyrdom are clarified and distinguished from the Christian propaganda that has been built around them.[29]

For the first centuries, the persecution of Christians was spasmodic, was local, and involved relatively few people. The most extensive persecution was in the middle of the third century, a time of widespread political corruption and unrest. By this time Christians had become a significant minority throughout the empire, even a majority in some places, and in a time of political instability it was believed that their refusal to participate in events of loyalty to the emperor could not be ignored. Even then, there were numerous opportunities for Christians to meet their legal obligation without public display. Many Christians took this option, purchasing a certificate saying they had sacrificed to the Roman gods.[30] Those who refused to do so became the martyrs, and the basis for the construction of the cult of the Christian martyrs.

The maintenance of commitment by Christians in the presence of this sporadic antagonism was maintained by Christian construction of these persecutions as inherent in their discipleship of Jesus, their lord who gave his life for them. Rather than make Christianity less attractive a proposition, the active persecution of Christians provided opportunities for the consolidation of Christian identity and, in effect, "god advertising" – the raising of public consciousness of Christianity's presence within the society.

A key site of contest between the two ideologies was the Roman Games, events of not only entertainment but also public executions. The Roman Games were an important element in enforcing political authority, maintaining public order, and promoting the noble qualities of composure and bearing in the face of adversity, threat, and misfortune. For people to die in terror legitimized authority, but to refuse to be frightened, to die willingly, and to master the performance of death constituted an attack on death itself through performance. Like modern sports fans, audiences of the games were skilled in discerning between those who died well and those who died badly.

These important social and political functions that the games served made the execution of Christians at the games an important site of contest for the new religion, and the importance of Christians dying well is frequently portrayed in oral and written accounts of Christian death. The writing, the Martyrdom of Polycarp, for instance, records that as Polycarp entered the stadium, "a voice came to him from heaven; 'Be strong, Polycarp, and play the man'."

By exploitation of the meaning of the dominant entertainment, verbal accounts and written stories of the deaths of Christian martyrs became important in building public opinion,[31] and they became another major literary genre of early Christianity. These were vivid and powerful literary constructions that were extensively copied, circulated, and consumed. They provided detailed insights into the inner lives of those executed, firsthand diary accounts written by martyrs on their way to martyrdom, legal transcripts of their interrogations, eyewitness accounts of their death, and descriptions of the impact of their deaths on those in the audience. The genre also included historical romances, popular imaginative elaborations of incidents, or even fictional events that were integrated with actual historical accounts without distinction.

An early account is that of Ignatius, the bishop of Antioch, who in the early years of the second century was arrested, tried for treason, and sentenced to death. During his journey to Rome for execution, escorted by a convoy of Roman soldiers, he wrote a series of letters to people and churches along the way, transforming his journey to execution into a community-building, public relations, and marketing exercise. He urged the Christians in Rome not to try to stop his martyrdom: "I beseech of you not to show an unseasonable good-will towards me. Suffer me to become food for the wild beasts, through whose instrumentality it will be granted me to attain to God."[32] His status as a martyr added extra weight to a number of propositions he made on his way to execution that became central to later Catholic-Orthodox theology: the concept of Christian leadership comprising three ecclesial offices of bishop, priest (presbyter), and deacon; the importance of the sacrament of the Eucharist; the replacement of the Jewish Sabbath (Saturday) with the Lord's Day (Sunday); and use of the term "catholic" or universal to describe the church where the male bishop was the leader.

Another influential martyrology was the account of the death of Perpetua, a twenty-two-year-old noblewoman and nursing mother executed in Carthage in 202 or 203 with four others, including her pregnant slave Felicity. Although her child was not yet weaned and despite repeated attempts by her father and the Roman procurator to have her change her mind at least for the sake of her child, Perpetua persisted in her intention to be martyred. Her slave Felicity, fearing that being pregnant would cause her not to be martyred, prayed for an early birth, gave birth two days before the games began, and was martyred with the others.

Perpetua kept a diary of her thoughts, dreams, and anxieties during her imprisonment. The account of her martyrdom, reproduced in the later book *The Acts of the Christian Martyrs*, intersperses her diary with an editor's narrative. The detail is intimate and touching.

> And as my father stood there to cast me down from the faith, he was ordered by Hilarianus to be thrown down, and was beaten with rods. And my father's misfortune grieved me as if I myself had been beaten, I so grieved for his wretched old age. The procurator then delivers judgment on all of us, and condemns us to the wild beasts, and we went down cheerfully to the dungeon. Then, because my child had been used to receive suck from me, and to stay with me in the prison, I send Pomponius the deacon to my father to ask for the infant, but my father would not give it him. And even as God willed it, the child no long desired the breast, nor did my breast cause me uneasiness, lest I should be tormented by care for my babe and by the pain of my breasts at once.[33]

The graphic eyewitness account of her death in the arena illustrates how the Christian martyrs subverted the dominant symbolism of the games and eventually of the empire by using it to their own purposes.

> And so, stripped and clothed with nets, they were led forth. The populace shuddered as they saw one young woman of delicate frame, and another with breasts still dropping from her recent childbirth. So, being recalled, they are unbound. Perpetua is first led in. She was tossed, and fell on her loins; and when she saw her tunic torn from her side, she drew it over her as a veil for her middle, rather mindful of her modesty than her suffering. Then she was called for again, and bound up her disheveled hair; for it was not becoming for a martyr to suffer with disheveled hair, lest she should appear to be mourning in her glory.[34]

The intimacy and graphic nature of the heroic account of Perpetua and Felicity's death and the dignity of how they met it made it a favorite for

Christians, to the extent that more than two hundred years later, Augustine cautioned his reading audience not to put *The Acts of Perpetua and Felicity* on the same level as the canonical scriptures.

The circulation of such martyr stories was so effective that it led some Christians not only to accept martyrdom but also in some cases to actively seek and even provoke it. The Emperor Severus in the third century observed that the martyrs of the early Church "desire death even more eagerly than the clergy desire a bishopric."[35] A Roman administrator in 180 in northern Africa, besieged by a pious mob of Christians demanding that he do his duty and consign them all to death, sent a few of them off to the arena but told the rest that if they were so eager to die they should jump off a cliff instead.[36]

This readiness of Christians to die, however, created potential problems. One was that an over-readiness on the part of Christians to die could present a message of life denial that could well subvert martyrdom's symbolism and impact. Another is reflected in the concern expressed by Hippolytus, a third-century Roman theologian, that the church could not expect to expand if its members too readily went to their deaths. Teachings emerged that drew a distinction between avoidable and unavoidable martyrdom, and that equal faithfulness was to be found in modeling a life of faith rather than going to an avoidable death.

Some suggest that the extent of persecution of Christians and the number of Christians actually martyred have been greatly exaggerated in the history of Christianity as a result of its development into religious folklore. Fredricksen, for one, has noted,

> The martyrs are a heroic minority. They don't represent a huge popular swelling. We don't have tens of thousands of people being martyred. What we do have, is tens of thousands of people admiring the few who are martyred.[37]

Certainly the greatest persecution of Christians was not by the Romans, but by Christians themselves once Christianity became the religion of the empire and they found themselves in positions of political power. But through the circulation of these written accounts, the martyred took on an elevated status as exemplars of faith and courage, a separate or better class of faith that all Christians should aspire to. The circulation and promotion of martyr stories also became the basis for the development of the phenomenon of sainthood and the cult of the saints, built around the view that the martyred were not only exemplars but also possessed or earned superior qualities of grace that was available to be called upon by others. Christians began visiting and holding services at the tombs and graves where martyrs were buried and seeking burial close to the remains of a martyr to benefit in the afterlife from their proximity. Martyrs were also a primary source of relics, with their remains later being dug up and distributed, further confusing and even horrifying many in the culture for whom contact with corpses was a defiling act. The miracles performed by the parts of the martyr's body became part of the story.

The reception and circulation of Christian writings

Coming into the second century, familiarity with writing was such that Christians were referring to it as an accepted part of the movement, reflected by Luke in the opening of his Gospel: "Many have undertaken to set down an orderly account of the events."[38] Writing was even the subject of possible humor: "if every one of them was written down, I suppose that the world itself could not contain the books that would be written."[39]

From an early time Christian communities would gain access to writings, make copies of them, and share those copies around other communities or individuals. Resources were allocated for necessities such as papyrus, parchment, ink, maintaining archives and libraries, and possibly paying for scribal services for writing and copying. Most Christian writers wrote with the expectation that their work would not only be read aloud to a group but also be copied and circulated, and the form of address of letters frequently allows for this. The second-century apocalyptic writing *The Shepherd of Hermas* includes the instruction:

> You will write therefore two books, and you will send the one to Clemens and the other to Grapte. And Clemens will send his to foreign countries, for permission has been granted to him to do so.

The reference to Clemens appears to be to a person in the Church in Rome, whose role it was to make copies of important documents and send them on to other communities in the region, reflecting the coordination already taking place. By the end of the first century, a number of collections of the letters of Paul were in circulation and being used as authoritative documents. Fragments of *Against Heresies*, written by Irenaeus in Lyons around 180, have been found in provincial Egypt and dated to the end of the second century, meaning they were copied possibly many times and made the journey across the countryside and Mediterranean in only twenty years. Mitchell notes, "The earliest Christians did not just produce texts, they created a literary culture."[40]

The earliest Christian writings were generally in Greek, but as they travelled and were taken up in different places they were also translated and circulated in other languages, initially Latin, Syriac, and Coptic, in some cases influencing development of the language.[41]

There was wide variety in how Christian writings were perceived, received, and used in these first two centuries. For many, writing was still sufficiently new and unfamiliar that it carried a mystique of having an inherent power. As Gamble notes, "In a society in which few could read, texts were esoteric objects to many, and if spoken words were powerful, so were inscribed words, for they had the advantage of duration and secrecy."[42]

Christian writers encountered the same problems with their texts as were encountered in the wider literate society: that errors could be made, and often were, in the process of copying. Often these were accidental – "slips of the pen, accidental omissions, inadvertent additions, misspelled words, blunders of one sort or another,"[43] reflecting the lack of skill or the tiredness of amateur copyists doing their best with unbroken script that was hard to read or illiterate copyists copying text letter by letter. Origen in the third century complained about the quality of the copies of the Gospel in his possession:

> The differences among the manuscripts have become great, either through the negligence of some copyists or through the perverse audacity of others; they either neglect to check over what they have transcribed, or, in the process of checking, they make additions or deletions as they please.[44]

Once works were in circulation, there were no protections or guarantees against the work being intentionally imitated, or in every instance of its reproduction being changed or corrupted to misrepresent the author or make it support an opponent's point of view. There are frequent warnings and even strong curses in early church writings against changing or corrupting the text.

> I warn everyone who hears the words of the prophecy of this book: if anyone adds to them, God will add to that person the plagues described in this book; if anyone takes away from the words of the book of this prophecy, God will take away that person's share in the tree of life and in the holy city, which are described in this book.[45]

Packaging could also influence the reception of writings. As noted, a number of letters in the New Testament attributed to Paul are now considered not to be of his making, being written by others and attributed to Paul in either honest admiration or dishonest deception. Different collections of Paul's letters that were in circulation gave different emphases to what Paul had written either through editing of the letters, deciding what letters to include and what not to include, how the letters were arranged within the collection, and the inclusion of letters written in Paul's name.[46]

An important aspect of the growth and spread of Christian literature was the widespread adoption of the papyrus codex form of the book – sheets of papyrus paper bound together between covers, similar to the book as we know it today. Mitchell sees the Christian use of the codex as "a distinctive mark on material culture in the realm of books."[47] All papyrus gospel fragments that have survived from the early centuries have been from codices.

The codex was not a new form. It developed several hundred years earlier and was used in Greco-Roman society primarily as a notebook or for pocket editions, not for literary purposes, for which the scroll was considered more appropriate. Its popularity among Christian writers was due to its material qualities and its facility as a medium. It suited the type of anthologized material, such as collections of letters and gospels, that Christians wrote. The text could be written on two sides of the page so that 2–3 scrolls could be integrated into one book, making it more economical to produce and less bulky for travelers and teachers to carry. The facility to quickly turn pages made it easier to use and refer to when one was in debates or a speaking situation.

Gamble[48] suggests that one of the influential factors in Christian adoption of the codex was its use in an early edition of the letters of Paul, with the respect given to Paul's letters transferred to the kind of book in which they were transcribed. The widespread use of the codex form helped establish Christianity's identity as a religion of the book (although, as Matthew Engelke incisively notes, not a religion of readers).[49] Use of the codex rather than the scroll differentiated Christianity materially from other groups such as Jews, other imperial religions, and the cultural literati, who didn't adopt the codex for literary purposes until several centuries later.

Resistance to writing

The growing use of writing within the Christian movement did not go without question or challenge. The questions raised about writing Christian teachings are brought to the surface in one of the writings of the second-century Alexandrian teacher, Clement.

Born of wealthy pagan parents around 155, Titus Flavius Clemens received philosophical training in the Hellenistic traditions before converting to Christianity and becoming head of the Christian Catechetical School in Alexandria. He was among the first to provide a systematic explication of Christianity into the influential Platonist framework of his time and was a leading figure in the development of Christian writings into what could be called Christian literature.

Even though writing had been used extensively in Christianity since soon after its beginnings, in the first chapter of one of his books on Christian teaching, *Stromata*, Clement gives an extended justification for why he was writing. His justification indicates that concerns about uses of writing in Christianity were still sufficiently strong that he felt it necessary, as a writer, to address them. A number of concerns are identified, most of which interestingly reflect similar concerns expressed whenever a new medium is brought into religious use.[50]

One was a persistent opinion that the personal human voice was the best and most appropriate medium for the communication of a personal faith such as Christianity – surely, it was argued, a personal relationship with God could only be communicated through people. A second was the perceived lack of control in how Christian teachings would be used when put in writing. As Socrates had noted centuries before, "once a thing is put in writing, the composition, whatever it may be, drifts all over the place, getting into the hands not only of those who understand it, but equally of those who have no business with it."[51] A third centered on the question of inspiration. It was easy for all to tell if a speaker was genuinely inspired or simply faking it through such things as their body language, their speech rhythms, their passion, and their responses to interlocutors and questioners. How did these markers of sincerity and inspiration apply to writing if you couldn't see the writer? A fourth was that writing threatened to distance the faith from attachment to Jesus, who was remembered for his oral stories, his down-to-earth theology, and his relationships with the poor and outcast.[52] Jesus didn't write, and his message was accessible to everybody whether they could read or not; why should his followers do something different? Would adopting a medium of communication that is accessible only to a small minority of people begin to exclude from leadership and teaching those whose leadership, like Jesus', was rooted in oral communication?

Clement in his work provided counterarguments for each of these objections based on a concept of media complementarity, seeing both oral and written teaching as working hand in hand in a total process. He drew attention to writing's advantages: its ability to share wisdom more widely, to preserve teachings that might otherwise be forgotten or corrupted, and to pass on the tradition. As long as the apostolic tradition is unwritten, he argued, the written tradition of the heretics cannot be disputed. He noted also an argument of pragmatic realism: writing is here to stay, wouldn't we be foolish to ignore it?

> It were certainly ridiculous for one to disapprove of the writing of earnest men, and approve of those, who are not such, engaging in the work of composition.

Clement's advocacy was a strong one and one of the first systematic attempts to address the issues around adopting a new medium in the communication of Christian faith. His doing so highlights the intimate connection there is between the ways in which a religion is mediated and its religious identity and, therefore, the objections and arguments that are commonly raised whenever there is a significant shift in how the faith is mediated.

What need to be acknowledged as well, though, are the foresight and wisdom in the heart of the objections. As Christianity developed and spread, writing grew in use and importance to the extent that in time being literate became an essential requisite of being a leader and a teacher within the Christian community. In the process, the hierarchical structuring of prestige and power that was associated with literacy in the wider culture began to be reproduced within the structures of Christianity, and the inclusiveness of community and leadership emphasized by the illiterate Jesus was being lost.

NOTES

1 Harnack, 1893, p. 11.
2 Stark, 1996, pp. 37–39.
3 Sawicki, 1994.
4 Borg, 2012, loc. 581.
5 Stark, 1996, p. 30. Stark quotes Harnack's point that Ignatius, writing on his way to execution in Rome in the early second century, urged Christians in Rome not to try to prevent his martyrdom only because he was aware that there were some in sufficiently powerful positions of influence to be able to do so.
6 Stark, 1996, p. 30.
7 Osiek, Macdonald, & Tulloch, 2006, pp. 157–163.
8 Meeks, 2006, p. 152.
9 Quoted in Gamble, 1995, p. 229.
10 Gamble, 1995, p. 41.
11 Watson, 1994.
12 Burns, 1989, p. 179.
13 Crossan, 1998.
14 White, 2004, p. 98.
15 Sawicki, 1994, p. 29. Some anthropologists, such as Lord (cited in Finnegan, 1988), see a similar phenomenon when modern scholars write down or record current living oral traditions. Although the traditions are by nature continually changing in performance, once recorded they become fixed at that point, and future improvisations in performance of the tradition are seen as distortions of the "true" tradition because they don't match the isolated recorded performance.
16 Sawicki, 1994, 54.
17 The differences in accounts between the Gospels are acknowledged in their titles in most English versions of the Bible: The Gospel "According to" Matthew.
18 Matthew 2:14–15.
19 Hosea 11:11.
20 John 1:1–5, 14.
21 Weber, 1968.

22 Crossan, 1998, pp. 31–40.
23 A polemically hybrid type of gospel such as *Epistula Apostolorum* (Epistle of the Apostles) or *John's Preaching of the Gospel*. In the *Epistula Apostolorum*, Jesus foretells that Paul would persecute the church and be converted to become apostle to the pagans.
24 Fredriksen, 1998.
25 Wilson, 2008, pp. 138–149.
26 Galatians 1:12.
27 Acts 9:10–19.
28 Acts 24:14.
29 See for example Moss, 2013.
30 Meeks, 1998.
31 Seaton, 2005, p. 71.
32 Ignatius, 107, chap IV.
33 Tertullian, 203.
34 Tertullian, 203.
35 Seaton, 2005, p. 74.
36 Seaton, 2005, p. 74.
37 Fredriksen, 1998. See also Moss, 2013.
38 Luke 1:1.
39 John 21:25.
40 Mitchell, 2006.
41 The Christian adoption of the simpler Coptic script in its texts contributed to the demise of older Egyptian scripts and their associated literature.
42 Gamble, 1995, p. 237.
43 Ehrman, 2006, p. 55.
44 Cited in Ehrman, 2006, p. 52.
45 Revelations 22:18–20.
46 Mitchell, 2006, p. 184.
47 Mitchell, 2006, p. 191.
48 Gamble, 1995, p. 56.
49 Engelke, 2009.
50 Insights into Clement's work and the concerns about writing are drawn from Fiskå Hägg, 2006; Kimber Buell, 1999; Osborn, 1959.
51 Hackforth, 1952, 25:274B.
52 White, 2004, pp. 122–125.

4

Men of Letters and Creation of "The Church"

When Roman Emperor Marcus Aurelius died in 180, the relative peace, political stability, and artistic, philosophical, and scientific development that had existed in the Empire for around a hundred years declined significantly. For more than a century following, there were continual wars as the army and other political alignments sought to control the Roman state. Religion became an important coping mechanism for people in uncertain times. The number of Christian communities had continued to grow to the extent that Christianity had become a recognized religion within the Greco-Roman world.

In this process of cultural imbrication, a number of issues central to the nature of the movement were being addressed: how to understand and explain Jesus in ways that were culturally and practically relevant, how to explain what exactly the salvation that Jesus brought was, and defending Christianity against criticisms and hostility. In addressing these questions, Christians in different places and with different philosophical backgrounds, interests, and alignments drew on resources from their own developing tradition and from the wider culture.

At this stage, there was significant diversity in Christian beliefs and practices. While a common view within Christianity is that there has always been one single "apostolic tradition," in these early centuries there was significant diversity. As Hatch has noted,

> If we were to trust the histories that are commonly current, we should believe that there was from the first a body of doctrine of which certain writers were the recognised exponents; and that outside this body of doctrine there was only the play of more or less insignificant opinions, like a fitful guerrilla warfare on the flanks of a great army. Whereas what we find on examining the

evidence is … a mass of opinions which for a long time fought as equals upon equal ground.[1]

That diversity included Christian streams such as the Jewish, Gnostic, Marcionite, Montanist, and Logos approaches, each of which interpreted the meaning of Jesus in different ways to address different contexts and existential demands. In contrast to later portrayals, not all were small or minority traditions. Gnostic Christianity had a wide and influential following across the Middle East and North Africa that persisted for centuries, as did Marcionism, which, in many places around the Mediterranean, was not just in the majority but *was* Christianity.[2]

Yet out of this early diversity of what Hatch calls "equals upon equal ground," by the end of the following century one of those cultural adaptations had largely succeeded in establishing itself as the only legitimate expression of Christianity. That stream was the Logos tradition, the one we now know as Catholic or Orthodox Christianity. To identify its partisan nature more clearly, and the early connections between the two, I am referring to it as the Catholic-Orthodox Party of Christianity.[3]

There were many reasons for why the Catholic-Orthodox Party was successful in defining and having itself recognized as the "only true interpretation" of the historical Jesus and his mission. Many of those reasons go beyond the scope of this study, but a number were distinctively media related. It is these in particular that I focus on in this chapter.

The Catholic-Orthodox brand

Installing a hierarchical authority structure

A crucial factor in the domination of the Catholic-Orthodox Party over other streams of Christian interpretation was their progressive consolidation of power and authority into a male-exclusive hierarchy, and the promotion of this authority structure as normative for the religion.

A hierarchical structure wasn't necessarily the natural organizational structure for Christianity. Jesus explicitly rejected the exercise of power over others by any one person within his group. He advocated instead a distributed communal authority characterized by a quality of mutual service.[4] The Jesus Movement communities reflected a variety of leadership and organizational styles. Leaders of new Jesus communities were initially appointed by the evangelists who established them, and thereafter were chosen by the members. Leadership was often distributed among men and women according to their particular practical or so-called spiritual gifts, such as apostle, pastor, evangelist, bishop (overseer), prophet, or teacher. The patron or patroness of the house in which the early Christ communities met also exercised a leadership role.

It is likely therefore that in the early Christian communities a variety of leadership patterns was followed, ranging from the more collegial to the more singular centered on a designated overseer. The earliest handbook for those running churches, the *Didache,* an early Christian manual, written around 100, identifies Christian leaders in terms of their function as teachers, apostles, and prophets.

The major proponents of the argument that the normative authority structure of Christianity was to be a hierarchical one were men already in hierarchical positions. Some, as we will see in the case of Cyprian, came from family or personal positions within the hierarchical structure of the empire and explicitly sought to reproduce that governance structure within the Christian churches.

One of the earliest advocates of a hierarchical model was Clement, the bishop of the church in Rome at the end of the first century and commonly claimed as the first Roman pope. In response to a dispute over leadership in one of the churches in Corinth, he advocated in a letter written around 96 that God through the apostles had established a particular order of bishops and deacons within the church, and their authority needed to be honored. He quoted an unidentified scripture sentence in support of his argument.[5] Irenaeus, the bishop of Lyons, in his book *Against Heresies* (180), promoted the position of bishop on the grounds that it was a bulwark against heresy. Repeating Clement's justification, he argued that bishops were the bearers of true Christianity because they were the ones to whom the original apostles who knew Jesus personally passed on the true tradition. The order and authority of bishops were the only way to preserve the truth of the apostles against heresy. Irenaeus supported his argument by constructing a list of those who had been bishops of Rome, to demonstrate their direct line of authority from the original apostles, Peter and Paul. While the same line of succession could be done for all bishops, he noted that to do so would be "very tedious in such a volume as this."[6] His focus on the succession of the bishops of Rome was because of what he saw as its preeminent authority, reflecting the hierarchical prominence that Rome was already taking in the minds of Catholic-Orthodox leaders.

The concept of a succession of bishops was an appealing idea to the legal and historical mind of Tertullian, the North African Latin theologian who argued for an institutionally organized universal church that alone has the truth, alone determines the core beliefs, and alone has the ability to use and interpret the scriptures, and where authority is managed through a succession of bishops. In Tertullian's view, a nonhierarchical view of Christian authority was one of the measures of Christian heresy.

An important site for the promotion of the hierarchical view of authority was the production and circulation of written manuals of practice. *The
Apostolic Tradition*, for example, a seven-thousand-word document from
the early third century, provides detailed directions on the choice and or-
dination of bishops, presbyters, and deacons; the preparation of people
for baptism and the conduct of baptism; the conduct of the Eucharist; and
guidelines for personal religious practices. A hierarchical authority structure is promoted in the manual, with detailed directions on who is to be
ordained and set apart and who isn't. Bishops, elders, and deacons are to
be ordained "because of liturgical duty." Widows, readers, virgins, subdeacons, and those who have received a gift of healing by revelation, on the
other hand, are not to be ordained. No justification is given for the different
treatment, apart from "for the matter is obvious." The hegemonic nature
of these particular interpretations of Christian authority is hidden by as-
suming a male hierarchical structure as the essence of the tradition that has
always been:

> Now, driven by love towards all the saints, we have arrived at the essence of
> the tradition which is proper for the Churches. This is so that those who are
> well informed may keep the tradition which has lasted until now, according to
> the explanation we give of it, and so that others by taking note of it, may be
> strengthened (against the fall or error which has recently occurred because of
> ignorance and ignorant people).[7]

Another influential manual was the *Didascalia Apostolorum*, or *Teaching of the Apostles*. Written later in the third century but attributing itself
to the first century to amplify its authority, it embeds a monarchical male
episcopate, which gives the bishop in effect unlimited symbolic and literal
control. This hierarchical authority is justified by a scriptural interpretation
that identifies the bishop as the successor of the kings of Israel. The practical
effects of the earlier reconstruction of Jesus as a ruling "lord" can begin to
be seen in this imperial framing of Christian leadership.

Building a Catholic-Orthodox branded church identity

Another important element in the Catholic-Orthodox Party's branding of
itself as "The Church" was in its cooption of exclusive use of the terms
catholic and orthodox. The term "catholic" comes from the Greek adjective
katholikos, meaning "universal." Although meaning literally all Christian
communities, it was appropriated early by Catholic-Orthodox Party male
bishops and given permanence in writing to refer exclusively to their particular interpretation of Christianity. In a similar way, the term "orthodox,"
which means literally correct or straight teaching or worship, was coopted

to describe only their activities. Opposing Christian interpretations were branded as *heterodox* and *heretical*, or "other" teaching.

One of the first uses of the term "Catholic" was by Ignatius, the bishop of Antioch, in a letter to Christians in Smyrna written around 106 on his way to martyrdom in Rome. Ignatius uses the term in a way that refers not to all Christian communities, but only those governed by male bishops.

> Wherever the bishop shall appear, there let the multitude [of the people] also be; even as, wherever Jesus Christ is, there is the Catholic Church. It is not lawful without the bishop either to baptize or to celebrate a love-feast; but whatsoever he shall approve of, that is also pleasing to God, so that everything that is done may be secure and valid. (Chap. 8)

The term is used again in *The Martyrdom of Polycarp* (155) and in the *Muratorian Fragment* (c. 170), one of the earliest lists of the books of the New Testament. In both cases, it is used not to refer to all Christians but to one particular type of ecclesiastical structure. By the end of the second century, the concept of Catholic Christianity was being used widely to refer only to those groups in line with the Catholic-Orthodox Party's hierarchical structure.

The exclusive right to the Catholic-Orthodox "brand" was entrenched politically in Roman law by the Emperor Theodosius I in 380, with a decree that the term "Catholic Christians" would be reserved only for the version of Christianity associated with the bishop of Rome. As for others holding a different opinion, the emperor wrote,

> [S]ince in our judgment they are foolish madmen, we decree that they shall be branded with the ignominious name of heretics, and shall not presume to give their conventicles the name of churches.[8]

This erasing of Christian diversity was embedded in Christian doctrine the following year at the Council of Constantinople. In the authorized creed that would be repeated by Christians for the next two millennia was the affirmation "I believe in one holy catholic and apostolic church."

Reducing difference

It was apparent in the first centuries of the development of Christianity that the memory of Jesus, embodied now in a growing number of stories, rituals, practices, and texts, was capable of generating unusual energy and transformative power in people's sense of meaning and moral behavior. As noted, initially there was significant diversity in this interpretive energy and vitality. The concern of the male leaders of the Catholic-Orthodox Party was to narrow this diversity into a single opinion in line with their view.

The reason commonly given for this, and the one that is reproduced in most Christian theology and histories, was that at this stage it was necessary to present a common face to the wider society and to protect the message and truth given by Jesus from its misinterpretation and corruption by heretical distorters. In this view, the Catholic-Orthodox Party is seen as the preserver and defender of the true "apostolic tradition" of Christianity.

This view ignores a number of things. The Catholic-Orthodox Party's view of the faith – *their* idea of the apostolic tradition – was not the original message of Jesus, but just one of a number of adaptations of the original story of Jesus into particular cultural, regional, and local contexts. The narrowing of Christian diversity into a single position reflected the particular view that there could only be one possible truth about Christianity, and that Catholic-Orthodox bishops were the definers and defenders of that single truth. This standardization process took place at a number of interconnected levels of the religion. As we will see in chapter 5, it also took several centuries to resolve.

The key elements of the Catholic-Orthodox Party's beliefs and practices were worked out, mainly by bishops and their advisers, in meetings and daily interactions, in circulated writings, in discussion and debate, in development of solutions to meet practical issues, in interaction with wider cultural thinking, and in attacking alternative opinions seen as being "in error."

Summaries of the key elements of the faith had existed since the earliest days of Christianity. Paul mentions some in his early letters. As the second and third centuries progressed, these early basic Christian beliefs developed in scope, complexity, and abstraction. By the late second century, *The Apostolic Tradition*, a written church manual, specifies that those who were to be baptized as Christians had to agree to a Trinitarian theological confession that involved at least sixteen different philosophical and doctrinal affirmations.

Written documents were crucial in this development. The growing abstraction of the theological issues involved in being Christian, as the bishops and their theological assistants were defining them, meant that in order to participate in leadership and contribute to the shaping of teaching within Christianity, one not only had to be able to read and write, but also had to be sophisticated in one's knowledge of classical written texts.

As beliefs grew in complexity, and as organizational control grew more restrictive, the potential for error increased. To the extent that the bishops had the power or political associations to do so, those people whose ideas were considered in error or heretical were constrained through censure, exclusion or social ostracism, removal from their positions, or strong counterattack. Irenaeus' *Against Heresies*, for example, was a five-volume set of books, each around forty thousand words long. Where possible, those considered to be in error had their writings removed from circulation or destroyed. As we will see in chapter 5, there were many doctrinal clashes to follow as the political power of the Catholic-Orthodox Party in the following century increased and contests to be appointed to a powerful bishop's position multiplied. But by the end of the third century, the Catholic-Orthodox Party had largely triumphed over other expressions and formations of Christianity, and had largely succeeded in establishing their concept of Christianity and their organizational structure as "the Apostolic Tradition" – the only legitimate expression and embodiment of what Christianity is.

As we have noted, writing was a crucial tool by which the Catholic-Orthodox Party bishops extended their hierarchical power and beliefs. This involved not just individual publications, but also the networking capabilities that having the resources and expertise to write made possible. While most bishops oversaw small Christian communities or groups of communities and many were poorly educated, they were reinforced in their positions by the bishops in the larger and more powerful city dioceses. These urban bishops used the greater wealth in their churches, the greater number of clergy under their command, the civil importance of their cities in the imperial order, and their access to the facilities and resources for writing to organize opinion and muster support. Male bishops were able to quote writings from each other in support of their own position and authority. A male bishop being installed in even a small rural diocese could count on letters of greeting from other male bishops around the world, enhancing perceptions of the global nature of their position even at the local level. As Fox notes,

> Literacy also allowed bishops to outmaneuver opponents, display a common front of opinion, abjure or cure mistaken Christians or "sign up" lists of names for creeds and disciplinary rulings, texts which allowed yet more power to be mobilized.[9]

This production and networking capability of the Catholic-Orthodox Party, and the contribution that media made to their dominance, are apparent in three influential figures from the second and third centuries: Tertullian, Cyprian, and Origen.

Tertullian

Tertullian was born in a well-to-do family in Carthage (in what is now Tunisia) around 160. He was educated in philosophy, history, and rhetoric; was literate in both Greek and Latin; and studied and practiced law in Rome. He converted to Christianity sometime between 190 and 195, a time of persecution and of martyrdoms of Christians in Carthage.

Although he also wrote in Greek, Tertullian made his mark as an independent lay thinker writing in Latin. He had a logical, terse, incisive legal mind and a strong moral outlook. Very practical in his concerns, all of Tertullian's thirty-one treatises, written between 196 and 212, address controversies in moral behavior, church structure and authority, theology, and heresy.

His writing style contributed significantly to the impact of his writings. He wrote as an advocate in a courtroom, utilizing in full the techniques of rhetoric in laying out a case, anticipating and answering objections, acting scathing and unfair toward his opponents, and arguing a point of view in a direct, terse, dense, witty, satirical, and eminently quotable style designed to grip his audience and be remembered.

> He preached, interpreted Scripture and wrote in order to argue. He was a pugilist with a pen.... In everything he wrote, there was some point in dispute, some quarrel to be had and some error to be corrected.[10]

Influenced by Stoic teaching, legal perspectives, and a Roman sense of order and authority, Tertullian constructed Christianity as primarily knowledge of God based on reason and authority expressed in the creeds of the Catholic Church, which alone has the truth and alone has the ability to use and interpret the scriptures. Valid churches were those managed by bishops through the succession of bishops. Tertullian saw Christian faith as a new law, calling people to a new way of life, and he was uncompromising on those who did not live out the moral demands of faith: sins after baptism were serious and in some cases unforgiveable, and martyrdom was a privilege that should be welcomed by Christians.

Tertullian's strong advocacy of an institutional organization of Christianity under the authority of monarchical bishops was a significant factor in the shaping of institutional church-centered Christianity, particularly of the Latin West. He was influential also in conceptualizing for Western Christianity some of the key theological issues that had been dogging Greek Christianity, particularly those of a Trinitarian view of God and the nature of Jesus. Though he wasn't the first to use them, his distinctive use of some Latin terms such as *sacramentum, trinitas, persona, substantia,* and *satisfactio* provided western theology with some of its basic theological vocabulary. The conceptual shift that he brought cannot be separated from its linguistic medium.

> What Latin it is that Tertullian dared to write! It was without precedent in the literary field. In Tertullian's writing, we come across the living language of the Christians of the time, the Latin of the growing Latin church, a language which accordingly is filled with loan-words and new coinage to describe the new facts and ideas of the Christian daily life.[11]

Ironically, appalled by the behavior of the bishop of Rome in restoring Christians who had committed and repented of gross sins, the great advocate of church authority withdrew from the Catholic Church in 200 and associated himself instead with Montanist Christianity, the strict charismatic Christian renewal movement that stressed moral rigor and asceticism and had been declared heretical by the Catholic-Orthodox Party. Ironically also, the ardent advocate of martyrdom as the expression of true faith died peacefully at the age of 60, although the influence of his ideas continued, particularly in Western Latin Christianity.

Cyprian

Born around 200, also in Carthage, Cyprian was a wealthy, aristocratic property owner, possibly of senatorial rank. He was trained within the Greco-Roman education system as a rhetorician and was experienced in politics, the law, and civil administration. He became a Christian when he was forty-six, partly as a result of disillusionment with the political instability of the empire and the decline in standards of civil society. Soon after his conversion, he was elected as bishop of the church in Carthage and overseer of the whole North African church.

Cyprian brought with him to the job of bishop his own personal resources, media skills, and experience in building political networks through personal contact and writing. In his eight years as a bishop (250–258), he wrote numerous letters and around a dozen treatises, some of them several volumes in length. Eighty-two of his letters are preserved; others are referred to but no longer exist. These, however, weren't just simple letters – many were long treatises, and many were produced in multiple copies with multiple attachments.

Cyprian was a strong advocate of episcopal authority, consistent with his aristocratic and senatorial background. To counter the weakening of episcopal authority by incompetent and dissident bishops, Cyprian promoted the concept of an objective authority of the episcopacy, based not in the individual bishop but in the college or council of bishops in their collective role as successors to the original apostles. By removing the possibility of authority being undermined by the humanness of the individual, Cyprian cemented the authority of the individual in the position by asserting the collective authority of the position.

Cyprian further reinforced the bishop's authority by making the institutional church, and therefore the bishop, indispensible to a Christian relationship with God, even though this contradicted Jesus' emphasis on an individual's relationship with God as a father. As Cyprian put it, "He can no longer have God for his father who does not have the church for his mother."[12] In Cyprian's model, divine forgiveness was dispensed by church clergy through a system of penances and pronouncements.

It was an extremely effective administrative solution with a wide range of applications. The effectiveness of the rite of baptism, for example, was not affected by the morality of the priest performing the rite because it was guaranteed by the whole college of bishops. The challenge presented to episcopal authority by other forms of religious authority, such as the charismatic authority of an oral prophet, were managed simply by saying that the "gift" of oral prophecy was a function of the college of bishops and was exercised through the bishop, regardless of his personal gifts.[13]

Cyprian's concept of the church was that of a hierarchical organization, reproducing the civil structure of the empire with which he had experience. In Cyprian's church, the bishop of Rome was the emperor, the clergy the aristocracy, and the laypeople the citizens. This structure, which came to be adapted by the western Catholic Church, laid the basis for a ready accommodation of Catholic Christianity to the political power of the empire.

Practically, this abstract concept of church authority was only possible and sustainable within a particular media system.[14] It presumes a scattered group of autonomous bishops forming a single corporate entity through a network of occasional face-to-face meetings and frequent written correspondence and circulation of written treatises. In this regard, Cyprian's use of media is illustrative.

Eighty-two of the letters Cyprian wrote (in Latin) have been preserved.[15] Most were not just private correspondence but public letters, intended to be read publicly, freely copied, and widely distributed. He wrote frequently to bishops and other leaders, encouraging them, telling him his opinion of things they're doing, and urging them to desist from behavior he considers divisive or damaging. His correspondence shows evidence of communication with Christian communities in Spain, Gaul, Cappadocia, Rome, and elsewhere in Italy. In one of his letters to Rome, Cyprian includes a list of all the African bishops and their sees, apparently to keep the central records and mailing lists held in Rome up to date.

Many of his letters are addressed to multiple recipients – one lists eighteen different recipients. Letter 73, written in response to an enquiry about the baptism of heretics, is a 6,500-word epistle, and includes as an attachment a copy of another long treatise, *On the Virtue of Patience*, "as a token of our mutual affection." Letter 20, written to the presbyters and deacons in Rome to correct misperceptions of his actions, includes copies of thirteen of Cyprian's former letters as well.

Several of Cyprian's letters give an indication of Christian uses of communication systems of the empire. Letter 49, written to Rome immediately after the close of a church council held in Carthage, for example, closes with the lines,

To you, my dearly beloved brother, we are sending over news of these events written down the very same hour, the very same minute that they have occurred; and we are sending over at once to you the acolyte Niceforus who is rushing off down to the port to embark straight from the meeting. (Epis 49.3.1)

Cyprian claims of an open letter written by the Roman clergy that "it has been circulated through the entire world and reached the knowledge of every church and every brethren" (Epis 55.5.2). He is able to cross-reference previous letters of his on the assumption that they have been widely circulated and their contents are part of the shared knowledge.

Fox refers to such a volume and exchange of Christian writing as "the organization of opinion," similar to what we would see today in a PR, media, or political campaign.[16] Haines-Eitzen argues that at this stage in the second and third centuries, the production of such an output was most likely the result of "circles of readers and scribes who transmitted Christian literature individually and privately."[17] A bishop such as Cyprian would not have been able to maintain such a volume of output and copying, nor exercise the influence he did from his base in North Africa, without access to significant personal resources to engage scribal support and without counting on the same support being available in "the circles of readers and scribes" he was writing to. It gives an indication of how access and facility with the affordances of writing undergirded the bishops' power.

Origen – the media magnate of Alexandria

Origen (c. 182–c. 251) was a Christian philosopher and theologian from Alexandria, one of the major cities of the ancient world. The second city of the empire, it was a major trading center where East met West, attracting both Greeks and Jews. It was also a major center of intellectual life with the most famous textual library in the empire, boasting a reported 700,000 books in its collections.[18] Included among its scholars were figures such as Euclid, Archimedes, Galen, and Philo. There was a strong and intellectually active Jewish community that had produced the *Septuagint*, a Greek translation of the Hebrew Scriptures that was adopted as the Christian Old Testament. The philosopher Philo had developed a philosophy of religion based around the logos doctrine that linked the wisdom of the Hebrew Scriptures with classical Greek philosophy. Philo's logos doctrine became an important tool in aligning the concept of Jesus as the Son of God with Hellenistic philosophy.

Origen received his education in the Christian catechetical school in Alexandria, which was engaged in an active project of reconciling Christian thought with the best of Greek philosophy. The focus of Origen's intellectual attention was to arrive at a definitive reconciliation between Christianity and the Hellenistic world. The ambitiousness of his intellectual ventures and some of his speculations made him suspect to many in the Catholic-Orthodox Party, and many of his ideas were condemned and many of his writings destroyed. Yet Christian scholars widely recognize him as one of the most influential formulators and thinkers of Christianity. Küng describes Origen as "the only real genius among the church fathers, a man with an insatiable thirst for knowledge, a wide-ranging education and tremendous creative power."[19] In Ling's view, his ambitious attempt to create a full Christian cosmology in his book *On First Principles* made him "the first theologian to put out a full and methodical exposition of the whole intellectual framework of the Christian faith."[20] His writings on asceticism and his own self-castration were influential in the development of the monastic movement.

Origen's intellectual influence is closely connected to his effective utilization of media. The volume and distribution of his written output were arguably unmatched in the ancient world.

Only a fragment of his works remain today. The list of his writings compiled by Eusebius is said to have contained two thousand books, although scholars suggest there may be as many as six thousand written works[21] on a vast range of topics: major works on theology, including a scientific doctrine of the Trinity and the first known systematic theology, *On First Principles*; writings on the Christian life; biblical studies; writings against pagan criticisms; and the basis for an orthodox theology of asceticism. His *Hexapla* was a manuscript of parallel columns setting out six versions of the Hebrew Scriptures. Laying out comparable translations side by side revealed the differences in literal meaning of the text, so Origen reconciled the differences by drawing on the resources of Greek philosophy and Jewish practice to develop a hermeneutical method recognizing three levels of textual meaning: the somatic, literal, or historical sense; the psychic or moral application to the soul; and the pneumatic, allegorical, or spiritual sense, referring to the mysteries of the Christian faith.

Even by today's standards, Origen was a media machine, gathering and consuming texts; teaching face to face in Alexandria, where his classes became so popular that he had to hire an assistant; and disseminating his ideas widely through an unparalleled utilization of writing. With the encouragement and financial support of an influential patron, Ambrose, whom he had converted to Christianity, Origen developed what was in effect a media studio to service and distribute his own intellectual output. Eusebius described it in the following way:

> Ambrose urged him not only by countless verbal exhortations and incentives but also by furnishing abundant means. For, as he dictated, he had at hand more than seven shorthand writers, who relieved one another at appointed times, and copyists no fewer in number, as well as girls trained in beautiful penmanship. For all these Ambrose provided the necessary means in abundance.[22]

Origen also travelled extensively, visiting Christian communities by invitation as a speaker or to mediate in church disputes. Like a current rock star going on tour to promote his latest CD, Origen took with him and distributed copies of his writing from his media center in Alexandria to supplement and reinforce his personal influence.

Around 230, Origen's ideas brought him into conflict with his bishop, and he moved to Caesarea (in current-day Israel), was ordained a presbyter, and established a school that led students through the study of philosophy to the study of scripture. He took with him to Caesarea his extensive and constantly expanding personal library, which made Caesarea a significant center of written output. He died in 254 as a result of injuries inflicted during persecution under Emperor Decius.

Although many of his works were destroyed, his extensive personal writings were widely reproduced and distributed in Greek and in Latin and Syriac translations. At times, his name was removed from copies because of their controversial nature. The library at Caesarea became a primary resource for Eusebius in compiling the canon of scripture commissioned by Constantine, and in writing his influential *Ecclesiastical History*.

Origen's extensive influence was not just that of a highly creative thinker but also that of a cultural and media visionary. Küng sees Origen as central in the development during this time of what was for Küng one of the major paradigms of Christianity: the Hellenistic paradigm.

> For there is no overlooking the fact that Origen's thought represents a shifting of the focal point of Christian thought under the influence of a Hellenism with a Neo-Platonic stamp.... The centre of Christian theology is now no longer, as in Paul, Mark and the New Testament generally, the cross and resurrection of Jesus. Now largely speculative questions stand in the center.... There is no mistaking the fact that already among the early Greek fathers the main theological interest shifted from the concrete salvation history of the people of Israel and the rabbi from Nazareth to the great soteriological system.... Now Christianity was understood less and less as existential discipleship of Jesus Christ and more – in an intellectual narrowing – as the acceptance of a revealed doctrine about God and Jesus Christ, the world and human beings. And it was to be above all the Logos Christology which increasingly forced back the Jesus of History in favor of a doctrine and finally a church dogma of the "incarnate God."[23]

Writing out women

One of the challenges in the establishment of the Catholic-Orthodox male hierarchical pattern of Christian authority was the containment of women's leadership. The issue provides an interesting case study in media and religious power.

Women played a significant role in Jesus' work and his religious vision. In the New Testament, women are mentioned among Jesus' followers and his inner circle. Women feature prominently in his parables and as models of the spiritual values he was proposing. There is evidence to indicate that women exercised a variety of leadership roles within the early Jesus and Christian movements, including as patronesses, missionaries, and leaders of local Christian communities. As Schussler-Fiorenza notes, "[W]ithout question they were equal and sometimes even superior to Paul in their work for the gospel."[24]

By the end of the second century, however, Christianity had become an almost exclusively male-led movement, with the maleness of Jesus identified as essential to his godness and extended into a paradigm of the essential maleness of normative humanity.

The suppression of women's leadership in Christianity took place within a wider social environment in which independent women were presenting a sufficient challenge to the male middle class that the nature and social position of women were under active debate and contention.[25] The men of the Catholic-Orthodox Party aligned themselves with the conservative side of this debate, promoting a hierarchical structure of male authority in Christianity that paralleled a male ideal of the Roman patriarchal family. Their patriarchal stance was mediated through Christianity in a number of ways.

One was the promotion of a shift in understanding of the Christian community away from the house church concept to the concept of the church as the "household of God" under the control of the patriarchal figure, the bishop. An example of this reworking can be seen in the widely circulated First Letter to Timothy. Although attributed to Paul, it is now widely seen as being written by a literate Greek Christian several decades after Paul's death. While the letter reflects what was then a common ambiguous attitude in Christianity toward those who were wealthy, the primary concern of the author is wealthy women and the influence they were having in the Christian community in Ephesus.[26] Against this, the author outlines a hierarchical and gender-based model of church order in which male bishops are to exercise the dominant role, linking that public role to the structure of the patriarchal family in which the morally superior male needs to exercise control over the morally inferior female.[27]

> The men should pray ... the women should dress themselves modestly and decently.... Let a woman learn in silence with full submission. I permit no woman to teach or to have authority over a man; she is to keep silent. For Adam was formed first, then Eve; and Adam was not deceived, but the woman was deceived and became a transgressor. Yet she will be saved through childbearing.[28]

There were other Christian writings endorsing women's leadership. The fact that this particular letter but not the others was included in the canon of authorized scriptures illustrates how the male bishops cemented their power over women through the selective legitimization and circulation of writings. A pseudonymous Latin work from the fourth century, Ambrosiaster's *Commentary on the Letter to the Philippians,* similarly promotes a male hierarchical structure of the church as a counter to vulgarity, referring back to a time when "a different order was instituted for governing the church because it seemed an irrational, vulgar and vile thing that all could do everything."[29]

Women's leadership was also subordinated through the written manuals of practice. Of particular concern to the bishops were single women, those not under the control of a husband or whose time wasn't fully occupied with home duties and had chosen to dedicate themselves to religious work. In *The Apostolic Tradition* (early third century), the detailed instructions relating to the subordinate role of widows are instructive:

> When a widow is appointed, she is not ordained, but is chosen by name. If her husband has been dead a long time, she is appointed. If it has not been a long time since her husband died, she may not be trusted. If, however, she is old, let her be tested for a time. For often the passions grow old with those who give them a place in themselves.... Widows and virgins will fast often and pray for the Church. The elders will fast when they want to, as is the same for the laypeople. The bishop may not fast except when all the people fast.[30]

The role and control of widows were defined even more extensively in the *Didascalia Apostolorum,* a third-century Syrian church order. The document reflects concerns about Christian groups in which women's authority was accepted.[31] The document adamantly puts women, particularly independent widows not under the authority of a man, in a place of subordination to the male bishop, whom they are told they are to respect and fear as if he were God [*sic*]. The argument for women's leadership on the grounds that it brings something complementary to men's is further dismissed in the document by presenting the bishop as incorporating both male and female qualities, including breastfeeding, rendering unnecessary any benefit to be gained by having women as leaders.

> Know thy bishops ... and love him who is become, after God, thy father and thy mother ... who reared you with the word as with milk, who bred you up with doctrine.

The *Didascalia* received wider circulation by being substantially reproduced in the *Apostolic Constitutions* (fourth century).

In the writings of Catholic-Orthodox Party men, women were frequently associated with passions and the body, sexual immorality, heresy, and wrong thinking. Hence, *The Apostolic Tradition* gives different rules for older widows on the grounds that for them "the passions grow old." In the third century, Origen (who castrated himself) observed, "What is seen with the eyes of the creator is masculine, and not feminine, for God does not stoop to look upon what is feminine and the flesh."[32] In the following century, Epiphanius, a bishop of Cyprus, observed,

> For the female sex is easily seduced, weak, and without much understanding. The devil seeks to vomit out this disorder through women.... We wish to apply masculine reasoning and destroy the folly of these women.[33]

Women's place and contribution in the development of Christianity were also submerged in the writing of Christian history. The subtlety of this process of displacement is observable in representations of women in the letters of Paul, compared to the writings of Luke forty or fifty years later. In his Letter to the Romans, Paul mentions in very positive terms a number of women as significant leaders, apostles, missionaries, and coworkers. Luke's account of the early years of Christianity in the Acts of the Apostles makes no mention of these women.

In the same letter, Paul identifies a number of people whom he considers to be apostles, including a woman, Junia.[34] In the subsequent copying of manuscripts, her name was frequently changed to a masculine form, a practice that wasn't finally corrected until the twentieth century. Luke, on the other hand, limits the term "apostle" to the twelve male disciples, but includes as apostles also those men chosen later to replace the disciples. This is in line with other aspects of Luke's portrayal of women. Although Luke's gospel has more female characters than the other gospels, they are portrayed playing a subordinate and supportive role, a view significantly different from that given in the earlier writings of Paul and a subtle rewriting of Christian history to make women's place in Christianity more acceptable to the conventions of the imperial world.[35]

The final strategy used by the Catholic-Orthodox Party men was to exclude women from access to writing to prevent circulation of their ideas. The Synod of Elvira (early fourth century) concretized in a canon what had been expressed in other places previously: "A woman may not write to other lay Christians without her husband's consent. A woman may not receive letters of friendship addressed to her only and not to her husband as well."[36]

Although most women's writings from the early centuries of Christianity were destroyed, a number have survived and were recently rediscovered. They give a different insight into the extent of this contribution. The apocryphal Gospel of Mary (early second century), for example, addresses the debate about women's leadership by giving Mary Magdalene's account of encountering the risen Jesus. The Acts of Thecla and Paul, part of the apocryphal book Acts of Paul (late second century), gives an account of the travels and activities of Thecla, a follower of Paul, whose experiences included escaping from being eaten by lions and cutting off her hair and wearing men's clothing so she could travel freely.[37] Her fame spread to such an extent that a shrine to her was founded in Syria. Some of the martyr stories in circulation reflect authorship by women, such as the diary account of Perpetua mentioned earlier.

The Apocryphal Acts of the Apostles is another body of work assumed to be authored by women. Written around 150–240, it reflects an alternative view of Christian life and organization through a genre that includes what Davies describes as "imaginative, at times even grotesque, compendiums of miracles, conversions, and adventures. Fundamentally hyperbolic, they are filled with obvious exaggerations, extravagant statements and fabulous journeys."[38] Although categorized as "apocryphal," Davies considers them significant as Christian writings, because of the social world they reflect and their subversive affirmation of a different perspective on Christian religious experience, community structure, and leadership. The concerns reflected are directed to the vulnerable within the community. Widows and elderly women are mentioned in positive terms and shown to be capable of visionary experience, and attention is given to their financial support and the structures in the community needed to do this. In contrast to the male hierarchy's emphasis on married women submitting without complaint to their husbands, *Acts* advocates women asserting their rights in relation to sexual demands on them, and rejects women seeing their bodies solely as instruments of procreation. It also supports a woman leaving her marriage in asserting this right if necessary. They were dismissive of church hierarchs and the ritualistic nature of institutional religion, looking instead to adventure stories of charismatic apostles.

> In the Acts, on the other hand, men are often seen, ethically, as dangerous to the female. Of course apostles, itinerant Christian preachers, were highly respected; but such men by the beginning of the third century were a vanishing breed. Men of charismatic works gave way to men of words. The Acts frequently show ordinary Christian men as foolish, confused about the faith, and liable to temptation.… To the widows in the Acts the Christian faith was a rebellious path to religious experience.[39]

In the face of the misogyny of the Catholic-Orthodox Party leadership, the Apocryphal Acts of the Apostles reflects an alternative of female self-assertion expressed from the context of a different community and authority structure in a subversive genre of writing.

NOTES

1   Hatch, 1957, pp. 10–11. See also Ehrman, 2003.
2   Woodhead, 2004, p. 33.

3 Although most commonly identified today as the Roman Catholic and the Eastern Orthodox Churches, I have deliberately identified them as a "Party" to keep apparent that, at the time, they were only one of a number of sincere adaptations of the Jesus Movement. The normalizing tendency to refer to them simply as "The Church" hides that they are a specific constructed theological and political position, not one innate in Christianity.

4 See for example Mark 10:42–44.

5 "For thus says the Scripture a certain place, 'I will appoint their bishops in righteousness, and their deacons in faith.'" Clement of Rome, 96.

6 Irenaeus of Lyons, 180, III:2–3.

7 "The Apostolic Tradition of Hippolytus of Rome," para 1.2.

8 Bettenson, 1943.

9 Fox, 1994, p. 134.

10 G. D. Dunn, 2004, pp. 9–10.

11 von Campenhausen, 1960, p. 8.

12 *On the Unity of the Church*, 6.

13 A clear example of Weber's concept of the routinization of charisma.

14 Innis provides a number of valuable studies in how particular media systems support the emergence of particular political structures. See particularly Innis, 1950, 1951.

15 Extracts from the letters are drawn from Clarke, 1984.

16 Fox, 1994, p. 137.

17 Haines-Eitzen, 2000, p. 84.

18 Barnes, 2000.

19 Küng, 1994, p. 163.

20 Ling, 1968, p. 172.

21 S. M. Miller, 1994.

22 Eusebius Pamphilius, 1890, p. VI.23.

23 Küng, 1994, pp. 169–171.

24 Schussler Fiorenza, 1983, p. 161. See also Byrne, 1988.

25 Schussler Fiorenza, 1983, pp. 182–183. See also Osiek et al., 2006.

26 Tamez, 2007, pp. 2–14.

27 Dewey, 1992; Tamez, 2007.

28 I Timothy 2:8–3:6.

29 Cited in Schussler Fiorenza, 1983, p. 303.

30 Hippolytus, 215, para. 10 and 23.

31 Connolly, 1929, section IX.ii.33.

32 *Selecta in Exodus* XVIII.17.

33 Adversus Colklyridianos.

34 Romans 16:7.

35 Schaberg, 1992, p. 279.

36 *Synod of Elvira,* Canon 81.

37 Good, 1992, p. 386.

38 Davies, 1986, p. 114.

39 Davies, 1986, p. 116.

5

Christianity and Empire

By the beginning of the fourth century, the Christian movement had substantially redefined itself and consolidated a position as one of the recognized cults or religions within the Roman Empire with communities widely distributed across regions we know today as Spain, France, Britain, Germany, Austria, Italy, the Baltic States, Greece, Bulgaria, Turkey, Syria, the Middle East, Egypt, and Northern Africa.

Though not the largest religion in the empire, Christianity was among the best organized and growing, with the original communal diversity narrowed significantly to a largely defined hierarchical organizational structure of male regional or city bishops overseeing congregations under the leadership of local male presbyters (elders) and deacons (servants).

Key to this organization was a recognized communication network of speech and writing. When the Emperor Diocletian attacked the Christians in 303 as part of a move to consolidate his hold on the empire, one of his decrees was for Christians to hand over all of their texts to be burned. His successor, Maximinus Daia, saw Christian literature as sufficiently powerful that he composed a counterliterature, *The Memoirs of Pilate and the Saviour*, and instructed that it be taught to schoolchildren for their memorization.[1]

Bishops, although scattered across the empire, kept in contact with each other through occasional regional meetings and messenger-delivered letters and writings. This networked oral and written communication was central in reinforcing the male episcopal organizational structure of Christianity and the narrowing of Christianity's early diversity.

Imperial patronage and imperial Christianity

In 311, Constantine became the emperor of the Western Empire at the Battle of the Milvian Bridge. He attributed his success to the one supreme god

From Jesus to the Internet, Peter Horsfield © 2015 John Wiley & Sons, Ltd. Published 2015 by John Wiley & Sons, Ltd.

of the Christians, citing a vision he had seen of a cross in the sky on the eve of the crucial battle. While maintaining an official policy of religious toleration, as emperor Constantine began actively promoting the cause of Catholic-Orthodox Christianity.

While Constantine's vision is often seen as the instigator of his support for Christianity, others see it in political terms. Christianity's increasing numbers and organizational structure were making it a rising political force and a valuable ally in Constantine's gaining control of the empire.[2] Constantine enlisted Christianity's strengths by coopting Christianity into the political structures and processes of the empire, as described by Brown:

> The empire was kept going not through intervention from on high by officials but, rather, as it were, "horizontally" – through collaboration with an empire-wide upper class, drawn from the elites of the cities.... These urban oligarchies formed a small and highly privileged group in every locality. The upper classes of the Roman Empire never amounted to more than 3 percent of the overall population. Yet they owned a quarter of all the land of the empire and 40 percent of its liquid wealth.[3]

The method of incorporation was the process of patronage, by which the emperor would choose and endow the top appointments from people he knew personally, who would in turn do the same, "right down the line to the humblest local officials."[4] This patronage included not only the gifting of money but also the means to become wealthy: ownership of land, access to services, and the authority to raise taxes.

Through his promotion and patronage of Christianity, Constantine drew the male bishops as the elite of the religion into the center of imperial life. He redressed the damage of the earlier Diocletian persecutions by restoring the property of Christians who had been martyred or exiled. He made all Catholic-Orthodox clergy salaried officials of the government in the way that pagan officials had been previously. He commissioned a number of major new Catholic-Orthodox churches to be built at sites of religious significance in Jerusalem, Bethlehem, Rome, and Antioch and bequeathed them with money-producing lands and estates to support their officers and their upkeep. The bishop of Rome was gifted the Lateran Palace as his Rome residence along with a large adjoining gold- and silver-adorned basilica church. The first day of the week, the Sun's Day and the common day of Christian worship, was made a public holiday, making possible greater popular participation in Christian worship services. An imperial edict allowed lands and other legacies to be bequeathed to churches by citizens, stimulating a rapid increase in wealth and greater financial security for churches.

Although the empire was still dominantly pagan, Constantine's patronage changed dramatically Christianity's relationship to the political empire.

Supportive Christian leaders were invited to the emperor's court and became part of the political apparatus of the empire, acting as advisers, judges, and distributors of social welfare, and praying for God's blessing on the emperor's military campaigns, displacing pagan leaders who had done the same previously.

Conversely, Constantine's patronage involved him in the interests of the religion. He identified himself as a bishop, "ordained by God to oversee whatever is external to the church," and in this capacity intervened in church matters that he considered disruptive or damaging to the welfare of the empire. Freeman notes that when Constantine visited the Eastern Empire, he found a form of Christianity quite unlike what he was used to in Latin-speaking Gaul, one that "buzzed with speculation on theological issues." Constantine had trouble grasping the seriousness with which the Greek mind considered these doctrinal matters and was constantly seeking theological and political solutions for these divisive doctrinal disagreements that threatened the unity of the empire.[5]

One of these was the lingering Donatist controversy, a disagreement between North African bishops and the bishop of Rome over the readmission of Christians who had repudiated their faith during the Diocletian persecutions. When the decision of a council of bishops was ignored by the African Donatists, Constantine used military coercion to try to change their mind, although the disagreements persisted long beyond Constantine.

One of the interesting media aspects arising in this dispute was over writing script. One of Constantine's actions in unifying his empire was unifying the variety of written scripts for Latin used in different regions of the empire into a common script. The Constantinian uncial was a merger of italic and Alexandrian Greek square scripts using a modified point system and phrase-by-phrase writing rather than *scriptio continua* (continuous letters without word breaks). The Constantinian uncial was adopted by the Alexandrian-Roman parties and, as well as the script of the imperial office, was the monopoly script for Latin liturgical and biblical texts until the ninth century.

As an act of resistance to the political coercion being exerted on them, however, the Christian Donatists across North Africa developed their own Latin script, the African half-uncial (the precursor of our modern lower-case serif scripts and fonts) and used it in their documents to signify their ongoing theological opposition.[6] Two hundred years later, Pope Gregory (540–604) made a similar effort to assert himself against the patriarch of Constantinople by reviving Roman capitals for Christian monuments and continental italic for Christian texts, but he did not succeed. Altman draws attention to this little-known religious phenomenon of script as authority:

> Prior to the invention of the printing press, liturgical letter forms had religious significance and their use, shape, and script-model were prescribed,

party-affiliated, and obligatory. There exist many examples of the rigidity of script-as-obligation. Biblical scholars need merely look at the script to know the religious affiliation of a group.[7]

In 324, Constantine took control of the eastern part of the empire from Licinius, building a new capital at the ancient Greek city of Byzantium and renaming it Constantinople. While this action was politically expedient, it aggravated tensions within Christianity between the Latin-speaking West centered in Rome and the Greek-speaking East centered on Constantinople, a rivalry that eventually split Eastern and Western Christianity.

After Constantine's death and a period of emperors suspicious or antagonistic to Christianity, Theodosius I in 379 reaffirmed Christianity as the official religion of the empire and Christianity became more closely intertwined with the imperial political system. Pagan religions were soon forbidden and became the targets of Christian persecution and violence. The state became involved in building churches, worship became more elaborate and institutional, and leadership became increasingly consolidated in the elite male clerical class. As it became fashionable and beneficial to be a Christian and more people became Christian, converts had less reason for personal commitment, and personal participation in religious activities by Christians became less obligatory.

In this political and economic climate Christian bishops, increasingly wealthy through their patronized benefactions, exercised spiritual, economic, legal, and political power as the equivalent of earthly princes or lords. Fourth-century Roman historian Ammianus Marcellinus described the bishops of Rome toward the end of the fourth century as "enriched by the gifts of matrons, they ride in carriages, dress splendidly and outdo kings in the lavishness of their table."[8] With such potential wealth, power, and influence, episcopal offices became highly sought after and the cause of extensive political intrigue and violence. Appointments to vacant bishoprics were intensely fought over – a hundred people are believed to have died in the fight for the vacant bishopric of Rome in 366.[9] With wealth from their imperial patronage, bishops, particularly those in the major cities, became patrons in turn, reinforcing their power and political positions through patronage and promotion of bishops of smaller towns, and acquiring their own cohorts of scholars and theologians.

Access to this political patronage was dependent on a bishop maintaining a theological position that was politically orthodox for those in power at the time. Yet with the specifics of doctrinal orthodoxy constantly changing from place to place and council to council, bishops or theologians could easily find themselves outmaneuvered or out of favor and losing their imperial patronage with all of its associated taxation, stipendary, and benefactional benefits.

This political context ensured that discussions about the substance of Christian belief became not just matters of doctrinal interest, but also struggles for political influence and power between bishops of important cities, people who wanted to be bishops of important cities, and the emperor. Being accused of or associated with heresy became weapons in this episcopal intrigue. Emperors from Constantine on found it necessary to intrude themselves into doctrinal disputes to ensure that the outcome was also in their best interests. Constantine, for example, played a leading hand in developing the foundational creed of Christian belief accepted at the Council of Nicea in 325. In similar fashion, the theological statement accepted by the council held at Chalcedon in 451, which resolved the issue of how the human and divine were related in the human being Jesus, was drawn up by court officials of the Emperor Marcian when they found the bishops' statement confusing and ineffectual.[10]

While many Christians welcomed this increased political power of Christian leaders as the work of God, others saw them as having compromised themselves and become weak and corrupt. The withdrawal of those critical of these developments into separated communities became the impetus for the development of a significant monastic movement in both Western and Eastern Christianity. This politicization of Christianity continued into the following centuries so that "by the end of the fourth century, bishops and emperors were relying on violence to subdue, coerce and marginalize dissident thinkers – a trend that continued on into the bloody Middle Ages and beyond."[11]

Councils, creeds, and canons

Once bishops had consolidated their position as the dominant authority in Christianity, bishops meeting together in council constituted themselves as the ruling body of Christianity. Meeting personally in council or through correspondence, bishops addressed questions of all kinds: the powers and responsibilities of bishops and other church officials; the conduct of church rituals; moral questions; the coordination of Christian dates and calendars; doctrinal questions, including what was heretical; and the interrogation, identification, and condemnation of heretics.[12]

While such a collegial concept of religious leadership appears exemplary, the association of bishops became a highly contested competition for dominance and superiority. There was frequent maneuvering in advance of meetings through written correspondence and envoys to muster support and to ensure that opponents were disadvantaged or even excluded from decision making. Decisions of councils were not universally accepted, and counter-councils were occasionally called to declare the other council's decisions heretical. Bishops from the large urban centers, particularly the key imperial cities of Rome, Constantinople, Alexandria, and Antioch, had greater resources at their disposal to muster support and exert or buy influence than those from smaller rural or regional dioceses, and many councils were organized by more powerful bishops using patronage or political influence to muster collegial support for their positions against opposing bishops.

The political nature of these councils is reflected in writings of the time. When Gregory of Nazianzus, the patriarch of Constantinople and a significant figure in the Council of Constantinople in 381, was asked by the emperor and several friends to return the following year to a reconvening of the council, he replied:

> If the truth be told my attitude toward all gatherings of bishops is to avoid them. I have never seen a good outcome to any synod, or a synod that produced deliverance from evils rather than addition to them. You must not think me tiresome when I write in this vein, but rivalries and maneuvers always prevail over reason, and in trying to decide between others it is easier to get accused of wickedness oneself than to deal with their wickedness. Consequently I have withdrawn to myself. I consider retirement to be the only means of saving my soul.[13]

A major agenda of the early episcopal councils was the resolution of the theological questions that had been created through the theological construction of Jesus as the Son of God. The elevation of Jesus in this way required the definition of how Jesus as Son of God was related to God the Father and to the conception of God as the Holy Spirit as well, and subsequently how Jesus could be both human and divine at the same time.

Those engaged in these theological developments were primarily the literate elite within Christianity. Wealthy patrons such as a bishop gathered around him literary friends, philosophers, and religious figures who counted on the patron for practical support and access to social opportunities.[14] In return, they enhanced their patron's stature and made available their literary and philosophical skills in service of their patron's interests. For these elite groups, the frame of reference and the focus of being Christian were not the practical demands of daily life but the traditions of Greek philosophy going back more than a thousand years.[15] But this was a precarious basis on which to try to find common ground. Freeman notes,

> Quite apart from the difficulties in interpreting the broad spectrum of scripture, there were too many varied sources and too many philosophical traditions, some very sophisticated and always in a state of development. This was the nature of the Greek intellectual world. It proved extraordinarily difficult to define the parameters of a theological issue and find ways of resolving it.[16]

Written texts were essential in this. The mastery of written texts was crucial for circulating one's ideas and putting and defending a case. Yet written texts could also be the cause of one's downfall. If the debate changed, one's position made permanent in writing could well lead to one being branded heretical, as happened on numerous occasions. Because every text was handwritten, it was also relatively easy to alter texts to misrepresent them or to make it appear they supported a different position. It was not uncommon for writings of opponents to be removed from circulation or burnt, and for those found in possession of suspect documents to be threatened with excommunication. Scriptural texts were also altered to support one's position to such an extent that one of the methods used by biblical scholars today to locate the history of particular scriptural texts is by tracing the history and reproduction of alterations. Arguments over whether to include a particular document in the scriptural canon were part of these debates.

The conflicts over such issues could be torrid and at times violent. In some cases, bishops in major cities or in the same city excommunicated each other because they thought they had it wrong. It was not a pretty picture. The fourth-century Roman historian Ammianus Marcellinus wrote at the time, "No wild beasts are such enemies to mankind as are most of the Christians in their deadly hatred of each other."[17]

The media form adopted to unify the religion also contributed to the division. The "creed," a short statement of core beliefs, gave few words to work with and made it difficult to summarize complex philosophical arguments, particularly when those words were translated from the primary language of Greek to the other Christian languages of Latin and Syriac. As a result, there were extensive arguments over minute details, in some cases over just one word, or, in the case of the *homoousios* versus *homoiousios* division (Jesus having the same nature as God compared to a similar nature with God), over just one letter. Yet those one or two words or one letter had wide-ranging political implications and produced violent confrontations. In some cases, the difference was resolved not theologically but politically. The Nicene Creed, for example, became normative in Christianity not because of general agreement or understanding, but because of its backing by the emperors. Doctrinal politics and their political risks were never far from bishops' minds. When asked a question about the meaning of part of the creed in 457, the bishop of Melitene in Armenia replied, "We uphold the Nicene Creed but avoid difficult questions beyond human grasp. Clever theologians soon become heretics."[18]

A number of councils are recognized as more important than the others because of the breadth of the participation of bishops involved and for the considered seriousness of the issues they address.

The Council of Nicea (325) was summoned and presided over by Emperor Constantine to resolve divisions over how to understand the relationship of

Jesus as the Son of God to God the Father. The main contenders were both from Alexandria: Arius, an elder, and Athanasius, the bishop. The council condemned the Arian position, which it considered made Jesus more human than divine. The resultant creed, the Nicene Creed, with support from the emperor, stood as a benchmark for future debates. However, support for "Arian" Christianity, which was actively missionary in emphasis, would continue for several centuries.

The Council of Constantinople (381) was called by Emperor Theodosius to address festering divisions over the conundrum of the Trinity and the nature of Jesus. Although no western bishops attended, the council reaffirmed the equal standing of the Father, Son, and Holy Spirit (known as consubstantiality) and rejected other alternatives such as those of the Arians, Apollinarians, and Macedonians. The council also issued a modified creed to provide greater clarification of the Nicene Creed.

The Council of Ephesus (431) was summoned by the Emperor Theodosius II at the request of Nestorius, the patriarch of Constantinople, to resolve the relationship of the divine and human in Jesus. The issue was also caught up in a festering dispute between the cities of Constantinople and Alexandria over their relative imperial superiority. After bribing the imperial court, Cyril of Alexandria started the council before the bishops of Rome and Antioch, who were supportive of Nestorius, had arrived. Nestorius was condemned and banished to a monastery in Egypt, and his writings were ordered to be burned. The council led to the separation of the Church of the East, which was supportive of Nestorius, from Eastern and Western Christianity.

The Council of Chalcedon (451) was summoned to solve the problem of dualism in Christ's nature (i.e., how he could be both human and divine). Because the bishops' resolution was considered to be too muddled, a solution was drawn up by an imperial official rejecting a monophysite position (Jesus had only one nature) in favor of a dyophysite (Jesus had two natures). To promote the creed and solve the political tensions being caused, the Emperor Marcian ordered his army officers to swear allegiance to it.[19] While the Chalcedonian creed became definitive in the West, it inflamed violent passions between competing groups in the East. The council deposed Dioscorus, the patriarch of Alexandria, because his position was considered to be too monophysite. When his appointed successor returned to Alexandria, however, he was murdered by a mob supportive of Dioscorus. A number of churches continued to hold a monophysite position and were declared heretical, but they have continued to the present day, particularly the Copts, Ethiopians, Armenians, and Syriac Jacobins.

Episcopal councils were significant media events. Prior to meetings of a council, there would be a flurry of correspondence as different bishops presented their views of the issues, argued their case, anticipated and countered opposing arguments, and projected themselves as the authoritative opinion maker. Then there would be a flurry of correspondence following the council providing information and interpretations. It is here that bishops of the larger and more influential cities were at a distinct advantage by being able to produce and reproduce multiple letters and distribute them widely and quickly.

> Christian intellectuals of the period had shown themselves to be well read and highly sophisticated and ingenious in argument.... Just as interesting was the efficiency by which new ideas, argument and ripostes were being spread through the circulation of texts. Many of the participants must have employed an army of scribes in order to keep up with the demand for copies of their works. An equivalent circulation of ideas of such complexity across such a wide region, would probably not be seen until the invention of printing in the late fifteenth century.[20]

Councils themselves were media pageants within the popular media of the time, and being associated with the wider occasion enhanced a person's status. About three hundred bishops from across the empire attended the Council of Nicea, called by the Emperor Constantine in 325. They travelled to the council at the emperor's expense accompanied by numerous support staff, and they entered the hall with their entourages through an entrance lined by the emperor's guard. The emperor presided at the opening session in a display subsequently immortalized by Eusebius in his obsequious biography of Constantine:

> As soon, then, as the whole assembly had seated themselves with becoming orderliness, a general silence prevailed, in expectation of the emperor's arrival. And first of all, three of his immediate family entered in succession, then others also preceded his approach, not of the soldiers or guards who usually accompanied him, but only friends in the faith. And now, all rising at the signal which indicated the emperor's entrance, at last he himself proceeded through the midst of the assembly, like some heavenly messenger of God, clothed in raiment which glittered as it were with rays of light, reflecting the glowing radiance of a purple robe, and adorned with the brilliant splendor of gold and precious stones. Such was the external appearance of his person; and with regard to his mind, it was evident that he was distinguished by piety and godly fear. This was indicated by his downcast eyes, the blush on his countenance, and his gait. For the rest of his personal excellencies, he surpassed all present in height of stature and beauty of form, as well as in majestic dignity of mien, and invincible strength and vigor. All these graces, united to a suavity of manner, and a serenity becoming his imperial station, declared the excellence of his mental qualities to be above all praise. As soon as he had advanced to the upper end of the seats, at first he remained standing, and when a low chair of wrought gold had been set for him, he waited until the bishops had beckoned to him, and then sat down, and after him the whole assembly did the same.[21]

The outcomes of these councils were published as canons and were considered to be law to guide the church's practice and understanding. Canons covered a wide range of topics from questions of moral behavior and handling lapses in such behavior, to spelling out the responsibilities, obligations, and limitations of clergy roles, and answering questions relating to doctrinal issues and the organization of churches. The canons were reproduced in writing and circulated widely, similarly to an imperial edict, with the aim of standardizing practice across all churches in the known world.

As this body of decisions grew, they became integrated into a highly developed system of legal decisions and prescriptions that governed the functioning and actions of the increasingly institutional and restrictive churches. Eventually, if one was to exercise any influence at all within Christianity, one needed to be expert in understanding and negotiating this complex system of canon law. Gaining this expertise required gaining expertise and access to the writing-based system of archives, cataloguing, cross-referencing, and interpretation, an access that was restricted to those approved by the bishops. In this way, the system of power within Christianity implemented by the bishops was reinforced and carefully controlled.

The official decisions prevailing at the time set a framework by which other works were judged. Those considered contrary to orthodox belief were condemned, leading to a widespread destruction of books and the emaciation of the rich literary culture that had been the pinnacle of the civilization of the empire. In 448, the Emperor Theodosius decreed:

> Since it has come to our pious ears that certain men have written and published teachings which are dubious and not precisely in accord with the orthodox faith ... we order that any such writings, coming into existence, whether formerly or now, should be burned and committed to complete annihilation, so as not even to come to public reading, with any who can be to own or read such compositions in books being liable to the extreme penalty.[22]

Many classical Greek works of science and philosophy central to the later Islamic and western Renaissances were preserved only in Syriac translations made by the Nestorian Church of the East.

These periods of doctrinal dispute had a further consequence in establishing a textual hierarchy within Catholic-Orthodox Christianity. In the early arguments over the relationship between Jesus and God, advocates of the Arian position quoted the Christian scriptures in support of their position – such as Jesus referring to himself as separate from and of lesser standing than God the Father. The Nicene formula overrode this scriptural evidence with a Greek philosophical term, *homoousios*, meaning "of the same substance," which elevated Jesus to a position equal with God. Once the Nicene formula had been adopted, and with the emperor's support, scriptural references were required to be read, not for their face value meaning, but through the lens of creedal formulae and church dogma. By the middle of the fifth century, this precedence in textual authority had been concretized:

> Everyone knew by now just how intractable an issue would become if the scriptures had to be consulted for elucidation. This shift to reliance on later sources and authorities marked an important development in the history of theology that was to reach its culmination in the declaration of the Council of Trent (1543–63) that scripture itself is not to be interpreted "in any other way than in accordance with the unanimous agreement of the Fathers."[23]

Many Christians today see the creeds of the fourth century as the pinnacle of theological precision, as something revealed by God about "his" own nature, and the yardstick of Christian orthodoxy. Others see it differently, as philosophical and linguistic word games devised by detached Christian intellectuals that contradict reason and hide those contradictions behind an aura of philosophical and theological mystery. In Küng's estimation, these conciliar decisions plunged Christianity into undreamed-of confusions that simply became more complex as they went along. "In four centuries the simple and easily understandable baptismal formula in Matthew had become a highly complex Trinitarian speculation."[24]

Constructing time – Eusebius' *Ecclesiastical History*

The establishment of Christianity as a legitimate religion required in time the creation of an official written Christian history. To a certain extent, this history was begun with the biography gospels and the history of the early church in the book Acts of the Apostles, and we noted earlier the specific interests that were served in the way in which the origins of Christianity were written. It was done to a more developed extent in the early part of the fourth century by the bishop of Caesarea, Eusebius, in his *Ecclesiastical History*.

Eusebius was born sometime between 260 and 264 in Caesarea, Palestine. He received his initial education within the Greek tradition, studying letters, classical literature, rhetoric, and Latin. Around the age of twenty, he commenced graduate studies with Pamphilus, a presbyter in the church at Caesarea and a leading biblical scholar of the time. The work of the school was disrupted by the Diocletian persecutions of 303–310, during which Pamphilus and others of Eusebius' friends were arrested and executed. After the end of the persecution, Eusebius was elevated to the position of bishop in 315. He was excommunicated at the Council of Antioch in 325 for his qualified support of the teachings of Arius, but restored to his position several months later at the Council of Nicea when he accepted the council's anti-Arius creed. Eusebius continued in pastoral, ecclesiastical, and scholarly work in Caesarea until his death in 339.

Eusebius' personal experience of persecution and the martyrdom of his loved teacher and friends were strong influences on his scholarly works. His scholarship over five decades included biographies, bible commentaries, apologetic works, and works of history. This scholarly work was facilitated by an excellent library at the church in Caesarea, which held at least four hundred works, mainly in Greek, many of which were brought by Origen when he resettled in Caesarea from Alexandria in 251. They included extensive works of Greek philosophers; books of poetry, oratory, and history; Jewish literature; Christian writings; contemporary documents, including the letters of Constantine; and multiple translations of Hebrew Scriptures and Old Testament *apocrypha* and *pseudepigrapha*. The collection included rolls and codices and a copy of Origen's *Hexapla*. The library's biblical collection and obvious facility to produce copies of documents were reasons for Constantine's choice of Eusebius and the library at Caesarea to produce fifty copies of the Bible for his imperial building program.

Eusebius is often referred to as the father of church history. The impulse of his historical writing was to defend Christianity in the wake of attacks by cultured critics and the Great Persecution. One of those cultural critiques was that Christians were traitors who had abandoned their Roman heritage and rejected their Jewish history but had no history of their own. At the time antiquity was more valued than the modern, and a significant line of attack on Christianity was that it was a recent innovation compared to the ancient religions of Rome and Judaism. Eusebius responded to these criticisms in a number of works but most fully in his ten-volume *Historia Ecclesiae* or *Ecclesiastical History,* which he began not with the birth of Jesus but with the beginning of time. He then traces Christianity's development through Moses and the Jewish prophets, the birth of Jesus, and the development of the church through the reigns of the different emperors.

There were numerous eloquent literary works of history in the world of late antiquity but no models for what Eusebius was seeking to do. He outlines his methodology as not just presenting a chronological list of events or working from scratch, but also building a history by bringing together the brief accounts that others had written into an integrated account of the development of the church. As he wrote,

So, having gathered from what they have mentioned here and there such matters as we think will be useful for the subject that lies before us, and having culled appropriate passages from the ancient writers, as if, as it were, from intellectual meadows, we shall endeavor to consolidate them in an historical narrative.[25]

Eusebius is modest in his claims, acknowledging that it is a first for Christians and requires him "to travel a deserted and untrodden road." He identifies six major themes that are explored through the work:

1. Apostolic succession: a written account of the succession of the apostles (bishops) from the time of Jesus to the present;
2. Events and people: those who were Christianity's illustrious guides and leaders in especially prominent dioceses, and those who have served in each generation;
3. An account of the heretics: "those who out of a desire for innovation launched into an extremity of evil";
4. The fate of the Jews: "as a result of its plot against our Saviour";
5. An account of persecution and martyrdom; and
6. The canon of scripture and development of its writings.

The work went through a number of editions, with changes and additions taking place between the first (which appeared in 313) and the last (which appeared in 326).

Mendels sees the *Ecclesiastical History* as a media revolution of its time, a new genre of history writing designed both as a defense of Christianity and as a missionary tool.[26] Anticipating his audience, Eusebius selects according to his purposes, shapes what he wanted people to know, omits what he wanted them to forget, and reinforces his key messages through redundancy and his use of at times extravagant language. Its impact has been significant. By collating a range of material into an overarching narrative, Eusebius gave Christianity for the first time a coherent and durable historical identity and, by being written, a reference work that could be reproduced and circulated. The *History* contributed to the building of a common Christian identity across a wide diversity of regions and people.

In doing so, however, he normalized a particular view of Christianity. Although only one account, the historical perspectives of Eusebius have proven remarkably durable, even in the face of sustained criticism. The accuracy of all the events and people and Eusebius' interpretations are the subject of significant debate. Disproportionate time is spent on particular subjects compared to others, and there is haphazard quoting of material and a range of styles and rhetoric in dealing with different topics. His advocacy of the concept of the succession of bishops is supported by wrong information and presents a static view of the church as existing in the same form rather than developing through the centuries.[27] Jews and Judaism are consigned to history in support of the succession of Christianity. His portrayal of Christianity is a clear and uninterrupted stream of orthodox Christianity, without engaging the ideas of alternative Christianities but instead permanently branding them as deviant – Montanist Christians, for example, are described as "strange heresies" produced by "the Enemy of the Church of God" that "crawled over Asia and Phrygia like poisonous reptiles."[28]

A number of the concepts presented in the *History* became formative in Christian thinking and western political theory through the Middle Ages. Eusebius rejects the classical historian's understanding of history as the arena of fate and created a Christian view of history that placed human action and initiative and their consequences as significant factors along with the action of God.[29]

The *History* reflects a reworking of the concept of the Roman emperor away from the pagan idea of the king as a god and the Platonic ideal of the philosopher king possessing wisdom and the self-denial of a sage, toward an understanding of the ideal monarch as "a pious, ascetic soldier monk."[30] This ideal of the emperor as an agent of God ruling with Christian piety in defense of the church became embodied in western and Byzantine political theory through the Middle Ages.

The scriptures as text and artifact

As part of Christianity's establishment of itself as a religion of the empire, the establishment of an authorized canon of scripture had also been underway. A significant narrowing of possible texts had been occurring through the frequency of their use, their perceived apostolic origins, and their perceived relevance. Different writers and councils through the centuries had identified a shortlist of books considered worthy of being given scriptural status. While there was general agreement on a core of texts, a number remained in dispute, among them books such as the Letter to the Hebrews and the Revelation of John.

A significant step ahead in this canonization process came with the Emperor Constantine's church-building program, when along with the buildings he also commissioned fifty bibles to be produced for placement in those churches. In 332, he wrote to Eusebius:

> I have thought it expedient to instruct your Intelligence that you should command to be written fifty volumes on prepared vellum, easy to read and conveniently portable, by professional scribes with an exact understanding of their craft – volumes, that is to say, of the Holy Scriptures, the provision and use of which is, as you are aware, most necessary for the instruction of the church. Letters have been dispatched from our Clemency to the accountant of the province, advising him to supply everything requisite for the production of the books, and it will be your care to ensure that they are prepared as quickly as possible. Using the authority of this letter you should commandeer two public carriages for their transport, for by such means will these fine volumes be most readily brought before our eyes, this duty being performed by one of

the deacons of your church, who on reaching our presence will experience our liberality.[31]

The emperor's commission of fifty official copies of the whole scriptures had a number of permanent consequences. Using Eusebius' list to determine what books were to be included had the effect of closing off any further serious discussion on the structure of the Christian canon. Even though a canonical list of scriptures had not been definitively decided by any official church council, from that point on no bishop would have dared used any other books as scripture apart from those used in the emperor's bibles. Terminology about Christian writings also changed, as Herklots notes:

> Where before scholars had spoken of "authentic," "spurious," "genuine," and "disputed" writings, now the terminology is dominated by two opposing terms: "canonical" (legal) and "non-canonical" (illegal).[32]

The emperor's bible project established the Bible as an integral part of the interior space of Christian buildings. Whereas previously most churches would have had bits and pieces of copies of the scriptures, Constantine's commission of the whole Bible to be produced as a single text stimulated other cities to commission similar copies of the whole Bible, to be placed in their churches as a matter of prestige. From this developed a perception of the scriptures not just as writings of inspiration and devotion but also as an artifact, to be decorated and put on display for observation and adoration.

What had been done publicly was reproduced privately. The educated classes brought their literate interests and practices of collecting books, both for private reading and for display, into their practice of religious faith. Full copies of the Christian scriptures were acquired by other manuscript collections, and a market developed to meet that demand.

This interest in religious books as objects to be collected rather than read was occasionally criticized by Christian leaders. John Chrysostom, the bishop of Constantinople, (347–407), was critical of some of these practices:

> [F]or they tie up their books, and keep them always put away in cases, and all their care is for the fineness of the parchments, and the beauty of the letters, not for reading them. For they have not bought them to obtain advantage and benefit from them, but take pains about such matters to show their wealth and pride. Such is the excess of vainglory. I do not hear any one glory that he knows the contents, but that he has a book written in letters of gold. And what gain, tell me, is this? The Scriptures were not given us for this only, that we might have them in books, but that we might engrave them on our hearts.[33]

Jerome (347–420) in one of his letters likewise bemoans the excessive concern with the appearance of the scriptures rather than their content:

"Parchments are dyed purple, gold is melted into lettering, manuscripts are decked with jewels, while Christ lies at the door naked and dying."[34] In another letter, written to a woman who had asked for advice on how to raise her daughter, Jerome cautions about not being distracted by the decorated form in which the scriptures were being produced: "Let her treasures be not silks or gems but manuscripts of the holy scriptures; and in these let her think less of gilding, and Babylonian parchment, and arabesque patterns, than of correctness and accurate punctuation."[35]

Christians had been encouraged to read the scriptures privately at least since the writings of Hippolytus (about 200). Origen encouraged Christians to read the scriptures at home for at least a couple of hours a day, although he did acknowledge that for the average reader the scriptures could be dull and obscure. Nevertheless, he encouraged them to persist "since even the sound of sacred words in the ear is beneficial even if you do not understand the sense."[36]

Private reading by Christians included not just Christian scriptures. There was a wide range of written materials available, and there is evidence that these writings, many of them apocryphal writings, were being read by Christians privately. The cost and accessibility of written texts restricted this practice to those who not only were literate but also had the resources to purchase the books and the privilege of leisure time to read them.

There was debate about the relative merits and dangers of Christians reading, and fears that if they did so they would be influenced by pagan writings or Christian writings deemed heretical. Cyril of Jerusalem (315–386) reflects a strict position taken by some – "What is not read in the church should not be read privately." Others saw benefits of Christians reading non-Christian literature; the *Constitutions of the Holy Apostles* from the late fourth century advises those Christian men who are in a position that they don't have to go out to work to read the scriptural books but to "abstain from all the heathen books."

The branding and condemnation of some Christian thinkers and writers as heretical and the burning of their works are indications that many Christians were readers and that there was a market or mechanism for the production, reproduction, and circulation of a variety of Christian writings. The General Letter from Emperor Constantine, circulated after the Council of Nicea in 325, reflects awareness that there was a wide circulation of religious writings:

[A]ll the writings of Arius, wherever they be found, shall be delivered to be burned with fire, in order that not only his wicked and evil doctrine may be destroyed, but also that the memory of himself and of his doctrine may be blotted out, that there may not by any means remain to him remembrance in the world. Now this also I ordain, that if any one shall be found secreting any writing composed by Arius, and shall not forthwith deliver up and burn it with fire, his punishment shall be death; for as soon as he is caught in this he shall suffer capital punishment by beheading without delay.

The majority of Christians who were illiterate were still able to engage actively with the scriptures in a variety of ways. They heard them quoted and chanted sufficiently regularly that, through memorization, even the illiterate could recall extensive passages. They also saw scriptural stories represented visually in drawings, paintings, and mosaics, and the meanings constructed through these visual representations actively engaged meanings constructed through the written text in debates or preaching. An interesting example of this can be seen in a letter written by Augustine to Jerome about his Latin Vulgate translation of the scriptures. Augustine relays to Jerome an incident in a congregation sparked by Jerome's translation of the Book of Jonah, where Jerome uses the word "ivy" to describe the tree under which Jonah rested, rather than the traditional word "gourd." Augustine writes,

> A certain bishop, one of our brethren, having introduced in the church over which he presides the reading of your version, came upon a word in the book of the prophet Jonah, of which you have given a very different rendering from that which had been of old familiar to the senses and memory of all the worshippers, and had been chanted for so many generations in the church.[37] Thereupon arose such a tumult in the congregation, especially among the Greeks, correcting what had been read, and denouncing the translation as false, that the bishop was compelled to ask the testimony of the Jewish residents [it was in the town of Oea]. These, whether from ignorance or from spite, answered that the words in the Hebrew manuscripts were correctly rendered in the Greek version, and in the Latin one taken from it. What further need I say? The man was compelled to correct your version in that passage as if it had been falsely translated, as he desired not to be left without a congregation – a calamity which he narrowly escaped.[38]

As a holy artifact and the container of divine words and revelation, the book of the Bible itself came to be recognized in a fetishistic way as having intrinsic power and used to bring good fortune and ward off evil. John Chrysostom (fourth century) alludes without criticism in one of his sermons to the popular view that "the devil will not dare approach a house where a Gospel-book is lying, much less will any evil spirit or any sort of sin ever touch or enter a soul which bears about with it such sentiments as it contains." Augustine considered it permissible in case of a headache to sleep with a copy of the Gospel of John under one's pillow.[39] Chrysostom also makes reference to people who "suspend (extracts from) Gospels from their necks as a powerful amulet and carry them about in all places wherever they go."[40] This wearing of amulets of Christian scripture on their bodies as a source of power was sufficiently widespread that a Church Council in Laodicea in 360 prohibited clergy from following the practice.[41] The Bible was also used by Christians for bibliomancy – seeking divine guidance or an omen by randomly opening the text of scripture and blindly selecting a passage (a practice that continues today) – as well as fortune telling, a practice that Augustine disliked, although he acknowledged he would prefer Christians do that "rather than run about consulting demons."[42]

With the artifact itself being seen as possessing power, extensive practices developed around honoring and protecting the book, ranging from protocols for handling and protecting it to curses and anathemas on those who damaged or misused it. The Third Council of Constantinople passed a canon that declared a year's excommunication for anyone who injured the books of the Old and New Testaments, or cut them up or gave them to book dealers to be erased for reuse. Protocols for the care of books became part of the rule of many monasteries, and written curses occasionally were inscribed in bibles to protect them from misuse, included threats of excommunication, leprosy, condemnation to hell, or having one's eyes put out.[43]

Part of the reason for this concern for misuse of manuscripts was the enormous energy and cost that went into their transcription and production, particularly as copies became more intricately embossed and illuminated. Part also was the perceived holiness of the text, in both the nature of its content and the physical form of that content. Part of these proscriptions, however, reflected the blurring that took place across the boundaries of material and spiritual practice, between text and form.

NOTES

1 Mitchell, 2006, p. 177.
2 Stark, 1996, pp. 10–11.
3 Brown, 2003, pp. 55–56.
4 Ste. Croix, 1981, quoted in Chow, 1992, p. 41.
5 Freeman, 2008, p. 51.
6 Altman, 2004, pp. 70–73.
7 Altman, 2004, p. 54.
8 Quoted in Freeman, 2002, p. 202.
9 Freeman, 2008, p. 67.
10 Freeman, 2008, p. 151.
11 Dungan, 2006.
12 Pusey, 1857.
13 Schaff, 1890.
14 Chow, 1992, pp. 72–73.
15 Freeman notes that Gregory of Nazianzus, one of the Greek "Cappadocian Fathers" who was a significant contributor to the Nicene debates, was absorbed

in classical writings, "often accumulating his own copies on papyrus rolls that he took around with him as he moved." In his writings, he quotes from texts going back almost a thousand years (Freeman, 2008, pp. 70–71).

16 Freeman, 2008, p. 53.
17 Quoted in Freeman, 2008, p. 66.
18 Freeman, 2008, pp. 74–75.
19 Freeman, 2008, p. 143.
20 Chow, 1992, pp. 72–73.
21 Freeman, 2008, p. 152.
22 Imperial law issued by Theodosius in 448, quoted in Palladius, 1985, pp. 41, 50.
23 Freeman, 2008, p. 150.
24 Küng, 1994, p. 194.
25 Eusebius Pamphilius, 1890, p. 1.1.
26 Mendels, 1999, pp. 5–9.
27 E. Cameron, 2005.
28 Eusebius Pamphilius, 1890, p. 5.14.
29 Chesnut, 1986, p. 33.
30 Chesnut, 1986, p. 33.
31 Quoted in Prescott, 1886, pp. 14–15.
32 Herklots, 1994, pp. 34–35.
33 Homily 32 in Chrysostom.
34 Epistle 22 in Jerome.
35 Epistle 107.12 in Jerome.
36 Hom in Nave Jesus 20.1, quoted in Gamble, 1995, p. 238.
37 Jonah 4:6.
38 Catech 4:36, quoted in Gamble, 1995, p. 235.
39 Gamble, 1995, p. 238.
40 Chrysostom, Hom 32, quoted in Gambler, 1995, p. 240.
41 Gamble, 1995, p. 238. Asamoah-Gyadu has written about similar practices occurring in present-day Ghana (Horsfield & Asamoah-Gyadu, 2011).
42 Gamble, 1995, p. 240.
43 Drogin, 1983.

6

The Latin Translation

Unlike some religions, Christianity had no single sacred language of origin. It emerged in a cultural context where a variety of languages were in use: Aramaic, Hebrew, Greek, and Latin. Each of these had different cultural and political associations and implications. In a relatively short time, as the Jesus Movement spread, the language used by Jesus, rural Aramaic, was displaced by the more cosmopolitan language of Koiné Greek, the major international language of trade and commerce and of the urban populations across the Roman Empire. For the first three centuries, Greek was the dominant language for almost all Christian letters, theological writings, and liturgies. In time, writings formulated in Greek were translated into other written languages such as Latin, Syriac, Coptic, and Ethiopian (Ge'ez).

The translation of Greek written materials into other languages reflected a willingness in Eastern Christianity to use vernacular translations to facilitate the spread of the faith. A different linguistic attitude developed in Western Christianity where the imperial associations of Latin, particularly in its written form, became a significant tool in the spread and dominance of Christianity in the largely oral-based regions of northern and western Europe.[1]

Latin roots

When Constantine took over as Emperor in 313, Greek-speaking Eastern Christianity was dominant, with seven to eight hundred bishops in the East compared to only sixteen for the whole of Gaul in the West.[2] Nevertheless, the Roman church held an important position, and the Bishop of Rome was seen as the elder statesman of bishops of the West.[3]

Although not the majority language of the Empire, Latin was the dominant language of the West, including Italy, parts of North Africa, parts of

From Jesus to the Internet, Peter Horsfield © 2015 John Wiley & Sons, Ltd. Published 2015 by John Wiley & Sons, Ltd.

Central Europe, Spain, Gaul, and Britain. It was also the language of imperial law and administration, even in the imperial court in Constantinople.[4]

Latin carried with it a different culture from that of Greek. From an
early time, Latin poets and philosophers saw Latin language as possessing
a beauty, order, and rationality that was a civilizing and unifying force in
itself, and the abilities to read and write in Latin were considered traits of
a cultured and civilized person. Roman officials were required to use Latin
in their dealing with conquered or alien people,[5] so the ability to speak
and understand Latin was an important practicality for participating in and
gaining the benefits of the systems of the empire.

These cultural differences began to be reflected in the approach and work
of a number of Christian thinkers who began to write in Latin. Their work
showed less concern for the highly speculative, metaphysical interests of the
Greek writers, and greater concern for practical theological matters such as
church order and organizational structure, pastoral care and discipline, ethics
and behavior, and the nature of Christian ministry and the sacraments. Two
of the earlier ones have already been noted: Tertullian and Cyprian. Three
others are interesting to consider: Jerome, Ambrose, and Augustine. Together,
through their thinking, their religious and political activities, and their distinctive media uses, they laid the roots for Western Latin Catholicism.

Jerome (c. 342–420)

Born of wealthy parents, Jerome was educated in Rome as a classical scholar, erudite in Latin, and fluent in Greek and Hebrew. In his thirties he adopted an ascetic way of life, which continued to his death and included three
years as a hermit in Syria. Around 382 he was summoned to be the personal
secretary of Pope Damascus, a position from which he actively promoted
his ascetic way of faith and attracted to him a number of wealthy and tal-
ented widows as patrons.[6] After Damascus' death in 384, he relocated to
Bethlehem, where he established a monastery for men with the support of
one of his Rome patrons, Paula, who established and led a monastery for
women nearby. Jerome continued to live in the monastery for the remaining
thirty-four years of his life.

Jerome wrote extensively. Along with his contributions in the development of asceticism, Jerome's ongoing influence on the Latin tradition of
Christianity lay in his translation work and biblical interpretation. His
translation of Greek writers such as Origen and Eusebius made their work
more accessible to the Latin Church. His writings on theology and ascetics were frequently controversial because of their polemical and aggressive
nature and stern ascetic views.[7] He gave a distinctive shape to Latin Christianity through the creation of 350 new Latin words, all of them "both
accurately formed and useful words, expressing for the most part abstract

qualities necessitated by the Christian religion and which hitherto had not existed in the Latin tongue, e.g. *clericatus, impoenitentia, deitas, dualitas, glorification, corruptrix.*"[8]

Jerome's writings were distinctive. While he wrote numerous biblical commentaries, he drew heavily, at times almost entirely, on other people's work.[9] This "reproductive" character of his work can be understood to a certain extent by writing protocols of the time but also by the volume of material he produced – he translated the *Book of Tobit* in one day and the *Book of Esther* in one night, for example. What Martin describes as his "negligences of style, overladen phrases and brusque shifts of topic" are also explained by the conditions of their production. Much of his work in Bethlehem was dictated to scriveners who knew shorthand or who recorded his sermons as they were preached:

> He could not stop to reflect when he saw the scrivener before him, awaiting his word with raised stylus. A number of sermons and homilies (with notations of the hearers' reactions) were taken down by stenographers placed among the crowd, traces of whose work remain in definitive versions of the texts.[10]

Jerome's enduring legacy lay in his Latin translation of the Christian Scriptures, produced under commission from Pope Damascus to solve the problem of confusion caused by a number of different Latin translations in circulation. Controversially rejecting the list of books of the Greek Septuagint version of the Old Testament, which was widely recognized as divinely inspired, Jerome chose the list of an earlier Hebrew canon, attaching the additional books in the Septuagint as *Apocrypha*. His Latin Bible, known as the Vulgate, became the authoritative biblical text for the Western Catholic Church.

Ambrose (c. 339–397)

As well as being known traditionally as one of the four "Doctors of the Latin Church,"[11] Ambrose is noteworthy from a media perspective for the breadth of his communication activities and their influence in the liturgical, pastoral, and political areas.

Coming from a distinguished and high-ranking political family, Ambrose was fluent in Latin and Greek and played a significant role in the translation of Greek culture and theology into the Latin context. As civil governor of Milan, in 374 he was called to intervene in riots that had broken out over the election of the new bishop. While mediating the conflict, he was invited and accepted the position of Bishop of Milan himself, even though he hadn't yet been baptized. Within a week he had been baptized, ordained and installed in the role, taking it up after a period of intensive study.[12]

Ambrose brought to the role a strong personality, rhetorical and organizational skills, knowledge and experience in politics, and an unshakeable determination to ensure that the Nicene version of Christianity was exclusively promoted and practiced and any alternative religious views such as Arian Christianity, residual paganism, and Judaism were actively opposed if not eliminated. To this end he employed powerfully a range of communication and media strategies. He wrote extensively, particularly biblical expositions or commentaries but also writings on virginity, widowhood, ethics, and the duties of clergy, and theological works on ascetics, the Nicene Creed, sacraments, penitence, and the martyrs. His letters, when arranged later for publication, filled ten books.[13] He authored a number of Latin hymns, and his influence is credited with hymns becoming "an integral part of the Western Church."[14] Although he is widely praised in Christian tradition for his writings,[15] Moorhead notes that "much of what he says in his commentaries is borrowed, sometimes _in extenso_ and almost always without acknowledgement."[16]

He was a powerful preacher and used his position not only to promote his orthodox views but also to denounce those who disagreed with him and to coerce those who opposed him, including emperors, into submission. He engaged in an active and extensive building program to establish the physical presence of the Catholic Church. The series of towering basilicas he had built included one for his own burial, the Basilica Ambrosiana, "set among the most celebrated of Milan's Christian graves."[17]

Ambrose holds a high position in the Catholic tradition for the contributions he made to the establishment of Nicene Orthodoxy and the independence of the Catholic Church as a political power. The Catholic Encyclopedia evaluates him as follows:

> From the very beginning he proved himself to be that which he has ever since remained in the estimation of the Christian world, the perfect model of a Christian bishop.... Rarely, if ever, has a Christian bishop been so universally popular, in the best sense of that much abused term, as Ambrose of Milan.[18]

Missing from this official evaluation are his intolerance of alternative religious viewpoints, his ruthless use of political power to eliminate his opponents, his deceptive manipulation of events and people to further his own ends, his bullying of those who disagreed with him, and his misrepresentations and punitive attitudes toward Jews,[19] each of which set a pattern for the political involvements and collusions of the Roman Catholic Church through the Middle Ages and beyond. There are many examples of this; two are illustrative.

In 389 a group of Christians at the instigation of their bishop burned down a Jewish synagogue in Callinicum. Around the same time a group of monks destroyed the meeting place of the Christian Gnostic group, the Valentinians. When the Emperor Theodosius directed the bishop to make reparation for the damage done and to have the monks disciplined, Ambrose intervened, insisting that Christians should not be expected to rebuild a Jewish house of worship. Exploiting his political influence, Ambrose identified himself as personally responsible for what was done, not the bishop: "I cry out that I set fire to the synagogue, certainly that I told them to do it, lest there be a place where Christ was denied."[20] In the face of Ambrose's popular support, Theodosius withdrew from holding the Christians accountable.

On another occasion Palladius, an educated bishop with Arian beliefs, arrived at a council of bishops ready to debate Ambrose's biblical interpretations and defend the Arian position. When he arrived, Palladius found himself ushered not into the basilica for an open debate but into a side room that was stacked with Ambrose's supporters seated in a prearranged order. Palladius was formally condemned. The clerics who recorded the proceedings and the decision were clerics of Ambrose's church.[21]

This uncritical praise in Christian writings of particular heroes and heroic actions such as those of Ambrose, but a failure to honestly acknowledge and examine the dark side of its legacy, has begun to be reexamined in recent scholarship. Freeman observes of Ambrose:

> This desire for control of others, whether these were virgins, widows, heretics, buildings or emperors, was to become the defining theme of Ambrose's reign as bishop.... Ambrose excelled in his brilliantly managed public performances. He was totally unscrupulous in seeking to publicly humiliate his enemies.[22]

Similarly Wiles, evaluating Ambrose's legacy, has the following evaluation:

> Ambrose's masterful authority and his moral courage are not in question. But the two dramatic stories of his exercise of that authority over Theodosius well illustrate the potential for good and the grave danger of abuse in the church's exercise of power in relation to the state that is evident from later history.[23]

Augustine (354–430)

Augustine was born in Algeria and lived in Algeria for all but five years of his life. After a youth of education, life with a concubine, and exploration of a number of religious alternatives, he came under the influence of the preaching and authority of Ambrose and converted to Christianity in 386. In 391 he went to Hippo with the intention of founding a monastery but in 395 was ordained as the Bishop of Hippo. He remained in that position for thirty-five years until his death in 430, as the Vandals were moving across the north of Africa and approaching the city.

Augustine was a committed pastor and one of the most prolific and influential writers of Western Christianity. Central in this influence was his
identity as a Latin speaker and writer. He knew little Greek and took the
extensive writings of Greek Christianity into account only when they were
available in Latin translation.[24]

Augustine's thinking and influence were shaped in response to a number of practical and pastoral issues that arose during the thirty-five years
of his episcopacy: the long-running dispute of Donatism, the challenge of
Pelagianism, debates about the oneness and threeness of the Trinity, and the
meaning and implications for faith of the impending collapse of the Roman
Empire. Beyond these, his *Confessions* introduced a genre of self-reflective
personal writing that anticipated modern psychology.

In the process of addressing these issues, Augustine defined a number of
key aspects of Christianity in a way that left a lasting influence on Western
Christianity. He emphasized the importance of unity of the church over individual holiness and advocated the use of force to maintain this unity in a
way that Küng sees as "the theological justification of forced conversions,
the Inquisition and a holy war against deviants of every kind."[25] He vili-
fied sexual libido and concretized a critical and repressive attitude toward
human sexuality, a perspective that was to shape Christian attitudes to the
present time. He developed the notion of original sin as a stain inherited
by all humans at birth, the solution to which was a concept of grace as a
spiritual commodity dispensed and received by people through the sacraments of the church. His skepticism about the ability of human will to be
effective in salvation led to a theological view in which God predestined
some people to salvation and others to damnation, encouraging a persisting
Western anxiety about personal salvation. His theology of the Trinity was
the first to utilize a psychological perspective. His political philosophy of
two cities – an earthly and a heavenly one – underlay the justification of a
theocratic state and influenced the political contests and structures of Christian and secular leaders into the modern period.

Augustine's reputation was built on his formidable intellect, command
of the medium of writing, and "long years of assiduous self-promotion."[26]
He was what we would identify today as a genuine global-local practitioner.
Long before becoming a bishop, he developed ways of building an audience
and bringing himself to the notice of literary Christians and patrons who
enhanced circulation of his works. This included a cultivated relationship
with Jerome.

Writing to Jerome in the early 390s was a way of calling himself to the older
writer's attention and entering into the literary public that Jerome dominated.
Over the years that followed, Augustine's books became well known outside
Africa in upper-class Christian circles.[27]

Augustine's situation and success illustrate how, even at this time, some Christian writers had perceived the importance of writing in building a larger reputation and exercising a wider influence, and the need as an author to be intentional in promoting one's name and building an audience.

His pastoral and judicial responsibilities as bishop inform his writings.[28] He preached regularly to large congregations, although he lamented on one occasion the large number of people who come to hear but do not necessarily take it to heart.

His arrangements as bishop were designed to support his ongoing literary and intellectual activity. The bishop's palace in Hippo was set up as a monastery with a disciplined community of priest-friends, many of whom went on to become bishops themselves.

> [B]ooks were read, study was pursued, learned conversation took place in a pleasant garden, in a town whose port brought many travellers. By the end of Augustine's life, visitors had become so many that a hostel was built to lodge them. These visitors would meet around the table in Augustine's house: there were hermits from little islands off Sardinia; Gothic monks.... Good conversation counted for more than food at this table.[29]

The community he established supported and contributed to his prodigious output. In total he wrote and distributed in multiple copies more than five million words, including dozens of books and hundreds of letters, greater than any other writer of antiquity. Nearly four hundred of his sermons were taken down in shorthand and reproduced in manuscript.[30] His correspondence indicates that bishops and learned laypeople across a wide geography engaged in an active exchange of ideas and concerns with him.

Given that many of his works were equal to several volumes of a printed book to us, and each copy had to be written individually by hand, the importance of Augustine's media management and his personal library facilities in Hippo cannot be underestimated. Some insights into this media effort can be found.

> Possidius speaks almost with tenderness of the magnificent episcopal library.... Augustine could command the services of so many copyists that on one occasion he was able and willing immediately to make a gift of his Confessions (13 books long) to a highly-placed literary enthusiast who was a complete stranger to him.[31]

Augustine himself comments that in Hippo new books were distributed quickly and easily, with a positive mania for reading and writing among the educated, both lay and clerical. The convent of the church in Hippo also had its own library with a lending desk that was open at certain hours.[32]

Augustine's self-consciousness of his role as a global leader beyond his local diocese extended to a concern for his legacy after his death:

> Augustine shaped his own survival with great care. Late in life he compiled a catalogue of his own written works under the evasive title Retractationes ["Reconsiderations"]. Each work was listed with some description of the circumstances of its composition and its purpose, as well as corrections or explanations of difficult or controversial passages.... Augustine left for the afterlife with a vastly better than average chance that his works would survive, be collected, and be read as his.[33]

Augustine's concern for his legacy was validated. His influence on western thought and the Latin translation of Christianity, both religious and "secular," has been profound, not only in his own time, nor only to religious leaders such as Charlemagne and Martin Luther, but also into modern times to important secular thinkers such as Descartes, Leibniz, John Stuart Mill, and Wittgenstein.[34]

After the fall

One of the major influences on the shape of Western Christianity was the collapse of the Western Roman Empire, a military and political process that took place over seven decades in the fifth century. It began with the crossing of the Roman boundary of the Rhine by a large number of Germanic tribes in 406; included constant battles in and over Roman provinces in Gaul, Spain, North Africa, and Italy; and ended with the abdication of the Western emperor, Romulus Augustulus, in 476.

There are different perspectives on how the aftermath of the collapse of the empire is to be understood. One is summed up in the common ascription of the period as "the Dark Ages," a time of the withering of culture, education, hope, and enlightenment.[35] Brown advocates a different view, one that sees the aftermath of the fall not as a single, unified degeneration, but as a diversification into different forms of culture occurring at different places and different times, and with different levels of intensity. It was, Brown argues, "not like the crash of a single building ... more like the shifting contours of a mud bank in an ever-flowing stream."[36]

Many of the Frankish and Germanic "barbarian" tribes associated with Rome's collapse had served in Roman armies, were familiar with and respected many aspects of Roman order and culture, and were open to foreign influence. Many of them also were Arian Christians, converted to Christianity as a result of earlier mission work from the East. The manner in which changes in power and political order were managed, therefore, varied significantly from place to place. In time the political structures shifted from the integrated and centralized Roman control to a number of separate barbarian kingdoms, with loyalty shifting from a single distant emperor to a variety of kings. The Roman gentry who had settled and remained in different parts of the old empire and people of the towns negotiated in various ways with these tribal groups.[37] In commerce, the centralized "pump" of the Roman command economy was dismantled and economic life decentralized into sluggish local and regional ones. The benefits and value of education as an investment steadily declined across most of Europe, and families decided that greater value was to be found in military skill than in being able to read and write.[38]

The impact on communication patterns was also marked, to the extent that a number of scholarly works see the interaction of literacy and orality as one of the primary lenses through which the Middle Ages need to be understood. Green, for example, writes,

> It is justifiable to see the medieval period as one in which literacy gradually expands, encroaching upon the hitherto oral area of Northern Europe, so that the period is characterized by the clash and interpenetration of orality and writing.[39]

The Roman Catholic Church played a central part in this. Through its organizational base grounded in literacy, it became the primary agent of literate education and practice, and as a result one of the dominant political influences in Europe for the next nine hundred years. In the process, Christianity itself was reshaped and refigured.

The Roman Catholic Church was a strongly mission-oriented church and over five centuries expanded its influence to cover most of Continental Europe, Britain, and Scandinavia, although the nature of missionary expansion was different for different regions. For those Germanic tribes who were already Christian, the mission was toward converting them from Arian Christianity to Nicene Christianity. For those who were pagan in their religious beliefs and practices, mission proceeded from Roman Catholic bases in cities and monasteries to the countryside. The methods of mission were material as well as ideological, with Catholicism seeking to present their faith not only as a superior belief system but also as a superior material culture. Pagan people were to be overawed with signs of strength and wonders of the superior material culture of Christian episcopal dress, wealth, and outfitting of churches.

> Spiritual authority was demonstrated, among other things, by spectacular displays of supernatural power. Saints, and their relics, worked miracles. Heroic performances of ascetic holiness would be rewarded and authenticated by

astonishing displays of quasi-magical power in life or after death. These were not entirely new phenomena but they achieved a degree of prominence they had not had for several centuries.[40]

Another element of the strategy was appeal to the powerful, with the educated, literate, and globally connected bishop offering mutually beneficial services to help the king politically. The artifacts of book and manuscript were part of this. Christian organizations and leaders gained enhanced prestige and power as the almost sole practitioners and preservers of literacy.

The barbarian tribes had no written script. Literacy and Christianity arrived together, and books were long regarded with superstitious awe. Knowledge of writing, the virtual preserve of the monasteries, became identified with authority, both religious and secular.[41]

Although literacy and manuscript production in the wider society didn't disappear altogether,[42] the general decline of schools and education and limited availability of books strengthened the political power of the Catholic Church. Its well-developed and carefully guarded processes of education, literacy, and manuscript production and circulation became powerful tools and were used strategically for the promotion and protection of the faith of the Church and its interests. Those interests were not so much the heavy doctrinal concerns of earlier Greek Christianity, but what Brown calls "the age *par excellence* of applied Christianity."[43]

Here the basic structures and offices of Latin Christianity, fashioned on the Roman political and social model, came into their own.[44] All roles – metropolitans, bishops, priests, subdeacons, acolytes, exorcists, readers, lawyers, notaries, doorkeepers, singers, and gravediggers – were clearly defined. Their relative status and authority, and the conditions under which they worked, were understood and preserved. As the administrative structures of the empire collapsed, this clearly defined religious structure became important for maintaining social discipline and welfare, and for meeting many of the practical, legal, and administrative needs of the cities and rural areas under their oversight.

Highly influential in this shaping of church order in the West was Gregory I, Bishop of Rome from 590 to 604. Coming from Roman senatorial aristocracy, as Pope he applied his administrative and diplomatic skills to the building of the church as the successor and bearer of the mantle of the empire. Described as "a highly energetic bishop with a very practical disposition,"[45] his involvements and influence covered pastoral work, mission, political diplomacy, church administration and finance, social welfare, worship and liturgy, the support and promotion of monasticism, and the building of the church's missionary activity. His manual of pastoral practice, the *Regula Pastoralis,* became highly influential in shaping church practice through the Middle Ages. Through his work and writings, some of the basic features of Latin Christianity through the medieval period were established: the idea of purgatory and that saying the Mass for the Dead could release them from purgatory, the basis of later practices of buying indulgences; that the Mass repeated the sacrifice of Christ; that original sin was washed away by baptism; that sins could be forgiven by meritorious works if accompanied by penance, utilized later in enlisting support for the Crusades; and the magical power of relics. Gregory also played a key role in establishing the political power of the Catholic Church in post-imperial Europe. Küng identifies him as laying the foundations for the secular and cultural power of the papacy in Europe – "Christian faith with a Roman stamp."[46]

Brown argues that what gave the Roman Catholic Church its strength and extensive influence in Europe throughout this medieval period, though, was not the Roman papacy or a centrally organized and controlled uniformity and structure, but a remarkable interconnectivity.[47] It is in the creation and maintenance of that interconnectivity that we can see the crucial role that media played in the development of the Roman Catholic Church into the most dominant European institution of the Middle Ages.

At the local level, the Roman Catholic Church had a readily transportable structure and communication model that could be quickly adapted into new situations, an adaptability essential in the fluid conditions that followed the collapse of the political empire.

> The basic modules of Christianity were remarkably stable and easy to transfer – a bishop, a clergy, a congregation … and a place in which to worship. Such a structure could be subjected to many local variations but, in one form or another, it travelled well.[48]

As well as a center for religious practice, the local parish was a center for welfare, social maintenance, and, often, political order. Every manifestation of this local church carried a larger identity as the local embodiment of a universal reality that was materialized in a range of visible ways. There was a common book of scripture and written service books that mediated local worship into a global interlinked community.

Bishops acquired significance as leaders of the towns and a significant agent in the building and maintaining of social order and security against the roaming bands of marauders that had emerged in the absence of Roman order. The church building itself, as one of the few substantial buildings, often became a refuge at times of threat. In exercising this role, bishops and priests kept in touch and supported each other practically through the constant circulation of news, books, and letters, making them representatives of a worldwide textual community.[49]

The bishop's palace in Rome facilitated this mediated interconnectedness. It had a library, ecclesiastical archives, and processes for managing the constant incoming and outgoing flow of correspondence. This included a designated group of papal notaries under a *primicerius notariorum,* trained in stenography and shorthand notation. In addition to taking down, writing, and dispatching all the Pope's correspondence, the notaries managed all aspects of document registering, processing, storage, access, and reproduction, using registry processes and practices that had been followed by the secular Roman bureaucracy.[50] They assisted deacons in church administration and acted as the Pope's delegates on diplomatic missions and in delivering important messages to other bishops and patriarchs. Other episcopal offices, particularly in the larger cities, had similar media offices and processes in place, although not necessarily to the same extent.

The fortunes and wealth of the Roman Pope and the political influence of the Latin Church expanded significantly with the conversion to Catholic Christianity of the Frankish King Clovis in 496. Clovis's conversion was influential in convincing other Franco-Germanic tribes to abandon Arianism in favor of Catholic Christianity in the decades to follow. This identification of the Franks with Catholic Christianity started a mutually beneficial political-religious relationship that would develop through the eighth century. In 754, in exchange for promises of military support, Pope Stephen II travelled to Paris to anoint Pepin III as king in a lavish ceremony, appointed him with the title "Patricius," and granted him eternal life.[51] In return, Pepin gained back strategic land in North Italy from the Lombards. Although the lands belonged to the Eastern Emperor in Constantinople, Pepin gave them to the Roman Pope, and they became the basis for the Papal States, income-generating territory owned and governed by the Roman Pope. The justification for doing so was a discovered set of documents, including one called The Donation of Constantine, a record of Constantine giving Pope Sylvester I and his successors supremacy over all churches of Christianity, making him the supreme judge of all clergy, and ruler of Italy and the Western Empire.[52] The documents were confirmed in the fifteenth century to be forged by a cleric in the Papal Palace in Rome.

Monasteries and manuscripts

Christian monasticism first appeared in Egypt toward the end of the third century as a form of solitary spiritual living. Its motivations included escape from persecution, an ascetic renunciation of the world, a form of independence for women, a withdrawal from a perceived corrupted church, and an aspiration to a higher form of spirituality. The idea of a communal ascetical life was first developed by Pachomius, a Coptic Christian in Egypt in the early part of the fourth century. Basil, the bishop of Caesarea in the latter half of the fourth century, continued its development with a rule that emphasized a contemplative celibate life of prayer and devotion to achieve union with God. Because of their disciplines of study and contemplation, eastern monks played a significant role in the development of theology and liturgy and were often recalled to take up positions as bishops and patriarchs.

Knowledge of the eastern monastic movement spread to the West through reports of travelers and pilgrims, and the reports became a popular genre in Christian Latin literature. One of the influential works was *The Life of St Anthony*, written by Athanasius in Alexandria – hearing *The Life of St Anthony* read in Milan in 386 sparked Augustine's path to conversion.[53] The literary works also stimulated a traffic of travelers between West and East, with Christian noblemen and women from the West travelling to live in monasteries in places such as Jerusalem and Bethlehem, and eastern monks coming to the West. One of the earliest monasteries in the West was established by Martin of Tours (316–397), who continued to live a monastic life even as a bishop.

The shape of western monasticism was influenced most greatly by Benedict (480–c. 547), the educated son of a noble family who at the age of twenty withdrew from Rome and became a solitary monk in a cave near Subiaco. His monasteries grew from followers who gathered around him whom he formed into communities, applying his keen knowledge of human nature and his Roman noble sense of order to shape what has become known as the Benedictine Rule.[54] Benedict conceived the monastery under the disciplined rule of an abbot as "a permanent, self-contained and self-supporting garrison of Christ's soldiers,"[55] with the day divided into seven periods comprising worship, work, and study.

Monasteries spread quickly and were an important source of social stability, particularly in the unsettled West. In troubled times, they were often a refuge for people under threat and centers for social services. Monasteries were also an important strategy of mission, particularly in the West. A small group of men or women mutually bound by a common discipline of study, worship, work, and obedience to their leader travelling and settling together in a new place without the distraction of accruing personal wealth became an effective means of spreading and establishing the Christian faith in new places. Their rule of industry, along with their communal view of property, led to them becoming significant centers of wealth and influence – by the start of the seventh century, there were at least 220 monasteries and convents in Gaul and around 100 in Italy.[56]

In the absence of other opportunities for political progression for the children of the surviving Roman aristocratic families still living in the provinces, the increasingly powerful monasteries became an attractive proposition. Drawing on family resources, they paid for their children to enter monasteries, where they were educated; inducted into the disciplines of obedience, humility, and ascetic living; and ordained into the religious-political community of the church. These disciplines, along with their wider organizational and leadership acquaintance developed within their family circles, enhanced their qualifications and suitability for religious leadership, and many of the recognized bishops of the time entered the church through this route. Lawrence identifies Luxeuil, the monastery in Burgundy, for example, as a "nursery of monk-bishops," with at least eleven of its monks appointed as bishops to Gallic Sees during the seventh century.[57] Their visual representation in churches served to promote their aristocratic status between heaven and earth.

> They were not always popular. But the townsfolk knew at least that their church was in the hands of men who knew what they wanted and what others wanted of them.... Bishops even looked their part. We see them in the mosaics of the time, which represented saints and former bishops. With their quiet eyes, solemn stance, and sweeping, silken robes, they are recognizably "last Romans." But they now hovered, in shimmering mosaics on the walls of churches, above the heads of the Catholic congregation. Their earthly representatives were supposed to look like them.... Such images of the bishop proved decisive in later ages. In many provinces of the west, they placed the aristocratic bishop at the center of the Christian imagination.[58]

From their earliest beginnings, monasteries became centers of Christian literary culture, with reading and memorization of religious texts seen as important in the shaping of a monastic mind and culture. Pachomius specified in his rules that new monks who couldn't read were to be taught how to do so at set hours of the day, and compelled to do so if necessary, to ensure that "there shall be nobody whatever in the monastery who does not learn to read and does not memorise something of the Scriptures, at least the Gospel and the Psalter."[59] In the Benedictine order, all monks were required to spend some time each day in reading – at least three hours a day in the summer and more in the winter.[60] In Lent they were given assigned reading, with oversight provisions to ensure it was done. While most reading was Christian and spiritual in nature, those judged able to manage it also read more widely, including in the Roman and Greek classics. By the ninth century, most of those recognized in the wider community as learnèd were monks, and the figure of the learnèd abbot was widely recognized.

Monasteries also became important sites for the rebuilding of education in Europe following the fall of the empire. The handing over of children from as young as seven years to monasteries became a useful way for propertied families to manage the care and inheritance issues of surplus male children and of providing for female children who were seen as having no marriage prospects. It also became an important source of recruitment by monasteries, and the donations required for the care of the child an important source of income or property.[61] The recognized eighth-century English religious scholar and historian, the Venerable Bede, for example, entered the monastery as a child. As this practice of *child-oblates* or child-monks grew during the Middle Ages, formal structures and processes for educating children developed that would extend in time into cathedral schools and universities.

One particularly influential monastic movement was that of the Celtic Church in Ireland, which grew from small groups that formed around individual ascetics, including women – Brigit of Kildare is identified as having founded one of the first monasteries in Ireland. Because the Celtic Church stood outside of the Roman Empire and avoided the barbarian invasions of the Continent, it developed its own character and spirituality. The monasteries in Ireland were strongly tribal related, and they became more important and powerful in the organization of Christianity in Ireland than the diocesan model followed on the Continent, which replicated the Roman civil administrative structure.

Celtic monasticism was radically austere and ascetic, seeing spiritual life as a warfare against self-will and sensuality. Legends abound of monks performing heroic acts of mortification,[62] and this ascetic zeal made Irish monasticism and Irish monks significant in the spread of Christianity throughout Europe. The ascetic discipline was reinforced by a rigorous schedule of penitentials for failures of behavior.

> A brother who drops food or spills drink while serving is to do penance in church, lying prostrate and motionless during the singing of twelve psalms; breaking the rule of silence at meals is to be punished with six lashes; forgetting prayer before or after work, with twelve lashes; smiling during the divine office, with six lashes; using the words "mine" or "thine," with six lashes; contradicting the word of another, with fifty lashes.[63]

These catalogues of sin and their appropriate acts of penance were gathered into Penitentials, guidebooks for the use of priest confessors. The circulation of these written Penitentials was influential in the shaping of medieval Christianity toward an emphasis on sin, its consequences of judgment and punishment in this life and the next, and its remedies in individual and private confession, penance, and purgatory. Brown notes,

> What was unique about Ireland was the vigor with which the sapientes, the Christian learned men of the island, codified and applied to every aspect of life a system of taboos which previously had been based upon the tacit agreement of local communities. The drawing up of the Penitentials did not represent the corruption of a more 'enlightened' Christianity. Rather, it marked a startling victory of the men of the pen who turned a widespread, almost nonverbal, sense of the distinction between the sacred and the profane, and between the

pure and the impure (shared alike by barbarian and by Mediterranean Christians) into a finely calibrated system to be used for the guidance of souls."[64]

Along with its missionary zeal and asceticism, Irish monastic Christianity was renowned for its enthusiasm for learning and education. Patrick, widely seen as the founder of Christianity in Ireland in the fifth century and its patron saint, is attributed with the establishment of a love of books and writing and classical Greek and Latin culture that was taken up by the poets and learned classes of Irish society. Brown describes Patrick's *Letters to Coroticus* and his *Confessions* as "the first pieces of extensive Latin prose to be written from beyond the frontiers of the Roman world."[65] By the sixth and seventh centuries, Irish monastic schools had developed a reputation for scholarship and learning throughout Europe.

Exemplary in this is the Northumbrian monk-scholar, Bede (672–735). Entering the twin Celtic monasteries of St. Peter's and St. Paul's in North Umbria at the age of seven, he remained within a monastic environment until his death at the age of sixty-three. He wrote more than forty books covering the fields of knowledge of his time: chronology, natural history, scripture, and theology. His major work was a comprehensive history of Christianity in England – the *Ecclesiastical History of the English People* – in which he reframed historical understanding of racial destinies. Bede's *Ecclesiastical History* is an exemplar of educated Christians during this period using their literacy skills to record and preserve the pre-Christian oral history of its conquered peoples:

> In Bede's writings we can watch, as seldom elsewhere in Europe, the process by which Christianity came to create notions of "national" unity that would (for good or ill) look straight to the present day.... Bede gave the nondescript patchwork of military adventurers who had settled in eastern Britain the common name by which they have come to be known in later ages – the "English." Centuries later, but also under the influence of readers of Bede's Ecclesiastical History, they would come to speak of their country as "England."[66]

As centers of literacy, monasteries became instrumental in conserving ancient culture and were a major source of documents for the rediscovery of classical Greek and Roman works during the Renaissance of the thirteenth and fourteenth centuries. Cassiodorus (485–580) established a monastery in Southern Italy for this purpose, seeing himself as the *Antiquarius Domini* – the Book-Producer of the Lord:[67]

> A place where the classics of Latin Christian literature would be copied and circulated, where translations of Greek works would be undertaken, and where the basic skills of Latin grammar and rhetorical analysis were maintained, as a *sine qua non* for the understanding and the accurate copying of

the Scriptures. Small textbooks were carefully prepared as "teach yourself" volumes, designed to meet the needs of the average reader.[68]

Monasteries such as that of Cassiodorus fed into the significant activities of the circulation and industry of textual reproduction. Illustrative of this is Benedict Biscop (628–690), a wealthy nobleman who founded and led the monasteries of St. Peter's and St. Paul's in North Umbria in which the Venerable Bede lived and wrote. Biscop made a number of trips to Rome and brought back with him to the monastery an entire library of classical and patristic books – all of which he had to organize to be produced by being copied on site in different locations where the copies were available. The library at St. Peter's and St. Paul's was the largest north of the Alps, with more than three hundred books, including some that came originally from Cassiodorus' *Vivarium*.[69] These were the references and resources on which Bede drew for his writings.

When one considers that every document had a limited life, the copying and recopying of documents that were essential for their preservation required a media industry, and the monastic network was central in one that remained organized and effective for around nine hundred years. Brown gives a good insight into the effort and costs of the industry required to service such a literary activity.[70] Thousands of sheep and calves were needed to provide the hides for making parchment – one large Bible required the skins of five hundred sheep. All of the skins had to be prepared, cut to size, folded, and stitched, and individual pages marked ready for writing by charcoal or stylus lines or by pricking holes. To copy the four Gospels took up to eight months, the same amount of time to build a building. To reproduce the works of Gregory the Great, for example, would require an eleven-volume set of 2,100 parchment folios weighing almost fifty kilograms (the modern printed edition weighs three). The *Codex Amiatinus*, an all-inclusive edition of the entire Bible created at Wearmouth to be placed on the tomb of St. Peter in Rome, took twenty-eight years to produce and weighed thirty kilograms.

While some suggest that copying was done only by literate monks with fine handwriting,[71] Tillotson suggests that for some work copyists need not have been literate, but trained only in a very mechanistic, letter-by-letter form of copying (hence the frequent mistakes).[72] There is evidence to indicate that women in convents also were actively involved both in the copying of manuscripts and in the writing of letters and codices. McKitterick identifies eighth-century copies of works, including Augustine's *Commentary on the Psalms*, which are signed by women, including one on which fourteen different women had worked. The quality of the copies is high, indicating the women scribes were competent and understood what they are copying.[73]

Included in the reproduction of manuscripts was the process of illumination or painting of the manuscript, through either the design and coloring of

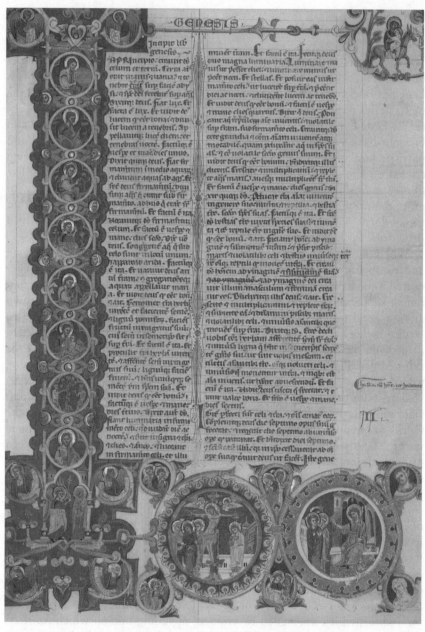

Figure 6.1 The initial page of the Book of Genesis from an illuminated bible produced in the thirteenth century, possibly in Bologna, Italy. The sweeping letter "I" introduces the text "In the beginning," and the images within it link the creation of Adam visually with the redemption of Christ. Source: The J. Paul Getty Museum, Los Angeles, Ms. 107, fol. 4. Digital image courtesy of the Getty's Open Content Program.

individual letters or words, or the incorporation of paintings within the text or on separate pages. Along with their artistic expressiveness, the illuminations served to enhance the authority and power of the artifact to impress both Christians and pagans, and Christian missionaries readily used "the books" to demonstrate Christianity's superior culture. Boniface, the British monk who became a missionary to Germany, on one occasion wrote to the Abbess Eadburga begging her to send to him the scriptural *Epistles of St. Peter,* written in letters of gold, so that "a reverence and love of the Holy Scriptures may be impressed on the minds of the heathens to whom I preach."[74]

Manuscript illumination became a specialist and expensive skill, requiring not just artists but also specialist materials; the deep-blue pigment lapis lazuli, for example, was made from a mineral available only from Afghanistan. Those designed for high liturgical use or maximum impact "were additionally embellished with gold, jewels and enamels, matching the splendor of the altar vessels."[75] This led to some monasteries gaining a reputation, and significant income, from specializing in the industry, with many of their orders for illuminated works coming from other monasteries.

While a major aim of the illumination of manuscripts was the enhancement of the spiritual content of the document by the ornamentation of the artifact, manuscript illumination was one of the few available opportunities for artistic expression, and in their illumination of religious themes many of the works reflect this artistic desire to incorporate aspects of everyday life. Backhouse draws attention to the opening page of *The Gospel of Luke* in the *Lindisfarne Gospels*, produced in the Lindisfarne monastic community in England in 698. Among the ornamentation on the page is a domestic cat, crouched in a corner with its eyes hungrily focused on a nearby group of birds. She notes that many of the illuminators' techniques were taken up in work by later artists.[76]

Written Latin and the consolidation of medieval Christendom

While the translation of Christian texts into vernacular languages was a strategy of mission in Eastern Christianity, Western Christianity followed a reverse linguistic strategy: the restriction of textual writings and religious activities to the one language, Latin. The reasons for this reflect the important ways in which the mediation of Christianity, even in what we would consider today as a relatively undeveloped media context, has been a site of political and cultural engagement and contest.

Theologically, Ecclesiastical Latin, as it came to be known, was suited to the purposes to which the Roman Church was putting it: clarity and directness for administration, conciseness for explaining theological doctrine, and logic for arguing and defending a position. Politically, the adoption of Latin by the Roman Catholic Church as its official language identified the Roman Pope and Roman Catholicism as the successor to the former Roman Empire and its civilization.

Practically, the use of a shared language made possible communication across different language and ethnic groups, a crucial requirement in the building and maintaining of any empire. Latin continued to replace local languages throughout Europe and North Africa even to the end of the sixth century, the exceptions being the continued use of Celtic in Britain and Basque in the Pyrenees.[77]

But spoken Latin, like all oral languages, was constantly changing through its usage and through taking up words and phrases from the different local languages it displaced. As the Middle Ages progressed, spoken Latin evolved into or was taken up in the different dialects and regional variants that we know today as national languages: Italian, Spanish, Portuguese, French, German, English, and Romanian. Along with this oral syncretizing of language practices, oral Christianity also incorporated practices and beliefs of oral-based regional religions into their fluid Christianity. By the end of the seventh century, as Butt observes,

> [A]nimistic and magical practices had become the norm for many who claimed to practice Christianity, including many of its clergy.... Customs that had been pagan were often absorbed into Christianity to make the new religion more palatable. Pagan gods were turned into saints. Pagan celebrations such as the winter solstice were combined with Christian holy days so that the birth of Jesus, a date that was not known nor of much concern to Christianity, became Christmas.[78]

On the other hand, in its written form, the ecclesiastical Latin of the Roman Church, carefully nurtured and preserved to retain its aesthetic qualities and theological and organizational precision, remained relatively unchanged. As a result, the two Latins, the Latin of the Catholic Church (written Latin) and the Latin spoken in the marketplaces (oral Latin), diverged into different languages.

The differences between the two forms came to a head in the reign of the Frankish ruler, Charlemagne. A formidable military strategist who used meticulous planning and, by the turn of the ninth century, was the undisputed ruler of western Europe, Charlemagne saw himself and his destiny through twin lenses: one in the tradition of the best of the Roman Emperors, and the other in the tradition of the godly kings of the Old Testament.[79]

In line with his vision of himself as both Emperor and God's agent on earth, Charlemagne implemented an extensive program of cultural, educational, and religious reform that touched almost every aspect of life: politics, civil administration, finance, law, moral behavior, education, learning, culture, the church, and religion. He imported scholars from around the Christian world and made his palace a center of study, discussion, and education. Charlemagne had read to him (he was functionally illiterate) on a regular basis Augustine's work, *The City of God*. He funded and promoted book production and the development of literacy.

Seeing Catholic Christianity as a unifying ideology and management structure for his empire, Charlemagne positioned himself as the governor and protector of orthodox Christianity and the authority on matters of faith throughout the empire. Politics served the ends of religion and religion served the ends of politics. Every Christian was required to be able to say from memory the basic elements of the faith, the Lord's Prayer, and the Apostles' Creed. He established local and regional bishoprics and archbishoprics as patronized administrative units, charged not only with religious duties but also with governmental responsibilities for implementing imperial directives and legislation and for collecting rents, taxes, and tithes. To equip them to do this, churches, dioceses, and monasteries were endowed with extensive lands, peasants, and income.[80]

With the assistance of a religious adviser, Alcuin of York, a variety of measures were enacted to counter the oral assimilation of pagan beliefs into Christianity and to restore orthodoxy of the Catholic faith. Ecclesiastical Latin became an important tool in these reforms. Bishops were made responsible for training their clergy to read and write Latin so they could properly lead services, preach, and interpret orthodox Catholic doctrine. The Roman Latin rite was installed as the official rite of the kingdom, replacing the various regional rites that had been in use.[81]

However, the Latin being used as the measure of Catholic orthodoxy was a particular form of written Latin brought by Alcuin from Britain, one that Alcuin learned and practiced from books but did not speak as a mother tongue – what Brown describes as "a perfect language because it was a perfectly dead language."[82] What Alcuin encountered in Continental Europe was a different sort of Latin, one spoken and written as a living and changing mother tongue by people who still saw themselves in some ways as Romans and speaking as Romans. Alcuin considered such Latin as "barbarous," and as part of his reforms set out to restore doctrinal and liturgical orthodoxy by re-instituting what he saw as proper Latin in its grammar use, orthography, and pronunciation. [83]

The impulse in instituting these reforms and enforcing the use of correct Ecclesiastical Latin was more than just pedantically linguistic. Serious issues of faith and piety were considered to be at stake. The vigorous, vernacular, popular piety practiced by people and priests in many of the churches was corrupted by pagan practices, and Alcuin considered they placed people's eternal destiny at risk. The risk to the Catholic faith was no longer coming from paganism but from vernacular Christianity. Against this corruption,

Alcuin restored what he saw as true Christianity through a wide-reaching reform of language and piety.

As Abbot of the abbey of St. Martin in Tours, he secured the most authentic scriptural and liturgical books from libraries in Rome and Monte Cassino for copying and distribution. Working with what he called a "crowd of scribes," he developed a smaller, more regular, and more legible Latin script called the Caroline minuscule script, with rules for scribes for writing each

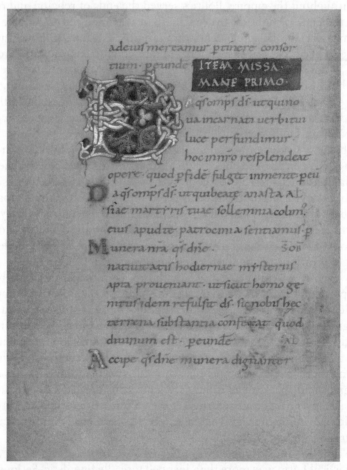

Figure 6.2 Caroline miniscule script, developed during the time of Charlemagne, used here in an eleventh-century French manuscript for the first prayer for the second Mass of Christmas day. The legibility of the letters, layout of the text, and ease of reading made it the most common book script for centuries. Source: The J. Paul Getty Museum, Los Angeles, Ms. Ludwig V 1, fol. 8v. Digital image courtesy of the Getty's Open Content Program.

letter and how the pen was to be held.[84] This easier and clearer script made book reading easier, reduced the potential for ambiguity, and facilitated the accurate reading aloud of the Christian Law for the illiterate.[85]

Along with the restoration of orthodoxy, Charlemagne and Alcuin's standardizing reforms in language, liturgy, and doctrine had the important political purpose of unifying the diverse Frankish tribes into a common kingdom.[86]

Charlemagne's promotion of book production and wider education in literacy and literature served a number of other purposes. One was to build a larger cohort of literate people to service the running of his far-flung empire. The other was to aid in the development of faith and the more intelligent understanding of scripture. In one of his official encyclicals, he explained his desire to increase literacy among the wider population on the grounds of better scripture understanding:

> For since there are figures of speech, metaphors and the like to be found on the sacred pages, there can be no doubt that each man who reads them will understand their spiritual meaning more quickly if he is first of all given full instruction in the study of literature.[87]

As Alcuin's version of proper Ecclesiastical Latin became widely implemented, a separation developed between the language of ecclesiastical Christianity and the vernacular languages of the people in the fields and marketplaces. All church documents and activities were to be in standardized Latin; vernacular languages were to serve the secondary purpose of interpreting the meaning of what had already been read in Latin. As decreed by a Council of Bishops in 813, preaching was to comprise the reading of authorized sermons by priests in Latin. These would be followed by the translation of the Latin text into the vernacular of the people – the *rustica Romana lingua*.

A number of scholars identify this process of reform as the time when the language of Christianity became alienated from the languages of the people.[88] A number of consequences ensued. One was that Christian worship came to be performed in what was to the majority of Christians a foreign language. The same applied to all official church documents and discussions, to the extent that only those chosen to be educated in Latin by the Roman Church could participate in the discussions and decisions of faith.

As verbal and aural participation diminished for laypeople, the visual became a primary means of their engagement with faith. To cater for this, physical performances became exaggerated and an increasing number of actions such as genuflections, signs of the cross, censing, the ringing of bells, and the raising aloft of the bread and wine developed in importance in the communication of faith. Ornamentation and visual storytelling in the form of stained glass, paintings, and statues increased. Altar tables at which the priest conducted his foreign-language rituals were built higher and higher and placed against the front wall of the church, so that the priest conducted worship with his back to the people, physically constructing the institutional church as the intermediary between God and people.

Although there is evidence of laypeople in the Middle Ages who could read and/or write,[89] the Church's dominance and control over the key medium of literacy gave them enormous political power. It made them indispensible as amanuenses, and their extensive ownership of property and command of people made Christian leaders such as bishops and abbots powerful figures at the highest levels of political power and administration. It also gave them a monopoly control on the interpretation and dispensation of faith, installing a hierarchical relationship of production and reception in which it was made clear that it was the Church's role "to read, interpret and pass on religious writings in Latin," and the layman's "to accept his inferior status as recipient." The oral culture of the layman became a diminution reinforced in language, with laymen commonly referred to as *illiterati, idiotae,* and *rustici* (illiterate, idiotic peasants) and clergy as *doci et cauti* (trained and cautious).[90]

The Roman Catholic Church was reluctant to share a medium that gave them such political and social power, and they protected their advantages vigorously. Education in literacy was restricted to those known to be supportive of the position and interests of the Catholic Church. The efforts by Charlemagne (as a layman) to establish monastic and cathedral schools to educate laypeople were abolished by the Synod of Paris in 829, just fifteen years after his death. Unlike Eastern Christianity, the Roman Catholic Church resisted the creation of vernacular literature and vernacular translations of the scripture, a situation that would continue in Europe until the Renaissance.

NOTES

1 The issue of how power operates through language has been the subject of extensive analysis, particularly in the Poststructuralist movement. See for example Bourdieu, 1977; Foucault, 1972; Harker, Mahar, & Wilkes, 1990; Lewis, 2005.
2 Freeman, 2008, p. 51.
3 Brown, 2003, p. 114.
4 Brown, 2003, p. 116.
5 Farrell, 2001, p. 3.
6 Wiles, 2005, p. 258.
7 See Brown, 2008, pp. 367–373.
8 Dégert, 1910.
9 Freeman, 2002, p. 275.
10 H.-J. Martin, 1994, p. 111.
11 Cross & Livingstone, 2005.
12 Wiles, 2005, p. 254.
13 Moorehead, 1999, p. 4.

14 Cross & Livingstone, 2005, p. 49.
15 "His indefatigable industry and methodical habits explain how so busy a man found time to compose so many valuable books" (Loughlin, 1907).
16 Moorehead, 1999, p. 5. Moorehead cites two occasions in his writings where Ambrose states that he had seen a poor man putting his children up to auction to pay his debts, an account copied from the Greek writer Basil.
17 McLynn, 1994, p. 226.
18 Loughlin, 1907.
19 See Moorehead, 1999, pp. 182–185, for examples of Ambrose's strong critical rejection of Jewish people and support for their disappearance.
20 Cited in Moorehead, 1999, p. 186.
21 McLynn, 1994, pp. 127–128.
22 Freeman, 2008, pp. 108–111.
23 Wiles, 2005, p. 255.
24 Küng, 1994, p. 289.
25. Küng, 1994, pp. 291–292.
26 O'Donnell, 2006, p. 12.
27 O'Donnell, 2006, pp. 12–13.
28 Kuhn, 2007.
29 Brown, 2000, p. 195.
30 Knowles & Penkett, 2004, pp. 159–160.
31 van der Meer, 1961, p. 132.
32 van der Meer, 1961, pp. 133, 223.
33 O'Donnell, 2006, p. 10.
34 Matthews, 2006.
35 See for example Shlain, 1998, p. 262.
36 Brown, 2003, p. 21.
37 Brown, 2003, pp. 7, 104.
38 Heather, 1994, p. 196.
39 Green, 1994, p. 3.
40 E. Cameron, 2005, p. 23.
41 Wood, 1981, p. 82.
42 Brown, 2003, p. 22 See also Kosto, 2005.
43 Brown, 2003, p. 25.
44 This summary draws on Wessel, 2008, pp. 21–24.
45 Küng, 1994, p. 334.
46 Küng, 1994, p. 334.
47 Brown, 2003, p. 13.
48 Brown, 2003, p. 14.
49 Brown, 2003, p. 14.
50 Wessel, 2008, pp. 23–24.
51 Cross & Livingstone, 1974, pp. 1062–1063.
52 Bowden, 2005a, p. 887.
53 Lawrence, 1984, pp. 10–11. Among other influential fourth-century writings were Jerome's colorful *Life of Paul the Hermit* and translation of the *Rule of Pachomius*, Rufinus' Latin translation of the *History of the Monks in Egypt*, and collections or written oral traditions such as Palladius' *Lausiac History*, Severus'

Dialogues, Cassian's *Conferences,* and various versions of *Apophthegmata,* or Sayings of the Fathers.

54 Modern textual research suggests that Benedict's Rule was not the work of a single original genius but one of a group of integrated monastic rules that were built up over time. The earliest extant written copy is an Anglo-Saxon manuscript from around 750 (Lawrence, 1984, pp. 20–21).

55 Walker, 1959, p. 127.

56 Brown, 2003, p. 221.

57 Lawrence, 1984, p. 44.

58 Brown, 2003, pp. 110,112.

59 Rule 140, in Fox, 1994, p. 147.

60 Lawrence, 1984, p. 30.

61 The practice of receiving children into monasteries was banned by a Lateran Council in 1215.

62 "[The monk] shall not do what pleases him; he shall eat what is set before him, clothe himself with what is given him, do the work assigned to him, be subject to a superior whom he does not like. He shall go to bed so tired that he may fall asleep while going, and rise before he has had sufficient rest" (Abbot St. Columban, 590).

63 Lawrence, 1984, p. 40.

64 Brown, 2003, p. 20.

65 Brown, 2003, p. 131.

66 Brown, 2003, pp. 351–352.

67 From the *Institutes,* cited in Brown, 2003, p. 197.

68 Brown, 2003, pp. 196–197.

69 Brown, 2003, p. 356.

70 Brown, 2003, pp. 357–358.

71 See for example Butt, 2002, p. 118.

72 Tillotson, 2006.

73 McKitterick, 1994, pp. VII.2–7.

74 Halsall, 1996.

75 Backhouse, 1979, p. 8.

76 Backhouse, 1979.

77 Brown, 2003, p. 232.

78 Butt, 2002, p. 107.

79 Hamilton, 2013.

80 Brown, 2003, p. 31.

81 Dowley, 1977, p. 148.

82 Brown, 2003, p. 447.

83 Brown, 2003, p. 449.

84 Bowden, 2005a, p. 168.

85 Altman, 2004, p. 70.

86 Küng, 1994, p. 356.

87 *Encyclia de litteris colendis,* in Loyn & Percival, 1975, p. 64.

88 See for example Farrell, 2001, p. 5; also Green, 1994, p. 43.

89 Green, 1994, p. 25. See also Kosto, 2005.

90 Green, 1994, p. 25.

7

Christianity in the East

The Church of the East

The canonical Letters of Paul and Acts of the Apostles present a view of Christianity's development as spreading primarily around the Mediterranean and progressively from the Eastern Empire to the West. Luke, as a Greek speaker and writer, in the Acts moves quickly in his narrative to the spread of Christianity from its Aramaic roots to the Greek-speaking world and toward his home city of Rome. What is omitted from this written construction that has shaped perceptions of Christianity's development (particularly for western eyes) is the extensiveness and significance of the spread of Aramaic-Syriac speaking Christianity to the East.

At the time that Paul was undertaking his missionary work around the Mediterranean towns of the Middle East, Christians were also traveling and spreading their stories and beliefs beyond the eastern boundaries of the empire into Asia. Antioch was an important center for this eastern-directed activity, and was one of the major recognized cities of early Christianity. Its geographic location on the coast (of present-day southern Turkey) made it the western end of the commercial trade routes that had existed, from at least the time of Alexander, connecting the eastern Mediterranean to Persia, central and east Asia, and the Indian Ocean along the Silk Road, the Spice Road, and the Royal Persian Road.

The spread of Christianity throughout Asia was extensive, and the general ignorance about this in Western Christianity justifies a brief overview. After journeys of several of the first disciples, Christianity was carried eastward largely by refugees, merchants on the imperial trade routes, and wartime captives deported to Persian territories. Christian influence spread also through Christian doctors, scribes, and artisans who found employment among Turks and Huns. By the end of the second century, Christian

From Jesus to the Internet, Peter Horsfield © 2015 John Wiley & Sons, Ltd. Published 2015 by John Wiley & Sons, Ltd.

communities had been established from Edessa (now Urfa in present-day Turkey), to Persia, Afghanistan, the Arabian Peninsula (including Mecca), and eastern Africa, with more than twenty bishoprics in Persia alone. A number of these attribute their founding to some of the disciples. The kingdom of Osrhoene, with its capital in Edessa was the world's first kingdom to become Christian (third century) and is the site of one of the earliest known church buildings. Armenia became a nominally Christian kingdom around 314 (the same time as Constantine's conversion and ascension to emperor of Rome) and in a short time had integrated its oral epic histories into a rich Christian literate culture.[1]

The spread of Syriac Christianity into Mesopotamia and Persia, where there were strong Jewish communities, brought it into closer contact with Jewish communities than churches in the West, and a more cooperative relationship with Judaism formed than the antagonistic one that formed in Christianity within the Roman Empire. The liturgy of the Syriac Church had a much more Jewish character than elsewhere, and the Old Testament section of the Syriac-language Christian Bible may have been created by Syriac-speaking Jews.[2]

By the fourth century a Syriac Church, which claimed the Apostle Thomas as its founder, was sufficiently established on the southwest coast of India (in the present-day state of Kerala) that it was placed under the care of a Syriac Church bishop on the Persian Gulf coast of Iran.[3] The early sixth-century traveler Cosmas Indicoplenstes reported witnessing Christians associated with the Syriac Church in Socotra (a small archipelago in the Indian Ocean), southwest and central India, Sri Lanka, Pegu (southern Burma), Cochin China (southern Vietnam), Siam, and Tonquin (northern Vietnam).[4]

A decisive influence on the shape and character of the Semitic churches was the Council of Chalcedon, the council held in 451 to resolve highly philosophical doctrinal disputes over the relationship of the human and divine in Jesus, and the proposition that Mary, being the mother of Jesus the man, should also be acknowledged as the mother of God (or *theotokos*). Nestorius, the Patriarch of Constantinople and formerly a monk from Antioch, opposed the proposition. In expressing his reservations, Nestorius argued that Jesus was both God and human but the relationship between the two was a unity of will rather than natures (a position labeled as *dyophysite*, or two-natured). Although his views were closely related to those finally agreed upon, the debate became caught up with political contests and maneuverings as well as philosophical reasoning, and Nestorius' position was declared heretical. He was removed as patriarch of Constantinople and exiled to a monastery in Egypt.

Many Syrians, bishops and others, supported Nestorius, partly because of his Syrian origins and because of his close association with the highly respected Syrian teacher Theodore of Mopsuestia. When Nestorius and his position were declared heretical, they moved east beyond the boundaries of the empire and consolidated a separate Church of the East, often called the Nestorian or Syriac Church of the East. It formed its own creed in 486.

The other significant groups alienated by the council's decisions were Christian groups in Armenia, Syria, Egypt, and Ethiopia, who also held different theological positions from the Chalcedonian decision. The differences are highly philosophical, complex, and nuanced, yet they have been strongly held until the present time. The dissenting Christian communities in Africa posed more of a political problem for the eastern emperor because they were located in the crucial economic regions of Africa, and efforts to resolve the theological differences were made more difficult because of these political and economic connections.

The Church of the East has continued to be *dyophysite* in its theology. One of the consequences of this is a quite different view of sin than the dominant western Augustinian view of original sin. For Theodore, one of the influential Syrian theologians, the root of sin lay not in human nature but in human will, that is, in people's choice of how they behave. Faith, then, was seen, not as a cure for the stain of sin but as a spiritual force enabling people to overcome the destructive forces of evil.

The rejection of the Church of the East's position by the Byzantine Orthodox Empire helped the church's acceptance into the social and political life of the Persian Empire, who were opponents of the Byzantines. By the sixth century, the Church of the East had its own principal bishop or *Catholicos*, who lived in one of the key cities of the Persian Empire and were independent of any control by the Byzantine Church.

It was an active missionary church that, because of its minority status, spread its faith by persuasion and influence rather than political coercion. Its spiritual and institutional life was sustained by active programs of education, community, and monastic life. There is physical and documentary evidence of Syriac Christian activity, communities, monasteries, and libraries along the whole length of the trade routes from Antioch through Persia to Kirgizstan, China, Mongolia, and Japan.[5] A Nestorian missionary, Alopen, under a commission of the Catholicos in Persia, met with the Chinese emperor in 635, leading to official toleration of "the religion of Syria," permission to make a translation of the Christian scriptures in Chinese, and the establishment of several Christian monasteries in China, including in the capital.[6]

The result of this spread was that, at the time of Charlemagne and the establishment of the Holy Roman Empire in the West (the turn of the ninth century), the Church of the East comprised around a quarter of the world's Christians. They had their own spiritual and political head living in the ancient city of Seleucia, in what is now central Iraq.[7] Until the Middle Ages, it also had the greatest geographical scope of any Christian church.[8]

Monasticism was a significant part of this mission activity. Syrian monasticism developed independently of Egyptian monasticism. In difference from the Egyptian monks, who retreated from the world into caves and cells in the desert, eastern Syrian monasticism was characterized by mission work. As Philip describes it:

> The central aspect of the main line East Syrian monasticism is not the fleeing from the world or despising the human body, but the exercise of self-discipline by the use of human will and acquisition of wisdom to be used for the salvation of the people.... His mission is not described as withdrawal, but as an advance against the forces of error and darkness.[9]

A number of aspects of the mediation of faith within the Church of the East are noteworthy. One is the part played (again) by language in the cultural mediation of Christianity, an issue we have looked at earlier. The language of the church, Syriac, is a dialect of Aramaic, which Jesus spoke. It was a widespread language within the Mesopotamian region – Brown notes that it was possible to travel from the Persian capital to Antioch in Turkey, a distance of more than 1100 kilometers, speaking Syriac all the way.[10] Its Aramaic character also maintained a cultural connection with the language of Jesus, and the first New Testament translation made from Greek was into Syriac.

The use of Syriac therefore was deeply embedded in Syrian Christianity, even when it spread to other regions. Although many biblical, liturgical, and other documents were translated into regional languages, Syriac was retained as its common liturgical and theological language, even as far east as China.[11] This was different from the *miaphysite* churches, for example, who translated their theology, liturgy, and Christian writings into regional languages such as Georgian, Coptic, Nubian, and Ge'ez.[12] The common use of Syriac helped to preserve a shared identity amongst Christians across this vast geography, as did Latin in the West. However, unlike the exclusive use of Latin in the West, where it was a tool of the Roman Catholic Church to maintain its political dominance, the continued use of what was a foreign language in situations where it was a minority almost guaranteed that the Christianity of the Church of the East would remain a minority and foreign religion.[13]

The influence of written script in the construction of Christianity is relevant also in relation to the Church of the East. One reason for the perpetuation of classical Syriac in the practice of the religion was the nature of the script used in its writings. The Syriac script was a Nestorian alphabetic script that did not have cursive or minuscule forms, script forms that enabled more rapid writing and thus were also more subject to change. As a result, the disjuncture between past and present writings that emerged in

Latin and Greek manuscripts where scripts occasionally changed did not occur in the well-stocked monastic libraries of Syria and northern Iraq, and any learned Syriac speaker could take up and read a manuscript written centuries before.[14] The unchangeability of its written text may be one of the reasons why Syriac Christianity remained unchangeable for so long.[15]

A second area of interest is the Church of the East's scholastic and literary activities. Brown notes that it was *Christian* literary activities that made Syriac (along with Coptic) a major literary language. Although spreading in regions that were in some cases strongly oral in character, Eastern Christianity quickly established literate cultures embodied in institutional forms such as monasteries and schools. The School of the Persians, developed in Edessa in the second century, was for several centuries the major center of higher education for Christians throughout the East, and reflects the emphasis placed by Syrian Christianity on literacy and education as faith activities. As Philip notes,

> The central aspect of the school was its spiritual discipline and Bible study. Within the framework of general biblical knowledge, the students were given systematic training in biblical exegesis after the manner of the great interpreter, Theodore of Mopsuestia. But the school was not only a school of spiritual discipline based on the study of the scriptures, its theology was also a missionary theology.[16]

When the Byzantine Emperor Zeno closed the school because of its heretical doctrinal positions, new schools for the development of knowledge and the training of clergy outside the empire were soon established in Nisibis (150 miles east, and across the border in the Sassanian Empire) and Gondeshapur (in present-day Iran). The schools developed an equally formidable reputation for their libraries, education, and research. As their students spread, they became a model for a variety of Christian educational and scholarly institutions at the local level. As Becker describes it:

> These institutions could range from gatherings in local churches for the elementary study of scripture to informal study circles which met in specific locations within monasteries to independent institutions with a multi-tiered hierarchy of offices, where students engaged in a detailed study of biblical exegesis and acquired an acquaintance with Aristotelian logic.[17]

One aspect of this scholarly activity was the preservation and translation of works into Syriac. This included pre-Christian Greek works to help in theological argument against Byzantine Christians. The influence of this scholarly work of the Church of the East was extensive. Cassiodorus, the Italian scholar who established a monastery in southern Italy for the preservation of classical works, modeled his cultural program partly on what he heard about the school in Nisibis. Syriac translations of classic Greek writings in philosophy, astronomy, geography, mathematics, and medicine were the source for subsequent Arabic translations that, when discovered in Spain in the thirteenth century, became a stimulus for the European Renaissance. A Christian scholar from Nisibis, Severus, a bishop and abbot of a monastery, was the first to identify a system of mathematical signs invented by Indians that came to be adopted into Islamic culture and known as our Arabic numerals. Christian physicians and translators from Gondeshapur became influential in the courts of the Persian and Islamic rulers.[18] Carter, in his extensive study tracing the origins of block printing in China in the eighth century and its gradual spread westward, notes the involvement of Nestorian Christians in that spread, long before printing exerted its influence in the West in the fifteenth century.[19]

Under quite different circumstances than in the West, the Church of the East persisted and continued to exercise a significant influence in the wide expanse of countries and regions where it was established. A number of the leading officials and princesses in the Mongolian court of successive Khans were Christians. Emissaries sent by the Mongol ruler in Baghdad to meet with Pope Honorius IV in Rome in the thirteenth century were Christians from the Church of the East.[20] When the Portuguese landed in Goa in the fifteenth century, intent on establishing Christianity in India, they were surprised to find a Syriac church in Kerala that had been there for over a thousand years.

Islam

The beginning and rapid spread of Islam in the seventh and subsequent centuries comprised a major political and religious challenge to Christianity. In what has been described as "one of the most rapid shifts of power in history,"[21] in only a century after Muhammad's death in 632, Islam had taken over many of the lands of the Persian and Byzantine Empires and become established as the ruling power in the Arabian Peninsula, Jerusalem, Palestine, Syria, Persia, Central Asia, Egypt, the provinces of North Africa, Cyprus, Rhodes, Malta, the Iberian Peninsula, parts of northern and southern Italy, and Switzerland. The three recognized Christian patriarchal cities of Jerusalem, Antioch, and Alexandria came under Muslim control in just a decade. This initial advance was halted in Turkey with the successful defense of Constantinople in 678 and in France in 732 by Charles Martel, the king of the Franks.

As "religions of the book," Jews and Christians were tolerated within Muslim-governed countries, many of which retained a Christian majority. However, Christians were subordinated as a class as *dhimmis* or non-Muslims, and were subject to particular guidelines and additional taxes. Within these guidelines, set out most explicitly in the Covenant of Umar, attributed to

Caliph Umar ibn Khattab in Syria in 633–644, Jews and Christians were allowed to keep their own religious authority structures and customs and practice their religion in private. Evangelization and conversion of Muslims were not permitted. The understanding is well elaborated in the authorization given by Caliph Muktafi II to Patriarch Abdisho III in Baghdad in 1138:

> The charter of the highest imamate of Islam is hereby granted to you to be the Catholicos of the Nestorian Christians inhabiting the City of Peace [Baghdad] and all the lands of the countries of Islam. You are empowered to act as their head and the head also of the Greeks [Byzantines], Jacobites and Melkites. If any of the abovementioned clerics [from the Churches named] treads in the path of revolt against your orders or refuses to accept your decisions, he will be prosecuted and punished. Your life and property, as well as that of your people, will be protected, likewise your churches and monasteries. We will be satisfied with your payment of the capitation tax. Be worthy of all these favors and set up prayers and invocations for the Commander of the Faithful.[22]

The extent to which the freedoms and protection given under the covenant were followed varied considerably from location to location and from time to time, influenced by economic, political, or religious circumstances. They ranged from a relationship of oppression and persecution to cultural exchanges and collaborations in the arts, literature, and scientific disciplines, as occurred in Baghdad in the eighth and ninth centuries and Andalusia in the tenth century. Political divisions on religious grounds likewise were not always clearly demarcated, with different Christians and Muslims at times forming alliances for political gain or as a political defense.

A number of reasons are given for why the early spread of Islam was so rapid and extensive and why Christian rule, even in regions that had been so central to the early development of Christianity, collapsed so quickly.

One aspect of it was the superior military power, drive, and organization of Islam, but the lack of strong resistance from dominantly Christian countries reflects deeper aspects to this spread. One of those was that, for many Christians in these regions, rule by Islam was perceived as a better option than rule by the Christian emperor. The Christian Byzantine state ruled its subjects with an authority that was at times tyrannical and oppressive, and Christians found freedoms in rule by Islam they didn't have in rule by Christians. Islam offered a political system in which, in response to political obedience, albeit as subordinate citizens, Christians were given protection and freedom to follow their own faith.

The complexity of text-based Christian doctrine, the fractious divisions that had been produced in the interminable doctrinal debates, and the intellectual and speculative complexities around doctrinal correctness and precision had made Christian thought and practice a confusing and at times risky business. Islam presented a much simpler monotheistic faith in which

God was one, Jesus was honored as having a special relationship with God, Muhammad was the prophet after Jesus, and the focus of faith was on practice and living.

The rise of Islam had a number of major consequences for global Christianity. It produced a weakening of the Eastern Roman Empire and the Orthodox Church, a decline of the Church of the East through its limited freedom to proselytize, and shifting of the center of power within Christianity to the West. Islam also had an effect in requiring Christianity to define itself again, politically and theologically, this time against the major competing global religious power of Islam. Doctrinally, from an original position of seeing Islam as a Christian or Jewish heresy, Christianity came to see Islam as a separate religion and a foil against which Christianity had to define itself. Islam had an influence in some areas on the mediation of Christianity, such as in the destruction of images in Byzantine Christianity because of Islamic challenges to icon practice as idolatrous. The Christian position of Arianism, which saw Jesus as a subordinate being to God the Father, was seen as too close to the Islamic view of Jesus and so lost its validity as an alternative Christian theological position, and remnants of Arianism in Europe increasingly became Nicene Trinitarian. Politically, in the Middle Ages, the threat of Islam provoked the Christian Crusades, fed by Christian propaganda and marketing.

Any acquaintance the Christian West had with Islam came mainly through pilgrims and traders. Reports from pilgrims initially focused on sites of historic Christian sacred value and showed little interest or information about Muslim people, customs, and conditions. At the time of the Crusades, there was an increase in writings, although in a particular frame that served the purpose of building support for the Crusades: "Pilgrims and scholars outdid one another in presenting Islam as an erroneous and idolatrous religion that must be condemned in any way possible."[23]

Writing the voice

The translation of Greek Christianity into local vernaculars involved, in a number of cases, the invention of a written alphabet for oral languages that did not have one. Finding ways to write the voice became a significant contribution of Christianity in the development of vernacular cultures.

One of the earliest examples of this was the work of Ulfilas (313–383), a Cappadocian whose family was abducted by the Germanic tribe of the Goths. Sent to Constantinople for an education in Christianity and Greek, in 341 he was consecrated by Eusebius, the Arian archbishop of Constantinople, and sent back as a missionary bishop to the Goths. Desiring to make the Greek scriptures available to the Goths in their own tongue, Ulfilas began what was likely a task not done before, intentionally creating a written version of an oral language. Realizing that there were sounds in Goth not represented by the Roman and Greek alphabets, Ulfilas invented his own Germanic alphabet, with a selection of Roman and Greek letters that corresponded to some of the sounds, and a selection of runes, an early Germanic alphabet in limited use for those sounds for which there were no Roman or Greek parallels.[24] Using his alphabet, he completed translation of the Bible, the first in a Germanic language, although it is said his translation did not include the two biblical Books of Kings, because "their warlike deeds might have a bad influence upon a nation so fond of war as the Goths."[25]

Highly effective in his mission, by the end of his life he had succeeded in conversion of the Gothic king and the whole nation to Arian Christianity, and their Arian identity was a significant marker in later political and military conflicts with the Roman Empire. Although highly successful, Ulfilas was never made a saint because of his Arian Christian views.

The alphabets of a number of other oral languages, such as those of the Armenians, Turks, Uighurs, and Mongols, owe their invention to the work of Christians keen to translate scriptures, liturgies, and other writings into local languages to make them more accessible to wider groups of people.

A similar path was followed by the two brothers Cyril (826–869) and Methodius (815–885) in their development of the Cyrillic alphabet. The two were sent by the patriarch of Constantinople in response to a request for help from Rostilav, whose rule in Moravia was being destabilized by Latin-speaking Frankish clergy loyal to Rome. The two were highly suited to the task. Among the intellectual elite in Byzantium, Cyril was a scholar, philosopher, and linguist and an emissary of the imperial court in Constantinople; and Methodius was the father superior of a monastery in Vitinia, Asia Minor. Both spoke Slav from childhood. Part of their mission strategy was the translation of the scriptures and liturgy into the oral Slavic language. This desire to utilize peasants' language reflected their view of the equality of all people before God. It also challenged the hegemonic view of religious language held by the Latin-speaking western missionaries.

To achieve the task, Cyril developed, or quite possibly had already developed, a new alphabet and script – named the *Glagolitic* – to convey accurately the sounds of Slavic speech. The alphabet, which MacCullough describes as "to say the least idiosyncratic, with only surreal resemblances to any other alphabetic form in existence,"[26] drew heavily on Greek but also used other linguistic symbols encountered by Cyril in his travels, including possibly Sanskrit.

While the resultant translation of the scriptures and conduct of the divine liturgy in Slavic was widely welcomed by the Moravians, they encountered such strong opposition from the Latin-speaking Frankish clergy that they were forced to withdraw. Both brothers went to Rome to present their case to Pope Adrian II, arguing that Slavic was an equally fit language for

Christianity as Greek, Latin, and Jewish. The pope gave his support for their mission and agreement to ordain priests for it. Gaining his agreement may have been assisted by the fact that Cyril had brought with him a gift of a piece of bone from the body of St. Clement, one of the earliest popes, recently discovered near the Black Sea. MacCullough notes that, more recently, it has been recognized that the body could not have been that of the early Clement, leading to his wry observation that "a turning point in Church history was thus dependent on some wishful thinking and some misidentified bones."[27]

Cyril died while in Rome. Methodius, consecrated as archbishop by the pope, returned to Moravia and worked there until his death. Despite the pope's endorsement, he faced constant opposition from the Frankish clergy. After his death, his followers were persecuted and finally forced to leave Moravia, and the Slavonic script and liturgy were replaced by the Latin.

The consequences for Christianity of this media-centered event, however, were profound. Methodius' followers moved to Bulgaria, where they continued their Slavic mission and created a second, simpler Slavic script, named "Cyrillic" in honor of Cyril, which became the script for a range of languages across large parts of Europe and Asia. They founded a strong literary and spiritual tradition, which became the basis for the spread of Slavic Christianity through the region, including to Russia, which, after the fall of Constantinople to Muslims in the fifteenth century, positioned itself as the new guardian of Orthodoxy.

Regulating the eyes

Despite the divisions caused by the doctrinal controversies of the Seven Ecumenical Councils of the fifth and sixth centuries, and in the face of frequent military threats from the Persian and Islamic Empires, Orthodoxy within the Byzantine Empire retained a strong, philosophically based theological tradition centered on its liturgical life, with little separation between the churches and the political empire. It saw itself as an empire of "the baptized people." Increasingly isolated from contact with the West and other Christian communities in the Middle East, frequent military pressure on the empire led to a desire to maintain stability and resist theological change – to such an extent that some scholars suggest the Orthodox Church did not develop theologically after the eighth century. Energy went instead into liturgy and preservation of the past.

> The Byzantine monks and scholars continued Greek classical literary scholarship and education side by side with Christian indoctrination. In the monasteries librarians and lexicographers preserved the Hellenic heritage until Western Europe, long after its long eclipse, was ready to receive it again.[28]

The texts of key theological thinkers were excerpted and arranged in encyclopedic anthologies: "trenchant collections of citations and the resolution of theological problems through manuals of Questions and Answers."[29] *The Fount of Wisdom* by John of Damascus (675–749), for example, was a compilation of the teachings of the councils; not original theology, but a summary of Christian theology and the teachings of the Greek fathers to John's time. It was used extensively but without comment, as it was considered there was no need to elaborate further on what John had said. Another was *The Myriobiblon* or *Bibliotheca* of the Patriarch Photius in the ninth century, a review of 279 books he had read, seen by some as the first encyclopedia of the East. Many of the books included by Photius, which are from the sixth through the ninth centuries, have since disappeared and are known only through the *Myriobiblon*.

This resistance to change remained, even when the center of power moved from Constantinople to Russia in the fifteenth century. As Küng observes, "everywhere it was simply a matter of going by the well-tried past and preserving what existed."[30]

This was the context for the iconoclastic disputes that ran from the sixth to the ninth centuries. It was one of the most dramatic clashes in Christian history over what constituted the proper mediation of Christian faith, particularly the place of the visual in Christian mediation and the relative priority of authority of the visual and the textual in that mediation. The iconoclastic clashes of the eighth and ninth centuries bring into focus the different issues.

Although they had existed since the early years of Christianity, the use of holy images or painted icons for devotional purposes increased in Eastern Orthodoxy during the sixth century. By the end of the seventh century, paintings had developed that showed portraits or images of Jesus and the saints from a frontal perspective, presenting a more engaging image. While there was a wide recognition that spiritual power could reside in objects such as bones, hair, or artifacts associated with saints, it wasn't until the later seventh century that painted portraits of saints came to be seen as similar channels of divine power, and they were venerated through actions such as bowing, kissing, lighting candles, and burning incense. The perceived power of icons was reinforced by the circulation of stories and traditions of miracles wrought by the portraits,[31] and icons became widely displayed on the iconostasis (the doors in the church separating the altar from the laity), in homes, and in the streets. As Briggs and Burke note, the visual imagery became an innate part of Byzantine culture:

> Developing in a part of Europe where literacy was at its lowest, Byzantine culture was a culture of painted icons of Christ, the Virgin and the saints. As an eighth-century abbot declared, "The gospels were written in words, but icons are written in gold."[32]

Figure 7.1 Russian icon, *Our Lady of the Great Panagia*, early thirteenth century, at the State Tretyakov Gallery, Moscow, Russia. Source: By jimmyweee (Moscow Uploaded by russavia) [CC-BY-2.0 (http://creativecommons.org/licenses/by/2.0)], via Wikimedia Commons.

The growing use and veneration of icons had its critics, particularly as the representations shifted from being symbolic to realistic in character. Criticisms involved arguments of idolatry, the infiltration of pagan practice, that the glory that filled Christ during his life made his visual representation impossible,[33] and that images in churches distracted Christians from purely spiritual realities.[34]

Early defenses of iconography and icon veneration were also given. Hypatios, the archbishop of Ephesus in the mid-sixth century, supported them on the basis that while visual images were not needed by the educated because they could read, they were of benefit to the faith of simple people who were illiterate:

> We ordain that the unspeakable and incomprehensible love of God for us men and the sacred patterns set by the saints be celebrated in holy writings since, so far as we are concerned, we take no pleasure at all in sculpture or painting. But we permit the simpler people, as they are less perfect, to learn by way of initiation of such things by sight which is more appropriate to their natural development.... For these reasons we too, allow even material adornment in the sanctuaries, not because we believe that God considers gold and silver and silken vestments and gem-studded vessels venerable and sacred, but because we permit each order of the faithful to be guided and led up to the divine being in a matter appropriate to it.[35]

Active antagonism and determined attack on the widespread use of iconic images emerged in the eighth century, when Emperor Leo III began destroying images and instructed his bishops to do the same. The reasons were both theological and political.[36] The empire was in a state of perpetual crisis and mobilization to counter the military threat from Islam in its Near Eastern and African provinces. While some saw icons as providing a means of empowerment and spiritual comfort in such conditions, others considered that the idolatry of icons was weakening the empire's spiritual power and bringing God's disfavor on their military campaigns. The use of images also brought criticism and disdain from Judaism and Islam, which saw them as idolatry. For some, the veneration of images was a theological innovation that threatened to displace the primacy of other material embodiments of Christ, such as the sign of the cross and the Eucharist. For others, the colors used and the likenesses created could not match the glory of Christ and were a limitation on the expanse of unseen imagined spiritual reality. For yet others, painting the image of Christ produced confusion about his two natures as God and human. Brubaker and Haldon provide a compelling case for seeing iconoclasm as part of the necessary political, economic, and military restructuring of the empire engaged in by a number of strong and reforming emperors to address military and economic problems.[37] By 650, after sustained Persian and then Islamic expansion, the Byzantine Empire had lost half of its territory and large portions of its rich agricultural bases in North Africa. Brubaker and Haldon's perspective is supported by the fact that the iconoclastic activity largely ceased when those reform agendas had been significantly achieved and the crises had been resolved.

In 730, Leo III called a council to ban icons and sack the patriarch of Constantinople. The pope of Rome reacted to this move and excommunicated Leo. Leo responded to this by seizing churches in south Italy and trying to have the pope assassinated. Initially, Leo's opposition was directed just to the use of religious images, but as the movement spread it led to widespread destruction of most forms of art: statues, murals, stained glass windows, and paintings. Painters, sculptors, and craftsmen were murdered, and some who simply appreciated art were killed or mutilated.

Leo's son, Emperor Constantine V (reigned 741–775), continued the iconoclastic agenda as a means of unifying political support and gaining control of the powerful monasteries and their monks, which he saw as a drain on the public purse and politically unreliable. In addition to icon veneration, Constantine attacked other practices or popular beliefs: the intercession of the saints, the cult of the physical relics of the saints, and the "theotokos" status of Mary. He attacked monastic asceticism and attempted to abolish monasticism, ridiculing, humiliating, and torturing monks and forcing them to renounce their calling through financial incentives or the threat of exile. Monasteries were confiscated and turned into public buildings. This bloody iconoclasm continued for more than twenty years until Constantine's death in 775.

Constantine's widow, Irene, acting as regent for her young son Leo IV, softened the iconoclastic action and called a council to address the issue. The Second Council of Nicea (787) reaffirmed the use and value of the veneration of images, and linked the material and spiritual dimensions of the practice. This action reflected not just theological justifications, but also a recognition of what icons had become in practice, that is, the means by which simpler folks accessed and were supported in their faith.[38]

In its resolution of the issue, the Second Council of Nicea opted for a complementary media perspective, but one in which one of the media was seen to be definitive: the text-based theologians were to determine the content of the icons, and the artists were to represent it. Conditions governing how icons were to be painted in order to be orthodox were also given.

> In the future bishops and clergy are to decide what may be depicted; the artists are simply to do the painting. This was a momentous decision for Byzantine art: "For the first time in the history of Christianity, a control of graphic art by the church" was resolved on here which tacitly presupposed "that the freedom of the Christian painter should be limited." The foundations had been laid for the theological control of Byzantine art, even if initially this control was only of subject matter.[39]

The issue of icon veneration reemerged again under Leo V in 814, prompted by another crisis in the Balkans and arguments that the use of icons was weakening the empire's military strength. Leo V reinstituted the ban on the use of icons, but it was not as severe and there was not a clear-cut division between iconophiles (those who loved and supported icons) and iconoclasts (those who sought to have them removed). A military loss in 838 undermined that argument, and in 843 the Empress Theodora, acting as regent for her young son Michael III, restored the use of icons, and iconoclasm was enshrined as a heresy.

The iconoclasm controversy was a significant influence in establishing the character of Eastern Orthodox spirituality and visuality. It affirmed the presence of God in the world, that God is manifest in sanctified material objects such as icons, and that how these objects work reflects in some way the mystery of the incarnation of Christ. But it also identified that in the Orthodox theological view there is a hierarchy of the spiritual world, and within that spiritual hierarchy icons fall below the more prominent artifacts of the Gospels and the Eucharist. It is perhaps the reaffirmation of the superiority of the textual word and its practitioners over practitioners of the visual that has given this conceived relationship of image and written text its durability within the Orthodox tradition.

Politically, iconoclasm is described by a number of historians as a watershed in Byzantine history,[40] marking the transition of the Byzantine Empire from the Ancient World into the Middle Ages and a full integration of religious life into the political life of the empire. For some, it reflects a failed opportunity for Eastern Orthodox Christianity to reform itself and an unfortunate triumph of the hegemony of orthodoxy. The visual arts became subject to serving the purpose of church tradition and orthodoxy, and their scope as a medium for innovation was significantly restricted. In Gero's estimation,

> The triumph of iconophile orthodoxy can, regretfully, be viewed as signaling the death of a belief in progressive revelation, of any willingness to adopt reformulations of Christian truth ... a momentous "failure of nerve" in Byzantine Christianity ... a crucial but unsuccessful attempt at a reformation which, given different circumstances, may well have utterly transformed Byzantine religious life.[41]

NOTES

1 Brown, 2003, pp. 266–276.
2 MacCulloch, 2009, p. 178.
3 MacCulloch, 2009, p. 248.
4 Philip, no date, p. 12.
5 Brown, 2003, p. 267; MacCulloch, 2009, p. 252.
6 Tomkins, 2005, p. 75.
7 Jenkins, 2008, p. 6.
8 Baum & Winkler, 2000, p. xi.
9 Philip, no date, p. 12.
10 Brown, 2003, p. 274.
11 MacCulloch, 2009, p. 251.
12 MacCulloch, 2009, p. 250.

13　MacCulloch, 2009, p. 251.
14　Brown, 2003, p. 251.
15　MacCulloch, 2009, p. 251.
16　Philip, no date, p. 12.
17　Becker, 2008.
18　MacCulloch, 2009, pp. 246, 266.
19　Carter, 1955.
20　Neill, 1986, pp. 105–106.
21　MacCulloch, 2009, p. 259.
22　Quoted in Baumer, 2006, p. 148.
23　Smith, 1999, p. 336.
24　Schaff, 1894; also Wood, 1981, pp. 85–86.
25　Cross & Livingstone, 1974, p. 1404.
26　MacCulloch, 2009, p. 461.
27　MacCulloch, 2009, p. 463.
28　Burns, 1989, p. 192.
29　Brown, 2003, p. 387.
30　Küng, 1994, pp. 265, 268.
31　See, for example, Cunningham, 1999, p. 74.
32　Briggs & Burke, 2002, p. 8.
33　Eusebius, fourth century.
34　Epiphanius, fifth century.
35　Quoted in Miles, 1985, p. 38.
36　See Brubaker & Haldon, 2011, p. 772.
37　Brubaker & Haldon, 2011, pp. 774–794.
38　Freedberg, 1989, p. 396.
39　Küng, 1994, p. 227.
40　Cunningham, 1999, p. 77.
41　Gero, 1977, pp. 56–57.

8

Senses of the Middle Ages

One of the areas of interest in the recent study of the mediation of religion is the place of the human senses in making abstract theological concepts and material practices "real" in the embodied experience of the believer. A number of scholars have been highlighting that to understand a religion one needs to look not just at the formal and authorized beliefs or practices of the religion, but also at how ordinary followers of a religion access, interpret, transform, and reinvent religious practices in their daily living.[1] Meyer has been foremost in advocating that this needs to include attention to the physical sensations made available by the religion, or created and experienced by people within it:

> Without the particular social structures, sensory regimes, bodily techniques, doctrines and practices that make up a religion, the searching individual craving for experiences of God would not exist. Likewise religious feelings are not just there, but are made possible and reproducible by certain modes of inducing experiences of the transcendental.[2]

When looking at people's immersion within a religion, therefore, the attempt to separate out the different contributions made by one medium or another to the religious experience is an artificial one. In an immersive or liminal religious experience, when boundaries between the material and immaterial and the mundane and transcendent become merged, media become so entangled with what they mediate that they are not visible to those who are involved. In these situations, Meyer argues, it becomes less relevant to talk about religion and media and more accurate to speak of the characteristics of the matrix of religious mediation.[3]

To this point, much of our study has focused more on how different media and forms of mediation have influenced the shape of Christianity from a more formal perspective. This chapter, focused on the Middle Ages, looks

From Jesus to the Internet, Peter Horsfield © 2015 John Wiley & Sons, Ltd. Published 2015 by John Wiley & Sons, Ltd.

more at the extensive sensory mediations of Christianity through which and within which people made connections between the professed virtual realities and stated beliefs of the Christian tradition, and the actual realities of their physical and emotional lives. This includes not just the official or authorized practices of Christianity, but also those invented, adopted, amended, or borrowed from other sources and injected into the religion through popular practice.

The medieval context

Although many early Christian writers and practitioners sought to sublimate the senses in favor of a strict asceticism,[4] the cultural environments that Christianity entered and settled into through the Middle Ages were highly sensory in character. Judaism had its own texts, religious buildings, sites, physical practices, and auditory and visual appeals, a number of which Christianity adopted in its material and textual practices. As Innis has noted of all empires,[5] the Roman Empire was built on effective processes of visual and physical communication, with its virtual realities of supreme power and order actualized through imposing temples, palaces, fortresses, flags, processions, religious rituals, imperial displays and symbolism, statues, coins, medallions, and other artifacts. Christianity incorporated many of these along with its own inventions into a rich tapestry of sensory and material practices.

The practices considered in this chapter need to be seen within the context of the realities of daily life. Apart from the aristocracy, everyday life for most people was unpredictable and precarious, with basic things such as the weather, pests, or infestations presenting constant threats to life or welfare. In 874, for example, one-third of the populations of Gaul and Germania died from hunger because of crop failure. Social life was also precarious. The feudal legal system imposed harsh physical punishments and impairments for a range of crimes and misdemeanors, particularly on slaves and peasants.[6] In this context, there was no separation of the natural from the spiritual: natural events were seen to have spiritual causes and meaning, with invisible demons a constant threat from which supernatural assistance was needed.

In such harsh conditions, greater religious comfort was to be found in tangible objects and rituals than in abstract theological ideas that occupied the attention of many of the Christian elite. Superstition and magical practices, including astrology, were widespread. Everyday religious practice was strongly practical in its engagement, orientated toward getting the support of the supernatural to provide protection against the unpredictable, cure disease, and ensure the survival of crops. The persistence of pagan practices well after formal Christianization reflected the appeal of their orientation toward these practical concerns. A number of these pagan practices were renamed and adapted into popular Christian practice, because of popular usage.

Christianity in the Middle Ages is most properly seen, then, not just as a religious ideology but also as a religious environment within which life was lived, food was grown, trade was conducted, politics were practiced, economics were managed, relationships were formed, and meaning was framed.

Making time

How time is experienced, perceived, and structured is an important component of cultural life and identity, shaping how people take meaning from the daily events of their lives. It was not accidental, therefore, that early in the life of Christianity, a Christian calendar was begun to structure time in a way that gave it a Christian meaning. The early calendar developed in complexity through the Middle Ages to incorporate practical requirements of social regulation.

Other calendars were in use when Christianity began. The imperial one was the Julian calendar, developed by Julius Caesar in 46 BCE. It commenced counting years from the founding of the city of Rome in what is now 753 BCE. Jewish Christians were also used to the Jewish calendar, which started counting from the assumed moment of creation (3761 BCE) and had a structured system of religious holy days, including two that became important to Christianity, Passover and Pentecost.

One of the earliest and most important calendar events for Christianity was Easter, the celebration of the resurrection of Jesus. It was also the most controversial in calendar events, due largely to differences between Christian groups in how the annual date of the resurrection of Jesus was to be calculated. The fact that Easter was being celebrated at different times in different places was seen to be a problem for a religion that wanted to see itself as a universal religion, and the Ecumenical Council at Ephesus in 325 sought to resolve the differences with an authoritative decree. But the dating issue was bound up in wider disagreements about regional identity and prestige, and on occasion caused sufficiently serious conflicts that emperors and kings felt it necessary to intervene to prevent the differences between Christians from disrupting their realms. A major division between Celtic and Roman Christians in Britain over their different calendars for Easter, for example, led to the calling of the Synod of Whitby in 664 by King Oswiu. The synod's resolution of the issue in favor of the Roman calendar was a seemingly small issue in itself, but it had ongoing effects in shaping the character of Christianity in Britain away from the more oral Celtic expression of Christianity toward the more literate Roman order.

As time progressed, other festivals were incorporated into the Christian calendar, again with differences between different regions that became problematic. By the early fourth century, the Eastern Orthodox churches celebrated the baptism and birth of Jesus on January 6, a date connected to a number of pagan festivals of water and birth in Alexandria. In the West a nativity festival had developed that was celebrated on December 25, the day of the pagan festival of Sol Invictus, the Roman sun god, a connection already established through Constantine's declaration of Sun-day, the day of Jesus' resurrection, as a nonworking day. December 25 was also the day calculated as being nine months after the proposed conception of the Virgin Mary at the spring equinox. Eventually the Eastern and Roman practices were brought together, with December 25 being recognized as the birthday of Jesus, and January 6 as the Day of Epiphany, celebrated in the East with an emphasis on the baptism of Jesus and in the West as the day of the visit of the Magi from the East.

A Christian monk in the middle of the sixth century restructured historical time into a Christian framework by renumbering historical years around the birth of Jesus, into AD ("anno Domini," or "in the year of our Lord") and BC ("before Christ"). This chronologically embedded Jesus as the turning point of history (although his calculation of when Jesus was born was out by six years).

Calendars steadily became filled with a variety of recognitions, festivals, and days allocated to various martyrs, saints, and local heroes, leading to variations from region to region. Reconciling these different calendars – calculations of dates for recurring festivals, the religious figures to be honored on what days, bringing them into line with more accurate astronomical calculations, and reconceptualization of the calendar under the influence of Protestantism – continued well into the twentieth century.

The impetus behind the efforts to standardize the calendar has been to cement the power and importance of Christianity universally by creating a sense of time as God-created, a sacred Christian domain that was true across all cultures and regions of the world. Appropriating significant pagan and agricultural festivals and Christianizing them have been part of that hegemonic process. The outcome was the mediation of Christianity in a calendar that surreptitiously embedded Christian ideology into the ordering and physical experience of everyday life.

Practically, the calendar further integrated Christianity into daily life by serving the social function of breaking up the monotony and arduousness of life with a regular interruption of feasts and festivals. Riché notes that in the village of Corbie, in northern France, in 822, the peasants stopped work for thirty-six commemoration days of the year, not counting Sundays.[7] In a situation where, for peasants, work was physically hard and demanding, the festivals of the Christian year provided important periods of recuperation, with the physical sensations of rest, feasting, and celebration becoming embedded with Christian meaning. As Küng notes,

> There is no question that the great festivals of the church in particular were community events which interrupted the social and economic wretchedness of the populace in medieval cities in a welcome way. But there is no question that the regular Sunday and feast-day liturgy at the same time represented a form of social control which gently forced everyone into a collective from which they could hardly escape at a time of limited mobility.[8]

The yearly rhythm was a liturgical year that recreated the life cycle of Jesus and the saints. Major festivals such as Lent and Easter, and Advent and Christmas, lasted for weeks and involved extended vigils, processions through the streets and in churches, special rituals and litanies around relics and sacred objects, periods of fasting, and feasting. In addition to these major annual events, each saint was remembered with their own day, with local feasts or festivals also celebrating local saints or the particular saint of the church. As the number of saints and relics increased, the occasions of religious recognition increased. Particular saints' days came to mark winter, spring, summer, and autumn harvest and had festivals associated with them. Special feasts and fasts were also instituted by kings or local lords at particular times of difficulty or crisis. Pagan rituals were appropriated when the church was unable to constrain their popularity or to cover gaps in the Christian schedule. The pagan fertility rite of Robigalia, for example, became the Catholic Rogationtide, a day of prayer for the crops. Birth, coming of age, marriage, and death each had their own sacrament.

The weekly rhythm was also ordered by the calendar. The climax was Sunday, a regulated day of rest and worship, with the celebration of Mass and other services such as Matins and Vespers. Work was suspended for the day, and people were encouraged to abstain from sexual relations, dancing, and commercial transactions and maintain only minimal domestic labor.[9]

The daily rhythm was ordered by church bells that sounded regularly, in some places every three hours, calling monks to times of prayer[10] and inviting workers to pray along with them in their workplaces. In the eighth and ninth centuries, breviaries or prayer books and pocket books of psalms were written for those who wished to join in the times of prayer with the monks.[11]

In the structuring of time, the mediation of Christianity was instituted as the framework for the mediation of daily life.

Seeing space

Until the fourth century, the gathering place of Christians for worship and fellowship was still predominantly in people's houses, often the more spacious house of a wealthy Christian or vacant or converted shop-fronts.[12] The concept of the Christian community created by and expressed within this domestic space was that of a family or an assembly of people (*ecclesia*) small enough for interaction and close relationships. The ordering of the space was functional to enable the major activities of the community to take place: eating together, sharing in an agape meal, hearing sacred texts being read and spoken, and baptizing new members.

As the movement grew, these spaces were adapted to accommodate larger and more permanent numbers. One of the earliest examples of such an adaptation is a house from around the 240s uncovered at Dura Europus in Syria. Built around a courtyard and from the outside looking like any other house, one inside wall had been removed to create a large space for the assembly with a raised platform at one end, probably for a table for the Eucharist and a lectern for reading. The house included a raised pool for baptisms under an arch decorated with stars. The surrounding walls were painted with religious images – Jesus as the Good Shepherd and his sheep, the fall of Adam and Eve, the women bringing spices to the tomb of Jesus, and Peter being saved from drowning – and other symbolic decorations such as grapes, wheat, and pomegranates.[13]

The decoration of the arch illustrates the development that was beginning to take place in early Christian visual expression. Up to the start of the third century, most Christian art was modest and largely private. The images used were frequently drawn from the surrounding culture, with the Christian meaning of the picture being implied by association in a way understandable to those within the movement. Many early Christian images reflected classical prototypes or pagan deities such as the shepherd figure, the philosopher, the *orant* or praying figure, the Sol Invictus, and meal and harvest scenes.[14] It wasn't until the third century that Christians had the physical security and resources to begin to develop their own visual language.

Another early form of Christian building was shrines erected around significant places associated with the faith. When Helena, the mother of Emperor Constantine, visited Palestine in 326, she found an active tradition of shrines and sanctuaries located at key sites of Christian significance, such as the purported Upper Room and places of Jesus' crucifixion and resurrection.[15]

After those initial centuries, Christian church building has been a strategic as well as practical activity. Some Christian structures were built deliberately on sites of earlier known pagan temples to capitalize on spiritual powers believed to be in the place.[16] Many Christian buildings were erected at the burial places of martyrs, serving as the site of martyr cults that built up around them. The first basilica of St. Peter's in Rome, for example, was erected over the traditional burial place of the Apostle Peter. Interestingly, the popularity of St. Peter's as a site of pilgrimage eventually caused the pope of Rome to move the bishop's seat and the papal residence from the

Lateran Church (given by Constantine) to St. Peter's basilica – a good example of Christian church leadership following popular practice.

A major step forward in Christian architecture and the construction of Christian space came with the legalization of Christianity as a religion by the Emperor Constantine in 313. In his promotion and patronage of Christianity, Constantine sponsored an extensive church-building program to give Christianity a material and visual presence to match its new spiritual prominence. Elaborate churches were built as part of complexes that could include also an audience hall in which the bishop presided as judge, a bishop's palace, warehouses for the charitable distribution of food, and impressive courtyards comparable to those of houses of the nobility.[17]

The intention to overwhelm the viewer and to attract pilgrims through the scale and grandiosity of these churches was palpable. The gold decoration alone in the church of Christ the Redeemer in Rome, commissioned by Constantine, has been estimated at in excess of £60 million (or around US $90 million).[18] As Brown notes,

> They spoke far more loudly and more continuously of the providential alliance of Church and empire than did any imperial edict or the theorizing of any bishop. They left visitors amazed.[19]

To maintain these new buildings, Constantine endowed the churches with wealth and lands to support their clergy and ensure their ongoing upkeep. The estates provided to service the operation and upkeep of the church of Christ the Redeemer in Rome and its staff gave the bishop of Rome an estimated income in excess of £20 million a year (or around US $30 million).[20] Constantine's actions set an example for others, and by the end of the fourth century most cities had at least one church, in many cases made up of multiple buildings with substantial endowments.[21]

The building form most commonly adapted for Christian churches throughout the empire was the Roman basilica, which for centuries had served a range of functions as a law court, covered market, military drill hall, reception hall, and throne room.[22] The spaciousness of the high ceiling was intended to evoke the expanse of heaven. The imperial associations of the basilica structure and adornment reflected the new ideological position of Christianity within the empire, and reinforced the imperial, ceremonial, hierarchical, and ritualistic characteristics that the performance of worship had now acquired. The space itself installed Christian leaders with a new imperial status and official role, including as judges in courts. Worship in the basilica in turn became an imperial ceremony.

In time, to heighten performance of the sacred and reinforce the status of the clergy, a screen was erected across the middle of the hall, separating the area in which the laypeople gathered from the area that only the ordained clergy could enter. At the far end of the restricted section was a raised altar housing the Eucharistic table, the bishop's throne, and seats for the clergy. The service began with a procession of the clergy in imitation of the triumphal procession of a victorious army, passing through the crowd to enter their exclusive space around the table of the Lord.[23]

While there were many variations to this specific layout, the new architecture and constructed space of Christian churches reinforced what was now the organizational theology of Christianity: two classes of Christians with the male clerical class determining, controlling, and performing the cultic rites and then dispensing the benefits under defined conditions to the subordinate laity who waited.

The creation of such dedicated and secure religious spaces provided the opportunity, resources, and stimulation for the fuller development of artistic expressions, including stonework and statuary, painting, carving, mosaics, metalwork, embroidery, and jewelry. Such ornamentation had multiple purposes: to impress through decoration of the constructed space, to create atmosphere that invoked a sense of the presence of the divine, and as a medium of education, contributing to a growing reverence for religious pictures as mediators of religious information and religious power. Christian decoration also absorbed aspects of the Roman imperial cult, with Jesus portrayed as the new emperor and Jesus and other Christian figures being represented in imperial motifs such as imperial processions and heavenly court scenes. The cultural and political transformation of Christianity through material construct in this period was marked:

> [The Christian clergy] began to think and act like Roman officials, living in stately villas and conducting public worship services, not in the little house churches they were accustomed to, but in huge new temples or basilicas, packed with masses of half-converted parishioners. These new Christian temples were decorated by Roman craftsmen with glorious mosaics in the dome or apse at the front that depicted the Lord Jesus Christ in the posture and clothing of the Roman emperor – which made sense, since the Sunday morning service was now conducted as if everyone was in the presence of Christ the Emperor.[24]

Given that Jesus had been quite critical of wealth, the development of ornate Christian architecture and decoration required a theological justification and re-moralizing of wealth and opulence. This was done through the invocation of Old Testament images of gold and silver being associated with God, and allegorical rather than literal readings of scriptural passages. So the building and ornate decoration of churches became justified on the basis of recreating paradise on earth or giving a glimpse of the heavenly city. The more elaborate, the more inspiring they were, the more they could be justified as invoking thoughts of heaven. The transformations of Christianity that took place in this period became decisive to Christianity's institutional presence throughout subsequent history.

After the fall of the political empire, church buildings became important strategic elements in the establishment of Christianity throughout Europe. Not only did they offer accommodation for religious activities, but also, in the social and political chaos that followed the fall of the empire, church buildings were symbolic statements of social order through religious power. Services in the basilicas bred a shared spirit and sense of endurance. Unlike the grand Christian buildings of the empire, the churches built in the European medieval period were more ancestral in character. Built on sites of significance from ancient times or the graves of local martyrs, they symbolically called on the strength of local heroes to provide an important defense against marauding tribes. As Brown describes it,

> The buildings of the church spoke of the day-to-day determination of cities to survive and to be seen to survive. The bishops of Gaul vied with each other in placing splendid basilicas in the fortified enclaves of their cities, and outside the city, above the graves of martyrs ... at a time when secular building had come to a standstill, these churches represented an impressive coagulation of wealth and collaborative effort. They were the "arguments in stone" appropriate to a new Christian age.[25]

In the West, images did not play the same role or encounter the same resistance as they did in Eastern Orthodoxy. Although relics were more popular as material bearers of divine power, images of biblical figures, biblical stories, and saints were widely used in popular Christian practice, reproduced on articles such as tablets, cards, and cloth, and in books. Christian images from the period have been found on domestic items, in streets, on bridges, at signposts, and at country crossroads.[26]

The widespread inventive devotional uses of visual and material artifacts by ordinary Christians caused some theologians at first to oppose them. Tertullian, for example, wrote on one occasion, "That which he has not produced is not pleasing to God, unless he was unable to order sheep to be born with purple and sky blue fleeces ... what God willed not, of course ought not to be fashioned."[27] But the widespread practices led others subsequently to invent theological justifications for it.

One of the earliest theological justifications devised in the West was that of Gregory the Great (540–604) who, in chastising one of his bishops for destroying images in his diocese, wrote:

> It is one thing to adore a picture, another to learn from the history of the picture what is to be adored. For what scripture shows to those who read, a picture shows to the illiterate people as they see it; because in it the ignorant see what they ought to imitate, they who do not know letters can read it.[28]

Bernard of Angers (eleventh century) wrote of how his attitude toward the veneration of images was changed by what he saw when visiting Auvergne:

> Hitherto I have always believed that the veneration of images and paintings to the saints was improper, and to raise statues to them would have struck me as absurd. But this is not the belief of the inhabitants of these parts, where every church contains a statue of its patron made of gold, silver, or base metal, depending on the wealth of the church.[29]

The tensions or contests between popular, materialist connections and practices of faith and the often-cerebral engagement with faith of Christian leaders have been one of the features of Christianity throughout its history, a feature that has only begun to be more fully appreciated in scholarship in recent times.[30]

Rituals and hearing

Most people in the Middle Ages accessed the life of Christianity as it was mediated through the drama and oratory of the regular public services of worship. By the fourth and fifth centuries, public Christian worship had developed into two parts. The first, open to the general public and those being prepared for baptism (catechumens), consisted of Bible readings, singing of psalms and hymns, prayers, and the sermon. The second part of the service was the service of Eucharist, open to only the clergy and baptized Christians.

As well as its precursors in Jewish temple worship, the development of the Eucharist took up elements of Roman mystery religions in its stress on mystery, sacrifice, drama, and sacrament, with the mystery further enhanced by the physical exclusion of laypeople from the altar section of the church.

The liturgy by this time had become a ritual dominated by the ordained. The use of ecclesiastical Latin made it difficult for people to follow what was going on, let alone join in it – laypeople were positioned, physically and linguistically, as primarily an audience to the clerical performance. Congregational participation was primarily in joining in responsively singing the Gloria, Kyrie, and Sanctus, which, although sung in Ecclesiastical Latin, had been learned through repetitive hearing. Aside from that, the gathered Christians stood in silence or talked. Lay participation in consumption of the bread and wine was also limited, partly because of stern warnings given to laypeople about what would happen to them if they didn't properly prepare themselves spiritually by prior confession and penance. Sharing in communion, with proper preparation, was generally expected on at least three occasions (Christmas, Easter, and Pentecost),[31] although for many it was a once-a-year event.

Rituals were heavy in symbolism, educating people in the faith in the process of their being enacted, such as kneeling before the altar, raising the host toward heaven, processions and images of processions that evoked imperial victory processions representing Christ as the new emperor, and the procession of saints and heavenly beings into heaven. Artifacts used in the rituals also carried symbolic meaning. Charlemagne's liturgical reforms utilized three categories of sacred sensory objects, as Riché describes:

> Bells not only summoned the faithful but had ascribed to them the power to chase demons and the intemperate away. Lamps, arranged around the altars or carried in procession, triumphed over one of the most redoubtable enemies, the night. Finally, standing or portable censers burned a perfume brought at great expense from the Orient. Rising like a prayer, incense enveloped the offerings disposed about the altar.[32]

Roman Catholic worship in the Middle Ages developed one of the more profound assertions about the ritual transformation of matter and sense, the concept of transubstantiation. In 831, the monk Paschasius Radbertus proposed in a book, *The Body and Blood of the Lord*, that at the time of consecration of the bread and wine during the Mass, the substances of bread and wine were transformed miraculously into the actual body and blood of Jesus – a literal, physical communication of the body and spirit of Jesus. In eating it, participants became part of the mystical church.

There was debate about the concept and its practicalities. The theologian Berengar of Tours in the eleventh century, for example, mused on how such a thing could be materially possible: "A portion of the flesh of Christ cannot be present on the altar unless the body of Christ in heaven is cut up and a particle that has been cut off from it is sent down to the altar," he wrote.[33] The concept, though, was made official doctrine at the Fourth Lateran Council in 1215.

In a way similar to the Ark of the Covenant in the Old Testament, the transformation of the bread and wine into the body and blood of Christ required sanctions to ensure the protection of its holiness and guard against its misuse. Decrees were produced that guided their proper handling, including prohibitions against removing any of the elements or parts of the elements from the church. Without a vernacular account of what was going on, and with incomprehensible mysteries associated with it, the ritual of what was once a reenactment of the Lord's Supper by believers became a "hocus-pocus,"[34] a magical event for people to watch rather than a communal activity to be participated in. The perceived holiness was such that many ordinary Christians ceased receiving the elements during worship out of fear of judgment and damnation because of their unworthy status. Others saw the raising of the host, the time when the transformation into the actual body and blood of Jesus occurred, as so powerful that there are reports of people running from church to church on a Sunday to see as many elevations of the host as possible.[35] The central place that the Mass, controlled by the clergy, came to play in Catholic Christianity became a powerful weapon used by the church for not just spiritual but also political control. Threatening to excommunicate a person from the rituals that communicated salvation was a powerful weapon used by popes to control dissenters and secular leaders.

Chidester advocates that the concept of transubstantiation also developed what might be called a Catholic "spirituality of eating God," reflected in later writings such as that of the thirteenth-century Flemish poet Hadewijch, who proposed that the closest union with God was achieved by eating and being eaten.[36]

Various symbolic physical actions also developed during this period: the practice of lying prostrate (in the East) or genuflecting (in the West) before the altar; standing, kneeling, or bowing at different times during worship; making a sign of the cross on your head and chest; and the raising of hands during prayer.

Two other auditory phenomena were important for what was overwhelmingly an oral population. One of those was preaching. Many of the early bishops, with their roots in Greek rhetorical education, were skilled orators. Bishops such as Ambrose, John Chrysostom ("golden-mouth"), and Augustine not only wrote extensively but also attracted audiences of thousands to their preaching on a regular basis. The interactive engagement of the audience in these oral performances is illustrated in one account of Augustine's congregation:

> Augustine's congregation were in the habit of reacting to whatever was read or preached with all the liveliness of their temperament. They shouted comments, sighed, laughed, like children at the cinema. When a few stereotyped expressions occurred such as "Have mercy on us," or at the word Confiteor, or at "Forgive us our trespasses" in the Our Father, they made a practice of very audibly beating their breasts. When the speaker made some telling remark they loudly acclaimed him, and protested as loudly when there was anything in his utterances of which they disapproved.[37]

This example of audience members interacting with the preacher illustrates that even in situations where one person held the power of the pulpit, audiences still exercised some power in the exchange through their vocal or demonstrative engagements of approval or disapproval. This is illustrated also in an instance in 380 in Constantinople, when disputes about the nature of the Trinity were running hot. During the dispute, the theologian Gregory of Nazianzus, one of the minority advocates of the Nicene version of the faith in largely subordinationist Constantinople, outlined his position in a series of five long theological sermons of around 3000 words each. Reproduced in written form as the Five Theological Orations, they are seen today as the best presentation of the Nicene position. The sermons, which included a critique of his opponents, were spoken in an open courtyard to a growing number of listeners, who interjected so frequently and passionately that the bishop of Alexandria provided Gregory with a group of sailors for bodyguard protection. Freeman has observed, "It would be exceptional today to find a public audience as alive to the nuances of theological debate and ready to argue such complex issues with confidence."[38] When Gregory of Nyssa visited Constantinople in the following year, he wrote:

> Every place in the city is full of them: the alleys, crossroad, the forums, the squares. Garment sellers, money-changers, food vendors – they are all at it. If you ask for change, they philosophize for you about generate and unregenerate natures. If you enquire about the price of bread, the answer is that the Father is greater and the Son inferior. If you speak about whether the bath is ready, they express the opinion that the Son was made out of nothing.

Singing also was widespread in Christian worship since its beginnings, carried over from its Jewish roots. In difference from common practice today, singing was not just a separate, discrete activity but also continuous with speech and reading, with stories and readings often told or read in a chanting or melodious way. It served a range of functions in the public and private practice of Christian faith: sensory involvement, participation, poetic and emotional expression, artistic and dramatic performance, community formation, and education.

Syrian Christianity was a major source of early Christian music, producing the earliest Christian hymnbook and shaping a variety of musical forms in the East and West. The Ambrosian chant, one of the officially endorsed chants of the Roman Catholic Church, was ordered to be sung "in the Syrian manner."[39]

Because they were central to worship, hymns and singing also became a battleground of doctrinal fights. One of the pioneers of Christian music and chant, the Syrian poet, astrologist, and philosopher Bar-Daisan of Edessa, wrote a number of metrical hymns that set Gnostic Christian beliefs to popular tunes. The rhythm and musicality of the hymns made them widely used and contributed to the increase of Gnostic Christianity among Syrian Christians. Their use and influence were such that in the following century, Ephrem, a monastic Syrian theologian, poet, and hymnographer, countered them by writing orthodox words for the same popular tunes and training choirs of young women to sing them in chorus. Ephrem's music became equally popular, and people travelled to hear them being sung. Ephrem's strategy worked, and gradually his orthodox versions replaced Bar-Daisan's on people's lips and in their minds.

In a similar way, the widespread following of Arian Christianity, even after it was declared heretical, was due in part to the effectiveness of its mediation. This included the greater clarity of its theological ideas, the expression of those ideas in memorable verse, and the setting of that verse to popular tunes that were widely sung. The sustaining power of this popular auditory mediation of Arian faith is illustrated by an incident that occurred almost sixty years after Arius' death. What is very clearly a media contest is recounted by Prescott:

> When ... the renowned John Chrysostom arrived as Bishop of Constantinople, he found a strange state of things. The Arians had, some years before, been forbidden by the Emperor Theodosius to have places of worship within the city. But on Saturdays, and Sundays, and great festivals, they were in the habit of assembling outside the gates, then coming into the city in procession at sunset; and all night, in the porticoes and open places, singing Arian hymns and anthems with choruses. Chrysostom feared that many of the simple and ignorant people would be drawn from the faith. He therefore organized, at the cost of the Empress Eudoxia, wife of Arcadius, nightly processions of orthodox hymn singers, who carried crosses and lights, and with music and much pomp rivaled the efforts of the heretics. Riots and bloodshed were the consequence. The chief officer of the Empress was wounded; and very soon an imperial edict put a stop to Arian hymn-singing in public. The use, however, of hymns in the nocturnal services of the Church became established; and this at once led up to a much freer and more constant use of them in Divine Service generally.[40]

Part of Charlemagne's effort in the ninth century to unify both Christianity and the empire involved imposing the Roman or Gregorian model to standardize chant and music practices across the empire. To achieve this standardization, cantors created a written musical script, including notation on the page to indicate how the voice was to move and be paced. This *prosa*, as it came to be called, spread quickly. By the end of the century, monks were supplementing their chant with additional musical, vocal, or instrumental accompaniments. According to Riché, the ornamentation of this in script by monks was "the first outline of what would become polyphony, the source of modern music."[41]

The advent of instruments in general use followed. Charlemagne took advantage of Greeks visiting his court on one occasion to have an organ built.[42] In time, "the naves of churches, like the rooms of a palace, were filled with the sounds of the lyre, zithers, harp, flute, horns, percussion instruments, cymbals, bone castanets, and hand bells (campanae),"[43] all of which were consequently given justification by quoting passages from scripture.

Nice touch: relics, saints, and pilgrimage

Cosmologically, Christians living in the Middle Ages saw themselves as living in a multilayered universe, which included a range of spiritual beings. As the Middle Ages progressed, the concept of "the saints" became an impor-tant part of this intermediate spiritual pantheon. Initially, the Christian con-cept of saints was used to refer to all members of the Christian household by virtue of their holy calling. Paul used it this way in his letters. In time, it came to be used to refer to a class of Christians seen as having particular merit, stature, or holiness and therefore closer to God. Having lived as hu-mans themselves and now in the presence of God, they were seen as having privileged access to God or as conduits of spiritual power.

The earliest evidence of a developing "cult of the saints" is around 156, when the bones of the martyred Polycarp were collected and his followers expressed their intention to celebrate the birthday of his martyrdom.[44] It was given a theological foundation by Origen in the third century within the doctrine of the Communion of Saints.[45] Saints and martyrs came to be com-memorated in prayers, services of worship, and calendar days, and in time they were invoked as intercessors with God on behalf of the one praying. The power of the saints to intercede on behalf of Christians was asserted by Cyprian in the third century, and he organized his own martyr's death to encourage this to happen.[46]

Important among these intermediaries was Mary, the mother of Jesus, whose giving virginal birth increased her stature as the ascetic tradition of sexual abstinence developed. Adoration of Mary as a heavenly Virgin Moth-er reached its fullest development during the Christological controversies in the fourth century, with the Council of Chalcedon in 451 declaring Mary as the mother of the Son of God – the *theotokos* or God-bearer.

Growing reverence for the saints and martyrs led to the fetishistic con-cept of heavenly power residing in parts of their body or any material object associated with them, so that contact with the martyr's earthly body was seen as mediating heavenly power contained in it.[47] Graves, places associ-ated with martyrs, or places housing one of their relics or physical remains, became popular places for the building of shrines or churches and the site for pilgrimages by those seeking to be influenced by their power. Gregory of Nyssa (fourth century) said of worshippers at the shrine of Saint Theodore that they "embrace (the relics) as though they were alive, approaching them with eyes, mouths, ears – all the senses."[48] As Aston notes, "[P]opular belief attached itself to the concrete and the seen, not because the faith of the people was materialistic, but because for them matter was an expression of spiritual forces."[49]

In recognition that relic worship, placing relics in sanctuaries, and build-ing shrines at the sites of martyrs' tombs were significant parts of popular piety, the practices were given legal or canonical status at the Second Coun-cil of Nicea in 787. The council also decreed that relics needed to be held in a consecrated place and that a church couldn't be consecrated without one. Disagreement was not tolerated – the penalty for a bishop consecrating a

Figure 8.1 The Reliquary of Mary Magdalene, at the Basilica Church of St. Mary Magdalene, Vézelay, France. The reliquary is supported by a bishop, a king, two angels, a monk, and a queen. Source: By D. Villafruela (own work) [CC-BY-SA-3.0-2.5-2.0-1.0 (http://creativecommons.org/licenses/by-sa/3.0)], via Wikimedia Commons.

church without a relic was being "deposed as a transgressor of the ecclesiastical tradition." For churches that had been consecrated without a relic, it was required that "the defect shall be made good."[50]

The growing importance of relics and visiting the shrines of saints and martyrs underlies the rise of pilgrimage, another sensory experience that became popular in Christianity. Christian pilgrimage falls within a wider orbit of common religious practice. Pilgrimages to recognized sacred places and for particular seasonal or religious purposes have been a common element in many religions since Paleolithic times.[51] In Christianity, pilgrimage began probably in the first century and was established by the second century, associated particularly with sites of martyrdom or the relics of martyrs. In different places, it melded with indigenous religious practice – a number of contemporary European sites of Christian pilgrimage, for example, are places that were once sacred to pagan deities.[52]

Common to all pilgrimage sites was the belief that they were "places where miracles once happened, still happen, and may happen again."[53] Even when miracles didn't occur, it was believed that faith would be strengthened and salvation better secured through the veneration of the saint of the site.

However, a hierarchy of pilgrimage sites developed, based on perceptions of their significance or power in general or for particular regions or language groups. As early as the fourth century, pilgrimage to the holy land was fashionable among Europeans and encouraged by churches as a penance and for the increase of faith it brought. Pilgrimage journeys were often long, arduous, hazardous, at risk of natural dangers and epidemics, and, as many pilgrim accounts record, fraught with robbers and confidence men.[54]

Along with spiritual motives, pilgrimage was encouraged for its economic benefits. The money brought by pilgrimage could be an important element in the economy of medieval towns, to the extent that competitiveness in relics and pilgrimage developed. It was in the interest of the local economy that any church building or shrine built had associated with it a relic of competitive significance. To be the bishop of a significant sacred site also increased the clergy's spiritual stature, social prestige, and economic wealth. This increased the pressure on clergy to find sacred significance in their buildings or sites or, if none could be found, to import it or if necessary invent it. Abou-El-Haj notes that the church built by Constantine in Jerusalem as part of his building program was begun on a site that had no recorded shrine. However,

> [D]uring construction, the site of Christ's resurrection was "discovered," and the intended cathedral was transformed into a martyrium. Thus the central Christian shrine and its cult was "invented." The discovery of the tomb was followed, shortly later, with the discovery of the True Cross. In the following century the bishops of the ancient administrative city in the hills developed a pilgrimage that became the city's main regional and supra regional industry for most of its history.[55]

One of the churches built by Ambrose as part of his extensive building program in Milan from 374 to 397 was a basilica intended by Ambrose to be his own burial place. When the building was being dedicated, a call came from the congregation that relics were needed in order for the church to be dedicated properly. McLynn notes that "perhaps the demand was spontaneous, perhaps there had been a subtle prompt."[56] The service was postponed, and the following day Ambrose led the way to one of the monuments in the cemetery and ordered digging to take place. In a seemingly miraculous way, two skeletons of "martyrs" were "found," and the bones were carried to Ambrose's church, the first recorded instance of a martyr's grave being opened and the bones translated to the altar of a church.[57] The relics immediately confirmed their authenticity by miraculous events taking place. McLynn notes of the occasion,

> Ambrose had organized the spectacle of the inventio with consummate skill, and the festivities had generated a momentum of their own. But he needed to put a seal upon the episode as quickly as possible. Quite apart from the illegality of

unauthorized translations of relics, affirmed in a recent law, the credentials of Ambrose's martyrs might not have stood prolonged or critical scrutiny.[58]

Along with the added prestige, Ambrose's "discovery" of martyr's relics before a large crowd may have insulated him from intended expulsion by the Arian Empress Justina.[59]

As the importance of pilgrimage and the competition for relics increased, a market in relics developed to service the demand. Relics were secured through gift or purchase, by stealing, or as "loot from ransacked Roman cemeteries."[60] Contrary to undermining their value, the stealing of relics was celebrated by the one who received them. Since it was considered that no saint would allow their remains to be translated without their approval, the stealing of relics was justified on the basis of "demands by saints to be removed to sites where they would be properly venerated."[61]

The flood of relics and questions about their authenticity threatened to undermine both their spiritual and economic value, and prompted the question of how to regulate the market to maintain the economy. Several tests were applied, including authentication through the presence of strips of parchment with the saint's name; another was a fire test, as relics were believed to be nonflammable.[62] In some cases, reports of opened coffins of saints were said to have found the body uncorrupted or the remains emitting a sweet perfume smell, indicating the purity of the relics and a readiness for the relic to be translated – the smell of authenticity.

In 1215, Pope Innocent sought to regulate the trade through a meeting of the Lateran Council, issuing a decree that forbade the sale of relics and ordering that all newly acquired relics be authenticated by the Vatican. The extent to which this regulation was effective is questionable, however. In 1543, the Reformer John Calvin observed:

> Saint Anne, mother of the Virgin Mary, has one of her bodies at Apt in Provence, the other at Notre-Dame-de-L'Ile in Lyon. Besides this she has one head at Trier, another at Düren in Jülich, and another in Thuringia in a town named for her. I omit those fragments which are found in more than a hundred places; and among others I remember that I kissed one part at the Abbey of Ourscamp near Noyon, where there was a great feast in its honor.[63]

The trade brought or promised by pilgrimage stimulated the building of roads and new church buildings, both to house the relics and to accommodate the crowds. The display of the relic changed to accommodate the larger crowds, and the ornateness of the reliquaries in which they were housed became part of the viewing experience. In the time of Charlemagne, the royal monastery of St. Riquier in France listed, among its inventory of 831 pieces of treasure, thirty reliquaries in gold, silver, and ivory.[64]

The profitability of the pilgrimage tourism trade often produced tension, contention, power struggles, and takeover bids between local churches, monasteries, local merchants, and political leaders. Records indicate that these conflicts could be very specific, down to percentages to be shared between town and church for such things as building construction and maintenance, accommodation for pilgrims, the costs of stalls, and tariffs and tithes to be given to the church by burghers during pilgrimage.[65] In 1060, after significant lobbying of the pope by the abbot of the monastery, the French village of Vézelay was declared the site of Mary Magdalene's tomb, stimulating its popularity as a pilgrimage site. Managing the logistics and income distribution of the trade, however, was the cause of continued conflicts between the abbots of the abbey, the bishop, the merchants of the town, and the local counts. A riot over taxes being demanded in 1106 led to the assassination of Abbot Artaud, with the assassin being sheltered by a count and the bishop.

By the eleventh and twelfth centuries in Europe, economic recovery and the development of local markets were so closely connected with pilgrimage that measures were taken to ensure their uninterrupted flow. Local councils and church leaders collaborated to address such things as the safe passage of pilgrims, with decrees and warnings issued that anyone robbing clerics, monks, travelling merchants, or pilgrims would be imprisoned or exiled.[66]

The peaceful movement and management of pilgrims were important to guarantee. At times, the crowds were so large that order was difficult and people were injured or killed in the press to get near the relic. In 1018, at a Lenten service at the tomb of St. Martial in the city of Limoges, confusion in the stream of people entering the church led to a stampede in which more than fifty men and women were trampled to death.[67] A fire at a pilgrimage vigil in Vézelay in the year 1120 killed 1127 people.[68]

The sensory perspective on how Christianity has been shaped through the way it has been mediated, explored in this chapter, is a valuable one to consider in contemporary discussions about how Christianity may be being changed by its adaptation to the new technologies and the technologies of mass and digital media. Some analyses of these contemporary changes frame them in terms of genuine Christianity losing its integrity and even becoming banal, under pressure from the logic, economic conditions, and practices of these powerful media. This chapter illustrates that throughout its history, what Christianity is at any time is a changing phenomenon, the consequence of interactive processes of the spiritual, political, economic, and practical conditions; the desires of its leadership and demands of its people; elite conceptualizations and popular practices of immersion, invention, and subversion; and engagements with cultures that produce transformation in some cases and concession in others.

NOTES

1 On this, see for example McDannell, 1995; Meyer, 2011, 2012; P. C. Miller, 2009; Morgan, 2005, 2010a; Plate, 2014; and the journal *Material Religion: A Journal of Objects, Art and Belief*, Bloomsbury.
2 Meyer, 2006, p. 9.
3 Meyer, 2011, p. 26.
4 Theodoret of Cyrrhus, in the mid-fifth century, wrote of the exemplary holy men and women monks of Syria, "[They] barred up the senses with God's laws as with bolts and bars and entrusted their keys to the mind." Cited in P. C. Miller, 2009, p. 5.
5 Innis, 1950.
6 Riché (1978, p. 253) provides graphic details of the litany of punishments for various misdemeanors or disfavors.
7 Riché, 1978, p. 241.
8 Küng, 1994, p. 436.
9 Riché, 1978, p. 235.
10 Matins, Lauds, Prime, Tierce, Sext, Nones, Vespers, and Compline. In some new mission situations, Catholic Christians were not permitted to live beyond the sound of the church bells.
11 Riché, 1978, p. 235.
12 Chesnut, 1986, pp. 34–35.
13 Borg, 2012, p. loc 651.
14 Stancliffe, 2008, p. 21.
15 Jensen, 2006, pp. 576–577.
16 For example, the current multileveled Basilica of Saint Clement in Rome comprises an eleventh-century church built over the top of a fourth-century basilica, which in turn is built over the top of a previous Mithraic temple.
17 Brown, 2003, p. 78.
18 Freeman, 2002, pp. 206–207, quoting Janes, 1998, pp. 55–57.
19 Brown, 2003, p. 76.
20 Freeman, 2002, pp. 206–207.
21 A. Cameron, 2006, pp. 546–547.
22 A. Cameron, 2006, p. 547.
23 Gaehde, 1981, p. 64.
24 Gaehde, 1981, p. 64.
25 Brown, 2003, p. 108.
26 Aston, 1981, p. 163.
27 Tertullian, c. 197, pp. Chap I, VIII.
28 Quoted in Freedberg, 1989.
29 Aston, 1981, pp. 169–170.
30 See, for example, Morgan, 2010b; Plate, 2014.
31 Riché, 1978, p. 237.
32 Riché, 1978, p. 232.
33 Chidester, 2000, p. 210.

34 The term *hocus pocus* is used by Küng. It is believed to be a perversion of the Latin words spoken in the Mass when the host is raised, "*hoc est corpus meinum*" ("This is my body"). The perception that the Latin words had a magical power to transform a piece of bread into the body of Jesus supported its later adoption in a corrupted or even satirical form of words used in magic.

35 Chidester, 2000, p. 213.

36 Chidester, 2000, p. 195.

37 van der Meer, 1961, p. 339.

38 Freedberg, 1989, p. 160.

39 Jenkins, 2008, p. 48.

40 Freeman, 2008, p. 88.

41 Riché, 1978, p. 236.

42 Riché, 1978, p. 236.

43 Riché, 1978, p. 236.

44 Angendt, 2002, p. 29.

45 Cross & Livingstone, 1974, p. 1227.

46 Aware that he was to be arrested and executed, in 258 Cyprian used his religious position and status as a Roman aristocrat to have the arresting Roman officer take him back to Carthage, where his martyrdom would serve as an example and encouragement for his followers. His beheading took place as a staged liturgical event in a public arena before many of his congregation, with Cyprian sitting on a covered chair as a bishop surrounded by his deacons. His execution block was covered by a linen cloth, and followers cast cloths on the ground where his head would fall to gather his blood as relics for future veneration.

47 Angendt, 2002, p. 29.

48 P. C. Miller, 2009, p. 5.

49 Aston, 1981, p. 159.

50 Canon VII.

51 Nolan & Nolan, 1989, p. 3.

52 Nolan & Nolan, 1989, p. 3.

53 Turner & Turner, 1978, p. 6.

54 Turner & Turner, 1978, p. 7.

55 Abou-El-Haj, 1994, p. 7.

56 McLynn, 1994, p. 211.

57 Angendt, 2002, p. 29.

58 McLynn, 1994, pp. 211–212.

59 Sumption, 1975, quoted in Abou-El-Haj, 1994, p. 8.

60 Abou-El-Haj, 1994, p. 9.

61 Abou-El-Haj, 1994, p. 12.

62 Angendt, 2002, p. 33.

63 Calvin, 1986, p. 193, quoted in Cottret, 2000, p. 25.

64 Abou-El-Haj, 1994, p. 11.

65 Abou-El-Haj, 1994, p. 24.

66 Abou-El-Haj, 1994, p. 13.

67 Abou-El-Haj, 1994, p. 16.

68 Abou-El-Haj, 1994, p. 22.

9

The New Millennium

The fusion of Frankish and Germanic tribes into the Holy Roman Empire achieved by Charlemagne declined after his death in 814. Security was continually unsettled by raids or invasion by the Vikings or Norsemen and the Muslim expansion across the Mediterranean and eastern Europe.

By the eleventh century, stronger regional feudal principalities and weakening of the Viking threat brought more stable political order to many countries. This greater political stability enabled developments in agriculture, new settlements of land, the rise of markets, and growth in the number and size of villages and cities. With increases in the number and size of towns, manufacturing, and trade came the rise of a middle class. Cities became new centers of wealth, power, and strategic value, with their political position variously negotiated within the national and international alignments of popes, kings, emperors, feudal lords, and princes. As Green has noted, "There can be no doubt that between the 9th and 13th centuries, Europe had been transformed. A money economy had come into being."[1]

This period also saw renegotiation of relationships between church and states. Charlemagne made the selection and investiture of popes and bishops the responsibility of the Holy Roman emperor, whose choice was influenced not only by spiritual appropriateness for the position but also by political expedience, loyalty, and money. In this situation the practice of simony, the selling of church offices, was common. Frequent confrontations occurred between rulers and popes over appointments to church positions, taxation, and political authority. Although different in different countries, the confrontations between new states and the Roman Catholic Church involved the negotiation of strategic political alignments, decrees of excommunication of rulers by popes, the forced abdications of popes by rulers, and a 16-year period when there were two popes, each supported by different political interests.

From Jesus to the Internet, Peter Horsfield © 2015 John Wiley & Sons, Ltd. Published 2015 by John Wiley & Sons, Ltd.

An agreement about the relationship of the sacred and the secular in the new millennium was reached in Germany in the Concordat of Worms in 1122, in which it was agreed that bishops and abbots would be elected by the church but confirmed by the emperor. The agreement overcame the subordination of the Roman Catholic Church in Germany and freed the papacy and bishops from direct control by the secular ruler. This gave greater scope to the distinctive political strength of the church, its integrated and media-based organizational structure.

> With control over its clergy, the papacy became an awesome, centralized, bureaucratic powerhouse, an institution in which literacy, a formidable tool in the Middle Ages, was concentrated.[2]

Defining separate areas of authority also gave scope for the development of a more secular view of society and the state. While the relationship between the Roman Catholic Church and feudal rulers would continue to be contested and negotiated for centuries, a more equal playing field had been established and Europe had entered a new phase.

Marketing the Crusades

The "Crusades," as they are called, were papal-authorized and generally papal-instigated military operations directed toward those considered antagonistic to the interests of the Roman Catholic Church. From the First Crusade instigated in 1096 by Pope Urban II, Catholic crusades continued for more than five hundred years.[3] While the primary focus was fighting Muslims in the East, which produced around ten crusades up to the fourteenth century, crusades were instigated against designated enemies of the Catholic Church in Spain, North Africa, Estonia, Finland, Poland, Bosnia, Germany, Italy, Bohemia, Greece, Russia, and England. These included heretical groups such as the Albigensians and the Hussites, and, when the papacy split in fourteenth century, pope against pope.

The crusading movement or mechanism marks a significant epoch in the historical development of Christianity. As Riley-Smith notes, it "had involved every country in Europe, touching almost every area of life – the Church and religious thought, politics, the economy, and society – as well as generating its own literature. It had an enduring influence on the history of the western Islamic world and the Baltic region."[4]

Augustine in the fifth century had justified the use of violence as an act of Christian charity, and engaging in war for a just cause had been seen as meritorious for salvation since the eighth century. But the Crusades reflect a new development, one in which the Roman Catholic Church moved from being an endorser or supporter of violence done by ruling agencies, to being the instigator and director of military violence for achieving spiritual ends. While some earlier military figures had achieved sainthood by abandoning their military activity, the Crusades established a new spiritual regime in which "the very act of being a soldier could create holiness," and new monastic orders arose whose primary vocation was fighting on behalf of Christianity.[5]

While many who joined the Crusades saw themselves as acting out of Christian charity, the Crusades built an atmosphere of excitement that resulted in uninhibited acts of extreme violence. One of the leaders of the First Crusade, Peter the Hermit, while gathering his army in the Rhineland, engaged in the first large-scale massacre of Jews. The whole Jewish population of towns such as Mainz was eliminated, on no other grounds than they were a group of impatient Christians waiting to go to war.[6] An eyewitness to the first Christian occupation of Jerusalem, Raymond d'Aguilier, gave a graphic account of the violence and an indication of its religious justification:

> Some of our men (and this was more merciful) cut off the heads of their enemies; others shot them with arrows, so that they fell from the towers; others tortured them longer by casting them into the flames. Piles of heads, hands, and feet were to be seen in the streets of the city. It was necessary to pick one's way over the bodies of men and horses ... in the Temple and porch of Solomon, men rode in blood up to their knees and bridle reins. Indeed, it was a just and splendid judgment of God that this place should be filled with the blood of the unbelievers, since it had suffered so long from their blasphemies.... Now that the city was taken, it was well worth all our previous labours and hardships to see the devotion of the pilgrims at the Holy Sepulchre.[7]

As well as the killing, invading crusaders also destroyed. Priceless treasures, including books, manuscripts, and scrolls belonging to not just Jews and Muslims but also Byzantine Christians, were destroyed or plundered, even though most of the plunder was discarded on the difficult journeys home. Nicetas Choniates, a Byzantine chronicler, wrote of the devastation of Christian artifacts wrought by the Western crusaders when they occupied Constantinople during the Fourth Crusade (1202–1204):

> For the sacred altar, formed of all kinds of precious materials and admired by the whole world, was broken into bits and distributed among the soldiers, as was all the other sacred wealth of so great and infinite splendor. When the sacred vases and utensils of unsurpassable art and grace and rare material, and the fine silver, wrought with gold, which encircled the screen of the tribunal and the ambo, of admirable workmanship, and the door and many other ornaments, were to be borne away as booty, mules and saddled horses were led

to the very sanctuary of the temple. Some of these which were unable to keep their footing on the splendid and slippery pavement were stabbed when they fell, so that the sacred pavement was polluted with blood and filth.... Even the Saracens are merciful and kind compared to these men who bear the cross of Christ on their shoulders.[8]

The first effort to hold a crusade to the Holy Land was made by Pope Gregory VII in 1074 in response to a request for help against Muslim attacks from the Eastern Emperor Alexius. His attempts to raise a crusade failed. His successor, Urban II, was a different person, a more persuasive diplomat who was able to work more effectively with lay rulers than Gregory. The concept of a crusade also served Urban's interests in consolidating his papacy. At the time he was one of two popes – the other, Clement III, had been appointed by the Emperor Henry IV after deposing Gregory VII. Unable to rule from Rome, and needing to stay away from the emperor in Germany, Urban concentrated his efforts to build a crusade in his native France.

Because crusades were a voluntary service, the successful enlistment of participants depended on persuasion, and Urban laid the basis with a strategic and effective marketing campaign to sell the concept and enlist support that was equal to any contemporary media campaign. He travelled through France and wrote a flurry of letters in which he recounted "imaginary atrocities against Christian pilgrims by Muslims in Jerusalem, so that he could arouse appropriate horror and action would follow."[9] At the opportune time, a "launch" was held in the town of Clermont in 1095, at a council summoned by Urban for the purpose. On the last day of the council, clergy from the council and laypeople from the town gathered in a field outside the town, where Urban preached a sermon in which he called for and authorized a crusade.

There are several versions of Urban's speech, but none are verbatim and most were written after the event. But there are a number of elements common across the different accounts.[10] Urban emphasized the appeal for assistance that had been received from the East and the need to help them; the special sanctity of Jerusalem for Christians; the victorious advance of the Turks, and the desecration or destruction of churches and holy places taking place; and graphic descriptions of the sufferings of Christians and pilgrims in the East under the contemptible Turks. In reply to these horrors, Urban presented a crusade as God's work in which rich and poor alike should go. He urged Christians to go and fight the Turks instead of fighting among themselves (!), gave praise for the Franks and a reminder of Frankish greatness, and promised as pope that all who went on the crusade would receive plenary indulgence or full remission of sins. The response of the crowd to what was said is reported as instantaneous, with people calling out together, "It is God's will! It is God's will!"

Along with its content, Urban's speech is noteworthy for its performance: it reflects a deliberately staged event to achieve a planned outcome.

> Although the eyewitness account of this assembly and the pope's sermon were written later and were coloured by the triumph that was to follow, they give the impression of a piece of deliberate theatre – a daring one, given the risk involved in organising an out-of-doors event at the start of winter – in which the actions of the leading players and the acclamation of the crowd have been worked out in advance.[11]

The "campaign launch" was a crucial element in the marketing of this crusade, and it was a feature of subsequent crusades as well. Because the pope was the only person with the power to authorize a crusade, and the only person able to authorize the spiritual benefits and protections that came with it (in this world and the next), the proclamation of his endorsement was a significant element in the event. A similar "campaign launch" can be seen in the Second Crusade, which took place at Vézelay in France in 1146 and was attended by King Louis and numerous nobles who had already committed themselves to the crusade. Bernard of Clairvaux was the featured speaker on that occasion, and the crowds were such that the launch was moved out of the church onto the side of the hill, where a special platform had been erected. The number of people joining the crusade at the event was so large that the organizers ran out of prepared crosses to pin on people's clothing and the abbot of the monastery tore up his own garments to make extra.

Following the launch of a crusade, an organized program of recruitment then took place. Preaching was a key element in this, to assemblies of clergy, lay rulers, and the common people. Following Clermont, Urban II travelled extensively around the regions of France promoting the crusade, enlisting recruits, and commissioning them. After the launch of the Second Crusade at Vézelay, Bernard, in spite of his physical frailty, "hastened about, preaching everywhere, and soon the number of those bearing the cross had been increased immeasurably."[12] In a letter written in 1146, Bernard spoke of his achievements through this preaching campaign: "You have ordered and I have obeyed and your authority has made my obedience fruitful. 'I have declared and I have spoken, and they are multiplied above number': towns and castles are emptied, one may scarcely find one man amongst seven women, so many women are there widowed while their husbands are still alive."[13]

This program of preaching to justify and promote a crusade was haphazard at first, but as crusades developed, formal structures were put in place. In 1198, for the Fourth Crusade, a general executive office for the business of the cross had been established in the Papal Office, with executive staff being dispatched to provinces of the church to manage crusade promotion and other matters. For the Fifth Crusade in 1213, an executive board was established in almost every province, with powers to manage aspects of the crusade and to handle promotion.[14]

At first any ecclesiastic could be called on to preach the crusade, although ordinary parish clergy rarely did so. By the thirteenth century papal legates, prelates, and dignitaries were being used in stage-managed occasions to launch promotional campaigns in local areas, with preaching to the people increasingly being performed by the mendicant orders, particularly the Franciscans and Dominicans, who were experienced in preaching in the streets in a popular way. Aids were also developed to facilitate "coordination of message" in popular preaching. Guidelines, including model sermons, manuals of themes, and collections of exempla, were produced and distributed.[15]

> After the Third Crusade, local preaching came to be closely planned in advance in the attempt to achieve maximum coverage, to utilise resources fully, and to avoid duplication of effort ... preaching offensives were rarely haphazard. Individual agents were deputed to preach the cross at specific places or over particular areas. To do this systematically, planned itineraries were called for, the first well-documented tour of this type being that led by Baldwin of Ford, archbishop of Canterbury, to Wales in 1188.... They went, inevitably, to places where a good turn-out could be expected. In their preaching they were assisted by the secular clergy, who were sent advance notice that the friar intended to preach on a particular day at a specified time. Ecclesiastical censure was threatened to compel both the parish clergy and their flocks to attend. If this was the stick, the carrot took the form of partial indulgence granted to those attending sermons.[16]

A further element in cultivation of popular support was circulated writings about the Crusades. The *Historia Francorum,* an eyewitness account of the First Crusade by Raymond d'Aguiler and quoted earlier, gave graphic details of the events of the crusade from within a framework of justified action. Later writers such as Robert the Monk, Guibert of Nogent, and Baldric of Bourgueil located the crusade in more sophisticated and theologically agreeable terms, such as a providential history or the ideals of monasticism, with the crusaders portrayed as "a military monastery on the move."[17]

The effectiveness of the marketing is illustrated in one of the unusual and tragic incidents of the period, the children's crusade. In 1212 a twelve-year-old shepherd boy called Stephen approached King Philip Augustus of France with a letter alleged to be from Christ ordering a crusade. The king dismissed him, but word spread and the number of young believers grew to twenty thousand, ranging in age from six years to maturity and coming from northern France and western Germany. In groups of twenty, fifty, or a hundred, they created banners and began to march to Jerusalem. They didn't arrive but suffered various fates along the way. Some were turned back at Metz, others at Piacenza. Some made it to Marseilles, where merchants offered the children free passage to the Holy Land but took them instead to Egypt, where they were sold into slavery. A group of German children made it to Rome, where the pope thanked them but sent them home again. A chronicler who wrote about it at the time ended his description by saying, "One thing is sure: that of the many thousands who rose up, only very few returned."[18]

While justified and romanticized in different ways, the Crusades had a lasting negative impact on Christianity that continues to the present day. They caused permanent damage to the relations between Eastern and Western Christendom – the Catholic Church used the Crusades to establish Catholic bishoprics in the East, and to sack the city of Constantinople during the Fourth Crusade and set up a precarious Latin empire on its ruins. They established a relationship of bitterness between Christianity and the Muslim world that continues to the present time – while Western Christianity may see the Crusades as events in the past, the concept of Christians as invading crusaders remains a vital interpretive metaphor for Muslims in current political events. The Crusades elevated and routinized the use of violence, including extreme violence, as a legitimate moral tool for achieving Christian spiritual ends – the use of violence as a spiritual tool would emerge again in subsequent actions such as the inquisition and execution of those deemed to be heretics or witches, the coercion used to convert indigenous people to Christianity in the colonial expansion of the fifteenth and sixteenth centuries, and mass killings in the European wars of religion in the sixteenth and seventeenth centuries.

The Crusades also embedded the practice of using indulgences, the purchasing of preferential spiritual benefits with money or by serving the interests of the Roman Catholic Church. Urban's indulgences for the First Crusade promised respondents preferential treatment in having their earthly sins either partially or fully dismissed in heaven. As we will see, this concept developed progressively to include gaining spiritual benefits for donating money for building programs and other assorted church needs.

Scholasticism and universities

Another major intellectual and cultural development shaping the mediation of Western Christianity in the new millennium was the Scholastic movement, which grew out of the cathedral and monastic schools established by Charlemagne in the late eighth century. Although the schools declined following Charlemagne's death, the improved political and economic conditions in Europe in the eleventh and twelfth centuries, and the rise in towns and the middle class, rekindled them. Large numbers of students from across

Europe would travel to schools, attracted by the reputation of the teacher or teachers at the school, and often moving to other schools to further their education in a particular subject or to study other complementary subjects.

The schools established by Charlemagne existed primarily to teach reading and writing in Latin through the classic Roman subjects of grammar and rhetoric. As the cathedral schools developed, they expanded into a basic curriculum of the *trivium* of grammar, rhetoric, and logic or dialectic; the *quadrivium* of astronomy, geometry, arithmetic, and music; along with law and medicine. Different schools gained reputations for specializations: Paris and Oxford for theology, Bologna for law, and Salerno for medicine, for example. The teachers and thinkers associated with this school movement are known as the Schoolmen, or Scholastics.

The growth of the Scholastic movement and natural philosophy wouldn't have been possible without the network of monastic centers of documentary preservation, reproduction, and circulation. While the role played by monasteries in the preservation of manuscripts is widely recognized, it is common to overestimate the number of manuscripts these schools and monasteries worked with. Compared to libraries in other civilizations at the same time, European Christian libraries were small. There are records of libraries in China holding in excess of a hundred thousand scrolls. Key Islamic centers such as Cordoba, Cairo, and Baghdad hosted large libraries in dramatic spaces. Baghdad alone had thirty-six libraries, the most famous of which was the House of Wisdom, which combined a library, school, and research institution and was said to contain 1.5 million books.[19] In comparison, libraries in Europe were small.

> In the 12th century the largest known monastic collections contained fewer than 1,000 books, only a very few had as many as 500 and most probably had fewer than 100. ... In 1338, the Sorbonne boasted the richest collection in Europe, with 338 books for consultation and 1,728 books in its register, of which 500 were marked as lost.[20]

For reasons that are not well known, the books and more than one thousand years of papal archives were dispersed in the early thirteenth century, and by the middle of the fifteenth century the Vatican Library had only 1,700 volumes.[21] In place of imagined large reading libraries in monasteries, popularized by Umberto Eco's novel *The Name of the Rose*, it is more likely that small monastic collections were distributed around the monastery in places such as the chapel or monks' rooms, and the common collection stored in a cupboard or book chests.

In addition to works of the church fathers and bible commentaries, the key texts for the Scholastics to draw on through the network were a limited number of Latin texts, and Latin translations of some basic Greek works from the fourth to eighth centuries. One of the reasons for this restricted availability of early Greek works was linguistic parochialism.

> The Romans had never been sufficiently motivated to translate the great works of Greek thought into Latin for the overwhelming mass of Romans who knew no Greek ... aside from a few translations of Hippocratic medical works and a bit of Aristotle's elementary logic, chances of acquiring Greek learning by translation into Latin were virtually nil by the end of the sixth century.[22]

What was preserved of Greek writings in Latin owes a lot to Boethius (c. 480–c. 524), a scholar and diplomat who ended up being executed as a traitor after falling out of favor of the Roman emperor, Theodoric. Along with translations of crucial works by Aristotle and a commentary on Aristotle by Porphyry, Boethius also wrote four commentaries himself on Aristotle and five independent treatises on logic. Boethius' translations and writings, and a number of works written before him, were known collectively as the *logica vetus*, or the "old logic."

Boethius' translations and commentaries on the ancient Greek thinkers were influential in rekindling some of the desire to apply classical Greek thinking in reason and natural philosophy to a better understanding of the world and society. Although reason as a methodology of understanding had been addressed to varying degrees in Christian thought since its first centuries, the development that took place in this late medieval period was the desire on the part of a number of leading Christian thinkers to apply it more rigorously in the exploration of the world and faith. Green proffers a number of possible reasons for this rise in interest:

> In the chaotic political and economic world of the tenth and eleventh centuries, perhaps logic "opened a window on to an orderly and systematic view of the world and of man's mind." In its rigour and organisation, logic stood in sharp contrast to the disarray of subjects like theology and law, which over the centuries had become filled with contradictions and inconsistencies.[23]

The lens of reason also offered greater scope for investigation and reconciliation of the complexities of the natural and spiritual worlds beyond the relatively closed systems of revelation and dogmatic assertion.

Further stimulus came through the exposure of scholars of the West to Islamic learning. Travel through pilgrimage and crusades had made European scholars aware of the expanse and higher levels of knowledge and learning in some Islamic countries. While some scholarly contacts had been made, and some translations had been made of Arabic texts into Latin, the European capture of Toledo from the Muslims in 1085, and of Sicily in 1091, gave direct access to this accumulated knowledge, primarily in science and natural philosophy. Translations into Latin of Arabic and Greek writings in logic, mathematics, astronomy, optics, mechanics, natural philosophy, medicine, astrology, magic, and alchemy introduced a new world of knowledge and learning to western thought.[24]

For theological thinking, it was the works of Aristotle that were particularly influential. A major issue of ongoing contention was how insights gained through Aristotelian reasoning related to tenets of Christian revelation. There were three principal philosophical positions adopted to explain the logical relationship between Christian ideals or theological beliefs and individual instances or practical situations:[25]

- *extreme realism*, where the universal ideal was seen as existing prior, and individual situations were instances of a universal ideal;
- *moderate realism*, where the universal ideal was seen as existing only in relation to individual instances of it; and
- *nominalism*, where the universal ideal was seen as existing only in thought, and was the abstract name given for what individual instances or situations had in common.

A number of Scholastics are seen as pivotal. One was Anselm (1033–1109), the archbishop of Canterbury. An extreme realist, he was convinced of the capacity of logic to prove faith. Although his work covers a wide range of Christian doctrine, he is most widely remembered and revisited for his much debated ontological proof of the existence of God as the ultimate ideal: presenting God as "that than which nothing greater can be thought." In Cannon's view, Anselm "saved Christianity from irrationalism and the absurdity of illogical and self-contradictory suppositions."[26]

Another was Pierre Abelard (1079–1142), a critical thinker standing between the extremes of realism and nominalism. Abelard embodies the media style of this group. A very popular lecturer with outstanding oratorical skills, from an early age he attracted followings of thousands to his lectures. Yet he was also a prodigious writer, with extensive works in logic and dialectic, ethics, philosophy, and theology. His disputational style is exemplified in his book *Sic et Non*, a list of 158 philosophical and theological questions in which he analyzes the arguments offered in support of and against the questions, including contradictory arguments from recognized leaders of the Church. He also led a turbulent life. While canon of Notre Dame in Paris, he entered into a secret marriage with Heloise, which resulted in the birth of a son. In the aftermath of this, Abelard was castrated by Heloise's angry relatives and both of them retreated to monastic life.

Because he left the questions he examined largely unanswered, he was frequently the subject of charges of heresy, and for a long time all his works were listed in the later Index of Forbidden Books of the Roman Catholic Church. Condemned at a Synod in 1140 at the instigation of Bernard of

Clairvaux, he died in 1142, "a broken man,"[27] in a monastery under the protection of the abbot of Cluny. His method of enquiry for the purpose of attaining the truth, however, became characteristic of the Scholastic method.

Perhaps the most influential of the Scholastics was Thomas Aquinas (1225–1274). Born into a knightly Italian family, he joined the Dominican order and studied at Cologne and Paris before becoming a teaching member of the Faculty in Paris in 1257. He also taught in Italy. As well as his teaching and writing, he was an active preacher and was constantly consulted on civil and ecclesiastical matters. His major work was the *Summa Theologica*, a work of sixty-one volumes (in English), which he began in 1265 and was finished after his death by Reginald of Piperno, Thomas' confessor and companion. The work's three parts address God's nature and as the principle of creation, God as the end of man [sic] and man's return to God, and Christ as the way of man to God.[28] Important in it is Aquinas' integration of what is called natural theology, or conclusions about God and faith that can reasonably be drawn from nature. In Aquinas' view, God's revelation does not contradict the lessons about God that can be drawn by reason from nature.

In Aquinas, Scholasticism is seen as achieving its greatest clarity, and his influence has been substantial. To him is attributed the easing of the official Roman Catholic Church's suspicion of Aristotle. As a result, the *Summa* became the basis of Catholic theological instruction and has been to the present time. Although criticized by various of his contemporaries, his framework for locating revelation and Christian belief within a wider framework of natural philosophy and theology, and his positions on original sin, redemption, the sacraments, and purgatory, became formative on the Roman Catholic Church as it moved into the modern era. In Cannon's evaluation,

> He became in the Middle Ages what Augustine had been to antiquity – its clearest and deepest thinker and its most comprehensive teacher and guide.... Reason and faith stand harmoniously together. Faith complements reason and goes far beyond it, but it never contradicts it.[29]

His system had a number of other profound effects, not least of which was giving the priesthood of the Catholic Church full control over the laity. In Aquinas' view, without priestly pardon no one guilty of a deadly sin has any assurance of salvation. This theological perspective instituted the Christian life as one that cannot be lived without submission to the will of the men in control of the institution.

What are now modern universities emerged from this Scholasticism. Although generally regarded as ecclesiastical institutions requiring authorization by the pope, the cathedral schools acquired the status of universities through formal recognition as self-governing corporations under law in a form of legal organization that was in use in business, trade, and the professions. The University of Paris was formally recognized by Pope Innocent III in 1211. Some, such as the University of Bologna, were able to keep their lay-dominated character, drawing on models of Islamic institutions of higher education.

> Their models were from outside the Christian world: they copied in a remarkably detailed fashion the institutions of higher education which Muslims had created for their own universal culture of intellectual enquiry, especially the great school of Al-Azhar in Cairo – now familiar institutions like lectures, professors, qualifications called degrees. These were the first Christian universities – Christian, but not under the control of the Church authorities.[30]

Similar to Islamic institutions, they also came to serve a consultative or advisory function on issues of social importance. In what was a new development in Christianity, theology faculties in universities such as the Sorbonne were called upon by popes for specialist expertise on disputed questions.[31]

Cathedrals

A major media form emerging in this period was the Gothic cathedral. Cathedrals are a product of a growing interest at the time to explore and experiment with new forms of building and to endow the production and acquisition of new arts to furnish their interiors.[32] They are also an indicator of the increasing wealth, intellectual expansion, and lay education of the period.

Panofsky identifies a close connection between the new architectural form of cathedrals and the emergence of Scholasticism, particularly in the correspondence between the Scholastics' methods of systematic division of thought and the cathedrals' cultivation of the visual arts and architecture through "an exact and systematic division of space."[33] That the cathedrals and Scholasticism should be connected is not surprising, as Scholasticism emerged from the cathedral schools and scholastic education was one of the major activities conducted within the cathedral space. The town of Chartres, for example, had a reputation as a leading center of education and learning long before the landmark cathedral was built.[34]

Cathedrals as a form invite analysis and appreciation from a variety of angles and many studies have done so: architecture, practical construction, sociological relationships, economics, and the visual arts.[35] Of particular interest to this study is understanding cathedrals' character as sites of Christian mediation.

The cathedral form and space were designed to engage and impact the senses of those who entered it through its diverse material and visual

Figure 9.1 Canterbury Cathedral, United Kingdom, twelfth century. Source: photo by Adam T. Shreve.

symbolism – a clear instance of McLuhan's proposition that the medium itself is the message.[36] The soaring vaulted ceilings were evocative of the expanse of heaven, with high clerestory windows symbolizing the light of God from on high. Biblical symbolism was incorporated in many ways, down to the physical measurements of the structure (which incorporated biblical numbers). Representations within the cathedral were eclectic, symbolizing the all-encompassing truth and completion of Christianity. In Chartres Cathedral, for example, one of the outstanding examples of thirteenth-century Christian building, a brass pin catches light that at the Equinox shines through the window of Apollo. On the floor there are carvings of the signs of the Zodiac, an Egyptian scarab, and a labyrinth. Statues in the entranceways include pre-Christian philosophers and scientists. Stained glass windows recount biblical stories but also include contemporary people in their imagery. Statues of biblical events or characters carved in wood or stone or cast in bronze are scattered around the area, stimulating memory of biblical narratives. The carved statues representing each of the twelve months of the year involve figures and activities from twelve corresponding moments of rural life.[37] Particular materials such as agate or marble are used, whose flowing grain and veins allow people to see in them their own visions, scenes, and meanings.[38] These multimediated environments in most cathedrals are so symbolically complex that they require long periods of time to absorb them, encouraging the participant to remain in the space and mediate. Or, in a way that prefigures twentieth-century media reception, they offer a wide selection of religious media symbolism from which the individual can select in line with their individual journey.

The impact of the Christian building as a sensory medium of faith at the time is captured by Luttikheizen in his study of Muslim medieval Spain:

Church architecture and Christian rituals fascinated medieval Muslims. Leaders frequently voiced their concerns, suggesting that the sheer spectacle of Christianity could dupe the spiritually weak into accepting false religion. As part of the agreement granting religious freedom to the Christian minority, Christians were not allowed to build new churches or remodel existing ones.[39]

Catholic reform

The improving political, economic, and educational conditions for those laypeople in a position to take advantage of them, generated a growing confidence and desire to explore their own beliefs and shape their own destiny. The dialectical methodology of Aristotelian reasoning that had grown in influence also encouraged individuals to discover and assess truth by logical criteria rather than passive acceptance. It was inevitable that traditional practices and beliefs would begin to have the scrutiny of reason cast upon them. A number of these beliefs and practices emerged as problematic: the practice of indulgences, the sacraments and transubstantiation, authority in Christian practice, the justification of war and violence, the position of laypeople, the accumulation of institutional wealth, the place of churches in the process of salvation, and sexual behavior. A number of powerful reform movements and individuals embodied this sort of challenge.

Women monastics: Denied opportunity to exercise formal leadership in the male hierarchal church, many women found the opportunity for leadership and reform within women's monasteries and, from there, into the wider church. A number stand out as exemplary: Hildegard of Bingen (1098–1179), Gertrude of Helfta (1232–1392), Bridget of Sweden (1303–1373), Catherine of Sweden (1331–1381), Catherine of Siena (c. 1333–1380), and Julian of Norwich (c. 1342–c. 1413).

A common claim of these women was to a direct knowledge of God gained not through the rituals or structures of the institutional church, but in personal mystical experiences of dreams, visions, auditory phenomena, or intuition.[40] Their power, therefore, came not from a formal position within the hierarchy, but from an embodied authority born of their personal experience and personality. As such, in the same way as the Christian oral prophets in the past, they had the potential to unsettle the male hierarchy who saw themselves as the ones through whom God spoke.

This initial crossing of the boundary between official authority and informal authority by women was commonly helped by sympathetic male clerics who personally recognized the authority of the women and served to make them more widely known through biographies, by serving as their amanuenses, or as collaborators in their writing. Coakley notes that far from using their formal authority to contain or direct the women, the male collaborators used it to facilitate the accessibility of women's authority and powers to a wider audience. In some of their writings, the men present the nature of the women's authority as something that men were not able to achieve. The biographer of Hildegard of Bingen, Guibert of Gembloux, for example, writes of her:

> The apostle does not permit a woman to teach in the church. But this woman is exempt from this condition.... For she has transcended female subjection by a lofty height and is equal to the eminence, not just of any men, but of the very highest.[41]

Hildegard of Bingen provides a good example of the scope and insight these women reflected. Born to an aristocratic family in the Rhineland, Hildegard was aware of visions or a keenness of perception at a young age. At the age of eight, she was sent to the recluse Jutta of Spanheim in a women's monastic community attached to a Benedictine monastery. She became abbess in 1136 when Jutta died.

Her visions continued, and Hildegard experienced frequent ill health until a monk confidant, Vollmar, encouraged her to accept and write down her visions. For this she invented a style of writing that embodied both descriptive text and symbolic images. Vollmar remained her amanuensis till his death. In 1147 she secured endorsement to make her visionary insights public from Bernard of Clairvaux, the archbishop of Mainz, and Pope Eugenius. After that, as Malone states, she "sought no further approval [and] from this time on, writings poured forth from Hildegard in a never-ending stream."[42]

Her writings included a visionary trilogy of theology, the *Scivias* (1151), *The Book of Life's Merits*, on ethics (1158–1163), and *The Book of Divine Works*, on science (1163–1173); a nine-volume *Physica* and *Causae et Curae*, handbooks on diseases and their remedies based on scientific writings and her own observations in the monastery hospice; *Lingua ignota* and *Litterae ignota*, books of an invented language related closely to her medical and scientific works; a steady stream of liturgical and musical texts for the use of her sisters; and *Ordo virtutum*, one of the earliest surviving morality plays.[43] Her categorization of herbs in *Physica* and *Causae et Curae* and her exact observations of how they worked in healing were foundational in the development of western pharmacy. *Causae et Curae* is also one of the first books on the psychology of personality based not on theoretical speculation but on actual observation of human beings.[44] Prudence Allen credits Hildegard with development of a consistent theory of the complementarity of male and female, including a complicated psychology of different kinds of persons within either sex, which challenged the dominant western view of men's superiority and women's inferiority with a view in which men and women were seen as equal but with significant observed and documented differences.[45]

In addition to these writings, Hildegard wrote almost four hundred letters to emperors, secular rulers, four popes, bishops, monks, and nuns. Even though she continued to describe herself as an unfortunate member of the "frail sex,"[46] in all of these letters Hildegard is forthright, critical, and unhesitating in condemning the failure of her correspondents to live up to the requirements of their state in life. Although abbesses were expected to remain in their cloisters, from 1158 she engaged in a series of four missionary and preaching journeys across most of Europe.

Despite the extent and insights of her writings, and her prophetic challenge to the male religious and secular leaders of her time, Hildegard's influence has been significantly overlooked in the history of Christianity – lesser male figures are more widely known. Küng attributes this directly to her gender, the nature of her concerns, and the more general suppression of the significance of women mystics by male leaders of the German mystical tradition such as Meister Eckhart, Johann Tauler, and Heinrich Suso.[47]

The Cathari or Albigensians were a largely urbanized ascetic movement focused in southern France. While Christianity had accommodated many ascetic movements in its history, the Cathari presented a particular challenge to the Catholic Church by dismissing the necessity of the church and the sacraments for salvation. When attempts at converting them back to Catholicism failed, Pope Innocent III in 1208 issued a papal bull for a crusade against them. In building support for the crusade, he offered captured Cathari land to anyone who joined the crusade. This drew northern French nobility into the conflict, and the crusade was marked by horrific massacres in which little distinction was drawn between the guilty and the innocent. By 1229, Cathari lands were finally taken and the conflict had left about a million people dead, much of the population of southern France.

An outcome of the challenge of the Cathari and its bloody resolution was reinforcement of the strong divisions between laity and clergy, with a ban on lay preaching and even more limited lay access to the Bible. In the process, with the threat of further violence not far below the surface, the clergy became even more protected from lay criticism and challenge to their authority. As we will see in chapter 13, this insulating of clergy from outside challenge or criticism was a strong barrier to the lay uncovering of extensive sexual abuse of adults and children by clergy in our present time.

The Waldensians began in 1176 as a protest by a Lyon merchant against the worldliness of the Church. Advocating the Christian life as a life of intentional poverty, the Waldensians became increasingly critical of many church practices – including aspects of the sacraments, purgatory, indulgences, support of war, the death penalty, and prayers for the dead. Included in their challenge to the male hierarchy was a view that women should engage in public preaching along with men.

Pope Innocent III won back many Waldensian followers by establishing an alternative Catholic organization of *pauperes catholici*. Those Waldensians who didn't return were actively suppressed and persecuted but survived in pockets of communities that became Protestant at the time of the Reformation and continue today in parts of Italy and South America.

John Wyclif (1324/31–1384) was an English theologian, university don, priest, preacher, and translator. Educated in logic and dialectic at Balliol College in Oxford, he became a doctor of theology in 1372. Influential largely through his extensive Latin writings, Wyclif attracted a group of followers known as the Lollards. The influence of his writings on reformists in Bohemia led to a Papal Bull in 1409 empowering the archbishop to act against Wyclifism.[48] Wyclif contrasted the universal reality of the church with the false visible church, challenging such things as the church's exercise of authority and ownership of property. In the place of church authority, Wyclif encouraged people to read the Bible and find the truth themselves. His criticism of the Catholic Church's view of transubstantiation led to a formal condemnation of his teaching, and he was forced to retire. To facilitate lay reading of the scriptures, in 1382 Wyclif began translating the Latin Vulgate Bible into common English, a work that was completed by his assistant and followers after his death in 1384. Wyclif's English translation was banned by the English Catholic Church hierarchy in 1407.

Jan Hus (1373–1415) was an influential Czech priest, philosopher, professor, and later dean of Charles University in Prague. Inspired by the writings of Wyclif, Hus began preaching sermons critical of the Catholic Church. The movement that built around him, the Hussites, gained popular support as it resonated politically with nationalist issues of Czech identity and resentment at Church interference in their affairs. Central in their opposition was their view of the Eucharist. They reinstituted the practice of laypeople participating more frequently in communion and distributing wine as well as bread to communicants, the first time this had been done in centuries. Hus was finally excommunicated in 1412 by Pope Alexander V because of his outspoken opposition to an indulgence-based papal fundraising campaign. While attending the Council of Konstanz to appeal his excommunication, under guarantee of Alexander's protection, Hus was arrested, put on trial, found to be heretical, and sentenced to immediate immolation. Escorted from the cathedral by an armed guard of a thousand men, he was burned in a nearby field, and his ashes thrown into the Rhine.[49] His death sparked a Bohemian nationalist movement and a civil war that included the violent destruction of symbols of traditional religion – "the first large-scale wrecking of monasteries and church art by Christians in the history of Christian Europe."[50]

One of the characteristics of these reformist movements was their ability to address popular concerns not being addressed by the official church, and to communicate in a way that attracted a popular response from large numbers of people. The opposition and persecution they received from the church authorities were often framed and incorporated into a narrative that strengthened rather than weakened them, in a similar way to the early Christian martyrologies. Following Jan Hus' death, for example, a passion narrative emerged in which his death was paralleled to that of Christ and Hus was portrayed as the ultimate Christian martyr.[51] The Catholic message of his death by burning, intended to discourage his followers and other dissenters through its horror, was subverted by narratives portraying his heroism in facing it. The subversive narratives seen in the early Christian martyrologies are referenced in the narrative of his death circulated by his followers:

> The executioners undressed Huss and tied his hands behind his back with ropes, and his neck with a chain to a stake around which would wood and straw had been piled up so that it covered him to the neck. Still at the last moment, the Imperial Marshall, von Pappenheim, in the presence of the count Palatine asked him to save his life by a recantation, but Huss declined with the words, "God is my witness that I have never taught that of which I have been accused by false witnesses. In the truth of the Gospel which I have written, taught and preached I will die today with gladness." Thereupon the fire was kindled. With uplifted voice Huss sang, "Christ thou son of the living God, have mercy upon me." When he started this for the third time and continued "who art born of Mary the virgin," the wind blew the flame into his face; he still moved his lips and head, and then died of suffocation. His clothes were thrown into the fire, his ashes gathered and cast into the nearby Rhine.[52]

Against these subversive communication practices of the reform movements, the Roman Catholic Church developed alternate media strategies to promote and protect its hegemony. One of those was the authorization of a number of new religious orders to counter the reformers' message on the streets. One of those was **the Dominicans**, formed from the work of a Spanish priest, Dominic (1170–1221). Challenged by the success of the Cathari and the ineffectiveness of the heavily institutionalized clergy against them, Dominic established a group of preachers and a campaign of preaching to counter and undermine the popularity of the Cathari on the streets. To counter the Cathari message, Dominic immersed his followers in education to equip them to mount an intellectually rigorous defense of Catholic faith. Against the ascetic self-denial of the Cathari, Dominic required of his preachers that they own no possessions and beg for their food.

Papal approval for an Order of Preachers was granted in 1216. With their strong vocational focus on preaching, intellectual rigor, and teaching, many Dominicans took up positions on the university faculties where they trained. Some of the leading figures of the Scholastic and mystical movements, such as Thomas Aquinas and Meister Eckhart, were Dominicans.

Another order was **the Franciscans**, formed by Giovanni Bernadone (Francis) (1182–1226) after a spiritual quest led him to adopt a simple life of utmost poverty, preaching repentance and the Kingdom of God, and working with the poor on the streets. Although advocating a life of simple poverty in a way similar to that of the Waldensians, the Franciscans' affirmation of the authority of the church led to their approval as a religious order by Innocent III in 1179.

The two orders became popular and widely recognized, largely because of their direct and close communication with ordinary people in preaching and pastoral work in the streets, particularly in the cities.

Walker attributes to the work of the Dominicans and Franciscans "a great strengthening of religion among the laity,"[53] but there were other consequences also. By their constant presence and effectiveness in the streets, the orders, who reported directly to the pope, lessened the control of local bishops and clergy and surreptitiously strengthened the direct influence of the papacy. The orders also allowed laypeople to participate as Tertiaries, that is, retaining their daily occupations while sharing in the monastic activities of fasting, prayer, worship, and benevolence. This blurred the boundary between monastic and daily life, facilitating access of laypeople to the benefits of monastic spirituality and in the process strengthening the status of lay life.

The Inquisition

Another media-political strategy of the Catholic Church against dissenters and reformers was the Inquisition, a strategy not only of physical control but also of physical control exercised in such a way as to communicate fear and compliance. Beginning as a response to the Cathari movement, it developed to become an organized agency of the Roman Catholic Church, responsible for discovering and eliminating heresy and other threats to the church (e.g., sorcerers, witches, and alchemists). Initially all inquisitions were decentralized, with departments of inquisition established in each diocese to stamp out heresy and ensure orthodoxy. In 1184, Pope Lucius III "made it mandatory for bishops of suspected areas to examine their flock at least once a year, requiring every member under oath to declare his orthodoxy."[54] Pope Innocent III in 1198 took it further, authorizing "that anyone who attempted to construe a personal view of God which conflicted with Church dogma must be burned without pity."[55]

The first papal-appointed inquisitor, the priest Conrad von Marburg, was so severe in his methods that the German bishops petitioned the pope to remove him. Their petition was not granted. When Conrad accused Count Henry of Sayn, one of the highest members of Germany society, of being involved in heretical activity (including riding on turtles), Henry submitted his case to an ecclesiastical council in Mainz and was found innocent. On his return to Marburg, the Inquisitor Conrad was murdered by a group of nobles. No effort was made to find the perpetrators, and contemporary chroniclers reported that "with the death of Conrad, peace and quiet returned to Germany once again."[56] The Inquisitor known as Robert the Dominican, sent by Pope Gregory IX to France in 1233, was reported to have burned or buried alive fifty people in one three-month period. Another, Robert Le Bourge, conducted a mass execution of 183 male and female heretics in France in 1239, summoning the nobles and prelates of Champagne and Flanders to witness the burnings.[57] While there were inquisitors drawn from the general priesthood and the Franciscan order, by the end of the thirteenth century the majority of the inquisitorial work had been entrusted to the Dominicans, who saw their founder as the first inquisitor and whose intellectual training made them ruthless in interrogation.

Concerns about the harshness of some inquisitorial practices, confusion about aspects of the process, and conflicts of authority between the bishops and the pope generated resistance by many bishops and threatened to derail it. In 1242, a council was assembled in Tarragona to resolve some of these questions. The council provided definitions of various forms of heresy and their penalties, processes to be followed, what constituted true and false confessions, and other things. Penalties were to include penance, the confiscation of property, imprisonment, and death by burning. The use of torture was authorized to elicit confessions where it was suspected the person was withholding acknowledgment of their guilt. Inquisitors were to be appointed by the pope independently of local bishops. The courts were reorganized and procedures regulated.

The new regulations were implemented by Innocent IV (1243–1254). While the council provided "a firmly and explicitly drawn code of procedure aimed at theological crime" in place of the haphazard practices of the past,[58] the secret conditions opened the process to significant abuse. While clergy were able to be present, the public was barred from proceedings and the accused had no right to know what they were accused of or question the evidence. The risks of being associated with heresy deterred lawyers from becoming involved in defending those accused.

As a media strategy, the Inquisition process had a number of other noteworthy elements. One was the secrecy of the process. The denial of information to the accused and to the wider public allowed the church to release information that served its purposes, multiplying its power by minimizing opposition and cultivating a repressive atmosphere of fear. This fear was enhanced by the encouragement of Catholic Christians to report each other to inquisitors, with promises of heavenly reward for doing so. The third canon of the Fourth Lateran Council, held in 1215, stated,

> Catholics who have girded themselves with the cross for the extermination of heretics, shall enjoy the same indulgences and privileges granted to those who go in defence of the Holy Land.

The other media event was the *auto-da-fé*, or "act of faith," a planned and performed spectacle in which an accused person found to be guilty was paraded publicly and formally sentenced. The spectacle of the *auto-da-fé*

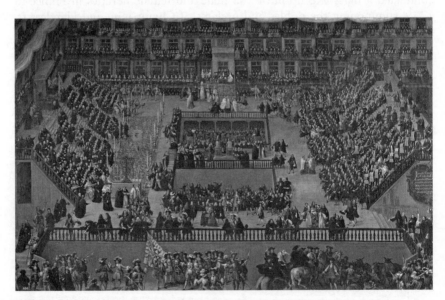

Figure 9.2 Francisco Rizi, *Auto de Fe en la Plaza Mayor de Madrid*, 1683. Source: © Heritage Image Partnership Ltd / Alamy.

reached its pinnacle in the Spanish Inquisition. In 1239, nobles, clergy, dignitaries, and a reported seven thousand people were present when 183 Cathari "were exterminated in one day to the triumph of holy church."[59] Often held in the presence of royalty, the *auto-da-fé* ceremony involved a procession, a solemn mass, an oath of obedience to the Inquisition, and a lengthy and detailed sermon castigating the sins of the convicted and warning others to amend their ways to avoid the same fate. The prisoners were then called upon one by one, and their crimes and sentences were announced. The culmination of the spectacle was the "relaxation" or handover of those to be executed to the secular authorities, to be taken away under guard to an open space beyond the city walls, the *quemadero* or burning place. Although separate from the formal part of the proceedings, the executions were an expected part of them, and there are indications of public disappointment if executions did not take place and a concern that attendance at the events would drop if executions weren't part of the events.[60]

The Inquisition was a highly effective media strategy for reinforcing the power of orthodoxy and the dangers of going against it. Invoking also the tropes of medieval theatrical performances, it was intended to instill fear in what Potter calls "a carefully-scripted and deeply serious – if in some respects highly insidious – ritual drama."[61] Bireley speaks of *autos-da-fé* in Spain lasting for two to three days and addressing 150 to 200 cases.[62] The last *auto-da-fé* was in Mexico in 1858.[63]

Research and rethinking of the Inquisition have expanded in recent decades with the opening of the secret Vatican Inquisition archives in 1998. Various efforts are made to justify the phenomenon of the Inquisition as a Christian spiritual activity: that they were in line with the social tenor of the time; that there were comparable practices in politics of the time; that they were motivated by the serious religious belief that people's eternal souls were at stake; that the legal processes were actually more careful and the punishments less extreme than have been thought; and that worse instances of abuse can be noted, such as the 40,000–60,000 women killed in Europe as witches.

From another perspective, however, the Inquisition can be seen quite differently: as the epitome of Christianity as an imperial religious dictatorship, working with political coalitions to maintain the dominance of its male oligarchy through the fearful suppression and torture of its citizens and the murder of its opponents. Part of this was a consequence, perhaps an expected outcome, of the early takeover of Christian leadership by men. The Inquisitions reflected a significant male construction of women as collaborators with the devil, a view promoted in the influential handbook for theologians, lawyers, and physicians, *Malleus maleficarum* (*Hammer of the witches*), written by two Dominican inquisitors, which was published in thirty editions between 1487 and 1669 and included a forged endorsement from the theological faculty of Cologne.[64]

The Inquisitions also had a repressive effect on social development through the suppression of initiative and intellectual life. The written word and some occupations such as map making became suspect, and laity were forbidden from possessing or reading the scriptures.[65] The seizure of vast amounts of property through arbitrary legal processes increased the wealth of the church. The creation of a climate of suspicion and fear undermined social relationships and trade. In the 1490s, a Spanish Scholastic lamented that people "were deprived of the liberty to hear and talk freely, since in all cities, towns and villages there were persons placed to give information of what went on." Another writer in 1538 lamented,

> Preachers do not dare to preach, and those who preach do not dare to touch on contentious matters, for their lives and honor are in the mouths of two ignoramuses, and nobody in this life is without his policeman.... Bit by bit many rich people leave the country for foreign realms, in order not to live all their lives in fear and trembling every time an officer of the Inquisitio enters their house; for continual fear is a worse death than a sudden demise.[66]

The inquisitorial process into false teachings or heresy continues today, albeit in a modified form, through the Vatican Congregation for the Doctrine of the Faith. Prominent recent Catholic theologians such as Edward Schillebeeckx, Hans Küng, and Tissa Balasuriya have been subject to processes of extensive scrutiny and discipline for things said in their writings considered to be contrary to official church teachings. The Congregation was also the source of the 1962 decree *Crimens sollicitationis*, which forbade anybody, under threat of papal excommunication, to talk about the sexual abuse of children by priests.

NOTES

1 Green, 1994, p. 21.
2 Green, 1994, p. 23.
3 A full chronology of the Crusades is given in Riley-Smith, 1995b, pp. 392–400. This section draws on a number of authored or edited works of Riley-Smith, whose work on the Crusades of the Middle Ages is extensive and thorough.
4 Riley-Smith, 1995a, pp. 4–5.
5 MacCulloch, 2009, p. 386.
6 MacCulloch, 2009, p. 384.
7 d'Aquilliers.
8 Choniates, 2014.
9 MacCulloch, 2009, p. 383.
10 Munro, 1906.
11 Riley-Smith, 1995a, p. 2.
12 Odo of Deuil, quoted in Phillips, 2007, p. 68.

13 Quoted in Phillips, 2007, p. 68.
14 Lloyd, 1995, p. 46.
15 Lloyd, 1995, p. 46.
16 Lloyd, 1995, pp. 47–48.
17 Riley-Smith, 1986, p. 2.
18 Coloniensis, 1213.
19 J. Campbell, 2013, p. 72. Campbell notes that none of these outstanding collections survived beyond the twelfth century, their collections ransacked by Mongol raiders or Christian Crusaders, or destroyed by orthodox Muslims who believed the only book Islam needed was the Qur'an.
20 J. Campbell, 2013, p. 79.
21 Vatican, 2014.
22 Green, 1994, pp. 28–29.
23 Green, 1994, p. 47.
24 Outstanding among the European translators were Gerard of Cremona (d. 1187), who translated around seventy works from Arabic to Latin, and William of Moerbeke (d. 1286), who translated around fifty from Greek to Latin, including a translation of the full works of Aristotle (Green, 1994, p. 86).
25 For further explanation of these, see Cannon, 1980.
26 Cannon, 1980, pp. 188–189.
27 Walker, 1959, p. 241.
28 Cross & Livingstone, 1974, p. 1322.
29 Cannon, 1980, pp. 257–259.
30 MacCulloch, 2009, p. 397.
31 MacCulloch, 2009, p. 397.
32 Favier, 1990, pp. 37–42.
33 Cited in Miles, 1985, p. 6.
34 Favier, 1990, pp. 37–42.
35 See for example, W. Anderson, 1985; W. Clark, 2006; Favier, 1990; Gimpel, 1983.
36 McLuhan & Fiore, 1967.
37 Favier, 1990, p. 13.
38 For a fascinating analysis of this phenomenon, see Rooney, 2011.
39 Luttikhuizen, 2005, p. 471.
40 Coakley, 2010, p. 85.
41 Cited in Malone, 2001, pp. 118–119.
42 Malone, 2001, p. 111.
43 See Maddocks, 2001, pp. 277–284.
44 Malone, 2001, pp. 115–116.
45 Allen, 1997, pp. 303–309.
46 Malone, 2001, p. 112.
47 Küng, 2001, p. 50.
48 Keen, 1986, p. 127.
49 Huschke, 2014, referring to Cannon, 1980, p. 309.
50 Palacky, 1869.
51 MacCulloch, 2009, p. 572.
52 Fudge, 2011.

53 Walker, 1959, p. 236.
54 Cannon, 1980, p. 209.
55 Papal Bull 1198.
56 Tompkins, 1981, p. 57.
57 Loos, 1974, p. 198.
58 Loos, 1974, p. 198.
59 Peters, 1988, p. 57.
60 The description is drawn heavily from Haskins, 1902.
61 Potter, 1996, p. 111.
62 Bireley, 1999, p. 68.
63 Bowden, 2005b, p. 345.
64 Küng, 2001, p. 73.
65 The Synod of Toulouse, 1229.
66 Kamen, 1985, p. 164, cited in Ellerbe, 1995, p. 84.

10

Reformation

The Reformation is the term now given to the complex of religious and political changes that occurred in Western Christendom during the sixteenth and seventeenth centuries. It was marked particularly by the fracturing of the singular Holy Roman Empire into a continuing European-wide Roman Catholic Church and a diversity of "Protestant" forms of Christian expression and organization. It is commonly seen as being initiated in 1517 by the nailing on the door of Wittenberg cathedral ninety-five theses of protest (in Latin) by Martin Luther. It is also seen as a major event of media significance within Christianity because of its connection with the expanding uses of printing. The nature and consequences of that connection are explored in this chapter.

Printing and its precursors

Printing emerged in the West in the fifteenth century as part of a wider convergence of cultural changes. The Scholastic movement had instigated a mechanism for rethinking the previously unquestioned assumptions of dogma. Developments in agriculture had facilitated new commerce and trade, the rise of a merchant class, the growth of cities and urban populations where new economic principles guided social relationships, and changing structures of authority. During the fourteenth and fifteenth centuries, new universities were established in major centers of Europe that expressed and fed the rise of Renaissance Humanism, a cultural movement of thought, technological change, and artistic expression that was generating a new sense of human individualism and scope to develop. New technologies such as the compass, lensmaking, and the telescope were changing people's perspectives on the universe and their place within it.

From Jesus to the Internet, Peter Horsfield © 2015 John Wiley & Sons, Ltd. Published 2015 by John Wiley & Sons, Ltd.

Within this ferment, the Holy Roman Church across Europe was rent by unrest. Political collusion and papal tolerance of corruption were creating problems of morale, trust, and integrity, reflected in a steady stream of individual reformers and reform movements as noted in chapter 9. Monarchs were becoming more efficient in the business of governing and asserting themselves against the dominance of the Roman imperial church. The three most powerful western monarchies emerged in this period: England in 1485, France in 1491, and Spain in 1492.

Media changes were also taking place that subsequently would be adapted to printing. Manuscripts, including illuminated manuscripts, were being produced in greater numbers. Visual art was developing, particularly in what would later be known as portraiture.[1] Poets and writers such as Dante, Petrarch, Boccaccio, and Chaucer were writing vernacular works for a wider reading audience. The book as a product had begun to take on differentiated forms: the great folio, the shelf book of the universities and serious study; the humanist book, a moderately sized book for classical texts and new works of literature; and the portable or pocket book, utilized for bedside or more popular use.[2] Silent reading had begun to replace the previous habits of vocalized reading.

Experiments in new forms of publishing were being undertaken. Jean Gerson (1363–1429), chancellor of the University of Paris and one of the early biblical humanists, was exemplary in this. He used his Carthusian Order as a copying network to create lending libraries. He spearheaded the creation of the literary genre of the tract, cheap "rapid response" religious pieces written in a style and on topics designed to reach a comparatively large audience.[3]

Well before printing, lay stationers began multiple copying of manuscripts for universities, with different copyists working on several copies of specific portions of a manuscript in different places.[4] Some of the earliest printed works were reproductions of these existing manuscripts. More than fifty years before printing, images made from woodcuts were in mass circulation, initially given out as commemorative illustrations of a pilgrimage to be displayed in the home and used as a memento, for prayer and meditation, or as a talisman.[5] Printing also took up existing formulas and patterns of oral speech, not only to facilitate comprehension of what was written, but also in recognition of the reality that many of the printed writings would be received by being read aloud by others. The development and influence of printing in the West fall within this wider cultural and media milieu.

The first person to use movable type in the West was Johann Gutenberg of Mainz, using a technology developed in China several centuries earlier. Working on a printing press made from a converted wine press, his first book, the Gutenberg Bible, took him six years to print and sent him bankrupt. Printing presses were quickly established in Italy in 1464, Paris in

1470, Cracow in 1474, and Westminster in 1476. By 1500 printing presses existed in over two hundred cities throughout Europe, and an estimated six million books had been printed.[6]

At first printers were secretive and cautious, printing mainly the classic Greek and religious texts that were being actively sought as part of the Renaissance movement. In 1471 and 1472 the presses of Venice, an important center of humanistic publication, produced 134 first editions of classical authors.[7]

As printing spread, it developed into a European-wide industry, with its own hierarchies and processes for regulating such things as competition and standards. Innovations were made in typography, content layout, title pages, and indexing. Content also began to expand beyond just the classical texts, with printers experimenting with new genres in cheap print – short books in small formats of sermons, prayer books, and devotional works – to attract a wider audience.[8] Booksellers developed expertise in reading the market, in advertising, and in promoting their publications through such things as booths at regional fairs.[9] Although the literacy rate across nations such as Germany was probably no higher than 5 percent, in the cities and towns it could have been as high as 30 percent.[10] With this size of market, printing and book distribution soon became an integral part of the commercial life of most cities.

Latin religious works were a significant portion of the new industry. Bestsellers included works such as Thomas à Kempis' *Imitation of Christ*, which had 172 print editions before 1501. *The Golden Legend*, a thirteenth-century collection of hagiographies by the Italian archbishop Jacobus de Voragine, had over 150 editions before the end of the century.[11] Liturgical materials were another mainstay, along with the printing of certificates of indulgence for use by bishops, with one estimate putting the number of printed indulgence certificates in circulation by the end of the fifteenth century at three to four million.[12] Yet these religious works were fewer than the secular materials published. Of all books published in Venice during the fifteenth century, 73 percent were secular, although outside Venice secular works accounted for only 52 percent.[13]

Printing had a significant impact in the development of vernacular literature, which had had a long but steady gestation. While oral vernaculars were used extensively in daily discourse throughout the Middle Ages and even had their own oral literature and narratives, it took centuries for them to develop written forms.[14] It wasn't till the thirteenth century that vernacular literacy began to be taught without recourse to Latin, and secular and religious literature in German began to be written and printed for lay men and women and clerics who wanted to read religious materials but weren't literate in Latin.[15]

Based on her study of publications in Strasbourg in the period 1480 to 1599, Chrisman identifies two reading and publishing cultures in existence before the Reformation. There was a Latin culture dominated by the universities and churches, in which books were written in Latin by scholars and theologians and published by the prestigious presses; and a vernacular culture, rooted in the interests of ordinary men and women, written in German, and published by a different set of printers.[16] The difference between the two was marked.

> The Latin writers' grasp of rhetoric and dialectic made it possible for them to write in logical, conceptual forms. The vernacular writers, ignorant of these skills, wrote descriptively rather than analytically. The two cultures used different sources and diverse criteria of evidence...the Latin culture was based on the ethics and philosophy of ancient Rome, the Bible, and the Church Fathers; the lay culture was based on the laws and commandments of Scripture.[17]

The groups and writers involved in the production of vernacular publications were less formalized and organized, and often were brought together by the printers' shops.[18] The lack of an identifiable institutional market for vernacular works led to more active promotion of them and experimentation with different genres. The commercial printers had greater freedom to do this than the universities, which were under tighter partisan control.

> The publishers advertised their books widely by sending out flyers and catalogues. Printers staged book fairs, sent their agents to the major cities of Europe and carried on a far-reaching correspondence with their potential clientele. Thus the literate public was kept aware of new editions and the latest literature on every subject ... knowledge and ideas were disseminated faster than ever before. Literacy rates multiplied. It is estimated that literacy rates in the more advanced countries by the end of the 16th century were better than 50 percent.[19]

Fairly quickly, printers also sensed that there was a market for vernacular bibles and began to produce copies of bibles in vernacular languages for a general audience. By the end of the fifteenth century, printed bibles had become available in German, Italian, Dutch, Spanish, Czech, and Catalan. In France, printers also produced multiple versions of abridged bibles, publications "concentrating on the exciting stories and leaving out the more knotty doctrinal passages."[20] An abridged bible, published in Provence in 1473–1474, was one of the early books printed in the French language.[21] Such abridged versions continued to be published till the middle of the following century, when they ceased to be profitable. Bernard Cottret reverses a common opinion by suggesting that "it was not the Reformation that created a need to read Scripture, but the reading of Scripture that brought about, partially at least, the Reformation."[22]

The growth of this independent activity by the printers caused concern to the Roman Catholic Church to the extent that the Lateran Council of

1512–1517 declared that no one was to print or have printed any book or other writing that hasn't been examined by a duly recognized authority of the church and given a signed warrant of approval. The penalty for not getting approval was excommunication, possession and burning of the books, payment of a fine, and suspension from further printing.[23]

In contrast to a common view that Luther initiated the Christian adaptation of printing, Pettegree[24] makes clear that much of what is attributed to Luther's initiative was in existence within the Catholic Church and the wider culture well before his activities: the use of pamphlets and small publications for propaganda purposes, experiments with cheap print religious publications for a wider audience, publications in the vernaculars, methods of quick printing and effective distribution, and printings of the Bible in vernacular translations. The Catholic Church and regional societies were also familiar with the use of quickly produced and distributed polemical writings in religious disputes well before Luther. The fierce disputes stimulated by Savonarola in Florence in the late fifteenth century are examples of this:

> A striking feature of these years is the manner in which Savonarola and his followers mastered the printing press. No sooner had he delivered his passionate sermons, often to enormous and excitable crowds, than the text was made available to the printers.... Publication was overwhelmingly in the vernacular, and almost exclusively in the quarto pamphlet form later made familiar by the German Flugschriften.[25]

Martin Luther

The major impact of linking Christianity with the printing press was the German Reformation instigated by the Augustinian monk, Martin Luther. Born in Saxony in 1483, Luther became acquainted with Scholasticism and the new Humanism at university. Intended for a career in law, after a frightening encounter with a storm he entered an Augustinian monastery, studied theology, and was ordained a priest in 1507. He took up a position as professor of biblical interpretation at the young University of Wittenberg in 1511, received his doctor of theology in 1512, and became pastor of the parish church of Wittenberg in 1514. Luther's sense of spiritual unease and his biblical studies led him to doubt traditional theology. In 1517 he posted publicly a statement of 95 theses against the selling of papal indulgences, beginning a history of conflict with the Roman Catholic Church and the Holy Roman Emperor.

Luther's distinctive understanding of Christian salvation and the answer to his long-running spiritual unease came two years after that, where in a mediation on Paul's Letter to the Romans he came to see Christian salvation as a gift of faith given by God rather than something that has to be earned or bought: "All at once I felt that I had been born again and entered into paradise itself through open gates. Immediately I saw the whole of Scripture in a different light."[26] Salvation by the grace of God received by faith became a central theological focus and difference of the subsequent Protestant movement.

The posting of disputatious theses on the door of Wittenberg cathedral was not in itself a contentious action. Wittenberg was a university town, and the door of the cathedral was in effect a public noticeboard on which teachers of the university posted ideas to invite discussion and debate. But the content of Luther's posting spread rapidly in a way that surprised Luther himself, as he expressed in a letter to Pope Leo X:

> It is a miracle to me by what fate it has come about that this single Disputation of mine should, more than any other, of mine or of any of the teachers, have gone out into very nearly the whole land. It was made public at our University and for our University only, and it was made public in such wise that I cannot believe it has become known to all men.[27]

Welcome to the new world of mass media! When challenged, Luther was unwilling to recant or disown what he had said, and proceeded to defend and promote his ideas publicly. Once started, he wrote prodigiously.

While the extent of Luther's influence was due to a variety of factors, two media-related factors were crucial: one was the support of the printers of Wittenberg and northern Germany; and the other was his adoption of the vernacular and media language in his writing. His desire to reach a wide audience coincided with the interests of the printers who saw in Luther and his dispute an opportunity to tap further the vernacular market.

Even before he posted his theses, Luther was familiar with the potential of printing for reaching a wider audience. The printing press of Wittenberg University was housed for a while in the Augustinian convent in which Luther lived. Along with textbooks, the press also published humanistic works, primarily in Greek and Latin. It had already printed two earlier works of Luther, which he had written in German with the specific intent of reaching a wider audience than just scholars and students. The style of writing he used to reach this wider audience was such that he discouraged his scholarly colleagues from buying the work, as he explained in a letter to the humanist Christoph Scheurl:

> They were written not for the Nurembergers, that is, for very fine and very cultured beings, but for the rude Saxons as you know them.[28]

His aim was successful. His *Die sieben Busspsalmen* (*The Seven Penitential Psalms*), published in 1517, was quickly reprinted in several cities to meet demand and went through a number of editions.[29]

At first Luther's disputes with the Catholic Church were written and published in Latin, the language of scholarly discourse. This soon changed as Luther and his printers realized there was wider public interest in the issues being raised in the German-reading market. It took only two years before Luther was publishing more of his works in German than in Latin. By 1523, 89 percent of his 390 published editions were in German.[30]

One of the reasons for Luther's early impact was the sheer volume of his writings. From 1517 till his death in 1541, there was a total of 544 first editions and 2639 reprint editions of Luther's works. This was eleven times more editions than the next Evangelical writer. Conservatively estimating each printing at one thousand copies, the total number of Luther's publications during his lifetime was 3.1 million copies.[31]

Another reason for Luther's impact was the type of publication he used. He recognized the importance of printing to his mission, calling it "God's highest and extremist form of grace, whereby the business of the gospel is driven forward." In his use of it, Luther accepted and adapted himself to the medium's demands. While Luther also published sermons and pastoral and biblical works, the most popular works were polemical publicity booklets or pamphlets, which were already in existence and perfected by Luther as a tool of propaganda and agitation. Most common was a quarto format (earlier used by Savonarola), with a soft cover and an average length of 16 pages. They were relatively cheap to produce, readily transported and concealed (for smuggling), and well suited for delivering a message to a large popular audience, as Gerson had found in the previous century. The small size of the booklets allowed printers to fit them in between larger jobs. Printers would even commission new booklets to be written to fill in short gaps in their production schedule of larger works – "an edition could be out on the streets and with its readers within a few days of Luther delivering the text to the printer."[32] Pettegree notes that a crucial element in Luther's success with the printers was his practice, as a profitable author, of spreading his work around smaller print shops to avoid conflict and maintain good relationships with the industry.[33] Luther was such a profitable author that "printers competed with each other to see who could quickly rush to market a new work by 'Martin Luther, Augustinian' or, as his fame grew, simply 'M.L.A.'"[34]

Because shipping and transport of materials were more expensive than reprinting, and because there were at this stage no copyright restrictions, it was common for printers in different towns simply to set and print their own editions of pamphlets.

Most publications were simply unadorned text, but many also carried visual propaganda. Scribner's analysis of woodcuts and engravings used in Reformation printed material shows that pictorial representations of Luther as a monk, doctor, or man of the Bible established him positively in people's minds well before they had read his writings. His opponents, on the other hand, were caricatured in derogatory woodcuts.[35]

There was, therefore, congruence between the medium Luther was using and the message he was arguing. His printed material combined media form and style with the content of the message. As Edwards has noted,

> Not only did the printing press broadcast the attack on traditional authorities to a broader audience and with greater rapidity than had ever been possible before, it itself embodied the subversive message it conveyed.... These pamphlets were in some sense what they contained: an address to the laity to become involved in an unprecedented way in their own religious destiny.[36]

The other element of media use begun by Luther and followed through by other Reformers was the linking of print with oral communication. Most people learned of the Evangelical message from oral sources such as sermons or conversation informed by disseminated printed material. Pamphlets of the early Reformation are replete with suggestions that the reader share his reading with the illiterate. Luther wrote in a way that his texts would read aloud well to facilitate this. Although there had been earlier instances where printing had been utilized to build public opinion, the sheer volume of publications has led Edwards to name it the first mass propaganda campaign.[37]

In the early years of the Reformation, Catholic responses to Luther's challenges were ineffectual. Not only were they fewer in number, but also they were written predominantly in Latin and therefore available only to a fairly limited audience. From 1518 to 1544, there was a total of only 154 Catholic works in German in the market, compared to 765 German works of Luther alone.[38] His German works were also translated quickly into other vernaculars – within his lifetime, eighty of his works were translated into Dutch.[39]

Luther's media use presented his Catholic critics with a dilemma. In order to counter Luther effectively, they had to do so where he was having greatest impact: in the market, in the vernacular. Not to reply was to leave Luther unchallenged. Yet to do so undermined the grounds on which the Catholic Church held its authority and power: that church leaders were the proper determiners of religious truth, not laypeople; that Latin, not the vernaculars, was the proper language of Christian discourse; and that the proper site for religious debate was within the church, not the marketplace.

The efforts by some Catholic apologists to counter Luther and other reformers in the early years failed to gain any support from the Catholic hierarchy. The hierarchy's primary response was to utilize their traditional power of position and authority by attempting to censor Luther and prevent the circulation of his alternative views. The success of such a response was limited. Condemning Luther and banning his publications were no match for the popular demand for his writings, the ready accessibility of their contents and form, and the commercial interests of the printers, traders, and smugglers in promoting and distributing him. The ban on his writings had the opposite effect of disadvantaging Catholic printers in the marketplace. In 1524 the Leipzig City Council petitioned their Catholic duke on behalf of the printers of the town to lift the ban on printing Lutheran materials because the ban was undermining their businesses. Luther's bestselling writings were being imported or smuggled in and purchased by people anyway, but the local printers weren't allowed to print and sell them. All that was permitted were Catholic treatises, which they had in abundance "but were desired by no one and cannot even be given away."[40]

It wasn't until the second half of the sixteenth century that a more determined effort was made in Germany and other countries in Europe to counter the effects of Protestant propaganda and political action. By that stage, however, the cat was well and truly out of the bag, and one of the major effects of the Lutheran Reformation was well underway: the breaking of the monopoly of the Catholic Church over the language of faith and the establishment of vernacular Protestant versions of Christianity in a number of European countries.

John Calvin

The reception of Luther's theological challenge and his reform proposals, and the support and protection given to them by political leaders, sparked a wave of alternative reform sects across Europe. One of those was that of the French reformer John (or Jean) Calvin.

Calvin was only eight years old when Luther pinned his theses of protest on the door of Wittenberg cathedral. Born in Noyon in Picardy, France, he is widely viewed as humanist in his intellectual roots. He studied the liberal arts in Latin at the University of Paris before undertaking studies in law at the University of Orléans and after that in Greek and Hebrew. Although tonsured at the age of twelve, he was never ordained. Sometime between 1532 and 1534, Calvin experienced what he called a "sudden conversion" in which he felt God's will must be obeyed. In 1536 he wrote the first edition of his major work, *Institutes of the Christian Religion*, the earliest systematic statement of the Reformed view of Christian doctrine and the Christian life.[41] His theology is a theology of God's sovereignty rather than God's love. Although the *Institutes* expanded in later editions, it did not change in substance. As the Christian historian Phillip Schaff has observed, "His *Institutes* came like Minerva in full panoply out of the head of Jupiter."[42]

After travelling in various parts of Europe in 1536, Calvin landed "accidentally" in Geneva, where he was first a lecturer on the Bible and then became one of the city's preachers. Opposition to some of his ideas led to his banishment by the city council in 1538. After a series of political struggles, the party that was favorable to Calvin returned to power and Calvin was invited back to the city. He returned in 1541, his re-invitation placing him in a position of significant power. He remained until his death in 1564.

Calvin's influence on the second generation of the Reformation was extensive, earning him the evaluation of some as being "the only international reformer."[43] The application of his reformed ideas were worked out in response to a number of pressing practical issues in Geneva. Along with what is reported as widespread immorality,[44] there were political instability and insufficient time for the newly reformed Christian community to establish a new organizational structure.

Calvin was placed on two committees to draft regulations for Geneva's church and to draft a secular constitution for the republic.[45] This gave him the chance to define a distinctively Protestant church–state working relationship. For the church, a Presbyterian model was devised, with four orders of ministry: pastors, doctors or educators, elders, and deacons. Authority for the church was vested in an assembly or company of pastors. For the city, a model was implemented in which the elected secular authority met with the company of pastors in a shared responsibility for social order and morality. The models Calvin framed became determinative for Reformed churches in different countries.

Calvin was a prodigious writer, the most widely published author in French of the Reformation, almost doubling the output of the next closest French writer of the time, the Paris Dominican theologian Pierre Doré.[46] His writings assembled in the early twentieth-century collection *Corpus Reformatorum* comprised fifty-nine volumes.

His writing covered five main genres: theology, bible commentaries, sermons, polemical writings, and letters. In theology, he established and distinguished the Reformed position on most of the fundamentals of belief: the Lord's Supper, the sacraments, worship and liturgy, church order, the Trinity, free will and predestination, and confessions of faith. The *Institutes of the Christian Religion* expanded from six chapters in the first edition, published in 1536, to eighty chapters in four books in the last revision of 1559. To assist in navigating the eighty chapters, Calvin provided a hundred aphorisms, or summaries of the key theological precepts of the work.[47]

Although not ordained, as a "doctor" of the church Calvin preached in Geneva on most days of the week and twice on Sundays, extemporaneously working his way systematically through exposition of biblical books. His preaching, according to reports, was consistently engaging and relevant, even though as the face and voice of authority in the city he frequently admonished, cajoled, and threatened the people of Geneva into submission.[48] In 1549 the deacons of the church appointed stenographers to record his sermons, and in the fifteen years till his death over 2,000 sermons were recorded.[49] New manuscripts of his sermons are still occasionally being uncovered in church archives.[50]

Although most comfortable writing in Latin, Calvin also wrote and translated his Latin works into French. In doing so he worked to make the language deliver the coherence, structure, and precision he required. Higman attributes to him invention of the short sentence in French:

> Each sentence represents no more than two or three subordinate clauses ... linked by a conjunction or adverb to the preceding sentence, and the reader is thus guided step by step through the argument.[51]

Calvin's influence has been extensive. In his work on church order, he molded the fundamental organizational and disciplinary shape of Protestant churches internationally. His *Ecclesiastical Ordinances* of 1541 became the model for churches within the Reformed tradition locally and within countries such as Scotland and the Netherlands. His theology was the basis for Reformed churches across Europe and dominant in the theology of the English Protestant churches of the Elizabethan period and through the English Puritans to the United States. The twentieth-century sociologist Max Weber attributes to Calvin's theology of predestination, his views on work, and the austerity of the Christian life as laying the foundation of the Protestant work ethic and the rise of western capitalism. The model of church–state relationships established in Geneva and reproduced in other countries has been credited as influencing the shape of secular democracies.

Two other influences on Christianity should be noted. One is the rigidity and narrowness with which Calvin framed the obligations and character of a Christian lifestyle, and the authoritarianism with which he and his ministers implemented them. While there are Reformed adulations of Calvin as "a quiet, sensitive man [who] said little about his inner life [but] was content to trace God's hand controlling him,"[52] a more considered estimation needs to address also the destructiveness of his ideas and influence. Calvin used his largely unchallengeable authority to justify domination and the use of violence to institute a form of Christianity that has become known for its repression and lack of joy. In his governance of Geneva, prohibitive and coercive laws were introduced that governed almost every aspect of life, including dress, reading material, the number of dishes to be eaten at meals, and names given to children. Attendance at worship was tracked, and the reporting of breaches was compulsory. Women, deemed by Calvin as "only an accessory" and "created for the sake of men," were required to direct their whole attention toward men's interests.[53] Punishments for offenses ranged from private admonition to public admonition or referral to the Council for more severe punishment. The death penalty and torture were applied for actions deemed to be heresy, idolatry, blasphemy, adultery, or insubordination.

Between 1542 and 1546, fifty-eight judgments of death were passed and seventy-five banishments. No exceptions were made for rank, class, or age – a girl was beheaded for striking her parents in contravention of the Fifth Commandment.[54]

Bouwsma attributes much of this to an innate anxiety in Calvin that expressed itself in a distrust of the world and human nature. Calvin often referred to sin not only in terms of good and evil but also in terms of order and disorder.[55] He justified his actions theologically as honoring and implementing the will of God.

> There is no question here of man's authority; it is God who speaks, and it is clear what law He would have kept in the Church even to the end of the world. Wherefore does he demand of us so extreme severity if not to show us that due honor is not paid Him so long as we set not His service above every human consideration, so that we spare not kin nor blood of any.[56]

A second major consequence, not just of Calvin's actions but of the Reformation in general, was the reframing of Christian unity into a Protestant concept of "confessionalization," one in which Christian groups established their difference and identity within the growing pluralism of Christian opinions by the definition of confessions or summary statements of faith. As the Reformation developed, a plethora of national or denominational confessions of faith were drawn up, duly printed, and circulated to give their followers a sense of identity in a forest of faiths: the Augsburg Confession (Lutheran, 1530), the Scottish Confession of faith (1560), the Belgic Confession of Faith (Netherlands and Belgium, 1561), the Heidelberg Catechism (German, 1563), the Thirty-Nine Articles of Religion (English, 1571), the Irish Articles of Religion (1615), and the Westminster Confession (English, 1646). They reflect what Higman describes as a shift in Protestantism from a devotional appropriation of Christianity to an intellectual one that appeals to the understanding rather than to the heart.[57]

Reworking the Bible

Although vernacular versions of the Bible were being printed before Luther, the Reformation emphasis on individuals interpreting the written text for themselves increased the urgency of getting accurate and authorized scholarly translations of the Christian scriptures to people in their own language. The first of the new versions was Luther's German New Testament in 1522, followed by progressive translations of the Old Testament and the first complete Luther Bible in 1534. These were followed in short order by New Testaments or complete bibles in French, Dutch, Italian, Spanish, Swedish, and Danish.

An overarching aim of Protestant bible production was to make the language of the translation accessible in an approved translation for a more general audience. In a number of situations, this provoked the development of largely oral vernacular languages into more literary forms. Blum describes Luther's German Bible as "a literary event of the first magnitude, for it is the first work of art in German prose."[58] The King James Bible, or Authorized Version, produced in England in 1611, was the work of fifty-four translators, most of whom were scholars. Although initially criticized for the unnaturalness of its language, in time it came to be appreciated for what was seen as "the inherent sublimity and beauty" of its prose.[59]

Protestant vernacular bibles were generally very successful for the printers. Luther's German New Testament became a sixteenth-century "bestseller." Its first, unusually large printing of between three and five thousand copies sold out immediately, despite its relatively high price. Approximately forty-three distinct editions appeared in forty months, including cheaper quarto and octavo editions totaling approximately eighty-six thousand copies.

The growing availability of the vernacular medium resulted in changes in how the Bible was received and consumed, shifting significantly the long-standing Catholic view of church clergy being the locus of spiritual authority and biblical understanding. No longer was the Bible read just in church, supervised by the clergy. Public readings took place in small congregations, families engaged in private readings, and, as literacy spread, individuals read alone.

The problem with putting such a complex set of texts as the Christian scriptures into the hands of new readers, however, was to ensure that the conclusions they drew from it were in agreement with denominational perspectives. Although an emphasis in Protestant bible reading was placed on the "plain sense" of the text, it became apparent that it was possible for people to gain a variety of plain senses from individual reading. This led to a number of hermeneutic aids being produced to assist readers in understanding the text the way Protestant church authorities wanted them to understand it. These aids – vernacular bible commentaries, devotional guides, study guides, cross-referencing aids, and concordances – became a major product of Reformation printing.

At times these aids were included in the biblical texts themselves. Luther's German translation of the New Testament, for example, includes introductions to each book (including an eleven-page foreword to Romans), marginal glosses, polemical illustrations, and interpretive paragraphing. He also illustrated his position and his antipapal message in twenty-one large full-page woodcuts. In total Luther's additions came to 298 pages, compared to the 401 pages of scriptural text.

Tyndale's English translation likewise included numerous prefaces to various books and marginal notes, including some that were strongly critical of the Catholic Church. In the margin of Exodus 32:5–7, where the people are told not to bring any more offerings for the building of the tabernacle because they have offered enough, Tyndale wrote, "When will the Pope say "Hoo! [Hold!] and forbid an offering for the building of St. Peter's Church?"[60] Not surprisingly, Tyndale was arrested by a Catholic monarch when he left England and, after a period of imprisonment, was strangled and burned to death in Brussels in 1536.

Although widely critical of the Roman Catholic Church's elevation of tradition above scripture as a source of faith, in the extensive directions and guides given to Protestants, we see a similar development and interposition of tradition over the text, albeit in printed materials.

The changing sensory landscape

The Reformation was a profound cultural and religious change. For those influenced by it, it involved stepping out into the unknown of the religious world, adopting a religious innovation, in many cases cutting oneself off from friends and communities, and facing potential persecution and death. While the new ideas of the Reformation are often put forward as the major influence, passions were also stirred through the variety of sensory experiences engaged.

One of those was preaching. The Reformation inherited a medieval experience of preaching as an engaging public event, and in the urban areas in particular people attended preaching events with an anticipation of performance. Good preachers could also be stimulators of tourism, and some towns would spend city funds to hire good preachers, particularly during the principal preaching season of Lent.[61]

The key Reformation leaders were active preachers, and their sermons largely biblical in focus. From 1517 to 1526, almost 40 percent of Luther's published works were sermons.[62] Despite difficult health, John Calvin preached in his central Geneva church on most days of the week and twice on Sundays. The sermon was generally the longest single element of the service, and being an effective preacher in style, voice capacity, and endurance was commonly a requirement for promotion to a larger or more central church.[63]

The centrality of preaching in Reformed practice was reinforced by the restructuring of church and worship spaces. Reformed church architecture was plainer, stripped of images and statues and often with clear glass in the windows. Side altars were removed so that people were not involved in a range of activities at different places in the church. Without images or material artifacts for distraction, the central focus of the church was the pulpit, which replaced the altar at the front and center of the church, and the Bible, which was often displayed in a central location in the front of the church.

As time progressed, pulpits became larger and more ornate, emphasizing the primacy of the preached word.

The Reformation also brought a revisiting of Christianity's understanding of the visual and material, with Reformed Christianity in particular introducing a much more austere, even ascetic attitude toward the visual and material. Differences in attitudes toward the visual and material reflect similar arguments and disagreements as those of the iconoclastic disputes of Eastern Christianity centuries earlier.

The cultural heritage of Protestantism was that of medieval Catholicism, one rich in visual imagery and material artifacts. As Aston notes, these visual and material religious cultures thrived because they gave people physical access to the immaterial ideas and virtual realities of Christianity:

> Images multiplied because they were popular. Ordinary people depended on them and loved them. The huge growth of imagery, was in large part spontaneous and the result of proliferating popular devotions. ... By the fifteenth century there was no part of a church building – walls, capitals, bosses, gables, windows – which was not ripe for artistic enrichment. ... This multiplication of imagery extended far beyond the walls of consecrated buildings...there was a great range of religious imagery, portable and otherwise, to be found in a variety of secular and domestic settings, extending from crucifixes at country crossroads and refined paintings and statuary in the palaces of rich merchants, to the small statuettes, pilgrim mementoes, and single-sheet depictions of saints to be found in the humbler dwellings and rougher hands of poor people.[64]

Calvinist Reformed Christianity was strongly antagonistic to this visual and material practice because of moral concerns for its perceived sensuality and decadence and its media difference from the perceived truths of the logical language of faith found in the written and spoken word. Luther was more moderate in his views, seeing value in visual artifacts as long as they weren't worshipped. Calvin, however, proscribed the use of images as mediators of the divine on the grounds that material images were insulting to and unworthy of God. Although he didn't endorse iconoclasm (it was too untidy for his liking), there was extensive destruction of religious art in many of the communities and countries that aligned themselves with Calvinism. This was most extensive in parts of Germany, Switzerland, the Netherlands, England, and Scotland. In England in the mid-seventeenth century, under Puritan political rule, 95–99 percent of all religious art was destroyed. In Scotland, less than 1 percent survived.[65]

The rigor and passion with which this Protestant iconoclasm were pursued is best grasped through an entry in the journal of William Dowsing, commissioned by a parliamentary ordinance in 1643 to travel around removing "various items of superstition from churches." His account describes his work in the church at Gorleston.

Twenty brazen superstitious inscriptions...broke twelve apostles carved in wood and cherubims, and a lamb with a cross ... four superstitious inscriptions in brass ...broke in pieces the railes, and broke down twenty-two popish pictures of angels and saints ...we did deface the font and a cross on the font ... took up a brass inscription there ...took up thirteen superstitious brasses. Ordered Moses with his rod and Aaron with his mitre to be taken down. Ordered eighteen angels off the roof, and cherubims to be taken down, and nineteen pictures on the windows. The organ I brake; and we brake seven popish pictures in the chancel window ...ordered the steps to be levelled by the parson. ... I gave orders to break in pieces the carved work, which I have seen done. There were six superstitious pictures, one crucifix, and the Virgin Mary with the infant Jesus in her arms, and Christ lying in a manger ...eighteen Jesuses written in capital letters, which we gave orders to do out. A picture of St. George, and many others ... divers pictures in the windows, which we could not reach, neither would they help us to raise ladders, so we left a warrant with the constable ... brake down a pot of holy water, St. Andrew with his cross, and St. Catherine with her wheel ... we brake a holy water font in the chancel. We rent to pieces a hod and surplices ... Peter pictured with his heel upwards, and John Baptist, and twenty more superstitious pictures, which we brake. ... In Bacon's aisle, twelve superstitious pictures of angels and crosses, and a holy water font, and brasses with superstitious inscriptions. And in the cross alley we took up brazen figures and inscriptions ... brake down a cross on the steeple, and three stone crosses in the chancel, and a stone cross in the porch.[66]

Such thoroughgoing destruction reflects the Reformers' view that such eradication was necessary for the rebuilding of a renewed system of faith to replace that of corrupted Catholicism. In that respect, the methods used in iconoclasm are instructive. Whitewashing images was one. Fire was another. Hundreds of wooden images and statues were burned in what Archbishop Cranmer called "jolly musters" – "a new kind of spectacle to replace the Catholic ceremonies of old."[67]

This rejection of the visual was selective, however. Much of the Lutheran propaganda utilized visual woodcuts in their publications, which portrayed people, narrative scenes, and elaborate title page decoration. Luther's endorsement and use of the arts led to a significant rise in creativity in the visual arts, sculpting, and woodcarving. Calvin and Zwingli used prints of biblical scenes in their publications. Paintings continued in many Protestant countries, therefore, albeit it in a different form, with paintings of biblical scenes replacing those of saints or allegories associated with Catholicism. Both England and the Netherlands adopted the Renaissance tradition of issuing commemorative medals to mark occasions and to reflect their religious identity. Another form of visual expression was "Godly tables," charts of texts painted onto walls or wall hangings – a painted listing of the Ten Commandments on the front wall was a common visual presence in Reformed churches.[68]

This contested relationship between visual, material, and textual mediations of Christian faith during the Reformation period left a legacy that would be carried into and worked out through the modern period. Aston calls it "a sediment of destructiveness" that retarded a life-affirming approach to living and creative expression that would express itself in subsequent destructive acts such as the religious wars, and the pathological search for witches and women whose social thinking and greater knowledge of practical arts such as healing stood outside the understanding and logic of the male leaders.[69] Besançon argues that Calvin's rejection of use of the visual in religious practice and his view of the imagination as "a forger of ideals" removed the imaginative from the realm of religious faith and laid the basis for the secularization of art and the artist.[70]

The other contention of the Reformers was with the vibrant and lively popular culture of Catholic Christianity, which was more oral, ritualistic, and sensory in its faith activities. Folk stories, ballads, songs, legends, and proverbs were primary sources of practical knowledge of the world, ethics, codes of conduct, and collective wisdom. Symbolically charged communal performances, gestures, theatre performance, patterns of speech, parodies, insults, and even ritualized protest and rebellion were stock elements. Craft guilds had their own rituals of speech and action. These were integrated with the rhythms of the liturgical year in saints' feast days, ecclesiastical holidays, Sundays, and popular festivals such as May Day, Midsummer, and Carnival. Festivals provided opportunities not only for celebration and recreation, including dancing, gambling, and sports, but also as circuit breakers for the effects of domination and subordination.

The "carnal profanity" of many of these popular culture practices and their Catholic entanglement made them problematic for the Protestant Reformers, particularly the Calvinists, and where the Calvinists were in positions of political control, the practices were progressively eliminated. The sensory impact was marked.

> In the place of recreation and its attendant disorder and mischief, reformers stressed sobriety, decency and order as the essential marks of godliness for the individual, the community and the state ... strict and decorous Sabbath-observance became a benchmark.... The reformers saw little distinction between orthodox pre-Reformation religion and its popular variants: all had to be reformed.[71]

Luther was not as absolute in his rejection of such popular practices. Luther set some of his hymns to secular music to encourage their being sung in the home and in taverns. Many of the woodcuts used in Luther's publications gained their effectiveness from their carnivalesque inversion, including the use of sexual imagery and language and scatological content to lampoon and mock the pope and Catholic clergy.[72] An obvious one, from one of Luther's tracts, is that of peasants defecating in the pope's inverted tiara, as seen in Figure 10.1.

Figure 10.1 *The Pope Is Adored as an Earthly God*, by Lucas Cranach the Elder, in the 1545 pamphlet of Luther's *Depiction of the Papacy*. Source: © Germanisches Nationalmuseum. Photo by Monica Runge.

Despite efforts to remove them, popular Protestantism also began to develop its own "magical" traditions. Objects such as bibles, hymnbooks, catechisms, and other religious books took on an aura of sacredness and were used for magical purposes such as divination, healing, or protection. The artifact and traditions of the increasingly popular family bible served to encase the family in spiritual significance, including the writing of the names and birth and death details of family members in a section at the front of the Bible, to be passed down from generation to generation. The recognition and honoring of Protestant martyrs through the laying of wreaths also began to reflect similar characteristics to the Catholic cult of the saints. Johnston sees the continuation of these popular practices within Protestantism, and resistance to them among the reforming elite, as creating a divergence of cultural outlook between the elite and popular classes, a divergence that would become one of the lasting legacies of the Reformation in the modern world.[73]

Another sensory feature of the Reformation was its transformation of Christian sound, particularly in communal singing. In place of the movement, diversity, and noise of a medieval Catholic church – the mass being celebrated at the main altar, confessions being heard, and other activities taking place at the side altars, all simultaneously – the sounds of Protestant ritual were more ordered and progressive, with more discrete separation of the sounds of preaching, congregational prayers, reading, and singing.

Pettegree highlights the origins and significance of Protestant singing:

> The Protestant tradition of communal singing drew on a deep love of song in medieval sociability, and at the same time articulated one of the core principles of the Reformation: that the people should be animated by an active, living faith. The leading reformers eagerly embraced the practice of singing as a primary expression of a lively commitment to an active religion.[74]

Singing also served a pedagogic role. Protestant hymns were a primary medium for carrying core beliefs, hopes, and aspirations, and the energy and needs generated by the movement stimulated a quick creative output of musical works in the vernacular. Luther was a significant composer of new songs himself, conceptualizing them as an alternative to the secular singing within the wider culture. His desire to write songs that people were able to sing in church, at home, and in the streets led to innovations in song form, among them the chorale, such as Luther's most well-known "A Mighty Fortress Is Our God," a song in stanzas set to music similar to secular songs that people were singing.[75] The first collection of Luther's hymns was published in 1524, just seven years after the start of the Reformation. In its introduction, Luther identified it as "Something to wean [the young] away from love ballads and carnal songs and to teach them something of value in their lives."[76] Publication of the hymns was also a profitable market for both printers and sellers, including street peddlers.

Part of the success of the new hymns lay in their intertextuality. The adoption of popular tunes for the singing of new content and the amendment of traditional content overlaid new meaning on traditional thought and practice. There were even collections of Protestant satirical songs focused on Catholicism.[77]

Other reformers adopted different approaches and styles. In Zurich, Zwingli believed music had no part in Christian worship and banned it from all services.[78] The Church of England, although strongly Reformed in its theology, retained a Catholic style of liturgy with congregational and choral singing. A distinctive musical form was the anthem, a choral piece often based on a scriptural verse sung after the collects.

In Calvinist churches, congregational singing was instigated, with a strong focus on content to protect against the potentially distracting effects of emotion stirred by the music. The primary genre of singing in Geneva and the Reformed tradition were the Psalms of David, which Calvin saw as representing the highest form of spirituality. These were arranged and set to music metrically for singing not only in church but also at home and in the fields. Calvin required that in church they be sung in unison in order to focus attention on the content, although he allowed them to be sung in harmony outside church.

The metrification of all 150 psalms was completed in 1562, using 128 different melodies written in 110 metrical patterns.[79] Printing of the psalms was extremely difficult because of the complexity of the project and the typesetting required to ensure that the notes, words, and score were accurately aligned. So highly was singing of the Psalms considered that the accuracy of their printing was rigidly enforced by magistrates and ministers, as illustrated in the following.

> When one musically literate printer spied a note that had slid down from its stave and silently corrected the error for a new edition he was reported and imprisoned for twenty-four hours. The symbolic point was clear: not only the words of Scripture, but also the translation and the appointed melodies, were regarded as having near canonical status. In this way they were appropriated to the Gospel principle of the "pure word of Scripture."[80]

The singing of the Psalms both within and outside of worship became a central part of Calvinist spirituality and identity. Reformed martyrs sang the Psalms while dying at the stake, Huguenot armies sang the Psalms when moving into battle during the French wars of religion (1562–1598), and refugees arriving in Geneva reported a great sense of joy and freedom at being able to sing the Psalms freely and publicly.[81]

The traditions of Protestant music had a number of lasting effects on western culture. The new emphasis on congregational participation produced in time a musically cultured population and traditions of domestic singing far wider than those of the pre-Reformation medieval period, when much of the music was professionally produced and performed. The wider use of the vernacular in music making also supported the broader rise of national linguistic cultures and traditions, contributing to a widening of musical culture whose fruits include popular musical culture of today.[82]

Catholic responses

The responses of the Catholic Church to the Protestant reform movements have often been titled the Counter-Reformation. This term has been challenged in recent decades on the basis that long before the Lutheran Reformation, there were reform movements within the Catholic Church also seeking to address some of the same issues. Scholars suggest alternative ways of describing the Catholic responses, such as the Catholic Reform[83] or, more recently, Catholic Confessionalization, a wider process of defining Catholic distinctives against alternative Christian viewpoints and the emerging secular consciousness.[84] Although there had been previous efforts at reform within the Roman Catholic Church, the Lutheran and Calvinist Reformations gave the Roman Catholic Church an added impetus to address issues that had long been recognized as undermining its effectiveness and integrity, such as moral laxity among the clergy, damaging political alliances, simony or the selling of ecclesiastical offices, the lack of clergy education, the selling of indulgences, and a growing desire among people for a more effective devotion or spirituality. The Protestant successes provided the shock for the papacy to act on these issues. Within seventeen years, the Catholic Church had lost its power in England, Denmark, Scotland, Sweden, Switzerland, and half of Germany and France, and the Netherlands and parts of Italy were unsettled.

One of those actions was a calling of the Council of Trent, a council of bishops that met in twenty-five sessions over three periods between 1534 and 1563. As well as defining a number of theological issues that had been challenged by the Protestants, the council addressed some of the organizational, moral, and pastoral issues that had been the focus of the various reformers, and a new attitude of moral rectitude was instigated. Bishops and clergy were required to live within their parishes and dioceses and give greater attention to pastoral work, preaching and the public interpretation of scripture. New seminaries for the education of clergy were projected. Abuses of wealth and power were addressed. Provisions for the moral supervision of clergy were made. Many of the abuses of the Papacy were identified, leading to a succession of future popes who were more disciplined, earnest in their faith, and "strenuously Catholic." The imperative of mission in a quickly expanding world was emphasized.

As a result, by 1565 Catholic earnestness had been revived, and there was a stronger resolve in its opposition to Protestantism, a recovery of some of the areas that had been taken over by Protestantism, and an active extension of Catholicism into the new worlds being opened up by European exploration.

The council also addressed the impact of the growth of printing and publishing. In its fourth session, the council began to define and frame regulations for the supervision and control of the printing press, "the operations of which as now uncontrolled tend to pernicious license and injury to the faith of the community and to the authority of the Church."[85] The outcome of its deliberations was *The Tridentine Index* – the *Index librorum prohibitorum* – which set out ten rules to guide printing in Catholic-dominated countries and a list of prohibited books. The *Index* was published in 1564, reprinted quickly by presses in seven European cities, and extensively republished over the next thirty years. The *Index* censored nearly three-quarters of all books being printed in Europe at that time. Pope Pius IV appointed a Congregation of the Index to update the list periodically. Catholic readers were limited largely to Catholic devotional books and the Vulgate Bible. Intending authors were required to submit their works for approval before publication, and in some Catholic countries printers couldn't get a license to print without making a profession of orthodox faith and promising to adhere to the requirements of the *Index*.

Implementation of the prohibitions of the *Index* was variously adhered to, and its success is questionable. In 1566, the Swiss theologian Josias Simmler wrote that "a new Index has been promulgated in which so many books are condemned that many Italian professors complain they will no longer be able to deliver their lectures."[86] Many Catholic printers went out of business or found themselves with unsellable stock when a new *Index* came out, whereas Protestant printers kept an eye on new editions of the *Index* to determine which books would be in demand and for which there would be no Catholic competition.[87] The *Index* and the congregation that administered it continued till 1966, when the *Index* was finally abolished.

By the middle of the century, Catholic writers also began to adapt not just their message but also their style of writing to counter the Protestants' popular appeal. Respected Catholic scholars, such as Pierre Doré in France, formed coalitions with Catholic printers to produce articulate works attacking the innovations, social divisiveness, and economic consequences of Protestantism and arguing the benefits of Catholicism in cheap, accessible editions and their own polemical tracts, including their own effective woodcuts satirizing the Protestants.[88] With these reforms, some of the advances made by early Protestantism began to be clawed back.

Ignatius of Loyola

Of particular note in the Catholic media strategy against the Protestants is the work of Ignatius (Iñigo) of Loyola, the founder of the Society of Jesus or the Jesuits. Rather than defensive protectionism, Ignatius addressed the new media culture of printing through engagement and rebuttal. The mixed media culture of his upbringing equipped him well for this multimedia activity.

Loyola was born into a Spanish military family with a long chivalric tradition and orthodox Catholic faith at a time of global changes. In the year of his birth, 1491, Pope Alexander VI managed the global expansion of Spain and Portugal by drawing a line on the world map and designating their separate areas of exploration and exploitation. In the following year, Columbus set off on his journey of exploration and discovered the Americas, and the Spanish reclaimed the remainder of Spain from the Moors after eight centuries of occupation. These early years were formative for Ignatius: "filled with reports of conquests that in one form or another were to colour his imagination for the rest of his life."[89]

Early on he learned an impressive handwriting and skills of correspondence, marks of courtesy in a chivalrous youth that he would later apply in envisioning a differently structured, decentralized religious order coordinated by the medium of letter writing. His early education took place within the king's court in Spain in the wake of the religious, literary, and artistic renaissance instigated by Queen Isabella, who along with founding the University of Alcalá encouraged the printing of books, including a flood of printed romance literature.[90] These included widely read novels of chivalry in modern Castilian translations, a genre marked by a spirit of adventure and conquest; the chivalric qualities of loyalty, courage, and courtesy; and the idealization of romantic love. Ignatius acknowledged that he became an avid reader of these books of chivalrous romance and was influenced by their worldview in his formation of the Society of Jesus. [91]

In 1521, badly injured in a battle and recuperating in his family home, he asked for more romantic chivalric novels to read. When there were none in the house, he was given two popular classics belonging to his sister-in-law: *The Life of Christ*, a four-volume work on the life of Christ with commentaries by Fathers of the Church, printed in 1502–1503; and *Lives of the Saints*, a thirteenth-century work by an Italian Dominican. Both presented Jesus within the ideals of knighthood and the saints as *caballeros de Dios*, or knights in the service of the eternal Prince, Jesus Christ.[92] A time of searching in a Dominican monastery led him to develop a set of guided visions that were to grow into what was to become one of his lasting influences, the *Spiritual Exercises*.

Working with the *Exercises* with a group of friends, Ignatius developed a vision for a society of people, structured along military and knightly lines, who would offer themselves in the service of Christ and the pope. The Society of Jesus was authorized by Pope Paul III in 1540, with Ignatius as the first general. In contrast to other religious orders, it didn't incorporate individuals into gathered, centralized, and conforming communities. Each member was formed by spiritual discipline, given work to do by his superior in line with his talents, and given significant freedom to do it.

The chief work of the society was preaching, the confessional, and education. Ignatius perceived that the cultural situation of Europe was changing: the book was ascendant, and the traditional Catholic strategy of "spectacle, images and rituals could not compete with printed books."[93] He advocated to the pope that Catholics should be taught the content of the scriptures, believing, like the Protestants, that reform would come about through studying the text.

Another lasting influence of Ignatius was in the development of education, although again it followed a different strategy. Growth in the numbers of applicants wanting to join the Society of Jesus led him in 1548 to establish a college in Rome to educate them. He devised a set curriculum for the purpose: four years in the humanities and seven more years in philosophy and theology. While what he conceived was similar to existing university practice, Ignatius added an innovation: assembling a staff of professors who were the most proficient in the world to give students from all nations the best Scholastic education available within a curriculum that grounded them in the orthodoxy of Catholicism and an environment of regular and cultivated spiritual practice.[94] In the confusion of religious ideas and debate taking place across Europe, Ignatius saw in a Catholic-grounded education the best measure and bulwark of orthodoxy.

In 1546, at the encouragement of benefactors, they accepted external students for the first time. The first college primarily for externals was established in Messina in 1548, with the Messina curriculum the first step toward the later Jesuit *Ratio Studiorum* or *Plan of Studies*.[95] Study in the humanities included literature, selected classics, and Greek. Extracurricular activities included opportunities for drama, music, and ballet, which were frequently performed outside in the town square, making Jesuit theatrical productions in many places major social and cultural events.[96]

Early on, Ignatius made two decisions about Jesuit education that would be influential on its subsequent character. One was that he would not charge fees. The second was to require boys to have had some prior training in Latin because there was insufficient staff and resources to teach the basics. Although the education was free, the Latin requirement made it difficult for the poor to find a place and Jesuit education evolved to become directed more toward the middle and upper classes. Although there were exceptions to this, it became a distinctive character of Ignatius' evangelization strategy: educating and winning the loyalty of the men who would become the civic leaders. The locating of colleges in larger cities with universities where people who exercised influence were more likely to be found was a further element of this strategy.

The schools became a major religious and cultural influence, as influential families saw in the colleges the best step for social advancement for their male children.[97] Although there were failures, by the time of Ignatius' death in 1556 there were approximately thirty-three colleges; and by 1773, when Pope Clement XIV suppressed the order, there were more than eight hundred Jesuit institutions in an international educational network unparalleled before or since.

The other enduring influence of Ignatius was a media artifact, the *Spiritual Exercises*. More than just a printed book, it was a book that was to be engaged with actively through conversation and under the direction of another person, with the focus on sorting out within a doctrinal framework the inner aspects of one's own religious faith and the wider directions of one's practical life. Caraman summarizes the *Exercises* as:

> It is in no sense a spiritual treatise, but more a genre of its own, a manual with the practical purpose of helping a man [*sic*] to save his soul and find his place in the divine plan. Even in its final revision in 1541 it is rough and rudimentary, not a book to be read but a guide to be translated into practice.... It was through his Spiritual Exercises that Ignatius influenced the course of European education and culture for two centuries and brought about a revolution in the Catholic world that is not a spent force today.[98]

NOTES

1 Briggs & Burke, 2002, p. 21.
2 Chartier, 1987, p. 3.
3 Hobbins, 2009, cited in Lerner, 2010.
4 Eisenstein, 1979.
5 Chartier, 1987, p. 6.
6 Andersson & Talbot, 1983, p. 35
7 Pettegree, 2010, p. 66.
8 Pettegree, 2013, p. 111.
9 Pettegree, 2010, p. 65ff.
10 Cited in Scribner, 1994, p. 2.
11 Pettegree, 2010, p. 58.
12 Pettegree, 2013, p. 112.
13 Burns, 1989, p. 202.
14 Green, 1994, pp. 50–54.
15 Green, 1994, pp. 9–10.
16 Chrisman, 1982, p. xx.

17 Chrisman, 1982, p. xx. The earliest was Raoul Lefèvre's courtly romance, *Recueil des historiens de Troyes*, published in Köln, Germany, in 1466. An English translation was the first book printed in English, by William Caxton in 1473–1474.
18 Chrisman, 1982, p. xxi.
19 Burns, 1989, pp. 212–213.
20 MacCulloch, 2009, p. 569.
21 Cottret, 2000, p. 94.
22 Cottret, 2000, p. 93.
23 Fifth Lateran Council, Session 10 1515.
24 Pettegree, 2013.
25 Pettegree, 2013, p. 114.
26 Luther, 1545.
27 Luther, 1518, loc. 590.
28 Grossman, 1970, p. 73.
29 Grossman, 1970, p. 73.
30 Edwards, 1994, loc. 262.
31 Edwards, 1994, loc. 501.
32 Pettegree, 2010, p. 95.
33 Pettegree, 2013, p. 114.
34 Edwards, 1994, loc.164.
35 Scribner, 1994.
36 Edwards, 1994, p. 58.
37 Edwards, 1994, loc. 128.
38 Edwards, 1994, loc. 381.
39 Pettegree, 2013, p. 116.
40 Edwards, 1994, loc. 214.
41 MacCulloch, 2009, p. 633.
42 Schaff, 1893, p. 262.
43 Walker, 1959, p. 357.
44 Schaff, 1893, p. 353. However, given Calvin's strict views on morality, the extent of the city's reported immorality has to be questioned.
45 Naphy, 2004, p. 313.
46 Higman, 1996, p. 5.
47 Calvin, 1599.
48 Naphy, 2004, p. 34.
49 Ganoczy, 2004, p. 23.
50 de Greef, 2004, p. 45.
51 Higman, 1996, pp. 27–28.
52 *Eerdmans' Handbook to the History of Christianity*, p. 380.
53 Calvin, 1992.
54 Schaff, 1893, pp. 491–492.
55 Bouwsma, 1988.
56 Cited in Shlain, 1998, p. 335.
57 Higman, 1996, pp. 18, 24.
58 Blum, p. vii.
59 Norton, 2011, p. 189. On the English Bible see also Tadmor, 2010.
60 Lane, 1994, p. 9.

61 Pettegree, 2005, p. 14.
62 Edwards, 1994, loc. 354.
63 Pettegree, 2005, p. 38. Pettegree notes one instance where a church in the Netherlands had to reject an otherwise satisfactory minister purely on the grounds that his voice was considered not robust enough to carry across the large auditorium.
64 Aston, 1988, p. 21.
65 Graham-Dixon, 1996.
66 From *The Journal of William Dowsing*. For the full quote see Aston, 1988, p. 78.
67 Graham-Dixon, 1996.
68 Pettegree, 2000, p. 485.
69 Aston, 1988, p. 17.
70 Besançon, 2000.
71 Johnston, 2000, p. 550.
72 Johnston, 2000, p. 555.
73 Johnston, 2000, p. 558.
74 Pettegree, 2005, p. 41.
75 Higman, 2000, pp. 494–495. The Lutheran tradition of the chorale would find its greatest expression in the work of Johann Sebastian Bach (1685–1750), and his Passion Chorale "O Sacred Head Once Wounded."
76 Luther's *Works*, quoted in Pettegree, 2005, p. 45.
77 Such as *Chansons des dix commandements de Dieu* by Antoine Saulnier in 1532. Cited in Pettegree, 2005, p. 67.
78 Higman, 2000, p. 495.
79 Pettegree, 2005, p. 56.
80 Pettegree, 2005, p. 58.
81 Higman, 2000, p. 499.
82 Higman, 2000, p. 503.
83 First suggested by Hubert Judin in 1946 (Bireley, 1999, p. 4).
84 Lotz-Heumann, 2013, pp. 35–36.
85 Cited in Putnam, 1906, p. 180.
86 Putnam, 1906, p. 196.
87 Burns, 1989, p. 259.
88 Pettegree, 2013, p. 119.
89 Caraman, 1990, p. 7.
90 Caraman, 1990, p. 11.
91 Caraman, 1990, p. 14.
92 Caraman, 1990, p. 27.
93 Shlain, 1998, p. 336.
94 Bireley, 1999, pp. 129–130.
95 Bireley, 1999, p. 125.
96 Bireley, 1999, p. 129. In Germany and Munich, casts of hundreds performed.
97 Although the Superior General in 1617, Mutius Vitelleschi, lamented "how many come to us in order to become rich, how few in order to become better" (Bireley, 1999, p. 127).
98 Caraman, 1990, pp. 41, vii.

11

The Modern World

The legacy of the Reformation

As noted earlier, the Protestant Reformation did not occur in a vacuum, but from within a convergence of social, political, economic, and religious changes that were coalesced by the Reformation. Similarly, although printing was only one part of that convergence, as Eisenstein contends it warrants special attention because it provided the means by which a range of other changes became possible.[1]

While there were numerous micro-changes that occurred during the Reformation, a number of enduring wider consequences are of particular relevance in thinking about mediation, Christianity, and religious change. One was the shattering of the single institutional authority structure of Roman Catholic Christianity in the West, an authority that had persisted for almost nine hundred years. The increased number of alternative Christian belief systems that emerged during the Reformation diminished the capacity of the dominant Roman Catholic Church to argue that it was the sole legitimate embodiment of Christianity in the West. The unity of the Holy Roman Empire was replaced by a "confessionalization"[2] of Christianity, one in which different Christian streams differentiated themselves through doctrinal, liturgical, ethical, and social emphases expressed in formal statements of belief. These were reproduced and distributed in printed texts – confessions of faith, articles of belief, catechisms, hymn books, bible commentaries, and devotional reading material – and served to build a sense of identity among their adherents, as well as a point of differentiation by which to evangelize and pitch themselves and their version of Christianity into the market.

These groupings of Christianity are now known as denominations, like notes in a currency. In line with the connections that Anderson makes between printed media and the different imaginations of community in the

From Jesus to the Internet, Peter Horsfield © 2015 John Wiley & Sons, Ltd. Published 2015 by John Wiley & Sons, Ltd.

modern period,[3] the denominational or confessional structuring of Christianity that emerged in the post-Reformation period may be considered as the social structuring of religion appropriate to a world where print is dominant.

The competing absoluteness with which the various Christian groups held their different beliefs, and the political relationships they formed to enforce these absolutes, made religious toleration or coexistence difficult. For more than a century after the birth of the Reformation, Europe was devastated by bitter and protracted religious wars over theological truth, church authority, property and resources, spiritual practice, and political power. Conflicts in France between Catholics and Protestants, in which tens of thousands were killed, were reproduced to varying degrees in most countries of Europe, to the extent that between 1560 and 1715 Europe witnessed only thirty years of international peace.

The trauma, devastation, and impact of these shifting, religiously aligned political conflicts produced two significant cultural outcomes. One was a series of political agreements by which the different versions of Christianity could coexist, although Christian intolerance, conflict, condemnation, and killing never remained far from the surface.[4]

The other was to produce a wider cultural search for a more impartial and certain basis of knowledge on which to build society, one by which the apparent arbitrariness and differences in religious doctrines and knowledge and the fights they produced could be managed intellectually and politically. The outcome of this search was what Toulmin calls a new "cosmopolis," a new intellectual view of the world (*cosmos*) as a basis for a different ordering of society (*polis*).[5] The influence and appeal of the sixteenth- and seventeenth-century Enlightenment thinkers such as René Descartes, Francis Bacon, and Isaac Newton were not just in their new ideas but also in the hope they gave people of finding a way out of the political and theological chaos that differences in Christian opinion and the groups that formed around them were causing. The Enlightenment alternative was to focus on knowledge that could be verified through objective information available to everyone (rather than in exclusively given revelations), using methods that were subject to human reason rather than the privileged or vested interests of tradition.

Initially the intent of the early Enlightenment thinkers was neither antireligious nor to do away with Christianity, but to find a more harmonious way of being Christian citizens together. But, as their thinking developed, their empirically based investigations opened up the way for new insights and understandings of the universe and human behavior, and new scientific and technological developments began to solve many of the problems that had previously turned people toward religious faith. In time, the outlook and methodologies of scientific rationalism and a secular worldview began to challenge some of the basic outlooks and religious perspectives of the Christian worldview. Although many Christian thinkers adapted the new tools of rationalism and empirical investigation to rethink traditional Christian theological propositions and biblical interpretation, for growing numbers of the population the insights and solutions of science and the technological products rendered such Christian beliefs increasingly unnecessary.

While religious figures have frequently criticized, even railed against, the progress of secularization through the Enlightenment and the modern period, and its impact on general religious belief, it is sobering to consider that the developments of secularization in the modern period were so influential because of the potential they offered for people and societies to escape the devastation caused yet again by destructive conflicts over power and vested interests of competing Christian groups and institutions.

Catholic mission

Although Western Christianity had always been missionary in its outlook, toward the end of the fifteenth century this outlook expanded to lands beyond Europe. This expanded vision was connected with the spread of European colonization that followed technological developments that made sea travel more trustworthy, economic growth that stimulated the commercial search for new resources and profits, and the prospects of a larger world offering potential for greater political power. Colonial expansion was also motivated by a sense of Christian mission. Catherine Keller, in her translation of Columbus' *Professies*, notes,

> Columbus expected the world to end in the year 1650; he therefore took his mission as "Christ-carrier" (as he began to sign his letters after 1498) very seriously, working to bring Christianity to as many of the "unsaved" pagans of the new world as he could before the end of the world and the return of Christ.[6]

From its beginnings, therefore, modern Catholic mission was integrated practically and ideologically with political expansion, military conquest, and commercial enterprise. Such evangelization through military conquest was continuous with attitudes of the Holy Roman Empire from Charlemagne through the Crusades, that force and violence were acceptable in the spread and maintenance of Christian faith.[7] The links between mission and Crusade mentality is illustrated by the establishment of a Portuguese mission in Goa in 1510, which included the slaughter of six thousand Muslims.[8]

The other major and unforeseen impact of mission and conquest was disease. Around half of the population of the Americas died in the waves of epidemics that the Europeans brought with them. The disease also communicated a powerful message to bewildered and terrified people: "that their gods were useless and that the God of the conquerors had won."[9]

The authority to conquer and Christianize was delegated by the popes to the Catholic monarchs of Spain and Portugal. As part of the management of this international expansion, a number of Papal Bulls were issued in the fifteenth century, allocating specific areas of Africa, the Americas, and Asia variously to Spain and Portugal to reduce the political and commercial conflicts that had emerged between them.[10] Where there was local resistance to Christian invasion or a failure to recognize European authority, violence was authorized. The violence was exacerbated by the fact that many of those taking part in the conquest were traders and ex-soldiers whose primary interest was commercial and acquiring riches. The brutality used in conquest in many places was horrendous.[11]

When the first group of Dominicans arrived in Hispaniola in 1510, they denounced the treatment of indigenous Indians. Their complaint was vehemently opposed by the conquistadors, who asserted that what they were doing was a right given to them by papal decree. The dispute was referred to the Spanish monarch, who responded in 1512–1513 with the Laws of Burgos, the first systematic code to govern the conduct of settlers in the Americas, particularly in their relationships with Indians. The laws replaced the existing practice of *repartimento*, where groups of Indians were allocated to individual Spaniards for compulsory labor, with that of *encomienda,* a colonially constructed relationship of supposedly greater mutuality and protection, where Indians were bound to offer service to Spaniards in exchange for being instructed in the Christian faith.[12] There are questions about the extent to which these laws and guidelines were enforced and followed, but even when they were followed they entrenched a relationship of servitude in which the only way for the indigenous Indians to survive and prosper was to accept the dictates and Christianity of the conquerors.

The Laws of Burgos also set out the terms for the communication of faith. The primary means of evangelization were to be constructing a Catholic social and religious structure within the mission area. Participation in the ritual practices of the church and instruction in basic elements of Catholic doctrine were enforced, and artifacts or practices of indigenous religion were suppressed or destroyed. Spaniards receiving forced labor under the *encomienda* system were obliged to make Christians of them.

[They were to] ... erect a structure to be used for a church ... place an image of Our Lady with a bell with which to call the Indians to prayer ... have them cross themselves and bless themselves and together recite the Ave Maria, the Pater Noster, the Credo, and the Salve Regina ... in case any Indian should fail to come to the said church at the said time, we command that on the day following he shall not be allowed to rest during the said period ... he shall also teach them the Ten Commandments and the Seven Deadly Sins and the Articles of the Faith, that is, to those he thinks have the capacity and ability to learn them ... and have all infants baptized within a week of their birth ... and, if the Indian should know how to confess, he shall confess him, without charging him any fee for it.[13]

One of the problems encountered in this form of communication of faith was that Indians who were evangelized during their forced labor tended to forget what they were taught when they returned to their own villages. So the Spanish king, after consultation with "several members of my council and by persons of good life, letters, and conscience (and) others who had much knowledge and conscience and experience of the affairs of the said Island," decreed that the chiefs and Indians would no longer return to their villages, but be permanently removed and resettled next to the Spaniards so they could continuously attend the Mass and divine offices, be instructed in the Catholic faith, and observe appropriate Christian behavior from their captors.[14]

Members of Catholic religious orders such as the Dominicans, Augustinians, Franciscans, and Jesuits were also involved in the work of colonial evangelization. At their best, some missioners learnt the local languages in order to better communicate with them, gathered indigenous people into Christian communities or "reductions" and put them to work, built schools and churches, and tried to protect them from being exploited, enslaved, or destroyed by European settlement.[15] Members of the orders often voiced their concerns about the brutality with which indigenous Indians were being treated and even slaughtered,[16] and many sought to model a more humane treatment. Some, such as Bartholomé de las Casas, an *encomendero*, or holder of an *encomienda* license, constantly spoke out against the system and later in his life freed his slaves and joined the Dominicans.

In such a way, Catholic Christianity spread through newly conquered countries of Central and South America, south and southeast Asia, and east, west, and central Africa. One estimate is that, by 1550, around ten million people in the Americas had been baptized as Catholic Christians, and Latin America has remained until the past few decades an overwhelmingly Catholic continent.[17]

While much is made of the "civilizing" effects and cultural advancement brought to "primitive" people through the spread of Western Christianity, it cannot be avoided that the processes of Christianizing indigenous people in the colonies took place in an explicit context of often brutal conquest and killing, economic exploitation, and enforced subordination and servitude. In a climate of European perceptions of the superiority of their cultures, the association of Christianization with political colonization and commercial expansion destroyed ancient indigenous cultures and religions, broke down traditional social order, brought diseases, separated families and communities, established artificial national boundaries that are still being disputed, and led to the insidious western slave trade that lasted for more than three centuries. For whatever advances becoming Christianized brought, enormous and permanent human damage was inflicted. It's estimated that by the turn of the nineteenth century, indigenous populations in the western hemisphere were a tenth of what they had been three centuries before.[18]

The impact of print

As the modern era progressed, printing and applications of printed writing became widespread and firmly embedded into the communication webs of western cultures, dovetailing with other developments such as increasing wealth, political stability, improvement in roads and transport, and travel. Increasing applications of printing were made in such things as news reporting and the mass production of newspapers, government and colonial administration, business, correspondence, education, entertainment, and religion. One estimate is that about 55 million books were produced in eighteenth-century England alone.[19]

The sheer volume of this production, circulation, and application produced changes in cultural practice and a new social environment within which Christianity and Christians were forced to rethink their faith.

Printing changed the economic basis on which the generation and distribution of social ideas were to operate. As printing expanded, ideas began to develop a commercial value. As we noted in chapter 10, the promotion of Luther's ideas by printers and peddlers was not just based on their ideological support for him, but also because his ideas were sellable and made them money. In development of their businesses, printers sought out ways to exploit the potential of this new market. Pallares-Burke cites an example of a publisher in eighteenth-century France who sent a man on a horse for five months to make contact with booksellers, visiting virtually every bookstore in southern and central France to find out what people were reading, and identify what the literary demand was.[20]

In this changed context, leaders of Christian institutions that previously held a dominant position in the generation and production of ideas within their societies found themselves having to contend with not just the different views of their Christian competitors but also competitive nonreligious ideas being generated by entrepreneurs for commercial purposes.

Producing ideas that were sellable began to provide a source of income by which a person could contribute to the circulation of ideas without the need for patronage or the support of an institution. The concept of the author as "author" emerged at this time as part of the move to stabilize supply and demand and economic management in the new cultural phenomenon of mass communication. When the commercial value of an author's name began to be recognized, a number of social processes followed to protect it.

One was the concept of copyright, which gave authors or publishers legal ownership of their named writings, slowly replacing the concept that ideas belonged to the community at large.[21] In line with the use of "trade marks" in marketing mass-produced goods, the trademarking of writings with an author's name similarly enhanced and stabilized their value in the marketplace.

Recognized authors began to develop cultural status as celebrities, a special kind of person, a moral exemplar or embodiment of an imagined national character;[22] this, in its turn, reinforced their commercial value. Samuel Johnson is emblematic of this development, on one occasion refusing an invitation from King George III to write for him on the grounds that "he was writing for a print-created reading public and not for the court." Ong has noted Johnson's significance in this regard:

> Johnson was a product of the new age, in many ways its most typical as well as its most distinguished product: a person who devoted his life to writing in order to have his works printed and thereby to make his living.[23]

Children were named after authors, homes were decorated with scenes from their novels, and public statues were erected in their honor, even in the far-distant British colonies.[24] William Hughes, later the Australian prime minister, in a speech in 1911 attributed to Charles Dickens the shaping of the Australian character and Australian democracy, through men "who imbibed his hatred of shams and humbugs of all sorts, and who wanted freer and better conditions."[25]

The decreasing costs of publishing, resulting from growth in the industry and precedents set in earlier cheap versions of religious material, led to wider public access to printed materials, which in turn stimulated a rise in general literacy and a broadening of the market for a wider variety of reading materials. In the competition for those growing audiences, books became more oriented toward the reader, with more popular content and more pleasing designs that served the reader's convenience. This broadened the base of participation in the production and consumption of social ideas away from just the elite.

This was most apparent in the growth of printed news across the sixteenth to eighteenth centuries, gradually displacing previous news sources such as the local church, newsmongers, and town crier. This wider dissemination of news and popular reading laid the basis for what Anderson calls "a new imagination of community,"[26] with wider public awareness and participation in social and political life being key factors in changing the nature of government from that of royalty and aristocracy to social democracies. The essential place of printed news within new democracies was politically embedded through the new social contracts of freedom of speech and freedom of the press, most clearly enunciated in the American Declaration of Independence.

The mass production of texts for heterogeneous audiences generated the need for greater standardization and accuracy, particularly in spelling, pronunciation, grammar, and textual accuracy. Publications such as dictionaries, grammar books, and books of etiquette were written to define and facilitate these new norms. In time, the norms applying to print discourse came to affect all writing and even speaking, with "proper" ways of writing, and speaking in ways that reflected knowledge of those writing norms, being identified as the sign of a literate and cultured person. Johnson's English Dictionary, which was instigated by publishers and published in 1755, was a significant marker in this process of standardizing and fixing norms of spelling and meaning.

Many of these standards enshrined discrimination and exclusivity into language structurally. In compiling his dictionary of proper spelling, Johnson consulted only printed works – oral usages and spellings of oral usages were not considered.[27] A further example is the influential grammar book, Richard Kirkby's *Eighty-Eight Grammatical Rules*. First published in 1746, it argued that the word "man" should be the standard collective for all human beings because men were preeminent and represented more of humanity than women. The principle was entrenched in law by an all-male House of Parliament in Britain in 1850, which decreed "that man should be the standard form, and that by law it would encompass woman." In time, standardization became an end in itself rather than an aid to communication, a set of rules and regulations imposed on the language that one had to learn how to use if one was to be seen to be communicating properly.[28]

Enmeshed in the spread of print culture was the growth of scientific understanding and technological development. Developments in science and technology were facilitated through the sharing and spread of new thinking and new discoveries among the scientific community through printed scientific journals and publications. Their wider influence was spread through newspaper reports, popular journal reviews, and books, as well as the appearance of new technologies in public use. The regular flow of new discoveries, new inventions, and new solutions to age-old problems held a magic that reinforced the superiority of the secular empirical method as a way of knowing, one that was available to all who wanted to understand, not just to "believers" through special or sectarian revelation. In the empirical gaze, the nature of the world changed from a bounded geocentric world governed and revealed by God, to an unbounded universe discoverable through human initiatives of observation and experiment.[29]

The Christian concept of humans as created by God but enmeshed in sinful humanity was challenged by a secular humanist individualism that affirmed people as unique human beings who could delight in life here and now. A new sense of human autonomy endowed the concept of being human with a freedom to develop, to solve problems, and to create their own destiny.

This wider distribution of a secular view undermined the ability of church leaders to control the creation and dissemination of ideas as they had in the past, through asserting their social and religious authority and limiting access to alternative ideas and practices through censorship and control. The rise of a more educated, literate, and engaged class of laypeople began to challenge centralized decision making within churches at the same time that media industries were undermining the hold of religious censorship. Galileo's masterpiece in Italian, *Dialogue concerning Two Chief World Systems*, in which he addressed in a satirical fashion the two conflicting views of the world, the Ptolemaic-Scholastic and the Copernican views, was an immediate success. By the time it was banned by the Roman Catholic Church because it contradicted church doctrine, all copies had been sold and had become hot black market items.[30]

The spread and influence of printing were not without their critics and opponents. The president of the Royal Society in England expressed the view in 1807 that educating the poor and teaching them to read could be prejudicial to their morals and happiness, by leading them to despise their lot in life and thus making them insubordinate, refractory, and insolent. Some saw reading as a risk to physical health – one 1795 tract listed seventeen possible consequences of excessive reading, including "gout, hemorrhoids, apoplexy, blocking of the bowels, migraines, epilepsy and melancholy."[31]

Churches expressed concern about the effects that mass-printed materials could have on church authority and the possible spiritual effects of people reading too much, particularly fiction. The Methodist Church in the United States, toward the end of the nineteenth century, held a campaign against novel reading on the grounds that it corrupted impressionable young minds, caused mental illness, and distracted people from engaging in the more serious work of spiritual practice.[32] Similar concerns arose in Australia, where the reading of novels was criticized by one clergyman as producing an "affectation of aristocratic ideas and prejudices, a disproportionate estimate of essentials and superficials [and] lukewarmness, indifference and neglect of religious duties."[33]

It was apparent, however, that Christianity had entered a quite different social context, once again, where the assertion of inherited rights no longer worked and methods of competing with worthy opponents for attention and loyalty had to be devised. As had been done on numerous occasions in the past, groups and churches within Christianity adapted to this competitive challenge in a variety of ways. While some resisted the new by asserting Christianity's distinctive cultural character and strengthening their efforts to enlist people into it, others reframed their Christian ideas and practices into the changed standards and practices of the print-based enlightenment culture of the eighteenth and nineteenth centuries. They developed their own publishing houses and print-based educational institutions and materials, and theological education and worship practices adapted to incorporate more print-based materials. Streams of theology also developed that reframed traditional theological concepts to incorporate the new insights and perspectives of secular thought, scientific discovery, and the greater emphasis on human autonomy. A distinctive response, and one that would lay the foundations for a major development of Christianity in the twentieth century, was Evangelical Revivalism.

Evangelical Revivalism

While there have been numerous periods and movements of revival of faith at different times throughout Christianity's history, Evangelical Revivalism is noteworthy for its extensiveness, media methods, impacts, and endurance.

A number of the factors identified previously are relevant for understanding the phenomenon of Revivalism. One is the post-Reformation legacy of Christian pluralism and the introduction of choice into people's religious lives. A second is the division that had emerged between those areas and activities of life that were seen as religious in nature and those considered to be secular. In combination, these factors opened the way for people to choose not only what form of Christianity they would adhere to, but also in what ways they would be religious (or not). A third factor was the rise of manufacturing, industrialization, and colonial expansion. In England, through the social dislocation of industrialization, large portions of the population had become disenfranchised and estranged from the established parish church system of Christianity. In the American colonies, the growth of cities and expansion into the wilderness and countryside created social networks that did not fit the traditional parish model and the Puritan heritage of their founding, leading to struggles to find more appropriate forms of spiritual expression. The revivals of the eighteenth century fall into this context.

Two important figures in modern Revivalism are John Wesley (1703–1791) and George Whitefield (or Whitfield) (1714–1770). Both studied at Oxford together and were part of a group of friends that became known as the "Holy Club." Earnestly religious, the group committed themselves to read and pray together regularly, be constant in private devotion and Communion, be diligent in meeting their ethical and religious duties, and visit prisons once or twice a week. The group was widely read, and met together each evening to discuss the Bible and other sacred books, so print was an important part in the shaping of their experience and convictions. Wesley's reading was eclectic and included the Church Fathers, monastic piety, ancient liturgies, continental mystics, Byzantine traditions of spirituality, the English and Scottish divines, the Moravians and Central European Pietists, Pascal, and classics of devotional spirituality. He also took an interest in science.

In 1735, Whitefield had an experience that he later described as a "new birth":

> I was delivered from the burden that so heavily oppressed me. The spirit of mourning was taken from me, and I knew what it was truly to rejoice in God my Saviour.[34]

Wesley had a similar experience in 1738 after returning from a pastorally and personally unsuccessful mission appointment in the American colony of Georgia. On the evening of May 24, he went to a Moravian society meeting in Aldersgate Street, London. While someone was reading from Luther's *Preface to the Book of Romans*, he had an experience that he later recorded in his journal.

> About a quarter before nine, while he was describing the change which God works in the heart through faith in Christ, I felt my heart strangely warmed. I felt I did trust in Christ, Christ alone, for salvation; and an assurance was given me that He had taken away my sins, even mine, and saved me from the law of sin and death.[35]

Such peak experiences of enlightenment or moments of religious ecstasy are well known in Christianity, although they're most commonly associated with Christian mysticism, monasticism, and asceticism. Puritan spirituality also placed a strong emphasis on conversion. What is unusual about the experiences of Whitefield and Wesley, which has also been characteristic of Revivalism, is the impulse these experiences gave the two men to communicate and try to reproduce the same experience of "conversion" in others. The mass movement of revivalism developed from these experiences.

The various forms of mediation used in the Wesleyan and Whitefield revivals were crucial elements in their success. Several are noteworthy. One was an emphasis on oral communication through open-air preaching, frequently to large crowds. Whitefield was the first to venture into what was then a novelty, although it had precedents in the street preaching of Christian groups such as the Dominicans and Franciscans. In his first appointment as a curate, responses to Whitefield's emotive preaching was such that the crowds overflowed church buildings and he began preaching outside the church. He came to the realization that preaching in open fields also captured the attention of many who were estranged from formal religion. From that point, preaching to crowds in the fields and marketplaces became a characteristic of his work. With a flair for oratorical performance and drama, his voice, which was said to be capable of being heard miles away, was able to construct imagination and evoke emotional responses in large mass audiences. In the thirty-six years of his ministry, Whitefield preached an estimated eighteen thousand sermons, attracting crowds of more than thirty thousand people in Britain and more than twenty thousand in the smaller cities of the American colonies. His preaching journeys included fifteen through Scotland, three in Ireland, and seven in America, where his preaching tours in 1739–1741 are widely attributed as instigating what is called the First Great Awakening.

Wesley was equally itinerant. At first he was hesitant about preaching in the open air, but he began doing so at the invitation of Whitefield, writing in his journal:

> I could scarce reconcile myself to this strange way of preaching in the fields, of which he set me an example on Sunday; having been all my life [till very lately] so tenacious of every point relating to decency and order.[36]

Once he began doing so, however, he was relentless. From when he began in 1738 to his death fifty-three years later, he travelled 4000–5000 miles a year on horseback through England, Wales, Scotland, and Ireland, travelling sometimes seventy or eighty miles a day, commonly preaching four or five times a day, while also visiting the local Methodist societies or class meetings that had been established in the area. The face-to-face interaction with people in the street that such preaching required became part of the performance of the message and an instigation of the experiential form of revivalist religion.

While they disagreed on some aspects of their theology, and their work separated because of it, central to the message of both Whitefield and Wesley was the assertion that salvation from sin and damnation was not a lifelong process of inculcation within a church, but a decisive and generally emotionally charged moment of spiritual rebirth in which a person volitionally accepted the forgiveness of God and chose to live a new life of spiritual and moral faithfulness. The prospect of a religious faith that leveled the spiritual status of all people, did not require a record of faithful churchgoing, could be activated by a person's own decision, and was practical and experiential rather than dogmatic and intellectual was a highly marketable concept of Christianity to those who were estranged from formal religion.

The object of revivalist preaching, therefore, was not just the communication of particular religious ideas, but doing so within a constructed situation of highly charged emotion (critics frequently used the term "hysteria") in which a person is persuaded to accept the preacher's argument and make a decision "to be saved." Whitefield was highly skilled at this emotionally charged persuasive communication – one report said he could bring tears to the eyes of grown men just by the way he said "Mesopotamia." It was similar with Wesley, although he retained a strong intellectual content to his message.

Since the primary legitimizing authority of the freelance revivalist was the number of such conversions he achieved, maximizing the factors that led to conversions became a refined skill. Charles Grandison Finney, one of the most celebrated revivalist preachers of the US Second Great Awakening in the early nineteenth century, structured the preaching environment to max-imize the effects of his communication. He set up arena spaces in a circular fashion so that everyone could see everyone else, which enhanced the sense of the self as exposed and scrutinized. He specified how music and singing were to be used to generate the conversion experience. He created an "anxi-ety bench" at the side or in front of the preaching dais, where people caught in between making a decision to be saved or not would be placed to anguish and teeter between resistance and submission (again, under the scrutinizing gaze of others looking on).[37]

This preaching methodology reflected the revivalists' perception, or chancing upon the realization, that the changed sociological situation re-quired a different communication of Christian faith. It also brought the revivalists a good deal of criticism, particularly from the established church-es of their time. Edmund Gibson, the bishop of London, contended that Methodist preachers encouraged social instability by meeting outdoors and breaking the rules that regulated the territorial rights of parish bounda-ries. Gibson argued that "regular attendance on the publick Offices of Reli-gion ... is better evidence of the co-operation of the Holy Spirit than those sudden Agonies, Roarings and Screamings, Tremblings, Droppings-down, Ravings and Madnesses into which their Hearers have been cast."[38] George Lavington, the bishop of Exeter, made similar critiques in a 390-page publi-cation in 1749, *The Enthusiasm of Methodists and Papists Compared*. The tone of the work is flagged in the Preface:

> That such freaks they are, will easily appear. And if in proving it I am some-times guilty of a levity of expression, 'tis to be hop'd some allowance will be made in consideration of the nature of the Subject: it being no easy matter to keep one's countenance, and be steadily serious, where others are ridiculous.[39]

The success of the revivalists (i.e., of those who were successful – many weren't) came from communication strategies that tapped into the oppor-tunities of what was a growing consumer market, with an innovative re-packaging of Christianity into an experiential commodity, tailored to the new cultural expectations of human autonomy by placing the individual in charge of their own salvation. In the first half of the eighteenth century, manufacturing and commerce in Britain and in trans-Atlantic trade were growing, fed by population growth, improved methods of agriculture and transport, innovations in commodity production, and rising consumer demand. These were fed by developments in communication and communication-based marketing. The first half of the eighteenth century saw a rapid growth in the number and diversity of newspapers, magazines, and cheap book production on both sides of the Atlantic. The combination of increased print availability and commodities led to the expansion of advertising and product marketing, and the growing acceptance of such marketing methods in people's consumer behavior.[40]

The revivalists, without the backing of established religious corporations to support them or hold them back, were quick to utilize these entrepreneurial opportunities offered by the new consumer market. Whitefield in particular utilized commercial strategies in his preaching journeys, assisted by his brother and nephew who had been highly successful in building and marketing a cross-Atlantic and Caribbean trade in alcoholic and other commodities. Although critical of a lot of consumer behavior, Whitefield used analogies of commercial and consumer practice in his sermons when talking about salvation, linking himself relevantly to the practicalities of the culture.

In 1739, a convert of Whitefield's, William Seward, took on responsibility for developing and handling Whitefield's newspaper publicity. Seward built a media image of Whitefield as a "selfless young evangelist who, forgoing lucrative opportunities in England, was undertaking a missionary journey to Georgia."[41] He provided papers with a steady stream of his own copy for their use, including daily stock reports on Whitefield's growing popularity, crowd sizes, and donations. He organized paid advertisements on newspaper front pages promoting Whitefield, in the form of news articles written by a third party. Copies of Whitefield's sermons, journals, and letters were sent to newspapers and magazines, booksellers, and evangelical ministers. Seward would also handle advance publicity, "flooding printers with publicity weeks before Whitefield's arrival to begin preaching."[42]

The sizes of the crowds that Whitefield and Seward provided to newspapers are now seen as subject to exaggerations, a cause of criticism by skeptics of the time and something that Whitefield modified when revising his journals later. Once he had become one of the most recognized men in the colonies and his presence in a city was noteworthy in itself, however, promotion and news reporting became self-generating.

More methodical than Whitefield, Wesley organized his new converts into local groups or class meetings under the leadership of a local lay leader. In these class meetings, old and new converts met regularly for bible study and prayer, moral accountability, spiritual discernment, education, and training.

It was within these class meetings that the momentary emotional experience of conversion was extended into spiritual concepts and people's fears of their decision in the cold light of day were addressed. The class meetings also served as the context for moral reformation through the Methodist concept of ongoing sanctification, or "growing in holiness."

It was in these small classes that the now-widespread evangelical communication practice of personal testimony emerged. These conversion narratives, a common feature of Methodist class meetings, revivalist services, camp meetings, and publications, became a recognized genre, still in use today, that replays the theological fundamentals of evangelicalism: being burdened with evil, fear, guilt, shame, or fear of damnation; becoming aware of and struggling with a spiritual challenge through preachers, friends, or class meetings; the moment of conversion as both a social and psychological sensory event; the fear of backsliding; the support of prayer, class meetings, and literature; the search for a higher spiritual experience of assurance and sanctification; and being of use in the spreading of the movement.

These class meetings and their lay leadership were under the oversight of regional ordained clergy who rode a circuit to visit the groups on a regular basis. It was these local groups, organized into circuits, into districts, and nationally as an annual conference, that became the basis of what was to become the Methodist Church. The local groups also became the source of another feature of Methodist communication, lay preachers, laypeople who preached locally in the absence of ordained clergy. The experience in public speaking provided by lay preaching made Methodist lay preachers significant leaders in some of the working-class reform movements in Britain and the United States.

Wesley's utilization of the emerging consumer market is most apparent in his organization, production, and circulation of print materials as a way of integrating and developing the growing movement of Methodism. Hempton describes its extent:

> One of the most striking features of Methodism is the extent to which Wesley tried to secure control over the discourse of the movement by remorselessly selecting, editing, publishing, and disseminating print. He commissioned and published biographies and autobiographies as exemplary lives for the edification of his followers. He selected and published books for a Christian Library to be used by his preachers. He edited hymnbooks, published tracts, and distributed a connectional magazine. An inventory of the books owned by Wesley's press in 1791 contains a formidable list of biographies, hymnals, commentaries, sermons, guides, thoughts, addresses, magazines, death narratives, and tracts. Moreover, Wesley refused to allow his preachers to publish works independent of his control. He literally tried to supervise the entire spiritual literacy of his connection by establishing a sort of Wesleyan canon beyond which his followers were encouraged not to go.[43]

The other important media aspect of Revivalism was its music and singing. Methodism in particular was a movement sustained in singing. An active collector, editor, and compiler of hymns, Wesley's *A Collection of Psalms and Hymns*, published in 1737 for use in churches in Georgia, is credited as being "quite possibly the first hymnbook published in America for use in public worship."[44] Over the next fifty years, Wesley and his brother Charles published around thirty hymnbooks, some for general use, some for specific occasions. While John was the compiler, editor, and publisher, Charles was the principal poet, writer, and lyricist and is estimated to have composed around nine thousand hymns and sacred poems in his lifetime.[45]

The definitive collection was the 1780 publication, *Collection of Hymns for the Use of People Called Methodists*. In his Preface, Wesley sets out the considerations that shaped the production of the book and the musical culture of Methodism.

Such a Hymn Book you have now before you. It is not so large as to be either cumbersome, or expensive: and it is large enough to contain such a variety of hymns as will not soon be worn threadbare. It is large enough to contain all the important truths of our most holy religion, whether speculative or practical; yea, to illustrate them all, and to prove them both by Scripture and reason: and this is done in a regular order. The hymns are not carelessly jumbled together, but carefully ranged under proper heads, according to the experience of real Christians. So that this book is, in effect, a little body of experimental and practical divinity. As but a small part of these hymns is of my own composing, I do not think it inconsistent with modesty to declare, that I am persuaded no such Hymn Book as this has yet been published in the English language.[46]

The tunes for the hymns were both original and borrowed from other sources, including recognized composers and folk melodies. Wesley expressed his intent that hymn tunes be "singable, teachable, memorable, functional and accessible to all," and that in their singing Methodists should "learn the tunes, sing the exact words, sing lustily, modestly, and in time, and above all to sing spiritually so that they would not be carried away by the sound."[47]

The ordering of the hymns in sections as indicated by Wesley, with each section named and most sections containing named subsections, gives an overview of all the important elements of Methodist doctrine, ecclesiology, and practical living. With many of the hymns strongly theological in their content, the hymnal was, in effect, the distinctive Methodist confessional statement in song and one of lasting influence in popular religiosity to the present time.

The dynamism engendered by Revivalism reformed worship at the local level into a quite different mediation experience. In difference from the ordered nature of a clergy-led liturgy, Revivalism introduced a dynamism of engagement and interaction, reflected well in a journalist's report published in the *Wales Western Star* newspaper in 1904, at the height of a Welsh revival:

> I felt that this as no ordinary gathering. Instead of the set order of proceedings to which we are accustomed at the orthodox religious service, everything here was left to the spontaneous impulse of the moment. The preacher [Evan Roberts], too, did not remain in his usual seat. For the most part he walked up and down the aisles, open Bible in one hand, exhorting one, encouraging another, and kneeling with a third to implore a blessing from the Throne of God. A young woman rose to give out a hymn, which was sung with deep earnestness. While it was being sung several people dropped down in their seats as if they had been struck, and commenced crying for pardon. Then from another part of the chapel could be heard the resonant voice of a young man reading a portion of scripture.... Finally, Mr. Roberts announced the holding of future meetings, and at 4.25 o'clock the gathering dispersed. But even at this hour the people did not make their way home. When I left to walk back to Lannelly I left dozens of them about the road still discussing what is now the chief subject in their lives.[48]

Revivalism has left a number of influences in the shaping of Christianity to the present time. One of those has been in the entrepreneurial accommodation of Protestant communication practice to the requirements of consumer marketing in an emerging consumer culture. The strategies employed by Whitefield provided a pattern for subsequent evangelical revivalists such as Charles Grandison Finney, Dwight L. Moody, Billy Sunday, and Billy Graham. It has also been the model for twenty-first-century Prosperity Christianity.

Revivalism has had a significant hand in shaping American religious identity in particular. McLoughlin sees in the regular recurrence of revivals within American society a process of cultural revitalization that begins in a time of crisis of beliefs and values, and continues over a period of a generation or so to effect a reorientation of those beliefs and values. Four particular mythologies of belief and value continue to be reworked in these Christian revivals: that Americans are a chosen people; that Americans have a manifest (or latent) destiny to lead the world to the millennium; that America's democratic institutions, abundance of natural resources, and freedom of the individual operate under a body of higher moral law; and that the Judeo-Christian ethic brings the greatest fulfillment of individual and social potential and welfare.[49]

Revivalism also created one of the enduring models for the adaptation of Christianity to the rise of industrialization and industrial capitalism. The greatest gains in Methodism were from the new industrial working class of miners, weavers, factory workers, seamen, potters, and rural laborers. It gave them in their social and economic dislocation a religious identity of equality, an emotional outlet, and a moral community that enabled them to deal with the changes.[50] In its turn, Methodism contributed to the emerging economic system of industrialization a sustaining religious spirit, expressed in social values of discipline, order, and productiveness. MacCullough provides an astute analysis of this religious-economic connection in his consideration of two lines from one of Charles Wesley's well-known salvation hymns, "And can it be that I should gain/ an interest in the Saviour's blood":

> Here Wesley's fertile imagination has sought his controlling metaphor in the language of a vigorously commercial society: sinners "gain an interest" in the Saviour's blood, just as they may gain an "interest," a commercial stake, in a little shop, a busy workshop — perhaps even, if they did well enough, a factory or a bank. Such would be the aspiration of many of the struggling, financially vulnerable people who sang Wesley's hymns, turning their sense of joy and relief at their salvation to making a decent life for themselves and their families. Hard work was allied with strict morality; if ever there was anything resembling the "Protestant work ethic," it came out of Methodism and the Evangelical Revival rather than the sixteenth-century Reformation.[51]

A lasting influence of revivalism was the formation of new networks of like-minded Christian people across churches, rather than within new churches. In the late eighteenth century, British Protestants sympathetic to the evangelical revival impulse began to form themselves into identifiable evangelical associations for particular religious or charitable purposes. Influential bodies such as the London Missionary Society, the Religious Tract Society, and the British and Foreign Bible Society were all begun at this time and reflect a development that continues today, the subdivision of Christianity into numerous "para-church" groups of like-minded Christians networking across formal denominational boundaries.

Producing evangelical material was a major activity of these para-church groups, and their activity was influential in setting the mindset and pattern for evangelical media strategy and practice.

The work of the Religious Tract Society gives an example of the strategy. The society produced massive amounts of inexpensive, typically short tracts that were commonly purchased in volume by evangelical individuals or groups and distributed widely, free of charge, as an act of witnessing to their faith. Distribution was limited only by the imagination of the person carrying them. Tracts would be placed in neighborhood letter boxes; left behind at shop counters, train stations, or public facilities; and handed out in the streets, at schools, in bars, and in the marketplace. Written in accessible and personal language, their short form and cheap economical production allowed print runs to be targeted specifically at particular groups or to address particular problems. In a way similar to earlier belief in the divine mediational power of icons and relics to work miracles, the distribution of media artifacts such as tracts was sustained by a belief in the power of God to work miracles through a person's exposure to a medium of evangelical information. The practice was sustained by biblical verses such as "My word will not return to me void, without accomplishing what I desire," and encouraged by frequent testimony in evangelical meetings and publicity of lives that were converted through a chance reading of an adrift tract.

This dynamism of evangelical entrepreneurship that developed in the latter part of the eighteenth century – producing readily accessible media products in vernacular language and style to be distributed by Christians as a part of a partnership with God to spread the faith – set a pattern for evangelical faith communication that would continue into the later media of film, radio, and television.

Protestant mission

The Protestant initiative in global missions developed with the colonial spread of Protestant countries, spurred by the evangelical missionary societies that emerged in the wake of the revivalist movements of the eighteenth century. English evangelical societies such as the Particular Baptist Missionary Society for Propagating the Gospel among the Heathen (1792), the London Missionary Society (LMS; 1795), and the British and Foreign Bible Society (1804), influenced by stories of British voyages of discovery and reports of non-Christian races, began to look to the wider world as a field of mission. Like Catholic missionary efforts, Protestant missions followed colonial pathways, a key reason why a large proportion of British missions were focused on India.

Reports from the first people sent as missionaries by these societies, such as William Carey in India, stimulated the imagination of others, and within less than a decade ten more Protestant missionary societies were established in the British Isles and on the European continent.[52] Engaging in and supporting "overseas" missionary activity in all parts of the world steadily grew to become a major focus of Protestant Christianity into the twentieth century.

Like their Catholic counterparts, Protestant missionaries reproduced in their mission work the communication methods they were familiar with from evangelical revivalism: public preaching (where it was permitted), personal engagement and witnessing, the founding of schools and churches, and the production and distribution of printed materials. As in their home countries, a print-based media strategy became a central feature of Protestant missionary activity. While preaching and personal conversation remained important, great emphasis was given to printing because of its

Figure 11.1 J.G.G., wood engraver, *The Missionary*, wood engraving, 1854, from *The Family Christian Almanac for 1855*. New York: American Tract Society, 1854. Source: photo by David Morgan.

multiplication effect in distribution, and its increased status as an artifact of superior cultural authority, visually depicted in Figure 11.1.

Robert Morrison, an LMS missionary to China, outlined the importance of printing in an address to the annual meeting of the LMS in 1825:

For the reading population of mankind let the PRESS be extensively employed. Knowledge thus conveyed can be scattered more widely than by living teachers. It can penetrate the palaces of kings and governors; as well as the studies of the learned; and the hamlets of the poor; to whom in some lands no foreigner is permitted admission. Knowledge conveyed in this way is more durable than that communicated by the living voice, and is more certain than that of tradition.[53]

The distribution of the Bible, now commonly named in its particular media form as "the" Word of God, in the language of the local people was from its earliest days central to the concept of Protestant Christian mission. For Morrison, the first priority in his Chinese mission was the translation of the Bible into Chinese:

> The vast and ancient literature of the Chinese and the established presence of Roman Catholics in Macao demanded the authority of the [Protestant] Bible, that is, the print-based authority of the faith, before the Church could be erected on its foundation.[54]

This print-based strategy reflects two fundamentals that came to characterize Protestant global missionary efforts: the production of print and the learning of vernacular languages. An important investment of missionary societies was the funding of printing facilities (printing presses, and supplies of paper, ink, and other material) and distribution networks in major mission centers around the world. Calls for money to support the supply of printing presses were often the focus of special fundraising efforts.

Enormous effort and resources were also put into the learning of vernacular languages so that communication could take place, and materials could be published, in local tongues. This included, in many cases, developing written forms of local oral languages that were native to small populations for which a written version of the language didn't exist. Independent organizations such as the British and Foreign Bible Society (1804) were established for this specific purpose, and reports from the mission field measured success in terms of the number of vernacular Bibles or Bible portions that had been produced and distributed.

Other works were also produced in the vernacular. William Ringeltaube, an LMS missionary to Tranquebar in India, found on his arrival materials translated into Tamil by Danish and German missionaries, including two editions of the Scriptures, collections of hymns, catechisms, scripture extracts, some religious tracts, and translations of European devotional classics such as a work by Thomas à Kempis, Bunyan's *Pilgrim's Progress*, grammars, dictionaries, and spelling books.[55]

Tracts were widely produced and distributed. They were a popular missionary genre for a variety of reasons: they were inexpensive, they were easy to read and memorize, they were able to reflect the local oral culture, they often included visual imagery they could be read in private, and they were easily distributed and circulated. In India in 1820, the LMS reported that thirty-three thousand tracts had been printed in Begalee, half of which had been circulated. The Madras Religious Tract Society reported printing fourteen thousand tracts in two major southern Indian languages, Tamil and Telugu, and another seven thousand tracts in English and Indian languages had been distributed at Bellary.[56]

NOTES

1 Eisenstein, 1979.
2 Lotz-Heumann, 2013.
3 B. Anderson, 1991.
4 The English Pilgrims, who immigrated to America to escape the lack of toleration of their Calvinist views by the Church of England, established a religious colony that was marked by an intolerance of difference that was worse than the one they fled from.
5 Toulmin, 1990.
6 Quoted in Maurer, 2009, p. 56.
7 Neill, 1966, p. 32.
8 MacCulloch, 2009, p. 689.
9 Bakewell, 1998; MacCulloch, 2009, p. 696.
10 For example, the Bull Romanus Pontifex (Pope Nicholas V, 1455), The Bull *Inter Cetera* (Pope Alexander VI, 1493), and the *Patronato* of Julius II (1508).
11 One eyewitness described how occupation of one area was made by fierce veterans of the Italian wars who were there in pursuit of gold and slaves. It devastated the whole region. "They tortured them, demanding gold, and some they burnt and others they gave to be eaten alive by dogs and others they hanged and on others they practised new forms of torture" (Brading, 1997, p. 121).
12 The Laws of Burgos.
13 The Laws of Burgos.
14 The Laws of Burgos.
15 Bahr, 2009, pp. 260–261; Bakewell, 1998.
16 A former provincial of the Jesuit Order in Peru, the Spaniard José Acosta, lamented in 1589 the extent to which the gospel and war were too often connected (Brading, 1997, p. 118).
17 MacCulloch, 2009, p. 696.
18 MacCulloch, 2009, p. 696.
19 Kernan, 1987.
20 Pallares-Burke, 2002, p. 173.
21 This became an issue with ideas or practices originally developed in dominantly oral cultures (e.g., the Australian aboriginal communities) or with trade or craft skills previously transmitted orally.
22 Askew & Hubber, 1988, p. 136.
23 Ong, 1982, p. 227.

24 In 1889, statues of the Scottish poet Robert Burns and the Irish writer Tom Moore were erected in the main street of Ballarat, a gold-mining town in Australia.

25 Quoted in Askew & Hubber, 1988, p. 136.

26 B. Anderson, 1991.

27 Ong, 1982, p. 239.

28 Spender, 1995, pp. 11, 19.

29 Methuen, 2000, pp. 424–425.

30 Burns, 1989, p. 263.

31 Spender, 1995, p. 8.

32 Herbst, 2007.

33 Askew & Hubber, 1988, p. 113.

34 Quoted in Davis, 1976, p. 56.

35 Curnock, 1909b, pp. 475–476.

36 Curnock, 1909a, p. 167.

37 David Morgan brought these elements of Finney's preaching style to my attention.

38 Edmund Gibson, *Observations upon the conduct and behavior of a certain sect usually distinguished by the name of Methodists* (1744), cited in Hempton, 2005, p. 33.

39 Lavington, 1749, Preface.

40 Lambert, 1994, pp. 37–38.

41 Lambert, 1994, p. 53.

42 Lambert, 1994, pp. 56–57.

43 Hempton, 2005, pp. 58–59.

44 Hempton, 2005, p. 67.

45 Hempton, 2005, p. 69.

46 Wesley, 1779, 1933.

47 Hempton, 2005, p. 70.

48 Kay & Dyer, 2004, p. 6.

49 McLoughlin, 1978, pp. xiii–xiv.

50 Thompson, 1963, pp. 355–356.

51 MacCulloch, 2009, p. 754.

52 Bahr, 2009, p. 333.

53 Cited in Morgan, no date.

54 Morgan, no date.

55 Morgan, no date.

56 Morgan, no date.

12

Electrifying Sight and Sound

The technologies of the audiovisual

What happened to Christianity in the nineteenth and twentieth centuries cannot be fully understood without understanding the significant media changes that occurred leading into the latter century. Those changes can be traced to the development of two key technologies: the means to generate and harness electricity, and photography.

Electricity's distinctiveness, as it developed through the nineteenth century, was in providing a superior, flexible source of energy for the powering of new technologies for industry and the domestic market. Not the least of these was the electric light bulb in the 1870s, whose impact on the ordering, rhythms, and conduct of human life by blurring the distinction between night and day was more profound than perhaps any other single technology.

In addition to its physical affordances, the invisible mystery of flow of the electric current provided a metaphor for rethinking some of the fundamental structures of life and its possibilities: time, light and darkness, human physiology, the order and dynamic of the natural world, and the nature of life itself. As this musing continued intellectually and artistically, cosmological thinking turned from the concept of the world as fixed and ordered to one with the fluidity, dynamism, and power of the current. As Sconce notes, electricity was for many in the eighteenth and nineteenth centuries "a mystical and even divine substance that animated body and soul."[1]

Photography began around the same time, developing from backyard-shed experiments in the early nineteenth century. Meaning literally "drawing with light," it came to wider public attention when Louis Daguerre developed the technique of fixing images on metal plates (1839) and photographs began to be used in newspapers and newsweeklies such as *The Illustrated London News* (1842). In 1888, George Eastman took the development a step further with the invention of the roll film and the Kodak camera.

From Jesus to the Internet, Peter Horsfield © 2015 John Wiley & Sons, Ltd. Published 2015 by John Wiley & Sons, Ltd.

Marketed with the slogan "You push the button – we do the rest," low-cost snapshot photography made the preservation of how life looked an accessible service for most members of the community, not just the well-off who had the resources to have their portraits painted. Photographic "images" of people and life soon became a part of everyday western culture.

The significance of photography for cultural development lies in its fundamentally different method of apprehending, preserving, and reproducing what reality looked like through the eyes, rather than how it was described in language through written and printed texts. Photography provided the technological means for visual culture to challenge the previously undisputed supremacy of alphabet culture.

The application of electricity and photography to the processes of communication during the nineteenth century stimulated the development of new audiovisual media technologies that would become the fundamental media of the twentieth century: the telegraph (1844), the telephone (1876), the phonograph (1877), the personal camera (1884), the wireless (1873–1896), and the motion picture (1887–1891). These were followed in short time in the new century with the first voice broadcast (1906), the first music broadcast (1919), the first talking motion picture (1927), and television (1923–1928).

These novel electric audiovisual technologies and the uses made of them brought experiences of technological enchantment, and new means of addressing the needs of people who were separated from family and village networks through employment, migration, and urban living but wanted to keep in touch or form new communities. Applications of the technologies expanded also because they were formed into commercial or social utility industries that exploited the distinctive potential of the technologies and the content they made possible.[2]

What the various applications of electricity and photography provided were the means of capturing and mass reproducing the senses of sight and sound, two transitory sensory experiences that previously were restricted to the immediate body. Electricity and photography enabled these transitory bodily experiences to be captured outside the body and reproduced on demand. With their address to the senses of sight and sound, electrified audiovisual media bypassed the restrictions of literacy required for written and printed media. In the process they reworked the media matrix of society and stimulated a recovery of oral competencies and influence in a way that matched the previous impact of writing and print. They also restored a sense of historicity to otherwise marginalized peoples and communities who lacked the literacies and resources to project their own history onto the world stage through written and printed media.

As the twentieth century progressed, these new media reworked the sensory and communication web upon which the various dimensions of societies and cultures had been structured, particularly in the West. Changes followed in how relationships were formed and maintained; how information was received, processed, stored, and reproduced; and how social organizations and institutions operated and were structured. The changes were profound.

Electrically mediated communications sped up the pace of communication and thereby changed concepts and perceptions of time, accentuating the cultural value of immediacy. For instance, in 1920, it took fourteen minutes and eight operators just to make a connection for a phone call from New York to San Francisco. In the last part of the twentieth century, a direct-dial call could be made instantly.[3]

Electric media also changed cultural concepts of distance and space. Beginning with the wired telegraph and progressing through submarine cables, radio, and satellite, electric media effectively removed distance as a barrier to communication. In the process, people's sense of identity became less space bound and more fluid. In a curious way, for example, the rise of the telegraph in the late nineteenth century triggered a rise in spiritualism. The possibility of communicating with unseen people far away through the medium of electrified telegraph wires – "psychical connection in spite of physical separation"[4] – prompted interest in spiritualism, in which the unseen spirits of the dead are seen as communicating with the living through invisible waves of spiritual energy channeled through a spirit medium.[5]

The models adopted in developed countries for the commercial exploitation of these media reshaped economies. While money in the audiovisual era was made by the manufacturers and sellers of the technologies, the greater amounts of money were made by those who produced and distributed the content that would be accessed through the audiovisual devices. In the case of motion pictures and the cinema, income from the technology was made by charging people to see the movies at the movie theatre. In radio and television, the content was distributed free, with the income from the technology being made by station owners selling time to advertisers to pitch their sales message to the mass audiences assembled. Mass electric media, therefore, represent a significant social shift, where the purpose in communicating was not to communicate a particular social message, but to invent content that would attract and assemble audiences that could be sold to advertisers. The larger the audience assembled, the more income could be produced and the more costs could be reduced through economies of scale.

This commercial imperative was influential in creating the concepts and dynamics of mass media, mass audiences, and mass society. Central to these was the creation of the powerful affiliated industries of advertising and marketing, individuals and corporations with expertise in converting audience listening and viewing into buying behavior. The commercial imperatives of building as large an audience as possible also encouraged the creation of a particular form of social content most suitable to the commercial interests of the mass media industries: content of general interest or attraction that the largest number of people would have in common, while avoiding particular or disagreeable material that would turn people off.[6]

Concern with this industry dynamic of mass media presenting only the most common social denominators has expressed itself in criticisms of mass-broadcast content as banal, having a culturally dangerous media logic, or even dulling people's intelligence.[7] Others question the singularity and pessimism of this concept of mass society, pointing instead to such things as the diversity that's available in mass media, the active nature of people's choice of media for particular purposes, and the active engagement people bring to their use of media, which includes critical engagement and the active process of constructing their own meanings and interpretations of what they're watching or listening to.

This interaction of Enlightenment culture with the emerging matrix of mediated communication being reshaped by the development of electric media was the context in which the institutions and individuals of Christianity in the twentieth century again found themselves working out their inherited faith.

Christianity and the twentieth-century media world

There are a number of theoretical perspectives put forward for understanding what happened to Christianity in the twentieth century. One of those is the secularization view, a perspective that argues that with an increased differentiation of the religious from the secular spheres of society (the political, social, scientific, economic, and educational), and the advances made in the secular sphere in such things as discovering new knowledge about the world and its processes, developing a better understanding of human behavior through the social sciences, solving practical problems, and improving the general quality of life, the grounds and relevance on which religion had justified itself intellectually and socially were steadily eroded. Sociological data are quoted to support the view that through the twentieth century there was a progressive decline in involvement, support, and resourcing for Christian churches and a corresponding decline or marginalization in the political importance and influence of Christian institutions.[8]

There is now significant questioning of this strong secularization perspective. Certainly, broad cultural changes took place in the relationship of religion to secular spheres of society through the twentieth century. However, the view that these changes involved a steady replacement of religious perspectives and activities with secular perspectives and activities has been called into significant question.[9]

A second perspective is the "mediatization" thesis, which deals more specifically with the shaping effect that mass media have exerted on Christianity and religion in general. The thesis posits that through the twentieth century, media developed into such an autonomous, independent, and influential institution that they have been able to shape most social practices in line with their particular institutional, aesthetic, and technological demands. This shaping effect includes religion, which is seen to have been either reduced to banality or steadily replaced by secular media as a primary source of information and enchantment.[10] This perspective has also been critiqued on a number of grounds, including a lack of appreciation for the mutually interactive relationship between religion and media that has characterized most religions from their beginnings.[11]

Two other perspectives are useful for thinking about the relationship of media changes and changes in Christianity in the twentieth century. One is the religious economy perspective, which sees religion functioning in society in ways similar to a fiscal economy, in which users are faced with a supply of religious faith options and make rational choices about the faith they commit to based on factors such as familiarity, relevance, and benefit.[12] Religious economies, like fiscal economies, can be variously regulated on a wider social level, and the level of regulation and choice available to people influences both the plurality of religion within a society and the commitment and involvement that people make to their religious choices.

From a religious economy view, for example, one of the profound effects of the Reformation was the introduction of choice into the western religious market in place of the monopolistic Christendom model where the Catholic Church automatically inherited all people as members at birth. In this new situation of religious choice, churches were put in the position where they were required to "win" members by what they offered. This situation of choice favored those expressions of Christianity that were able to attract and retain adherents not through coercion or restriction, but through their ability to freely persuade and convince people on the basis of their attractiveness, the benefits and relevance they offered to members, and their accessibility for people to participate in.

Within this pluralistic religious marketplace, the secular/scientific/consumer worldview also offered its own attractive, relevant, and accessible nonreligious alternative. The effects of this competitive ideological marketplace were not the same across the western world. In some areas, there was a significant decline in churches. This was noticeable in parts of Europe particularly, where churches held privileged social positions as established churches that disguised their need to act competitively in engaging and addressing the needs of their members.

Yet at the same time as some churches were declining in numbers and influence, others were growing. What these growing churches appeared to have in common was that they accepted the new conditions of a diversified secular and religious marketplace, and adapted to those changed conditions by defining a new role for themselves within it, renewing what they offered to be of relevance to the marketplace, and establishing effective mechanisms for recruiting new members.[13] Some have seen this adaptation as an example of undesirable media influence on Christianity, encouraging churches to become competitive with each other in promoting and furthering their own sectarian interests, although as we have seen such competitiveness has existed within Christianity since its early decades. Another view of this shift is that the wider social changes that took place during the twentieth century, in which media changes were an important part, created a different fertility in the cultural ground that allowed aspects within Christianity's diversity that had previously lain quiescent to become relevant and sprout again. Nor were all of the changes sectarian, competitive, or antisecular in nature. In some cases, churches found a new social relevance in defending Enlightenment values of human autonomy, justice, and human dignity against authoritarian (religious and irreligious) and anarchic regimes that were denying them.

As many of the changes of the twentieth century were closely connected to media changes, the response by Christian groups to twentieth-century media and the media context has been central to their health or survival. The nature of Christian responses have been influenced also by related factors such as the regulatory frameworks of media with which they were working, mythologies of media systems and how they related to particular Christian mythic systems, patterns of consumer choice and interests, and individuals who were able to facilitate bridges or new ventures in media and Christian practice. A number of key Christian positions can be noted.

Mainline mediation

Mainline churches are those seen as significantly integrated into the mainstream culture of their host societies. Some had formal recognition as the established church of their country and, as such, were a recognized part of the national establishment. The mainline status of churches such as Baptist, Church of England or Anglican Episcopal, Lutheran, Methodist, Presbyterian, and Roman Catholic reflects a consolidation of their confessional position coming out of the Reformation and Revivalism. These ranged across a spectrum: from liberal positions where many of the values of secularism and rationalism were aligned to Christian thought and practice, to conservative positions where the secular humanist values of the state were constantly contested or actively negotiated on cultural or doctrinal grounds.

Mainline Christian churches tended to be strong in their emphasis on literate-based education as a key means of improvement, in both faith and secular life. A strong emphasis was given, therefore, to the production of printed materials for the development of faith for members and their families. The Presbyterian Publishing Corporation in the United States, for example, identifies the strong educational focus of its mission: "Most of its publications are used in the spiritual formation of clergy and laity, the training of seminarians, the dissemination of religious scholars' work, and the preparation for ministry of lay church leaders. One of PPC's principal aims is to help readers of its publications achieve biblical and theological literacy."[14] As a result of this educational emphasis, with a strong basis in print, religious publishing was a major industry in many western countries.

This strong emphasis on literate education in faith has tended to align the theology and practice of many churches, particularly the liberal Protestant ones, with the values and aspirations of the literate middle classes. It has also encouraged alignments to be made between Christianity and Enlightenment thought, with scientific advances in medicine, the social sciences, and textual criticism being variously integrated into understandings of faith.

This literate focus of mainline Christian faith was influential also in their responses to the electric mass media. While there was ready adoption of those electric media that were primarily instrumental or personal in nature, such as the telegraph, the telephone, and photography, and of radio also because of its orientation to the spoken word, the literate basis of their cultural positions created an ambivalent relationship with the more visual and mass character of television.

The limits of the airwave spectrum forced most western countries to regulate radio and television through allocation of licenses to communicate in a way that was not needed for print publication. The broadcasting of some form of religion was one of the programming requirements in most license allocations.

In those countries with a strong national broadcasting service, such as the United Kingdom, Canada, and Australia, the production and broadcast of religious material were placed in the hands of the national broadcaster as part of their comprehensive service. As it was a publicly funded service, the focus in the public broadcasting of religion was not on presenting specific forms of Christianity but on general Christian beliefs and activities of value to the whole community. This also permitted the governments of nations that were expressly Christian, such as the United Kingdom, Canada, and Australia, to make use of religious programming to strengthen affiliation to national values, thereby reinforcing the power of the state. So the state broadcast of religion was not just a public service but also a means of reinforcing inherent nationalism.

On commercial radio stations, it was a common requirement of their license to broadcast in most western countries for a station to make airtime available free for the broadcasting of religious (i.e., Christian) programs. Given the potentially contentious nature of religion, commercial stations generally met this requirement by making time available for the broadcast of church-produced programs. This free time was generally distributed proportionally to churches based on the denominational composition of the national population. This benefited the more populous mainline denominations, who gained more access to broadcast time than smaller Christian denominations or churches.

The consequence of this beneficial public service arrangement and the ecumenical nature of the Protestant programming was that the Christian message projected into the public sphere on commercial stations was one that could be agreed across the different doctrinal positions, and that emphasized those aspects of Christianity that corresponded to the wider values of the community. While this message of general good on the part of mainline churches met the spirit of the free public service time slot, it had significant implications for Christianity in reducing its capacity to project any sense of distinctiveness into the marketplace.[15]

Radio as a medium was not as problematic for the mainline churches as television. Radio invoked the oral and musical qualities of worship, and a lot of Christian communication through public and commercial radio consisted largely of transferring Christian activities from the church building to the airwaves – worship services, preaching, Christian music, pastoral conversations, and education. Many radio-broadcasted religious programs were simply recordings of worship services in local churches.

In the United States there was an early acquisition of stations by churches: by 1925 at least sixty-three stations were owned by church institutions.[16] By the 1930s most of these had been sold to commercial companies, due to increased costs of federal regulation and the difficulty of maintaining the stations during the Depression years. In many cases, agreement was reached as part of the sale that time be given free for the continuation of religious programs.[17]

The Roman Catholic Church was more active in acquiring local radio stations, particularly in countries where Catholicism was the established religion, such as in Latin America and parts of Asia. Vatican Radio in Rome, begun in 1931, identified itself with such a global mission. The first words spoken on the station were a message of peace and blessing by Pope Pius XI: "We address ourselves to all things and to all men. May the earth listen to the words of my mouth; pay attention, remotest people."[18] Ironically, but revealingly, the pope's message inviting "the earth to listen to the words of my mouth, and pay attention" was spoken in Latin, a language understood by no one but male leaders of the Roman Catholic Church. In some countries with a dominant Catholic population, the Catholic stations at times became important alternative voices to domineering governments, such as in times of political unrest. Catholic radio stations in Latin America or broadcasts from Radio Veritas in the Philippines at the time of the overthrow of President Ferdinand Marcos played such a political role.

Similar arrangements were carried over when television began comprehensive broadcasting in the 1950s. In countries with a strong national broadcasting system, such as the United Kingdom, a common programming format was the broadcasting of church services from local churches, either live or prerecorded and edited. The other popular format was hymn singing – the BBC religious program *Songs of Praise*, begun in 1961, continues today as the most continuous and popular religious program in the world. An early concession to the established place of Christianity in the United Kingdom was that there were no programs broadcast at the time of Sunday evening services in order not to distract people from their religious duties.[19]

Changes to this pattern of regulation began in the late 1950s and early 1960s, when increases in the number of television stations and commercial networks increased competitiveness and diversity in the media market. In the United States, Australia, and other countries, the obligation on stations to provide free airtime to mainline Christian denominations to broadcast their religious programs began to be replaced by stations selling airtime for religious programs to whomever was willing to pay for it. This opened the way for more entrepreneurial independent Evangelical groups, who previously had little access to television, to buy time for the broadcast of their Evangelical programs. Their readiness and ability to pay fairly quickly displaced mainline Christianity from television.

This displacement of mainline Christianity from television reflected a broader ambivalence of mainline Christian leaders toward television itself as a medium.[20] Because much of their leadership power was held by virtue of their highly literate, Enlightenment-framed theological education, mainline Protestant leaders were frequently critical of a medium that was visual in nature and was associated with mass popular culture and its perceived consumerism and commercialism. Rosenthal cites as an example the liberal Protestant magazine, *The Christian Century*:

> For *The Christian Century* editors, television viewing was at best a waste of time, and at worst a direct assault on the American (that is, Protestant) way of life.... For the editors, little on television warranted positive praise or even critical evaluation. Even religious television was largely ignored by *The Christian Century*. True to its rather highbrow, intellectual character, the magazine was reluctant to cede to this new medium its due cultural weight. For the most part, readers were counseled simply to "turn it off!"[21]

Television stations tended to be too expensive for churches to buy or run, so there was little church ownership of television stations to provide any potentially alternative models. From their different cultural perspective, mainline churches occasionally issued pronouncements setting out philosophical, theological, or ethical reflections on the nature of media in society, and the obligations of its producers and users in the light of those perspectives. Some of these statements were substantial reflections on the nature and social responsibilities of both public and commercial media, and principles for a just distribution of media access within society. The Vatican II pronouncement *Inter Mirifica*, issued in 1963, and its follow-up *Communio et Progressio* in 1971 are good examples of this, as are Protestant statements and publications such as the World Association for Christian Communication's *Communication for All: Christian Principles of Communication* (1986) and its *Media Development* journal.

Interestingly, mainline church leaders did not have the same critical reservations about the medium of film, whose narrative format had more in common with a book than did the programmatic/advertising style of television. The liberal Protestant journal *The Christian Century*, although highly critical of television, had regular film reviews over the years providing various theological perspectives on individual films or film's cultural significance.[22]

An exception to the lack of serious engagement with the media by mainline churches was the Roman Catholic bishop, Fulton Sheen. Sheen began broadcasting on US radio in 1928 with a series of radio sermons and became the regular speaker on the nationally broadcast *Catholic Hour* program. He moved to television in 1951 at the invitation of a commercial television network, which gave him a weekly slot of half an hour with commercial sponsorship. Sheen took the role seriously, spending thirty hours each week preparing for it, including presenting it to friends in French and Italian to clarify his mind. His program was markedly different from religious programs of the time. It was solely a speech or classroom lecture on a religious or moral subject, presented live without a teleprompter, in a study-type setting with the aid of only a blackboard on which he occasionally illustrated points he was making. The program was broadcast live and for the years 1952–1957 maintained a competitive share of the evening television audience, sustained solely by Sheen's meticulous planning, vocal variety, facial expression, and gestures; the relevance of his content; and the visual and oral dynamic of his authoritative personality and presence. No other religious program has ever gained such sustained commercial sponsorship or the consistently high audience numbers that Sheen did. In many ways he can be considered to be the first televangelist. Interestingly, when Sheen appeared as a guest at the 1997 convention of the National Religious Broadcasters, the association of doctrinaire evangelical and fundamentalist Protestant broadcasters, he was given a standing ovation – a symbol of the dream of media success shared by most of those present.

The Evangelical Coalition

The concept of modern Evangelicalism is a difficult one to deal with, partly because it is so diverse and idiosyncratic in its nature that a single definition is hard to arrive at. Historically, the term "Evangelical" was applied to Protestant churches per se, because of their claim to base their message on "the Gospel" or *euangelion*. In Germany and Switzerland it was applied historically to the Lutheran church, to distinguish it from the Calvinist Reformed churches.[23] The term "Evangelical" as it is used today incorporates a wide variety of Christian expressions, including Fundamentalism, Pietism, Evangelicalism, Revivalism, Conservatism, Confessionalism, Millenarianism, and the Holiness and Pentecostal movements.[24] Yet even within that variety a continuum exists, such as left-wing, progressive, moderate, and right-wing positions.[25] The term "Evangelical" can refer to particular organized churches, whole denominations, independent associations, or individuals within a church.

Because it is such a broad phenomenon, and still the subject of specialist scholarly study, I will be using the term "the Evangelical Coalition" to recognize that as a movement running through modern Christianity it coalesces a wide diversity of organizations, groups, and individuals who associate themselves with a shared theological and cultural emphasis. A number of those shared emphases are relevant to an understanding of the communication of Christian faith in the modern audiovisual era.

One point of commonality are particular emphases about the Christian faith – a stress on individual salvation and conversion, a high view of biblical text as the inerrant Word of God, and a belief that God acts supernaturally in everyday life and can be influenced through prayer to act on one's behalf – although there are significant tensions and differences in how these are understood in detail. For some, such as fundamentalists, the Bible is inerrant in every detail, including scientific and historical facts; for others, the Bible's inerrancy relates only to matters of doctrine or salvation.

A second point of commonality is a shared suspicion or rejection of liberal modernism and Roman Catholicism. This polemical position commonly includes a rejection of Darwinian evolution, a suspicion or rejection of secular humanism and rationalism, and a suspicion of ritualistic liturgy and versions of Christianity in which salvation is presented as a process of life formation rather than conversion. Again, though, there are a variety of stances in attitudes toward secular humanism and Roman Catholicism, from outright rejection to a critical but sympathetic engagement. It is worth noting that none of these positions is particularly novel to the modern Evangelical Coalition: each can be found in various forms throughout Christian history.

What has made the Evangelical Coalition particularly effective in the audiovisual twentieth century has been its third emphasis: a strong missionary emphasis with a stress on the obligation on every Christian to actively witness and communicate their faith in order to bring others to salvation. The expectation that every individual Christian should communicate their faith personally, and the institutional support given to them in doing so, has produced an amazing utilization of human resources and innovation that have been ideally suited to the communication of Christianity in a mass media age.

Again, this is not new. MacCullough sees similarities to the evangelical emphases in German Pietism, particularly the work of August Hermann Francke, a Lutheran pastor who, concerned by the increasing demands being placed on parish clergy, sought out concerned laypeople as partners in ministry. He gathered them together outside their local churches in what he called *collegia pietatis* for times of bible reading, prayer, and hymn singing, and new ventures in welfare, education, health, and communication. In evangelical ventures such as these, MacCullough sees a Protestant equivalent of what had been achieved in Catholicism through their religious orders: a methodology for innovation and individual initiative in specific areas or for specific projects without becoming bogged down in the regulations and processes of larger Christian institutional forms. [26]

What has characterized modern Evangelicalism as a movement has been its ready and energetic adaptation of new media of the audiovisual age in the communication of their faith. With a strongly pragmatic and instrumentalist view of media, what the Evangelical Coalition found in the audiovisual media were new and highly effective means for marketing widely its messages and products of salvation. Many Evangelicals saw electric media in similar theological terms as Luther did printing: as a divine intervention specifically to further God's work. Ben Armstrong, the executive secretary of the Evangelical association National Religious Broadcasters, reflected this in his affirmation:

> I believe that God has raised up this powerful technology of radio and television expressly to reach every man, woman, boy and girl on earth with the even more powerful message of the gospel.[27]

With the same pragmatic Evangelical focus, Armstrong saw God through these media creating a new kind of church, an electric church – "a great and new manifestation of the church created by God for this age."[28]

One of the early exemplars and models for Evangelical media initiatives was Dwight L. Moody, the American Chicago-based revival evangelist who began establishing an evangelistic ministry in Chicago in the 1860s. In 1869 he helped found Fleming H. Revell Publishing Company, which became the primary publisher of Moody's sermons and writings and a major religious publisher of the twentieth century. In 1873–1875, he went on the first of several evangelistic campaigns in Great Britain with the gospel singer and composer Ira Sankey, whose musical compositions of emotive and rousing gospel hymns contributed significantly to the success of Moody's evangelistic campaigns. The Moody and Sankey collaboration continued for the remainder of their lives, and their collection *Sacred Songs and Solos* includes more than 1200 works.

Early in his campaigns, following the examples of Whitefield and other revivalists, Moody took out newspaper space to advertise his revival meetings. In 1887 he started the Chicago Evangelization Society and in 1889 the Chicago Bible Institute to provide biblical education. The institute, renamed the Moody Bible Institute on Moody's death in 1899, grew to become a major educational institution that continues to the present day. Along with its regular courses of instruction, the institute began regular residential bible conferences (1897), offered the first program to train church musicians (1889), and in 1901 offered the first correspondence courses by an Evangelical school (and the third in the United States).

In 1895 Moody established the Bible Institute Colportage Association (BICA) to print and distribute small inexpensive reprints of established books or new books for the common reader. The cost of the books was ten cents, a revolutionary cheap price for religious literature, to compete with the "dime novels" of the day. The association employed students at the MBI to travel through the country's hinterland to sell the books from horse-drawn wagons. The books were also promoted by Moody at his revival meetings. In 1941, 12 million copies had been sold and the Colportage Association became Moody Press.

In 1926 the MBI began radio station WMBI-AM, the first noncommercial educational and religious radio station in the United States and today a network of thirty-six stations. In its first year it began the Radio School of the Bible, the first correspondence school courses offered on radio, which continued in syndication for eighty-six years. In the post–World War II period, MBI began the production of films promoting salvation within the context of scientific investigations. Although not shown in theatres, the thirty films produced were viewed extensively in schools and churches, and were required viewing for US Air Force recruits as part of President Truman's Character Guidance Program.[29]

Moody's evangelical work is indicative of the media entrepreneurship of the Evangelical Coalition. Not hamstrung by elite media-cultural reservations, and with a focus principally on the goal of saving people's souls, the Evangelical Coalition saw media principally through an uncluttered instrumentalist or utilitarian lens.

In contrast to earlier institutions of Christianity where the truth was upheld by the suppression of alternatives, Evangelicals saw the open competitive system of free-market capitalism as part of God's gift. As Ben Armstrong argued,

> That's the great genius of the American system. There is a choice of radio and TV stations, each working to capture its share of the audience. Broadcasting in this country is unique because it operates as part of the competitive system of private enterprise.[30]

This competitiveness of the open US media market, and the capitalist drive of it, gave optimum scope for the competitive mindset of the Evangelical sense of mission, one that has continued to the present time.[31] The voluntary coalition nature of evangelicalism also gave scope for individual Evangelical entrepreneurs to create their own opportunities without having to work through the sometimes laborious processes of established institutions.

This Evangelical competitiveness explains their success over the mainline Protestant churches in radio and television. Although in the United States mainline denominations garnered the valuable free airtime for several decades, minority coalition groups with their evangelical drive continued to increase their presence and to attract significant audiences on radio, buying their broadcast time. While numerous of them failed, many established a durable presence, such as Paul Radar in Chicago, John Roach Straton at Calvary Baptist Church in New York, Walter Maier and station KFUO in St. Louis, Aimee Semple McPherson and station KFSG in Los Angeles, and the fundamentalist Donald Grey Barnhouse, whose *Bible Study Hour* program in 1928 began to be broadcast weekly across the CBS network. Dr. Charles Fuller's *Old Fashioned Revival Hour*, a nationwide radio program originally broadcast from Hollywood, aired for over thirty years on over 650 stations. In 1931 the World Radio Missionary Fellowship began broadcasting from its makeshift shortwave radio station in Quito, Ecuador, with station HCJB. It continues to operate today, broadcasting twenty-four hours a day in thirteen languages and reaching virtually every point of the globe.[32] The weekly radio program from the Billy Graham Evangelistic Association, *The Hour of Decision*, begun in 1950 in association with Graham's wider program of crusade meetings around the world, has continued uninterrupted since then on numerous stations and in different languages around the world.

In 1942, a group of Evangelicals formed the National Association of Evangelicals as part of a deliberate cultural and political strategy following what was seen as a major public defeat for conservative Christianity in the Scopes Monkey Trial. Its goals were to reshape the direction of Evangelical Christianity in the United States through increased evangelistic efforts and establishing "a thriving evangelical subculture, centered around engaging personalities and independent institutions."[33] Against the perceived cultural dominance of what was seen as liberal mainline Christianity, it shifted Evangelical focus away from a purely individual salvation to a cultural one. Two years later, the National Religious Broadcasters (NRB) was formed to address the media arena and to promote the interests and cultural agendas of the loosely aligned individual religious radio entrepreneurs and their organizations.

As has happened on numerous occasions through the history of Christianity, Evangelical radio broadcasters drew from the diversity of Christian performative and aesthetic resources those most suitable to the medium of mass radio: preaching, interpersonal conversation, storytelling, and singing and music. Outspoken Evangelical preachers found out early that sectarianism and controversial polemics, a feature of a lot of Evangelical preaching, were not as conducive to building a large mass audience. Pohlman notes that all of the radio preachers who succeeded in becoming prominent broadcasting figures, even the Evangelical ones, "made their peace with the constraints of broadcast media" by avoiding substantive theological issues and embracing a more nonsectarian approach.

Charles Fuller distanced himself from militant fundamentalism and achieved an enormous audience. Walter Maier forsook Lutheran particulars to bring "Christ to the nations" and gained a remarkable number of listeners throughout the nation and across denominational boundaries. Harry Emerson Fosdick preached simple virtues to a large, general Christian audience. Aimee Semple McPherson promoted a charismatic ecumenism and became one of the most recognized entertainers in the nation.[34]

A similar pattern can be seen in American television when it was introduced in the 1950s. While mainline denominations initially dominated religious television through the mandated free-time provisions, Evangelical entrepreneurs purchased time from stations to broadcast their programs and, following common Evangelical practice, raised funds from their audiences or consumers to do so. Among the earliest was Rex Humbard, who began his television enterprise in 1953 by broadcasting his local church service in Akron, Ohio; and Oral Roberts, a tent revivalist who began in 1954 with a revivalist program syndicated over sixteen television stations.

The major advance in Evangelical programming on television came in 1967, when Roberts perceived that television was a medium that required a different approach from the revivalist genre that had brought him controversial fame on radio. In 1967 he closed down his television program and began redesigning it, reopening two years later with a new variety show format featuring well-known guests and performers and a message delivered by Roberts in a much smoother, "cooler" style. His Thanksgiving Special in the following year, using this new format, reached over 27 million people. Televangelism, as it is now known, was born. By 1978 there were seventy-two such programs on air in the United States using 92 percent of the religious airtime, largely shutting out mainline programming.[35]

Part of the success of Roberts' cultural shift from tent revivalist to television entrepreneur was because he tapped into the rising social confidence of the Evangelical Christian identity and the momentum of the deliberate Evangelical cultural and political agenda. This rising confidence and momentum were supported by a number of intersecting economic and demographic changes in the United States through the middle of the twentieth century.[36] One was the militarization of the Second World War, and a call for the United States to claim its destiny as God's agent for transformation of the world. A second was the profound economic changes taking place in global economies and the challenges they posed to people's livelihood. A third was the migration of people from the northern states of the United States to the South, bringing an improvement in the economic conditions of the previously marginal evangelical populations of the South and their rise into the middle classes. With this migration came also a growth in southern religious institutions, a new confidence in the Evangelical perspective on Christianity against perceived liberal contaminations, and a wider cultural claim for their key moral emphases of sexual purity, the sacredness of marriage and the family, and the God-given gender hierarchy of patriarchy. As Dochuk describes the changes:

> Such conspicuous encounters with new wealth drew southern evangelical transplants toward a theology of blessedness that assured them of their divine calling.... Certain of the absolute rightness of their doctrine, impassioned with the cause of evangelical democracy, and dedicated to those leaders most willing to flex their muscles on behalf of such sacred causes, evangelicals who were nurtured in this belief system exuded a gritty determination. Unlike mainline liberal Protestants, they possessed little patience for intellectual nuance or social progressiveness; in comparison to northern evangelicals, who turned "serious, quiet, intense, humorless, sacrificial, and patient" in the peak religious experience, they were always "busy, vocal and promotional" and "task-oriented." Amid the vicissitudes of migration in which a frontier spirit or pragmatism trumped all other concerns, these tendencies moulded southern evangelicalism into an aggressive, enterprising force.[37]

The media presence of the independent Evangelical broadcasters, with the lobbying support of the NRB, was an important part of this Evangelical sense of destiny. The growth of the large evangelical broadcasting ministries was marked also by a particular shift in the cultural character of the Evangelical religious message. As the individual and independent television ministries grew, with weekly and in some cases daily television programs syndicated across hundreds of stations, the costs rose dramatically and broadcasters were faced with the challenge of building and maintaining the size and loyalty of their audiences and their financial contributions, particularly in competition with other Evangelical programs. As a result, the programs became significantly audience driven and fundraising became a significant element of the programs. In a way parallel to the medieval practices of selling indulgences or purchasing spiritual benefit, methods of fundraising were developed that linked giving money to a religious broadcaster to a spiritual or material benefit. Oral Roberts' idea of "seed faith" was one of the earliest of these, where financial contributions to his program would operate as a seed of faith being planted, which would be honored by God with the giver receiving a larger amount of money through some other channel, such as an unexpected bequest or a new job. Part of most programs was broadcasting viewers' "testimonies" (picking up the earlier revival tradition of testimony) of miracles that had occurred to them because they gave money to the broadcaster.

As the analytical capacities of computerization were added to their management systems, issues that triggered audience contributions were more quickly identified and these issues were emphasized in future messages. Extensive market research was undertaken to identify audience preferences, down to such details as whether audiences preferred the broadcaster on screen to pray with his eyes open or closed and the posture he should adopt when praying.

Along with their dominance of the religious radio and television spectrum, and in line with their cultural agenda, the aggressive, enterprising force of Evangelicals moved into the competitive market of American popular consumer culture, transforming Christian ideas into broader popular subculture commodities of Christian music, printed materials, and movies. Heather Hendershot, in her book *Shaking the World for Jesus*,[38] demonstrates how Evangelical Christianity has had a marked influence on both secular and religious American culture simply by the preponderance of popular culture materials and commodities they've injected into the media and retail marketplace – replicating Martin Luther's influence four hundred years earlier. The dominance globally of American popular culture has meant that the capitalism-aligned, religious commodity culture of American Evangelical Christianity has also had a marked influence on the practice of Christianity elsewhere, such as in Latin America, West Africa, India, and Eastern Europe.

The criticism is at times made that these developments, the commodification of Christianity and adaptations of the message to the demands of the market, are perversions of true Christianity – a process of commodification or simulacrum shaped by the power and logic of the media that has little to do with "real Christianity."[39] While there is much that one could find to criticize in this particular version of Christianity, it is necessary to recognize that it is continuous with the Christian tradition of adapting messages, behaviors, and artifacts from the vast repertoire of Christian options, to make them fit the requirements of a new situation. As Hoover notes,

> Many people who are unfamiliar with American religious movements assume that the formats, technical sophistication, on-air fund raising, and general "hype" of the electronic church is an effect of the "medium" on the "message." While this may have been true with respect to some elements of these programs, by and large what the audience saw were tried and true formulas of the

revival circuit, put to use in a new medium which was hospitable to them. In short, electronic church broadcasting springs from a religious tradition – frontier evangelicalism – which has always stressed a simple and straightforward message, carefully packaged for maximum effect.[40]

The question, then, is not whether twentieth-century electric Christianity was continuous with the Christian tradition or not. It was. The question is: what were the cultural and political implications of this particular adaptation? One consequence that has already been identified was a smoothing over of the distinctive challenges of Christian ideological and theological perspectives – some that were previously for Evangelicals important signifiers of difference – to make the message more acceptable to large mass audiences: what Martin Marty has critiqued as a loss of Christianity's transformative "improper opinions."[41] A second was an alignment of Christian ideology with the ideologies of western capitalist consumer commodification, with all of the exploitation, inequality, dehumanization, and environmental damage that brings with it. As Dochuk has insightfully observed, while American Evangelical Christianity arose as a reaction and opposition to the creeping threat of secularization, its abandonment or lack of theological insight and substance has ironically promoted the secularization of the American church, albeit while retaining its Christian appearance."[42] As we will see in chapter 13, this has reached its zenith in the phenomenon of Global Pentecostalism and Prosperity Christianity.

Fundamentalism and Pentecostalism

Although Fundamentalism and Pentecostalism are both aligned with the wider Evangelical Coalition, they are of interest because of their distinctive uses of the Bible text, the distinctive aspects of their mediation of Christian faith, and the significance of those uses to the changing nature of western culture under the impact of electrification.

Fundamentalism emerged from the social and religious aftermath of the horrors and destruction of the American Civil War and what was seen as the undermining of the Christian foundations for recovery by the spreading influence of Enlightenment secular rationalism and liberal Christianity's perceived accommodation to it. The concerns were not limited to Protestantism, with Pope Pius X in 1907 also condemning the ideas of modernism as a collection of heresies and rejecting the application of historical criticism to scripture and the elevation of human reason over the supernatural.[43]

In the first two decades of the twentieth century, a series of pamphlets entitled *The Fundamentals* was published by the Moody Church in Chicago, challenging what were seen as the heresies of modernism and secularism and establishing the foundation for the United States to return to the true faith of Christianity. Five Christian fundamentals were identified:

- The virgin birth of Christ
- The substitutionary atonement of Christ for the sins of humanity
- The reality of the physical resurrection of Jesus
- The reality of miracles and the second coming of Christ
- The literal inerrancy of the Bible

Whereas other streams of Christianity charged Christians with responsibility for the improvement of social conditions, the dispensationalist views of emerging Fundamentalism denied any value in trying to save the world from what was seen as its predestined decline into disaster and ruin. While this would shift in later decades to a more pro-patriotic one of American exceptionalism and support for the US mission in the world, a persistent aspect of fundamentalism has been what Maurer describes as "the appearance of a new, darker, and much more pessimistic view of the Christian relationship with the world."[44] This worldly pessimism guided Fundamentalist political views of what should be done against ongoing threats such as the spread of communism and military attacks against the United States.

While it highlighted a number of indispensible fundamentals of belief, the key identification of Protestant Fundamentalism has been with their advocacy and defense of the inerrancy of the Bible text. In its defense of the Bible against attacks by modern historical biblical criticism, Fundamentalism elaborated a particularly modern Christian construction of the nature of sacred text.

Fundamentalism's challenge to secular humanism reached public attention in the Scopes Monkey Trial, a contest over whether understandings of human origins taught in American schools were going to be based on the biblical account of the creation of the world recorded in Genesis, or on scientific theories of origins, particularly that of evolution. The Scopes Trial was a major media event, broadcast on live radio and covered by hundreds of newspapers. It created a perception of Fundamentalists in the wider public mind as ignorant, backward laughing-stocks and led to their significant retreat to the fringes of society.

Dismissing Christian Fundamentalists as ignorant and backward, however, ignores the fact that there are many highly intelligent people, including scientifically educated ones, who hold these beliefs. It also hides the significance of its different media/textual understanding, that is, the absolute accuracy of the written text as an unchangeable and sure foundation for Christianity in a world of electric dynamism and fluidity.

The Fundamentalist view of the biblical text arises from a particular assumption that can be disputed but cannot be disproved: that is, that the biblical text in its original production was dictated by God to the consciousness of people who wrote it down as they were given it. As such, it is without error and is therefore the benchmark for subsequent human knowledge. Where subsequent human discoveries appear to contradict the biblical text, they are judged as either in error or not having discovered the full truth yet, a position that science in its theories of probability should theoretically be open to. Movements in Fundamentalism more recently, such as Creation Science, have sought to reformulate and reinterpret scientific data in a way that in their mind proves the Bible right in all things.

As a modern theory of text, Fundamentalism asserts a methodology of a literal meaning of the text, against earlier Christian views of historical, literary, or allegorical interpretations. The problem faced by Fundamentalism lies in the text itself: its complexity, the contradictions within the text itself, and the implausibility of some of its statements if taken literally.[45] It is here that Fundamentalism, like Catholicism and early Protestantism before it, interposes its own tradition above the text, bible commentaries and sermons that guide the reader into the "proper" Fundamentalist way of reading. Commenting on this, Morgan describes Fundamentalism as a theory of text that, far from simply taking the literal meaning of a text, integrates the open complexity of literal meanings into a closed ideological construction to serve a particular political and cultural purpose.

> Literalism is a mode of interpretation that conceals behind the façade of scripture a much more extensive interpretive machinery whose purpose is to generate a seamless fabric of reading from a spotty weave of text.[46]

Pentecostalism followed a quite different view of text and a quite different strategy of bringing the faith to life in an electric age, similar to that of the earliest Christian prophets and evangelists, that is, by using the text as a springboard. With roots in the Evangelical and Holiness revivals of the nineteenth century, modern Pentecostalism originated in the United States in the early twentieth century. Strongly oral in its communication style, it features a distinctive group experience of what is called "glossolalia" or "speaking in tongues," the ecstasy expressed by a person speaking in nonlanguage sounds, referenced in the Book of Acts account of the disciples of Jesus speaking in different languages when they were visited by the Holy Spirit.

From these early roots, the movement spread fairly quickly around the world, and it is now one of the fastest growing and most influential streams of Christianity in the United States, Europe, Latin America, Africa, and Asia. With the main commonality being a belief that God as the Holy Spirit "baptizes" people in the Spirit and empowers them with supernatural gifts, less stress is placed on specific theological beliefs and more on being dynamically alive in and guided by the Spirit.

As in other oral-based movements, there is a close connection between ascribed authority and the perceived integrity of the leader. Authority is strongly charismatic in character, indicated by achievements of success in conversions, healings, powerful oral preaching, and the ability to induce ecstatic religious experience. The instability of charismatic authority characterized by Weber is also present, leading to a high turnover of adherents through migration to other groups where the leaders are seen to be more inspired.

In the Pentecostal movement, the Bible is engaged as a sourcebook and springboard for insight and guidance given to the individual by the direct intervention of the Holy Spirit. In contrast to the deductive, rational approach of Fundamentalism and liberal Christianity, the meaning of the text in Pentecostalism is an individual meaning activated by God's direct intervention.

This emphasis on charismatic authority, rather than formal authority based on position or post in the Christian institution, opened Christian leadership to those who had previously been largely shut out of it, in particular people with little education, and women. One of the most exemplary and influential Pentecostal personalities of the twentieth century, although also among its most controversial, was the Canadian-American Pentecostal evangelist Aimee Semple McPherson. Converted at a Pentecostal rally in Ontario in 1907, she married the preacher and went with him as a missionary to China, where he died soon after arrival. After a period of evangelistic work in Canada, in 1921 she moved to Los Angeles and built a church, the Angelus Temple, where she gathered a large congregation through a mix of worship services that involved imaginative positive preaching, theatrical sets and performances, a large choir and brass bands, healings and Pentecostal demonstrations, book and magazine publication, and radio performances and ownership. By the end of the 1920s, she was preaching up to twenty times a week to overflow crowds that crossed class lines. Although one of the most recognized religious figures in the United States, she was unsuccessful in evangelical campaigns outside of the United States. Her impact and influence began to decline due to a number of public scandals in the late 1920s, but grew again in the 1930s with a blend of Christianity with American patriotism in the face of the threat of communism and leading up to the Second World War. She died in 1944. The Angelus Temple in Los Angeles rode the wave of Pentecostalism and grew into a denomination of Pentecostal Christianity called the International Church of the Foursquare Gospel that today claims sixty-six thousand churches in 140 countries.[47]

In summarizing McPherson's influence, Sutton identifies her as the first religious celebrity of the mass media era, setting precedents that would be taken up by later evangelical celebrities such as Billy Graham, Oral Roberts, Pat Robertson, and the megachurch movement. Her wider influence was in moving conservative Protestantism from the margins to the mainstream of American urbanized culture.

McPherson's religious revival caught the nation off guard. With rapid urban-ization, the discovery of new technologies, the perfecting of powerful forms of mass media, the rise of the modern university system, and the growth of a celebrity-centered culture, many Americans in the early years of the twen-tieth century predicted the extinction of classic evangelicalism. Yet from her location in the burgeoning show business capital of the world, McPherson changed the way American religion is practiced. She combined the old-time faith, showbiz sensibilities, marketing savvy, and passionate Americanism to revive a seemingly dead movement.[48]

The responses to her death provide a good illustration of the differences in attitude toward such media performance held by the literate-print cultur-al position of mainline Protestantism and the populist oral-cultural move-ment of Pentecostalism. The Protestant magazine *The Christian Century*, in an anonymous obituary, gave recognition to the fact that she "put on a good show" but then largely lambasted her.

> On the other side of the ledger were the fallacious and dogmatic simplification of Christian teaching, her glorification of ignorance, her mouthing of pious slogans and catch phrases, her fraudulent faith cures, her reliance upon the spectacular and the sentimental.[49]

On the other hand, in the three days that her body lay in state in the An-gelus Temple, forty-five thousand people of all classes and colors stood in long lines, sometimes till two o'clock in the morning, to view her coffin and pay their respects. All major US magazines and many international ones, including *Time, Newsweek, Life*, and *New Statesman*, did long stories on her life and ministry. While many mainline churches have been in decline, the Angelus Temple continues its work today with two hundred different ministries, a food program that feeds twenty thousand people a week, a drug and alcohol rehabilitation program that serves four hundred men and women, work with gangs and youth at risk, and neighborhood beautifica-tion programs.[50]

NOTES

1 Sconce, 2000, p. 7.
2 For a thorough investigation of the social adaptations of electricity and electrical technologies, see Marvin, 1988.
3 Sawhney, 1996.
4 Sconce, 2000, p. 7.
5 Stolow, 2007.

6 For further insight on this, see Lundby's analysis of the 1994 Winter Olympic Games Opening Ceremony in Lillehammer (Lundby, 1997).
7 See for example Adorno & Bernstein, 2001; Hjarvard, 2008b, 2011; McComb, 2004; Postman, 1987.
8 See for example Bruce, 1996, p. 2.
9 For a further discussion of this, see Casanova, 1994; Finke & Stark, 1988; Greeley, 1972; D. Martin, 1969; Swatos, 1999; C. Taylor, 2007.
10 Hjarvard, 2011, p. 124.
11 See for example Horsfield, 2013; Morgan, 2011.
12 The perspective was developed by a number of American sociologists of religion, particularly Roger Finke and Rodney Starke; see Finke & Stark, 1988; Finke & Starke, 1992.
13 Finke & Starke, 1992.
14 From their website: http://www.ppcbooks.com/about.asp
15 For an early discussion of this, see Marty, 1961.
16 Barr & Fore, 2005a, p. 1007.
17 Barr & Fore, 2005a, p. 1007.
18 Barr & Fore, 2005a, p. 1008.
19 Barr & Fore, 2005b, p. 1171.
20 The paradoxical relationship of American Protestantism with television is well explored by Rosenthal, 2007.
21 Rosenthal, 2007, p. 22.
22 See for example Hurley, 1970; Kahle, 1971.
23 Cross & Livingstone, 1974, p. 486.
24 Marsden, 1993, p. 37.
25 Bebbington & Jones, 2013; Kay, 2011; Marsden, 1984; Wallis, 2009.
26 MacCulloch, 2009, p. 738.
27 Armstrong, 1979, p. 7.
28 Armstrong, 1979, p. 8.
29 Hendershot, 2004, pp. 145–147.
30 Armstrong, 1979, p. 134.
31 James Taylor, 1977.
32 Barr & Fore, 2005a, p. 1008.
33 http://www.nae.net/about-us/history/62
34 Pohlman, 2011, p. 5.
35 Horsfield, 1984, p. 9.
36 Dochuk, 2007, pp. 300–303. See also Hoover, 1988.
37 Dochuk, 2007, p. 302.
38 Hendershot, 2004.
39 Baudrillard, 1993. See also Hjarvard, 2008a.
40 Hoover, 1990, p. 24.
41 Marty, 1961.
42 Dochuk, 2007, p. 303.
43 Maurer, 2009, p. 62.
44 Maurer, 2009, p. 53.

45 There are few Fundamentalists who pluck out their eyes or cut off their hands if they happen to see or do something sinful, as Jesus apparently instructs his followers to do in Matthew 18:9.
46 Morgan, 2014.
47 From http://www.foursquare.org/about/history
48 Sutton, 2007.
49 Cited in Sutton, 2007, p. 272.
50 Sutton, 2007, p. 276.

13

The Digital Era

The empire of digital capitalism

The extensive cultural changes that have occurred around the turn of the third millennium have their roots in a number of intersecting technological developments.

One of those has been digital computerization. Building on theories of eighteenth-century philosopher Gottfried Leibniz, the foundation of computerization lies in digital language, the technological conversion of all information and sensory data into a binary code of on-off, 0-1 pulses. Utilizing this electronic language has enabled exponential growth in the capacity to process and store large amounts of multisensory information and data in smaller and smaller pieces of equipment in a way that can be accessed on call and reconfigured into new sensory forms and applications.

A second has been the development of hypertext, a term invented by Ted Nelson to describe what he saw as "non-sequential writing – text that branches and allows choices to the reader, best read at an interactive screen."[1] Hypertext consists of nodes or writing spaces created in a document, linked technologically in a way that enables the user or reader to jump from node to node, document to document, and textual space to textual space. Instead of reading being marked by progress through a single text in a linear fashion, one at a time in a physical library of single texts, digital reading is marked by an individual creating their own reading trail through a network of interlinked texts or "docuverse."[2] The instantaneousness of the appearance onscreen of a totally new text, image, sound, video, or animation creates a lateral, multisensory, user-directed textual engagement in place of the more singular, sequential pattern of most hard-copy reading.

A third is the development of new technologies of digital data transmission. Technologies such as fiber-optic cabling, satellite relays, wireless transmission, and digital switching systems have provided the means for the

From Jesus to the Internet, Peter Horsfield © 2015 John Wiley & Sons, Ltd. Published 2015 by John Wiley & Sons, Ltd.

high-speed continuous transfer of these digitized data and voice across all areas of the globe, making possible the accumulation, storage, access, and reproduction of these data through a technological web of networked global communication.

The fourth is the adaptation of these technologies into mobile media that allow despatialized personal access to this universe of information. It is the speed, the mobility, the accessibility, and the convenience of mobile media devices that have enabled the constructed network services that now largely organize contemporary life in developed nations, a digital culture marked by complexes of activities and attitudes commonly identified through single words (e.g., Google, Facebook, SMS, Instagram, Twitter, online, email, voicemail, smartphone, laptop, or tablet) or their related practices of googling, facebooking, and tweeting.

The increased capacity, diminishing size, and increasing mobility of technologies of information and communication have insinuated computerization into almost every aspect and activity of daily life.

A number of commentators identify the symbiosis of this global digital communication and economic organization as a new form of capitalism, one in which the local and global are reformed. Jameson sees it as a third stage of capitalism, characterized by multinational corporations with global markets and mass consumption creating a world space of multinational capital.[3]

Castells likewise sees a new form of capitalism, marked by the globalization of core economic activities, greater organizational flexibility, and greater power for management over labor. The demands for greater corporate flexibility in order to compete globally have undermined the rights and leverage of workers and are undermining the boundaries and protections of the geographically bounded welfare state, "the cornerstone of the social contract in the industrial era." Castells sees this form of capitalism as integrally linked to what he calls "informationalism."

> New informational technologies played a decisive role in facilitating the emergence of this rejuvenated, flexible capitalism, by providing the tools for networking, distant communication, storing/processing of information, coordinated individualization of work, and simultaneous concentration and decentralization of decision-making.... In spite of a highly diversified social and cultural landscape, for the first time in history the whole planet is organized around a largely common set of economic rules. It is, however, a different kind of capitalism than the one formed during the Industrial Revolution.... It is a hardened form of capitalism in its goals, but incomparably more flexible than any of its predecessors in its means. It is informational capitalism, relying on innovation-induced productivity and globalization-oriented competitiveness to generate wealth, and to appropriate it selectively. It is, more than ever, embedded in culture and tooled by technology.[4]

This global dynamic of capitalism is sustained by a number of key transformations. One is a shift in the character of public communication from being an expressive human activity and common good to a valuable commercial product. The concept of society as a commonwealth of citizens united by communication is under pressure from a concept of society as an aggregate of individuals or demographic markets constructed by marketers. Within this model, a key issue for the production of public communication, whether for broadcast, print, or online, is whether one can find or attract a market sufficiently large to financially sustain the publication.

A second important value and dynamic is that of commodification, where social or cultural activities are coopted, stolen, or invented, and then packaged and sold as commercial products or commodities. The commercialization of most social and cultural activities is displacing previous social structures that supported noncommercial activity that was of benefit to the wider community, placing pressure on most social and cultural activities not just to produce but also to capitalize or monetize the activity. Even online communication activities, such as blogs, which may begin for a self-expressive reason, can find themselves courted or taken over by commercial interests eager to monetize their audience. In this competitive commercial communication environment, noncommercial public institutions that communicate in the public interest, such as publicly funded national broadcasting systems, can become subject to political or legal challenge because their public funding presents unfair competition for commercial organizations working in the same area.

The multitude of options in the marketplace can now only reasonably be managed through the social philosophy and processes of consumerism (i.e., reframing and resocializing tribal members or citizens to be individual consumers who are to be ostensibly self-directed in their acquisitions based on their own narratives and needs). It is through the mechanisms of consumerism – expanding the production of goods and services through marketing and the cultivation of desire – that the potentially fickle markets of capitalism are sustained and stabilized.

One of the marked features of Christianity in the current digital era has been the negotiation of beliefs, practices, and standing that has taken place by different Christian groups, not just in the use of new media technologies, but also in relation to this new global empire of digital capitalism. Within the historical context, this process of negotiation of beliefs and values can be seen to share many features with Christianity's earlier encounters with empires such as those of the Romans, Byzantines, and Franks. In a way similar to Christianity's acceptance of patronage into the empire of Constantine, there are rewards and benefits for Christianity for cooperating with the empire and disadvantages for not cooperating.

The opportunity that's open to willing Christian groups is that the successful functioning of late capitalism needs a cooperative spirit to provide the motivation for people, who are disadvantageously affected by capitalism's necessary inequities, nevertheless to continue to participate and contribute to the system in the hope of gaining benefits from it. Drawing on Boltanski and Chiapello's work *The New Spirit of Capitalism*,[5] Willis and Maarouf outline this dynamic:

> There is a recognition that capitalist relations of production cannot function entirely through their own intrinsic logics or through direct coercion. They are always socially and culturally embedded and require appropriate attitudes and feelings in their agents to move the whole system at the human level. Capitalism needs lots of 'spirit(s)' to make it work on the human plane. Often thought through from above in terms of the need for managerial or entrepreneurial skills, equally vital for the functioning of capitalist social formations is a subordinate 'spirit' from below, a willing submission, at some level, or at least withdrawal of subjective negation, to the formal relations which subsume labour power to the labour process under the direction of capital or its managers.[6]

The opportunity for Christianity to play a vital role within the dominant new empire of capitalism by providing its energizing and motivating spirit in support of economic production has been taken up by some bodies within Christianity, and, in a way similar to what we observed with Catholic and Orthodox Christianity in the fourth and fifth centuries, theology has developed to justify this cooperation with the dominant system in order to gain the benefits that come with it.[7] We will explore these dynamics and issues further in this chapter.

Digital practice

Before looking in more detail at some specific Christian responses and initiatives in the current period, it is helpful to look at some of the practices that have developed as people, industries, and institutions have utilized the affordances of digital technologies, and some of the ways in which these practices are presenting themselves as challenges to existing Christian cultural practice.

Digital practice as immersive environment

While communication has always been an omnipresent phenomenon in human societies, the digital era deepens the character and experience of that omnipresence. With mobile telephony, mobile computerization, and the increasingly small and specific applications of computer chips to more and more daily activities, mediated communication has taken on the characteristics of an enveloping technological and symbolic environment within which life is lived. This environment has a number of characteristics. One is a constant flow of information. The volume of information available through search, reference, and download, and the volume of information pushed through programs such as email, SMS, Twitter, Facebook, and Instagram, create a felt imperative of being in constant contact with cultural information delivered and accessed digitally. Yet given the volume of information flow, one needs to become culturally and technologically adept at selecting, processing, and evaluating information for relevance and importance – a dynamic Couldry identifies as keeping all channels open while also screening out.[8]

Another characteristic of digital practice is its interactivity. Changes in technologies of production and reception have reduced the time and cost of the circulation of information to such an extent that interacting quickly with others around information is as important as, if not more important than, pondering it in depth. Underlying this interactivity of digital practice is its sensory character. Digital technologies address the aural, oral, tactile, visual, and kinetic functions of the body in ways that are reworking the relationship between reason, imagination, and the emotional in the evaluation and integration of information, experience, and perception. They have also brought a changed relationship and balance between noise and silence, and between stimulation and inaction. For many, if not most, digital natives today, to be is to be in noise and constantly in touch. To be in periods of silence is boring or suspicious.

A third aspect of digital practice is the acceleration or condensing of time. Developments in the technologies have enabled digital communication to be virtually instantaneous, changing cultural perceptions of time in ways similar to other occasions in history when the mediation of time has changed (e.g., the invention of calendars and the mechanical clock). Speed in particular has become an important social value that is linked with the fluidity of hypertext; cultural perceptions of time are changing from time as something ordered and following its own duration, to time as something immediate, fluid, and fast.

These new cultural practices of information management disrupt some of the foundational cultural practices on which Christianity shaped some of its basic structures of institutional life, religious authority, and theological thinking. While many see these historic aspects of Christianity as essential Christian practices, in fact, as we have seen, they developed in quite specific mediated contexts and have essentialized culturally specific characteristics of those contexts.

For example, while interactivity in community has been a sustaining feature of Christianity, it has commonly been managed within defined conditions. Important in this has been a concept of Christian authority as a particular type of communication activity, where a designated leader is institutionally authorized to make authoritative statements that carry, or are assumed to carry, a quality of definitiveness or command that could be enforced by social, political, or military power if necessary. This institutional view of directive authority reached its apogee in the Roman Catholic Church's dogma of papal infallibility, which was created in the late nineteenth century and asserts that when making official statements as pope, the pope is incapable of error – no question or interaction on the issue was possible.

The interactive nature of digital practice subverts this construct of authority. Not only may a designated Christian authority not even be heard in the wider ocean of information, but also, if their so-called authoritative pronouncement is heard, it is likely to be immediately interacted with through social media: commented on, pulled apart, criticized, defended, and perhaps even lost in a rapid shift to a related topic. The authority ascribed in digital practice is one earned in the process of interaction on specific topics or issues, a type of authority that is more common in oral-dominant communities than in the aloof, institution-based authority that most churches have carried into this third millennium.

Social risks of digital practice

Each form of communication carries risks. We've noted earlier some of the different practices that those in power in Christianity have put in place to manage or minimize the risks that communication activities posed to their power. Digital practice brings a different set of risks, and these present challenges also to current Christian practice. In her study of families and digital media, Lynn Schofield Clark identifies a number of these in relation to families,[9] which are also of relevance to Christian practice.

- *The persistence of communication.* Once entered on the internet, information, including personal information, can be difficult to remove. As we saw earlier, part of the strategy by the Catholic-Orthodox Party to gain ascendancy over other streams of Christianity in the third and fourth centuries was to destroy their writings or remove them from circulation. Christian strategies of handling alternative opinions through destruction, censorship, or restricting circulation that was possible in a manuscript or even print cultural context cannot be used in a digital environment today.
- *Changeability.* Digital information is easily replicated and modified, and therefore easily misrepresented. This presents a problem for Christian institutions, which have been able to a significant extent to control the imputed meaning of their messages and their symbols. Digital practice largely removes that control.

- *Scalability.* The proportion of something is easily misrepresented in digital practice through either reduction (i.e., rendering something that is serious as trite) or amplification (i.e., expanding something out of its original context and proportion – the current term "going viral" describes this amplification). Those Christian institutions and leaders whose native culture is a literate one of order, reason, and patriarchal calm lack the cultural literacies to communicate effectively within this new digital environment.
- *Searchability.* The interactivity of digital media works on an expectation that people will present themselves publicly through social media. Without such a public presence, it is assumed that one does not exist socially. A consequence of this, however, is that one can also be searched – a dynamic Couldry describes as showing and being shown.[10] Through Google, GPS, and visual and voice recognition, almost all actions are capable of being found out. Corporations have developed significant crisis management strategies for handling exposures of contradictions between the public and the private perceptions of corporate practice. As we shall consider further in this chapter, the exposure of hidden sexual abuse by Christian leaders is a good example of the new conditions being created by digital practice.

Digital language

Changes to the fundamental nature of textual language brought by hypertext has and continues to have implications for Christianity, whose religious thought, construction of meaning, symbolic practice, structures of authority, and unifying systems of theology, since at least the end of the second century, depend heavily on textually based grammatical structures of language. Those building blocks of textual language are changed by hypertext, which destabilizes meaning toward something more fluid, multiple, variable, and polysemic,[11] and without a clear beginning or ending.[12]

Martin Marty presciently noted this shift and its implications for Christianity in the late 1980s in comments on the central Christian practice of theology. The practice of theology in Christianity, he noted, was built on a particular media structure that is fundamentally subverted by the processes of digital media:

It is time to say that theological expression was reliant upon the stable, purchasable, book-length literary products of theologians in community within free societies. Those were books written by people whose vocation climaxed in reading and writing them. Now they present a fragile, endangered species.... Technologically, economically, politically, religiously, and in respect of status, conception, and the use of time, the concept of theology expressed through a moderate diversity of books is called into question by hyper-modern and counter-modern tendencies.[13]

What is interesting in this current situation is that while the destabilization of meaning through hypertext presents challenges to current institutional Christianity, it has a lot in common with the oral communication style of Jesus, which was largely dispensed with in the Gentile creation of Christianity as a hierarchical, theologically defined, institutionally ordered phenomenon. The characteristics of hypertext identified here, as being more fluid, variable, and polysemic, and without a clear beginning or ending, have strong resonances with the language practices of Jesus, as Woodhead has described them:

> When he spoke he used riddles and parables which even his contemporaries had a hard time understanding. When he referred to himself he used ambiguous titles like "son of man," or turned the question of "who do you say I am?" back to his questioners. He laid down few clear rules, left no systematic teaching, and founded no institution to pass on his message. Rather than supplying answers he provokes people to make their own response.[14]

Deinstitutionalization and new community formations

The exponential increase in choice and the digital practice preference toward networking are changing previous formations of social order that were strongly institution centered to formations in which loyalty and commitment to any one community or institution are more tentative. Increasingly, people are involved in a mix of communities, drawing from and contributing to each what is enjoyable, useful, or dutiful for particular stages of life. In this process of deinstitutionalization, those social institutions that in a previous cultural regime were the principal agents or determiners of social information, services, and resources are having to adapt by packaging and marketing their services and products to meet the needs or demands of individuals or collectives in what is now a highly competitive, selective, and increasingly well-informed social market.

Various concerns have been expressed about this transitory nature of people's relationship to community. Some see it simply as selfish individualism or consumerism. Bar-Haim's concerns are more nuanced. While he sees this networked form of collective as possibly necessary in these new cultural conditions, he cautions about an absence of what he calls "compulsion," the practical interdependencies and a sense of a compelling history or destiny that calls the individual out of herself or himself into a durable collective for the mutual benefit of the whole.

While there is decline in some traditional forms of community and institutional structure, Wuthnow notes the growth in relevance of other forms of social formation, which he identifies as communities of support, communities of residence, communities of service, and communities of memory.

Because choice of community is available, he notes that volunteers now ask more questions than they did in the past in return for their participation, such as questions regarding expectations of achievement and satisfaction, greater accountability on the part of the community, the need for recognition and some personal reward for what is given (that previously came from inherent interdependence), and a decreasing tolerance of nepotism and self-serving institutions.[15]

This changed situation is a significant challenge to many parts of Christianity, which see their current structures of church institutions as important, if not indispensible, to the ideology and practice of the religion. In many understandings, the church as an institution is not just a resource or site for faith, but also a supranatural entity, a cosmic mother even, to be loved and served.

What is becoming apparent, particularly in the West, is that people, including Christians, increasingly are not seeing the institutions of Christianity as crucial to their religious practice, or seeing churches as an essential source of information about Christianity. Nor are they seeing that placing oneself within a church is the way one becomes a Christian. Redefining the nature and place of its institutional formation is a major challenge being faced by most parts of Christianity today.

Openness to enchantment and transcendence

One of the surprising aspects of contemporary digital practice is its openness, and even active search, for experiences of enchantment and transcendence. It is surprising because in the influential processes of secularization, it was thought that as scientific understanding, the nation-state, and improved social conditions progressed, religious and pseudo-religious phenomena would cease to be attractive to people. While interest in organized religion may have diminished, digital practice appears to be ignoring those formal boundaries between the secular and the religious, and actively exploring and playing with enchantment and transcendence.

Bar-Haim links this openness to transcendental possibilities to widespread disillusionment with utopian promises and unfulfilled hopes of secularized consumer culture.

> In summary, the social ideals that once defined and focused political energies, inspired new challenges for reform, paved the way to a more flexible stratification, and gave legitimization to a secular morality have reached a point of ineffectiveness, incapable of mobilizing and fulfilling expectations.[16]

In the wake of this disillusionment, or perhaps boredom, one can see in many digital practices a rejection of pure rationalism or empiricism and a renewed interest in religion, mystery, myth, and magic. This interest is reflected in a flurry of new religious movements, most of which have been facilitated by and operate within the networking capacities of the internet and social media, which have enabled the congregating of people of like minds who previously would have remained isolated.[17] A number of these are recovering traditional indigenous and "pagan" beliefs and practices that were displaced by Christianity during its missionary expansions, and the challenge they pose to Christianity replicates in some ways the challenge of popular religious practices to orthodox Christianity during the Middle Ages; some of these popular practices were opposed, but others were simply rebranded with a Christian label and adopted into Christian practice.

The commercial media and culture industries have recognized in this broader cultural desire for reenchantment a profitable new market, capable of being commodified and sold. Issues of transcendence, mystery, myth, and magic have become common themes in popular television programs, movies, products and product marketing, advertising, and the immersive virtual realities of popular video games.[18] The search for reenchantment also finds expression in increased participation in civic rituals and mega-spectacles:

> It is the grand spectacle which has become the epitome of contemporary celebration; with its large-scale technical wizardry and stunning effects, logistical complexity and vast publicity that attempt to compensate for the loss of mythology and absence of a metaphysical presence ... the disintegration of traditional small communities and with them the gradual disappearance or transformation of religious and agricultural rituals, has left a void that is gradually being filled by mostly secular celebrations along with some civic rituals.[19]

It is apparent that a significant challenge to Christianity today lies not so much with secular rationalism, but with commercial products of commodified enchantment, such as the Olympic Games and World Cup quadrennial events, new year and millennium celebrations, national day celebrations, and immersive virtual reality games.

With this cultural framework of the new millennium, the dominant economic systems of global capitalism, and the cultures of digital practice, three aspects of Christianity's engagement with this new cultural context are examined: global Pentecostalism, the media exposure of sexual abuse by Christian clergy, and transformations taking place in Christian traditions and practice that speak to the new cultural situation.

Global Pentecostalism

One of the most noted and public Christian phenomena of the contemporary period has been the rise of the Christian stream of Pentecostalism.[20]

While Pentecostalism associates its distinctive emphases and practices such as glossolalia, dramatic miracle healings, prophecies, exorcisms, and spiritual gifts directly to the New Testament, it has aspects in common with historic Christian traditions, such as ecstatic mysticism and Evangelical revivalism. From its modern beginnings in the early twentieth century, it has grown to become the fastest-growing branch of Christianity globally, driven largely not by churches but by entrepreneurial Christians.

It is identified most publicly by its large mega-churches, not just in the United States but also globally. Examples can be cited on every continent. The City Harvest Church in Singapore, with twenty-eight thousand members and an annual budget of $49 million in 2007, spent $300 million to become a part-owner of the Suntec shopping and convention center in downtown Singapore with the intent of relocating its gatherings into the heart of Singapore's shopping district.[21] The Yoido Full Gospel Church in Seoul, begun in the 1950s with a mission to present Christianity in a practical way that alleviated suffering, solved problems, and helped people become wealthy, today has a membership of over a quarter of a million people.[22] Pentecostalism is the most rapidly growing religious expression across Africa,[23] to the extent that Africa is exporting its spirituality: the largest church in Kiev, Ukraine, is a Pentecostal church of twenty-five thousand members with seventy branches, started and headed by a Nigerian, Sunday Adelaja. Christian Pentecostalism has become the dominant religious force in Latin America, displacing what had been the traditional dominance of Roman Catholicism. The founder of one of the key Pentecostal groups in Brazil, the Igrega Universal do Reino de Deus (the Universal Church of the Kingdom of God), was able to bring sufficient political influence and financial resources to bear to secure personal ownership of one of Brazil's largest broadcast networks, Rede Record.[24]

These, however, are the tip of the iceberg. Below the surface are innumerable medium-sized regional and city churches and small town or village churches that nevertheless name and identify themselves as global. Operating within the opportunities and needs created by the global spread of capitalism, these local-based, media-extended Christian movements compete in the open media market with packages of faith-colored solutions to dissatisfactions and opportunities created by the rise of cultural pluralism, failures in postcolonial national rebuilding, and the economic and political uncertainties of globalization. Lehmann notes that despite differences in their national and cultural contexts, Pentecostal churches "exhibit astonishingly similar patterns of growth, use similar techniques of oratory and proselytization, similar forms of organization and leadership, and also resemble each other strongly in their ritual practices."[25] Asamoah-Gyadu, from his studies of African Pentecostalism, elaborates shared characteristics in more detail. The churches are mostly urban-centered congregations, with English as the principal language of communication, an absence of religious symbolism in places of worship, and a special appeal to and attraction for "upwardly mobile youth." A strong emphasis is placed on church growth, with extensive and innovative use of modern media technologies. Leadership is predominantly by laypeople, with ecclesiastical office based on a person's charismatic gifting. There is an ardent desire to appear successful – the churches project a modern outlook, there is a relaxed and fashion-conscious dress code for members, and significant effort goes into cultivating an international image.[26]

We noted earlier connections that have been drawn between Protestantism's religious ethics and the growth of modern capitalism. The connections between Pentecostalism and global capitalism are different. Whereas Weber saw well-being and prosperity as indirect consequences of Protestantism's faith in a higher power and emphasis on living an ordered, thrifty, and industrious moral life,[27] global Pentecostalism is overtly materialist in its practice and emphases, unashamedly promoting Christian belief and practice as means of individuals becoming healthy and wealthy.

In contrast to the indirect, rationalist, abstracted stance of much of western Christianity, the theology and spirituality undergirding these movements are direct, active, interventionist ones. In many ways they reflect a regeneration of historic oral-based, rhetorical Christian practices, but with distinctive economic perspectives. There is, it is claimed, an active spiritual force in the universe that can influence daily events. The desire of that power, among other things, is that believers be healthy and wealthy. This power can be enlisted and used by those who believe to improve their personal and financial circumstances. All a person has to do is to claim it by saying it (the power of the spoken word) and acting in a way that gives that power the opportunity to work. The global Pentecostal movement reflects the maturation of the Evangelical, Revivalist, Pentecostal entrepreneurship of the nineteenth and twentieth centuries.

The rise and spread of global Pentecostalism cannot be fully understood without understanding its place within and relationship to the global empire of digital capitalism. A number of researchers locate the rise of these religious movements, particularly in Africa, Latin America, and Asia, in needs generated through the collapse of social and economic systems, political corruption, and disillusionment with the functionality of institutions of government in the postcolonial period. Meyer, in her studies in Africa, for example, notes that the rise of these churches in Ghana corresponded to a period of severe economic decline and starvation in the postcolonial period of the 1980s.[28] The Yoido Full Gospel Church in Seoul likewise was born in the economically depressed 1950s with an expressed intention to provide religion as a way of improving people's material conditions.

There have been other responses made by Christianity to address the poverty generated by western capitalism's exploitation of the laboring classes and third world countries. Advocacy movements in the West have agitated for social justice and economic development. Indigenization movements in Christian mission churches have sought to strengthen local cultures and cultural responses. The movement of Liberation Theology and the development of base Christian communities in Latin America were active centers of resistance to economic domination. The failure of these Christian efforts to redress entrenched poverty laid the ground for Pentecostalism. Rather than valorizing poverty as a way of ameliorating its dehumanizing effects, Pentecostalism has offered a form of Christian faith and faith community that is dynamic, emotionally engaging, accessible, and globally oriented, and that promises a way to secure God's help to access the benefits of western capitalism and become wealthy.

The appeal of Pentecostalism lies in its perceived relevance to the global economic system and the cultural patterns of digital, electronic media. More than just using media extensively, Pentecostalism has relocated Christianity within a quite different sort of media culture: electronic, visual, spectacular, mobile, sloganeering, dynamic, and fluid. As Asamoah-Gyadu notes, "Pentecostals, as modern day evangelicals, have taken the use of media for religious purposes to a new level."[29]

Highly technological in their media use, they subordinate the stability, order, and linearity of textual Christianity to the dynamics of oral culture. Community worship services and prayer meetings are loud, dynamic, participatory, interactive, and constantly in motion. It is a culture of "flow" – of words, and of people moving in and out of services, workshops and groups, and experiences.

> Words spoken in faith are regarded as objectifications of reality, establishing palpable connections between human will and the external world. They form a kind of inductive fundamentalism. Believers are supposedly enabled to assert sovereignty over multiple spheres of existence, ranging from their own bodies to broad geographical regions.[30]

Monetary exchange is a part of this flow and verbal performance and an indicator of one's trust in the spiritual power that governs the universe. Money is readily given away, generally to the church or the preacher, in faith and expectation that within the global flow of capital, God will cause a larger amount of money to flow back again. One needs to give in order to receive. Whether one is prepared to do so or not is one of the indicators of whether one has faith or not. As Coleman notes,

> The speaking out of words and the giving away of money are therefore akin to each other in the way they provide means of reaching into a world of opportunity as well as threat.... An ideology of uninterrupted flow and reception is reinforced by the global charismatic habitus in combination with particular ways of structuring linguistic and financial "transactions."[31]

This concept of flow also informs the charismatic engagement with the empire of global capital. Pentecostalism is a global movement in identity and perspective – even small churches claim the word "global" or "international" as part of their title. The pastors of the larger churches dedicate significant parts of their website to images of their international recognition, such as photographs with world leaders and celebrities. Significant time is given in church services to praying for and celebrating success in such things as gaining international visas or business deals.

While some of the claims made on websites may be questionable, there is an international circuit of Pentecostal leaders regularly visiting each other, with Western-based charismatic leaders trading funding support in exchange for association with the raw spiritual power and energy of charismatic leaders from Africa, Latin America, and Asia. There is also significant interchange between diaspora Asian and African communities in the United Kingdom and United States and their home religious communities.

Ethically, Christian Pentecostalism focuses on personal morality with an emphasis on chastity or heterosexual marriage in a patriarchal-headed nuclear family. Its social ethic is oriented toward structures that support these values and facilitate church growth and wealth creation. This generally finds expression in the support of governments and political parties that serve those sectarian interests. Singapore provides an interesting case study in this regard. Daniel Goh notes that in order to build Singapore as a modern industrial state, it was necessary for the Lee government to suppress those who undermined that development.[32] This included Protestant and Catholic wings of Christianity that presented challenges to government action on the grounds of social injustice, the preservation of indigenous culture, or the promotion of democracy. The government strongly opposed these Christian challenges, in some cases jailing their leaders. The economic development agenda being promoted built a climate in which Pentecostal groups, whose moral concerns for sexual morality, promotion of the family, and support for wealth creation supported government plans, were able to prosper.[33]

Although justified within a Christian theological framework, Christian Pentecostalism contributes significantly to the spirit of aspiration and hope that capitalism needs to maintain its attraction and workforce. In developing countries, Pentecostal churches have become significant training centers for basic skills and services to facilitate the rebuilding of social and economic communities within a global context. Maxwell, in his study of the Zimbabwean Assembly of God Church, identifies a variety of practical steps taken by this Christian body to convert existing cultural practices into a Christian culture of making money. These include shifting relationship support away from traditional tribal supports to church communities, education in literacy and morality, training in economic management, making profit and enterprise a spiritual calling, teaching money making through workshops and worship, interpreting Christianity into the financial marketplace, and promoting lifestyle changes that reflect one's aspirational path.

Despite its emphasis on the spirit, Pentecostalism is a commodity-oriented religious expression, with significant investment made into the acquisition of consumer goods to indicate, or create the impression, that one has been blessed by the spirit. As Maxwell observes,

> Free from kin and community to accumulate wealth, the new believer is smart in appearance, trustworthy, hard working and literate, and hence employable.... Being born again can create a "redemptive uplift."[34]

Because of the biblical caution against the dangers of wealth and possessions, Pentecostalism has established processes for the exorcism of evil from wealth and consumption to make them spiritually safe for believers. Meyer describes these processes from her studies in Ghana,

> By invoking God's power over every commodity bought, they perform "exit rites" for the commodity, through which it is purified from its polluting past in the global market – in short, it is de-fetishized. Stripped of its history, it is safe to carry into its owner's house. Through this process, the object is subordinated to its owner; now it can no longer act as a fetish nor turn its owner into a satanic sign.[35]

A similar development can be seen in the rise of Christianity in China, where the number of Christians is now estimated at between 77 and 100 million, more than membership of the Chinese Communist Party.[36] Among the fastest growing of these are Christian groups that Fenggang Yang identifies as the "grey religious market," the unofficial but tolerated urban, Protestant house churches that now make up the largest nongovernmental organization in China. Many meet in McDonald's restaurants to avoid undesirable attention from residential neighbors, although Yang sees another significance in the McDonald's meeting location of these new Christian groups. In his interviews, Yang found that for many of this aspirational urban business and youth demographic, western Evangelical Christianity, accessed through the global media system, is seen as providing a more useful ideology for making money than Marxism. The global movement of Pentecostalism provides practical supportive connections for them in making the transition between the rapid changes in the developing Chinese market economy and the global economic community.

> By frequenting McDonald's and converting to Christianity, young urban Chinese get psychological peace, security, and certainty. They also gain a sense of participating in the new and glamorous dimensions of contemporary cultural change without exposing themselves directly to the vagaries of the global market.[37]

Media and Christian sexual abuse

One area where media have had a marked impact on Christianity in the current period is in the exposure of sexual abuse of children and women by Christian leaders, and exposure of the protection of those abusers and cover-up of their crimes by other Christian leaders. The phenomenon has a number of significant media connections: it marks a change in the previously deferential stance of news and public media toward Christian leaders; it brings to the surface some of the media and communication strategies that churches have used to cultivate and project a particular Christian image into the public sphere; and it illustrates the impact that social media have had in coalescing individuals in action against powerful social institutions.

Sexual abuse by leaders of Christian churches is not a new phenomenon. Its occurrence was sufficiently widespread to justify explicit attention being given to it on numerous occasions, beginning with the Synod of Elvira, held in 306 CE, which prohibited clergy and other men from having sex with young boys.[38] The *Penitentials* of the Irish monasteries make a number of references to sexual crimes committed by clerics against young boys and girls. The eighth-century *Penitential of Bede* in England recommends harsh penalties for priests who commit sodomy with boys.[39] Elizabeth Abbott, in her study of celibacy in the Roman Catholic Church, notes that in monasteries on the eve of the sixteenth-century Reformation,

> [T]he monks' "lapses" with women, handsome boys and each other ... became so commonplace that they could not be considered lapses but ways of life for entire communities.[40]

Among the reforms of the Council of Trent were measures to address clergy abuse. Clergy charged with "grievous crimes" were to be tried by an ecclesiastical court but with a secular judge present, and if found guilty the priest was handed over to civil authorities for punishment according to civil law, which could include beheading. "Clergy privilege" – that is, the church rather than the secular state having the esponsibility for disciplining clergy who commit crimes – had been a running issue since the time of Constantine (who decreed that clergy would be dealt with only by ecclesiastical courts). All vestiges of clergy privilege were legally abolished in the United States and the United Kingdom and its colonies in 1790 and 1827,[41] although the social standing and influence of churches have meant that the police and the press have not pursued crimes by clergy with the same rigor as they have for other law enforcement issues.

There was a marked rise in the secrecy with which the Roman Catholic Church handled this issue in the early twentieth century, with media being both a reason and a method for this. As had been the case in the past, controlling communication was a key church strategy. Tapsell attributes this rise in secrecy to an increase of clericalism within the church, and the beginning of radio, which the church feared had the potential to spread "scandal" about the church that could affect its cultivated reputation and membership. In 1922 Pope Pius XI issued the decree *Crimen Sollicitationis*, which directed bishops to handle cases of sexual abuse by clergy themselves in secret and to report them to the Holy Office but not civil law enforcement agencies. Priests found guilty were to be "amended" in monasteries or religious houses. What is noteworthy is that the papal focus was not on the damage done to victims of the abuse, nor to putting preventive measures in place to prevent such abuse from happening, but on maintaining its tight control of communication about the issue. Not just information about cases came under the secrecy provisions, but also the decree's contents and the existence of the decree itself. Failure to keep secrecy would be subject to excommunication:

[I]n dealing with these causes, more than usual care and concern must be shown that they be treated with the utmost confidentiality, and that, once decided and the decision executed, they are covered by permanent silence ... under pain of incurring automatic excommunication, ipso facto and undeclared, reserved to the sole person of the Supreme Pontiff. (Article 11)

The decree was affirmed by every pope following, with extensions made to its secrecy provisions to cover allegations as well as charges of abuse, a wider number of abuse situations (including abuse of intellectually disabled adults), and a five-year limitation clause placed on cases to be considered. Pope John XXIII's reissue in 1962 carried the rubric, "To be kept carefully in the secret archive of the Curia for internal use. Not to be published."

The decree was the handbook for the Roman Catholic Church for handling cases of abuse globally. The secrecy, not just of the processes but also of the decree, became a powerful weapon to hide from public awareness the widespread occurrence of abuse, and to apply the church's superior communication power and public image of superior moral standing to keep isolated and disempowered the questions and challenges of victims of abuse and their advocates. Similar institutional power was brought to bear by other Christian denominations to suppress public awareness, keep victims isolated, and limit the ability of adult and child victims to have the abuse recognized and have its consequences acted upon.[42] This included denominations that historically had a reputation for social justice advocacy in other areas.

That institutional religious power was overcome in the late twentieth century by the actions of three separate centers of communication activity: small support groups of survivors and their advocates (utilizing activist networks and later social media), the legal system, and the media, including the press and the various agencies of social media. Beginning with a landmark case in the United States in 1985, through press coverage and legal investigation, the public exposure of the extent of the abuse and its cover-up has spread internationally. Persistent media activity has now brought into public awareness extensive sexual crimes and sexual abuse of children by individual and collaborating priests, clergy, and church workers; widespread professional sexual abuse of adults by priests and clergy; prolonged and systematic abuse of children in church institutions; and persistent denial, containment, cover-up, defensive transfer of offenders, and obstruction of investigation by church leaders. These different forms of abuse and containment have been uncovered, to varying degrees, in all Christian denominations.

The extensiveness of the hidden abuse, gradually brought into public consciousness, has prompted parliamentary enquiries in a number of countries, and Royal Commissions in Ireland and Australia. In the United States, where the legal system is more accessible for legal challenge to churches, *The Economist* magazine in 2012 reported that in the past fifteen years the Roman Catholic Church in the United States had paid out more than $3.3 billion in settlements, forcing eight dioceses, the American arm of the Irish Christian Brothers, and a regional branch of the Jesuits into bankruptcy.[43] The Royal Commission being held in Australia is investigating sexual abuse of children across the spectrum of Australian churches, including the Roman Catholic Church and its orders, the Salvation Army, the Anglican Church, the Aboriginal Inland Mission, and Hillsong, the largest Pentecostal Church in Australia.

Despite the public exposure of criminal activity within their institutions and by their leaders, many churches are still attempting to manipulate their legal systems and processes to avoid public accountability and to hinder reparation being made to victims.[44] *The Economist* reports that the New York bishops, the US Catholic Conference of Bishops, and the California Catholic Conference are spending between $100,000 and $1,000,000 a year lobbying different legislatures to avoid changing the statute of limitations on child molestation cases to avoid increasing the number of cases to be dealt with. Churches are shifting funds into cemetery and other unrelated trusts to make them inaccessible for redress of damage done by the church and its officers.[45] In Australia, the Roman Catholic Church has vested all its assets in a Property Trust that is immune from suit. In 2007, it spent $1.5 million to protect this legal privilege by opposing a claim for redress from a man whose abuse by a priest they had already acknowledged. The Victorian Parliamentary Enquiry into Sexual Abuse by Religious Organizations in 2013 concluded in its report:

> There is no doubt that the unincorporated structure of the Catholic Church has not only prevented victims of criminal child abuse from bringing legal claims against the Catholic Church as an entity. It has also been exploited by the Catholic Church to avoid financial liability."

The public exposure by support groups, news, and social media not just of the extent of abuse, but also of priority being given by Christian leaders to protect their colleagues, church wealth, and reputation rather than hold offenders accountable and use their wealth to restore the damage that's been done, has been a contributing factor in the decline in the standing of Christian organizations and perception of the safety and trustworthiness of institutional Christianity in the public mind.

Tradition and change

We've noted in this chapter that the rapid growth of Pentecostalism has led to the perception by some that Pentecostalism is the appropriate form of Christianity for a digital age. While Pentecostalism has been growing, there has been significant decline in membership and participation in what had been the dominant structural forms of Christianity in the West, the mainline Protestant and Roman Catholic churches. Some sociologists, such as Steve Bruce, contend that the decline in mainline churches is indicative of a wider lack of interest in what he refers to as "the plausibility, popularity, and power of shared religious or spiritual beliefs."[46] He sees Pentecostalism as being a distraction from what is an irreversible trend.

Certainly there is significant turmoil in Christianity today, instigated by a number of wider social factors: a growing disenchantment with organized or institutionalized religion, a decline in the obligation people feel to support a particular religious tradition as a social or moral responsibility, a decline in social volunteerism in general, and a wider acceptance of the exercise of choice in one's religious, or nonreligious, involvements (the optionalism introduced by the Reformation movement and intensified by revivalism). We have noted also that the changes taking place in Christianity are connected to changes in the media structures and practices of contemporary societies, and their impacts on older patterns of thought, social relationships, institutional formation, and social experience on which Christianity had previously defined itself. How these changes are working themselves out within Christianity is not uniform, however.

The Hartford Institute for Religion Research[47] has found in its research on churches in the United States that, despite their growth, Evangelical mega-churches still account for less than 1 percent of weekly worshippers in the United States. Against that, 59 percent of weekly worshippers worship at a church of less than one hundred members, and 94 percent at churches of less than five hundred members. The United States Congregational Life survey found that, despite their financial difficulties, smaller congregations scored higher than the biggest churches on measures such as fostering spiritual growth, sharing faith, having empowering leaders, being places where more worshippers are actively involved, and caring for children and youth.[48]

One way of considering the changes taking place is to consider what happened in social media patterns when television was first introduced in the 1950s. Television quickly became such an accessible and popular medium that it was widely predicted that it would soon displace the existing mass media of radio, newspapers and magazines, book reading, and moviegoing. The immediate decline in radio audiences and the closure of a number of major mass-market magazines seemed to validate this prediction. After an initial period of adjustment, however, each of these other media rebounded by redefining a new role for themselves within the media market. They did this, not by competing directly with the more dominant medium of television, but by diversifying and offering media services that were complementary to television. In doing so, they assembled smaller audiences with more specific interests in a way that was sustainably profitable.

This experience led to awareness that the social structuring of media within a society needs to be seen as a whole, not just through the lens of its major players. The media market constantly adjusts itself to accommodate new media or new media players. In some cases this adjustment leads to the closing of some media that cease to be relevant, but more often it leads to a process of media complementarity in which citizens package a variety of media in idiosyncratic ways according to their interests, availability, access, resources, and content preferences.

The perspective is an interesting one to bear in mind in considering the changing shape of Christianity in the current period. While Global Pentecostalism seems to be more successful in attracting members, and is growing while other churches are in decline, there are interesting processes of redefinition taking place also in non-Pentecostal Christianity, marked by a wide variety of institutional and community forms, a more flexible view of theology and tradition and their relevance, and a wide variety of alternative media uses. Along with the corporatist, church growth model of contemporary Evangelical and Pentecostal Christianity, one also finds:

- Local or parish churches, which are still the most common form of Christian organization. Although their roots are in a declining order of parish or village community, and as a result are rapidly declining in support, some are being rekindled by addressing their local cultures in relevant ways, and by tapping into opportunities coming from the revived desire for the value of the local in a global-local worldview.
- House churches, communities formed on the concept of the extended family, which find their relevance by bringing together different generations and family types to support each other in the daily business of living.

- Intentional Christian communities, small live-in communities of not just individuals but also mixed family groups, with similarities to the lay monastic movement.
- Political or social interest mixed religious communities, where communities gather, worship, celebrate, and engage in education around issues of shared interest or political commitments, such as LGBT (lesbian, gay, bisexual, and transgendered) affirmative communities, environmental, or social justice groups.
- Electronically networked communities, which Groot calls "the church in liquid modernity."[49] Networked religious communities, such as The Emerging Church, are formed loosely around shared interests through newsgroups, blog sites, Facebook, and other internet services.
- Church school communities, where community, social services, and worship takes place around church-run schools, with families intermingling during the time of their children's education and then moving on.

Within these contexts, there is significant experimentation taking place to convert what were previously clearly defined traditions into new expressions and practices that draw on those traditions for relevant resources to address new cultural situations. A part of that reinterpretation of tradition involves taking seriously the cultural practice of packaging, where people are putting together mixes of traditional and contemporary spiritual belief and practice in what Ellingson refers to as "multi-layered spirituality."[50] These reflect a greater eclecticism, a greater engagement of the senses, and a greater openness to interactivity than existed previously. Some form as resistance communities challenging the inequitable structures of doctrinaire religion, gender, race, and economic capitalism. Many integrate other religious practices such as meditation, yoga, goddess religion, Jewish practices, and nature religion into a Christian framework. In many cases, the smaller numbers of these groups allow for an experimentation and flexibility that aren't possible in larger churches.

This diversity characterizes also the experimentation taking place with new media in new forms of Christian mediation. After a slow start on the part of many traditional churches, new media such as Twitter, Facebook, Instagram, YouTube, podcasts, and virtual reality gaming, as well as legacy media and the arts, are being utilized in line with defined community agendas.[51]

It is in this context of religious change, instigated by the ubiquity of media as the environment of social life, that the influence of the Pentecostal, nondenominational mega-church movement upon Christianity may be better understood. What global Pentecostalism may be contributing to Christianity is not "the" new or the only model for Christianity in a digital culture, but a clearer practical reading of the changes that are taking place within the wider culture that Christianity in its diversity needs to address. This diversification of Christianity is happening, not by reproducing the apparently successful Pentecostal model, but by institutions, groups, and individuals drawing on traditional Christian intellectual, communal, liturgical, and symbolic resources for relevant and transferable concepts and practices, and integrating them into new practices for new situations. While successful Pentecostal churches appear to have put together a cultural package of Christianity that attracts the largest numbers of people into single organizations, the television metaphor mentioned above suggests that there is a wide variety of activity taking place in the reworking of previously dominant traditional churches into niche markets that, although smaller, are sustainable and can be influential. The decentralized and more fluid nature of this diversity can hide the extent of it.

Two factors appear to be crucial in this major process of tradition and change. One is for churches to identify the extent to which previous Christian truths and organizational practices that were considered to be unconditioned, universal Christian truths were actually mediated phenomena, rooted in specific and often invisible media practices and perspectives that are now passing.

The other crucial factor for Chistianity in the current period of change is resource conversion. The historic mainline churches are the holders of the majority of the current wealth of Christianity, with most of it tied up in property assets that are of decreasing use as the numbers of members and activities within those buildings diminish. A key question for Christianity in this present time, therefore, is whether the historic mainline churches can convert those assets and make them available for sustainable new ventures and new community formations while their aging populations still have the energy to imagine them and get them started.

NOTES

1 Nelson, 1992.
2 Landow, 1992, pp. 4–5.
3 Jameson, 1991.
4 Castells, 2000, pp. 368–369.
5 Boltanski & Chiapello, 2005.
6 Willis & Maarouf, 2010.
7 See chapter 5. Also Thompson, 1963, pp. 355–356.
8 Couldry, 2012, p. 55.
9 L. S. Clark, 2013, p. 7.
10 Couldry, 2012, p. 47.
11 Capable of multiple meanings.
12 Landow, 1992, pp. 66–67.
13 Marty, 1989, pp. 186–187.

14 Woodhead, 2014, p. 3.
15 Wuthnow, 1993, pp. 100–113.
16 Bar-Haim, 1997, p. 141.
17 This rise in new religious movements has been extensively studied, stimulated particularly by the early work of Jeffrey Hadden at the University of Virginia and his colleagues in the American sociology of religion network. The interest has spread globally. See for example Bromley & Hadden, 1993; Cusack & Kirby, 2014; Hadden & Cowan, 2000; Kirby, 2013; Possamai, 2003, 2005.
18 The MMORPG *World of Warcraft*, for example, in 2010 had a global subscription of 12 million players (Vallikatt, 2014, p. 14). The topic of a cultural search for reenchantment has been widely explored in recent research on media and religion. See for example Apolito, 2005; H. Campbell, 2010; L. S. Clark, 2003, 2007; De Vries & Weber, 2001; Hadden & Cowan, 2000; Hoover & Venturelli, 1996; Lynch, 2007; Meyer, 2006; Meyer & Moors, 2006; Morgan, 1998, 2008, 2010b; Stolow, 2005, 2013; Wagner, 2012; Wertheim, 1999.
19 Bar-Haim, 1997, p. 137. See also Lundby, 1997.
20 There is a significant overlap in demarcation of the terms Pentecostal, Charismatic, and Evangelical Christianity and churches. In some contexts, including in the churches' own identity demarcation, differences between them are identified and may be seen as crucial, but these identifications can then be disputed when discussed in other contexts. I am using the term "Pentecostal" not to stake a position, but as an inclusive term to cover both Pentecostal and Charismatic Christians.
21 At the time of writing, the founder of the church and five of his deputies were on trial for the misappropriation of funds.
22 Kim, 2007.
23 See Asamoah-Gyadu, 2005, 2012.
24 Hoover notes that Catholic identification in Brazil has fallen from 93% in the 1960 census to 63% in the latest census, and that actual participation in church activities by Catholics could be as low as 4%. Most of that loss has been to Protestant Pentecostal churches and those identifying as "no religious identification," something unheard of two decades ago, which has risen to 12% (Hoover, 2013).
25 Lehmann, 1996, cited in Coleman, 2000, p. 67.
26 Asamoah-Gyadu, 2005.
27 Weber, 1930.
28 Meyer, 1998, p. 759.
29 Asamoah-Gyadu, 2012, p. 128.
30 Coleman, 2000, p. 28.
31 Coleman, 2000, pp. 202–203.
32 Goh, 2010.
33 This political stance is well illustrated by Article 17 of the statement of faith of City Harvest Church in Singapore: "We believe that Government is ordained of God, and the powers that be are ordained as ministers of God to us for good. To resist the powers and the ordinances is to resist the ordinance of God.... We declare our loyalty to our Government and its leaders, and will assist in every way possible, consistent with our faith in the scriptures as Christian citizens."
34 Maxwell, 1998, p. 14.

35 Meyer, 1998.
36 Micklethwait & Wooldridge, 2009, p. 4.
37 Yang, 2005.
38 A full chronology of Roman Catholic Church actions against the sexual abuse of children by priests is given in Tapsell, 2014, pp. 9–48.
39 Doyle, 2014.
40 Abbott, 2001, p. 108.
41 Tapsell, 2014, p. 11.
42 For some of the research done on this suppression, see Adams & Fortune, 1995; Born, 1997; Carlson Brown & Bohn, 1989; Fortune, 1989; Horsfield, 1992; Keenan; The Commission to Inquire into Child Abuse, 2009.
43 "Earthly concerns; The Catholic Church in America," 2012.
44 Although, as alluded to in this volume, the model for this was set by St. Ambrose in the fourth century. Ambrose used his position of power to force the emperor to back down from his insistence that Christians pay for restoration of a Jewish synagogue they had destroyed, including lying that he had ordered the destruction himself. The Catholic Encyclopedia's description of Ambrose as "the perfect model of a Christian bishop" takes on a new meaning in retrospect.
45 "Earthly concerns; The Catholic Church in America," 2012.
46 Bruce, 2013, p. 278.
47 "Fast facts about American religion," 2014.
48 "Is bigger always better?" 2014.
49 de Groot, 2007.
50 Ellingson, 2007, loc 131.
51 For more extensive work on new media and religious bodies, see H. Campbell, 2004, 2005, 2010.

Conclusion

This book has investigated the ways in which processes and characteristics of mediation have contributed to the development of the original talk and actions of a short-lived Jewish Galilean peasant called Jesus into the global religion(s) of Christianity.

The intent in doing so is to add an historical perspective to current scholarly discussion and wider public interest in what is happening in religion and Christianity today, and the place of new and legacy media in that. The approach has been to understand the part played by media in religion by studying the mediation of one religion, Christianity, from its beginnings to the present time. Given the immense diversity there is in the phenomena of both media and Christianity, and the length of time under consideration, it's recognized that what's been covered has been highly selective and that things of equal relevance have been either omitted or simply missed. It's considered, though, that the benefits justify the risk. From this historical perspective, a number of findings relevant to the current questions being asked about media and religion can be identified.

Firstly, media and Christianity are revealed as symbiotic cultural phenomena. It's important to state this explicitly, as there are tendencies to overlook this interconnectedness. Many Christian groups see Christian faith as something uniquely different from other cultural phenomena, with its own unique origins and its own distinctive sources of truth and belief. In the modern period, the Protestant theologian Richard Niebuhr was influential in framing Christian faith this way with his book *Christ and Culture*,[1] suggesting from the title alone that theology can be seen as separate from the culture in which it takes place. This perspective, though, comes through in a wide variety of Christian expressions, including Catholic enculturation theology, mystical and revelational theology, theological idealism, Pentecostal ecstatic experience, and Fundamentalist biblical literalism.

From Jesus to the Internet, Peter Horsfield © 2015 John Wiley & Sons, Ltd. Published 2015 by John Wiley & Sons, Ltd.

This is likewise the case in the discipline of media studies where, if Christianity is considered at all, it is generally studied as a bounded cultural phenomenon, separate from the secular, and studied largely in terms of how new (secular) media are affecting it.

It becomes apparent, in looking at the mediation of Christianity historically, that Christianity was born, developed, and is constantly evolving in environments of changing mediated social communication. In the process, it feeds on, interacts with, and absorbs characteristics of those environments. Even the fundamental intellectual process of framing and expressing Christian ideas and beliefs uses linguistic and symbolic resources that are circulating through communication in the wider cultural environment, and implements them in ways that in turn resonate back to those cultures.

In conceptualizing the relationship between media and Christianity, therefore, it is more accurate to see Christianity itself as *a mediated phenomenon*, one in which the matrix of mediation within which it takes shape at any particular period of history is integral to its character.

A second observation is that Christianity is a diversified phenomenon, and needs to be understood and studied in this diversity. This is germane because a constantly recurring dynamic within Christianity has been individuals or groups trying to deny that diversity and impose a narrow understanding of Christianity that serves particular interests, beliefs, or power. Sometimes that narrowing process has been done by persuasion, but many times by force.

This diversity is manifest in the myriad ways Christians have adapted and integrated different technologies and modes of mediated communication into their faith practices. Some Christian groups have been open to particular media practices but closed to others. Some have utilized similar media to others, but used them differently or ordered them in different hierarchies of value. Some have approached media from a purely utilitarian mindset, using whatever's available on the basis of its usefulness and effectiveness. Others have been selective in the media they use because of a given medium's different cultural associations. Some have seen technological forms of mediation as a priority; others have given higher priority to bodily, interpersonal forms of mediation.

This variation in response and adaptation of practices is influenced by factors such as the groups' previous practices, attitudes toward stability and change, cultural alignments, current financial positions, and the ideological association of their Christian beliefs and values with particular forms of mediation. This not only is apparent with new digital media but also is seen historically in almost every form of mediation.

The diversity of Christianity makes it difficult to make definitive statements about how Christianity as a single entity is affected by, or has responded to, media use at any particular time. It also makes it problematic to support the proposition that, in the modern period, media have been so powerful and are imposing their logic so relentlessly that Christianity is becoming "mediatized" and losing its distinctiveness. Such a view can only be supported if Christianity is essentialized into one particular sociological entity or ideological form rather than viewed in its current and historical diversity.

Certainly, Christianity is affected and changed by changes in the media environment. It is a cultural phenomenon, and like all cultural phenomena it constantly adapts itself to the legal, political, economic, and media realities of its environment. But, historically, the response of Christianity to wider social and cultural changes can be seen to be very diverse, interactive, and adaptive. In some situations, the response is one of unquestioned acceptance and utilization of new media – such as Luther's recognition of printing as "God's highest and extremist form of grace," or Armstrong's view of television as an express gift of God. Some responses can be seen to be more qualified and negotiated in their adoption of new media technologies and practices, in some cases by overlaying new practices on the old – such as Clement's justification of his use of writing as a complement to oral communication, or mainline Protestantism's use of free-time radio and television. Some Christian groups have responded to changed media situations with resistance and even subversion – seen in incidents such as oral resistance to written directives, scribes making changes to manuscripts they disagreed with, book burnings, the smuggling of vernacular religious literature in the medieval period to subvert the hegemony of Latin, or Christian radio stations that have become points of resistance to authoritarian regimes. In some cases where Christians have been in positions of political control, such as Byzantine Orthodoxy, medieval Catholicism, or Calvin's Geneva, we see Christianity using its social or political power to impose its own media regulation on the rest of society.

To speak of a single shaping effect that media have had on Christianity, therefore, ignores this diversity and the enthusiasm with which Christianity has grasped opportunities that new media make available.

A third insight is that, as in other parts of society, securing or maintaining the right or ability to communicate has been a constant factor in the construction of power and authority in Christianity. How the religion should be mediated has been a recurring cause of conflict and contest throughout Christianity's history, in relation to not just modern technology but almost every dimension of communication practice.

The inherent power that the ability to communicate brings means the structures of power and authority within Christianity have been closely connected to particular practices, values, and structures of communication that constitute and reinforce that power. Historically, this has been effected in moves to link Christian truth to particular forms of mediation, to restrict access to privileged communication or distribution networks to particular groups or people, or to associate authority with particular language forms or media practices.

Because media and communication are such critical sources of power and authority, the emergence of new media or new media practices from within or outside the religion commonly prompts a situation of change or even crisis in religious organization, practice, and authority.

It was noted earlier[2] that the hierarchical institutional structure that has marked Christianity for much of its life was not a natural organizational structure for a movement that identified itself with Jesus, whose authority was more oral-charismatic in nature and whose comments about organization and authority were of an inclusive, nonhierarchical community regulated by mutual service. As we have seen, the hierarchical, institutional authority concept of much of Christianity is an authority structure that was created and sustained by written media, and subsequently printed media, and used its cultural media superiority to assert itself against other authority practices.

A major challenge being faced by Christianity today is that the media structures and practices that have supported its historic organization and authority have shifted, and social organization is taking place and authority is being ascribed in different ways. One of the problems that many Christian leaders have in dealing with this shift constructively is that they are unable to see the media-specific nature of their religious authority and are therefore unable to facilitate, if they were inclined to do so, the transfer of their authority to something more appropriate for the new situation.

A fourth finding of relevance is that the challenges and opportunities that new media technologies and practices present to Christianity are generally part of a much wider matrix of social and cultural changes that need to be reckoned with.

Media changes are generally part of broader movements of social ferment and convergence across areas such as cultural practice, economics, politics, and civic life. As detailed in chapter 10, the technology of printing existed in Asia and Europe well before Gutenberg. There were also reform movements within Catholicism prior to Luther, some of which were more radical than Luther's. The technologies of printing only made their impact felt when other political, economic, and cultural conditions had developed to such an extent that the social applications of the technology became viable.

The implications of new media developments for groups in Christianity, therefore, lie not only in how to adapt to new modes of communicating but also how to align themselves with new political conditions, new cultural perspectives, new intellectual perspectives, new economic arrangements, and new industry requirements associated with the media shifts.

It is necessary, therefore, to consider various Christian responses to media change not just in a narrow sense of "comfort" with new ways of doing things, but also in terms of how the different ideological preferences of Christian groups align with the political, economic, or cultural conditions associated with new media changes. Here there may be more affinity between the responses of some Christian groups with others outside Christianity than there is with other groups within Christianity. The alignment of Christian evangelical groups in the United States with right-wing political and economic groups around common concerns for family-based values and the "American way of life," and their joint desire to have these concerns reflected in US popular culture, is but one example.

A fifth finding suggests that the challenges and opportunities presented to Christianity today by new media and the new media industries are not unique in Christian history. Certainly the characteristics of the media situation are different than those of previous media situations. However, the nature of the challenges and opportunities has existed in previous historical periods of transition. The absorption of Catholic-Orthodox Christianity into the media, political, and economic structures of the Roman Empire in the fourth and subsequent centuries, and the Protestant accommodation to the literate urban print cultures of Renaissance Europe, the political structures of nation-states, and the economics of mercantilism and emerging global imperialism, are instances of this. Yet in these times of change also, one can perceive persistent Christian counter or reform movements challenging these dominant political and economic adaptations and asserting alternative cultural interpretations of Christian ideology, practice, and media uses.

An historical reading suggests, therefore, that in the current situation particular streams of Christianity are likely to become more successful and grow because their mythologies, theological formulations, cosmology, ideology, and practices correspond to those of the dominant political and economic order.[3] It suggests also that there will continue to be alternative embodiments of Christianity that, while not the largest, may become the source of innovation for the future.

A final insight follows: that Christianity is perhaps best understood historically, and in the present time, not as a single, coherent religious movement but as a diverse and rich repository of symbolic media resources that are continually being drawn from and reworked in the construction of new and relevant religious meaning.

The newsworthy growth of Global Evangelicalism and Pentecostalism has become paradigmatic of Christianity in the present electronic and digital era. This view is certainly promoted by Pentecostal groups as evidence of God's blessing and approval of their enterprise. Yet though a modern phenomenon, there are precursors readily available from the diversity of Christian tradition for its ideas, its methods, and its sense of global destiny.

However, this is only one of the many adaptations of the Christian tradition being made today to reinterpret and re-institutionalize Christianity in a way relevant to the times, with each one also drawing from the tradition, albeit in a different way, to support the historical continuity and legitimacy of its enterprise.

As a reading of Christian history also demonstrates, it is often not from the dominant expression at any time but from the minority opinions, that creative ideas for new future directions emerge – not unlike the way yeast works in bread making or a small mustard seed that's sowed in a field.

Afterword

> *If you're cutting timbers the same length, always measure against the original, otherwise you'll multiply your mistakes.*
>
> Carpenters' axiom

My evolving understanding of the interaction of media and Christianity has been a journey of nearly thirty years. I began as a student and Christian theologian and have reached here as a media and religion scholar. I have come to the evaluation in the course of the journey that while what presents itself as Christianity is a remarkably robust, adaptable, and energetic phenomenon, capable of significant good but also immense evil, it has very little connection with the character, self-understanding, and mission of the Jewish Galilean man called Jesus. Too many aspects of Christian beliefs, organizational structures, corporate ethics, institutional practices, and leadership behaviors are incompatible with or contradict what Jesus did and taught and with how, as a faithful, monotheistic Jewish prophet, he saw himself. Numerous examples are apparent of these contradictions, which lie not just in isolated, peripheral, or aberrant instances, but also in areas that are central to the religion. It is as if Jesus was the subject of a corporate takeover, where the new company retained his name and reputation but the values and aspirations of what he started were replaced by a totally different corporate ethos and agenda that have nothing identifiable to do with him.

If there was a decisive moment in this corporate takeover of Jesus, in my reading, it was in the reinvention of Jesus by Paul of Tarsus after Jesus had died. Why Paul's idiosyncratic ideas had such a lasting impact can only be understood fully through a media lens. As well as setting a model of religious community relevant to the needs of dislocated urban populations, his novel ideas were fixed in written letters that were copied, recopied, and widely circulated and gained a heightened value because they were among the first shared interpretation Christians had of their faith in the authoritative cultural medium of writing. Paul's letters in writing helped give Gentile Christians a vision of the cultural legitimacy of their faith.

There were other possible ways in which the significance of Jesus could have been applied to non-Jewish contexts. The Jewish disciples of Jesus held a different understanding and were critical of Paul's interpretation, which is why Paul largely stayed away and had little contact with them. But the transitory, oral methods of the largely illiterate disciples who the Rabbi Jesus chose to continue his work were no match for the circulating permanent writings of the Rabbi Paul and his disciples.

Later Christian writers worked to reconcile Paul's new ideas with those of Jesus, and it's their perspectives that have been given authenticity to Paul's perspectives through later selection and rewriting of material. The Gospel writers used the oral traditions of Jesus' teaching and activities, but integrated them into different theological and cultural narratives that included a divine conception and physical resurrection. The Gospel of John promoted Jesus as the preexisting Hellenistic philosophical structure of the world (logos) that became a person. Luke rewrote the history of Christian origins in a way that minimized the disagreements between Paul and Jesus' disciples and made Paul's message complementary to rather than conflictual with that of the disciples.

This presents Christianity with a fundamental problem: the scriptures that Christians look to as their authority are the ideas of a second generation of writers, not those of the original speakers themselves. Later theologians post facto have justified Paul's interpretation on the basis either that Paul gave shape to the true nature of Jesus that Jesus didn't fully understand himself, or that he simply made overt what Jesus was thinking about himself but either hadn't fully worked out or wasn't prepared to say. Others have justified Paul's interpretation of Jesus on the basis that if Paul hadn't translated the ethnically specific Jewish message of Jesus into the more universal Hellenistic message of Jesus the Christ, Jesus' message would not have become as widely influential across the centuries as Christianity has made it. However, there's an inner contradiction involved in explanations that a religion, which has at its heart a belief that people should trust in Jesus, does not trust Jesus enough to believe that he knew fully what he was doing or that his teachings wouldn't survive or be effective in history unless they changed him from being who he was into a Hellenized mythological figure.

What is of interest from a media perspective though is the persistence of the attraction and influence of Jesus and his oral communication, preserved though it may be in written records. While institutional Christianity proceeds on its own corporate doctrinal complexities and institutional strategies, there is a large number of people, many within churches, who care little for those complexities and strategies, but continue to be attracted to and to varying degrees shape their lives by the character of Jesus and what he sought to do, as they access him through his stories, his memorable provocative teachings, accounts of what he did, and his invitation to have the faith to see things differently. They may or may not call themselves Christian.

NOTES

1 Niebuhr, 1951.
2 Chapter 4.
3 James Taylor gives a good analysis of this correspondence of mythological frameworks in his analysis of American religious broadcasters (J. Taylor, 1977).

References

Abbot St. Columban. (590). The monastic rule. http://www.scrollpublishing.com/store/Columbanus.html

Abbott, E. (2001). *A history of celibacy*. Cambridge: Lutterworth Press.

Abou-El-Haj, B. (1994). *The medieval cult of saints: formations and transformations*. Cambridge: Cambridge University Press.

Adams, C., & Fortune, M. (Eds.). (1995). *Violence against women and children: a Christian theological sourcebook*. New York: Continuum.

Adorno, T. W., & Bernstein, J. M. (2001). *The culture industry: selected essays on mass culture*. London: Routledge.

Allen, P. (1997). *The concept of woman: the Aristotelian revolution, 750 B.C.–A.D. 1250*. Grand Rapids, MI: Wm. B. Eerdmans.

Allison, D. (2010). *Constructing Jesus: memory, imagination, and history*. London: SPCK.

Altman, R. (2004). *Absent voices: the story of writing systems in the West*. New Castle, DE: Oak Knoll Press.

Anderson, B. (1991). *Imagined communities: reflections on the origin and spread of nationalism* (Rev. ed.). London: Verso.

Anderson, W. (1985). *The rise of the Gothic*. London: Hutchinson.

Andersson, C., & Talbot, C. (1983). *From a mighty fortress: prints, drawings and books in the age of Luther, 1483–1546*. Detroit: Detroit Institute of Arts.

Angendt, A. (2002). Relics and their veneration in the Middle Ages. In A. Mulder-Bakker (Ed.), *The invention of saintliness* (pp. 27–37). London: Routledge.

Apolito, P. (2005). *The internet and the madonna: religious visionary experience on the web*. Chicago: University of Chicago Press.

Apostolic Tradition of Hippolytus of Rome. http://www.bombaxo.com/hippolytus.html

Armstrong, B. (1979). *The electric church*. Nashville, TN: Thomas Nelson.

Asamoah-Gyadu, K. (2005). *African charismatics: current developments within independent indigenous Pentecostalism in Ghana*. Leiden: Brill.

Asamoah-Gyadu, K. (2012). Hearing, viewing and touched by the Spirit: televangelism in contemporary African Christianity. In P. Thomas & P. Lee (Eds.), *Global and local televangelism* (pp. 126–145). New York: Palgrave Macmillan.

Askew, M., & Hubber, B. (1988). The colonial reader observed: reading in its cultural context. In D. H. Borchardt & W. Kirsop (Eds.), *The book in Australia: essays towards a cultural and social history*. Melbourne: Australian Reference Publications in association with the Centre for Bibliographical and Textual Studies, Monash University.

Aslan, R. (2013). *Zealot: the life and times of Jesus of Nazareth* (Kindle ed.). Sydney: Allen & Unwin.

Aston, M. (1981). Popular religious movements in the Middle Ages. In G. Barraclough (Ed.), *The Christian world: a social and cultural history of Christianity* (pp. 157–170). London: Thames and Hudson.

Aston, M. (1988). *England's iconoclasts: laws against images*. Oxford: Oxford University Press.

Backhouse, J. (1979). *The illuminated manuscript*. London: Phaidon Press Ltd.

Bahr, A. M. (Ed.). (2009). *Christianity: the illustrated guide to 2,000 years of the Christian faith*. Elanora Heights, NSW: Millenium House.

Bailey, K. (1976). *Poet and peasant and Through peasant eyes: a literary-cultural approach to the parables in Luke*. Grand Rapids, MI: Eerdmans.

Bakewell, P. (1998). 1512–1513. The Laws of Burgos. http://faculty.smu.edu/bakewell/BAKEWELL/texts/burgoslaws.html

Bar-Haim, G. (1997). The dispersed sacred: anomie and the crisis of ritual. In S. Hoover & K. Lundby (Eds.), *Rethinking media, religion and culture* (pp. 133–145). Thousand Oaks, CA: Sage.

Barnes, R. (2000). Cloistered bookworms in the chicken coop of the Muses: the ancient Library of Alexandria. In R. Macleod (Ed.), *The library of Alexandria: centre of learning in the ancient world* (pp. 61–77). London: I. B. Tauris.

Barr, A., & Fore, W. (2005a). Radio. In J. Bowden (Ed.), *Christianity: the complete guide* (pp. 1006–1009). London: Continuum.

Barr, A., & Fore, W. (2005b). Television. In J. Bowden (Ed.), *Christianity: the complete guide* (pp. 1171–1174). London: Continuum.

Baudrillard, J. (1993). The evil demon of images and the precession of simulacra. In T. Docherty (Ed.), *Postmodernism: a reader*. Hemel Hempstead, UK: Harvester Wheatsheaf.

Baum, W., & Winkler, D. (2000). *The Church of the East: a concise history*. London: Routledge Curzon.

Baumer, C. (2006). *The Church of the East: an illustrated history of Assyrian Christianity*. London: I. B. Tauris.

Bebbington, D., & Jones, D. C. (Eds.). (2013). *Evangelicalism and fundamentalism in the United Kingdom during the twentieth century*. Oxford: Oxford University Press.

Becker, A. (2008). *Sources for the study of the School of Nisibis*. Liverpool: Liverpool University Press.

Besançon, A. (2000). *The forbidden image: an intellectual history of iconoclasm*. Chicago: University of Chicago Press.

Bettenson, H. (1943). Theodosian Code XVI.i.2. In H. Bettenson (Ed.), *Documents of the Christian Church* (pp. 31). London: Oxford University Press.

Bieringer, R., & Pollefeyt, D. (Eds.). (2012). *Paul and Judaism: crosscurrents in Pauline exegesis and the study of Jewish-Christian relations*. London: T & T Clark.

References 295

Bireley, R. (1999). *The refashioning of Catholicism, 1450–1700: a reassessment of the Counter Reformation*. London: Macmillans Press Ltd.

Boltanski, L., & Chiapello, E. (2005). *The new spirit of capitalism* (G. Elliott, Trans.). London: Verso.

Borg, M. J. (1987). *Jesus: a new vision*. San Francisco: Harper.

Borg, M. J. (1994). *Jesus in contemporary scholarship*. Valley Forge, PA: Trinity Press International.

Borg, M. J. (2012). *Evolution of the word: the New Testament in the order the books were written* (Kindle ed.). New York: HarperOne.

Borg, M. J., & Wright, N. T. (1999). *The meaning of Jesus: two visions*. New York: HarperCollins.

Born, M. (1997). *Why does he hug us so tightly?* Melbourne: YWCA.

Bourdieu, P. (1977). The economics of linguistic exchanges. *Social Science Information, 16*(6), 645–668.

Bouwsma, W. (1988). *John Calvin: a sixteenth century portrait*. Oxford: Oxford University Press.

Bowden, J. (2005a). Books. In J. Bowden (Ed.), *Christianity: the complete guide* (pp. 166–170). London: Continuum.

Bowden, J. (Ed.). (2005b). *Christianity: the complete guide*. London: Continuum.

Brading, D. (1997). Prophet and apostle: Bartholomé de las Casas and the spiritual conquest of America. In J. S. Cummings (Ed.), *Christianity and missions, 1450–1800* (pp. 117–138). Aldershot: Ashgate.

Briggs, A., & Burke, P. (2002). *A social history of the media: from Gutenberg to the internet*. Cambridge: Polity.

Bromley, D., & Hadden, J. (Eds.). (1993). *Handbook on cults and sects in America*. Bingley, UK: Emerald Group Publishing.

Brown, P. (2000). *Augustine of Hippo: a biography* (new ed.). Berkeley: University of California Press.

Brown, P. (2003). *The rise of western Christendom: triumph and diversity, A.D. 200–1000* (2nd ed.). Oxford: Blackwell.

Brown, P. (2008). *The body in society: men, women and sexual renunciation in early Christianity* (20th anniversary ed.). New York: Columbia University Press.

Brubaker, L., & Haldon, J. (2011). *Byzantium in the iconoclast era c. 680–850: a history*. Cambridge: Cambridge University Press.

Bruce, S. (1996). *Religion in the modern world: from cathedrals to cults*. Oxford: Oxford University Press.

Bruce, S. (2013). Secularization and church growth in the United Kingdom. *Journal of Religion in Europe, 6*, 273–296.

Burns, A. (1989). *The power of the written word: the role of literacy in the history of western civilization*. New York: Peter Lang Publishers.

Butt, J. (2002). *Daily life in the age of Charlemagne*. Westport, CT: Greenwood Press.

Byrne, B. (1988). *Paul and the Christian woman*. Homebush, NSW: St. Paul Publications.

Byrskog, S. (1994). *Jesus the only teacher: didactic authority and transmission in ancient Israel, ancient Judaism and the Matthean community*. Stockholm: Almqvist & Wiskell International.

Calvin, J. (1599). *The institutes of the Christian religion* (H. Beveridge, Trans.). Grand Rapids, MI: Christian Classics Ethereal Library.

Calvin, J. (1986). Traité des reliques. In J. Backus & C. Chimelli (Eds.), *La vraie piété*. Geneva: Labor et Fides.

Calvin, J. (1992). *Men, women, and order in the Church: three sermons*. Dallas, TX: Presbyterian Heritage.

Cameron, A. (2006). Constantine and the "peace of the church." In M. Mitchell & F. Young (Eds.), *The Cambridge History of Christianity (Vol. 1: Origins to Constantine*, pp. 538–551). Cambridge: Cambridge University Press.

Cameron, E. (2005). *Interpreting Christian history: the challenge of the churches' past*. Malden, MA: Blackwell Publishers.

Campbell, H. (2004). Challenges created by online religious networks. *Journal of Media and Religion*, 3(2), 81–99.

Campbell, H. (2005). *Exploring religious community online: we are one in the network*. Leiden: Peter Lang.

Campbell, H. (2010). *When religion meets new media*. London: Rouledge.

Campbell, J. (2013). *Library: a world history*. London: Thames & Hudson.

Cannon, W. (1980). *History of Christianity in the Middle Ages*. Grand Rapids, MI: Abingdon.

Caraman, P. (1990). *Ignatius Loyola: a biography of the founder of the Jesuits*. San Francisco: Harper & Row.

Carlson Brown, J., & Bohn, C. (Eds.). (1989). *Christianity, patriarchy and abuse: a feminist critique*. New York: Pilgrim Press.

Carter, T. F. (1955). *The invention of printing in China and its spread westward* (2nd ed.). New York: Ronald Press Company.

Casanova, J. (1994). *Public religions in the modern world*. Chicago: University of Chicago Press.

Castells, M. (2000). *The information age: economy, society and culture (Vol. 3: End of millenium)*. Oxford: Blackwell.

Chartier, R. (1987). General introduction: print culture (L. G. Cochrane, Trans.). In R. Chartier (Ed.), *The culture of print: power and the uses of print in Early Modern Europe* (pp. 1–10). Princeton, NJ: Princeton University Press.

Chesnut, G. F. (1986). *The first Christian histories: Eusebius, Socrates, Sozomen, Theodoret, and Evagrius*. Macon, GA: Mercer University Press.

Chidester, D. (2000). *Christianity: a global history*. San Francisco: Harper San Francisco.

Choniates, N. (2014). The sack of Constantinople. *Medieval Sourcebook*. http://www.fordham.edu/halsall/source/choniates1.asp

Chow, J. K. (1992). *Patronage and power: a study of social networks in Corinth*. Sheffield, UK: Sheffild Academic Press.

Chrisman, M. (1982). *Lay culture, learned culture: books and social change in Strasbourg, 1480–1599*. New Haven, CT: Yale University Press.

Chrysostom, J. Homilies on the Gospel of John. http://www.newadvent.org/fathers/2401.htm

Clark, L. S. (2003). *From angels to aliens: teens, the media and belief in the supernatural*. New York: Oxford University Press.

Clark, L. S. (2013). *The Parent App: understanding families in the digital age*. Oxford: Oxford University Press.

Clark, L. S. (Ed.). (2007). *Religion, media and the marketplace*. New Brunswick, NJ: Rutgers University Press.

Clark, W. (2006). *Medieval cathedrals*. Westport, CT: Greenwood Press.

Clarke, G. W. (1984). *The letters of St. Cyprian of Carthage*. New York: Newman Press.

Clement of Rome. (96). First epistle of Clement to the Corinthians. *Early Christian Writings*. http://www.earlychristianwritings.com/text/1clement-roberts.html

Coakley, J. (2010). Women's textual authority and the collaboration of clerics. In A. Minnis & R. Voaden (Eds.), *Medieval holy women in the Christian tradition, c.1100–c.1500* (pp. 83–104). Turnhout, Belgium: Brepols.

Coleman, S. (2000). *The globalisation of charismatic Christianity: spreading the gospel of prosperity*. Cambridge: Cambridge University Press.

Coloniensis, C. R. (1213). The children's crusade, 1212. *Medieval Sourcebook*. http://www.fordham.edu/halsall/source/1212pueri.asp

Commission to Inquire into Child Abuse. (2009). *Commission report*. Dublin: Government of Ireland.

Connolly, R. H. (1929). *Didascalia Apostolorum*. Oxford: Clarendon Press.

Cottret, B. (2000). *Calvin: a biography (M. W. McDonald, Trans.)*. Grand Rapids, MI: William B. Eerdmans.

Couldry, N. (2012). *Media, society, world: social theory and digital media practice*. Cambridge: Polity Press.

Cross, F. L., & Livingstone, E. A. (Eds.). (1974). *The Oxford dictionary of the Christian Church* (2nd ed.). Oxford: Oxford University Press.

Cross, F. L., & Livingstone, E. A. (Eds.). (2005). *The Oxford dictionary of the Christian Church* (3rd ed.). Oxford: Oxford University Press.

Crossan, J. D. (1994). *Jesus: a revolutionary biography*. San Francisco: Harper.

Crossan, J. D. (1998). *The birth of Christianity*. San Francisco: Harper.

Cunningham, M. (1999). The Orthodox Church in Byzantium. In A. Hastings (Ed.), *A world history of Christianity* (pp. 66–105). London: W. B. Eerdmans.

Curnock, N. (Ed.). (1909a). *The journal of the Rev. John Wesley* (Vol. 2). London: Robert Culley.

Curnock, N. (Ed.). (1909b). *The journal of the Rev. John Wesley* (Vol. 1). London: Robert Culley.

Cusack, C., & Kirby, D. (Eds.). (2014). *Sects, cults and new religions*. London: Routledge.

D'Angelo, M. R. (2006). *Abba* and father: imperial theology in the contexts of Jesus and the Gospels. In A.-J. Levine, D. Allison, & J. D. Crossan (Eds.), *The historical Jesus in context* (pp. 64–78). Princeton, NJ: Princeton University Press.

d'Aquilliers, R. Historia francorum qui ceperint Jerusalem. *Medieval Sourcebook*. http://www.fordham.edu/halsall/source/raymond-cde.asp - jerusalem2

Davies, S. (1986). *The revolt of the widows: the social world of the Apocryphal Acts*. Carbondale: Southern Illinois University Press.

Davis, R. (1976). *Methodism* (Rev. ed.). London: Epworth Press.

de Greef, W. (2004). Calvin's writings. In D. McKim (Ed.), *The Cambridge companion to John Calvin* (pp. 41–57). Cambridge: Cambridge University Press.

de Groot, K. (2007). Rethinking church in liquid modernity. In K. de Groot (Ed.), *Religion inside and outside traditional institutions* (pp. 175–192). Leiden: Brill.

De Vries, H., & Weber, S. (Eds.). (2001). *Religion and the media*. Stanford, CA: Stanford University Press.

Dégert, A. (1910). Ecclestical Latin. *The Catholic Encyclopedia.* http://www.newadvent.org/cathen/09019a.htm

Dewey, J. (1992). 1 Timothy. In C. A. Newsom & S. H. Ringe (Eds.), *The women's bible commentary* (pp. 353–358). Louisville, KY: Westminster/John Knox Press.

Dochuk, D. (2007). Evangelicalism becomes southern: politics becomes evangelical: from FDR to Ronald Reagan. In M. Noll & L. Harlow (Eds.), *Religion and American politics: from the Colonial period to the present* (pp. 297–326). Oxford: Oxford University Press.

Dowley, T. (Ed.). (1977). *Eerdmans' handbook to the history of Christianity.* Grand Rapids, MI: W.B. Eerdmans.

Doyle, T. (2014). A very short history of clergy sexual abuse in the Catholic Church. *Crusade against Clerical Abuse.* http://www.crusadeagainstclergyabuse.com/htm/AShortHistory.htm

Drogin, M. (1983). *Medieval scribes and the history of book curses.* Montclair, NJ: Allanheld and Schram.

Dungan, D. L. (2006). *Constantine's bible: politics and the making of the New Testament.* London: SCM Press.

Dunn, G. D. (2004). *Tertullian.* London: Routledge.

Dunn, J. D. G. (2003). Altering the default setting: re-envisaging the early transmission of the Jesus tradition. *New Testament Studies, 49,* 139–175.

Earthly concerns: The Catholic Church in America (August 18, 2012). *The Economist, 404.*

Edwards, M. U., Jr. (1994). *Printing, propaganda and Martin Luther* (Kindle ed.). Berkeley: University of California Press.

Ehrman, B. (2003). *Lost Christianities: the battles for scripture and the faiths we never knew.* Oxford: Oxford University Press.

Ehrman, B. (2006). *Whose Word is it? the story behind who changed the New Testament and why.* London: Continuum.

Eisenstein, E. (1979). *The printing press as an agent of change: communications and cultural transformations in early modern Europe* (2 vols.). Cambridge: Cambridge University Press.

Ellerbe, H. (1995). *The dark side of Christian history.* San Rafael, CA: Morningstar Books.

Ellingson, S. (2007). *The megachurch and the mainline: remaking religious tradition in the twenty-first century* (Kindle ed.). Chicago: University of Chicago Press.

Engelke, M. (2009). Reading and time: two approaches to the materiality of scripture. *Ethnos, 74*(2), 151–174.

Eusebius Pamphilius. (1890). Church history. In P. Schaff (Ed.), *Eusebius Pamphilius: Church history, Life of Constantine, Oration in praise of Constantine.* Grand Rapids, MI: Christian Classics Ethereal Library. http://www.ccel.org/ccel/schaff/npnf201.html

Farrell, J. (2001). *Latin language and Latin culture from ancient to modern times.* Cambridge: Cambridge University Press.

Fast facts about American religion. (2014). Hartford Institute for Religion Research. http://hirr.hartsem.edu/research/fastfacts/fast_facts.html - sizecong

Favier, J. (1990). *The world of Chartres.* London: Thames and Hudson.

Finke, R., & Stark, R. (1988). Religious economies and sacred canopies: religious mobilization in American cities, 1906. *American Sociological Review*, 53(1), 41–49.

Finke, R., & Starke, R. (1992). *The churching of America 1776–1990: winners and losers in our religious economy*. New Brunswick, NJ: Rutgers University Press.

Finnegan, R. H. (1988). *Literacy and orality: studies in the technology of communication*. Oxford: Blackwell.

Fiskå Hägg, H. (2006). *Clement of Alexandria and the beginnings of Christian apophaticism*. Oxford: Oxford University Press.

Fortune, M. (1989). *Is nothing sacred? When sex invades the pastoral relationship*. San Francisco: Harper & Row.

Foucault, M. (1972). *Discourse on language*. New York: Pantheon Books.

Fox, R. L. (1994). Literacy and power in early Christianity. In A. K. Bowman & G. Woolf (Eds.), *Literacy and power in the ancient world* (pp. 126–148). Cambridge: Cambridge University Press.

Fredriksen, P. (1998). The martyrs. *From Jesus to Christ*. http://www.pbs.org/wgbh/pages/frontline/shows/religion/why/martyrs.html

Freedberg, D. (1989). *The power of images: studies in the history and theory of response*. Chicago: University of Chicago Press.

Freeman, C. (2002). *The closing of the western mind: the rise of faith and the fall of reason*. New York: Vintage Books.

Freeman, C. (2008). *A.D. 381: heretics, pagans and the dawn of the monotheistic state*. New York: The Overlook Press.

Fudge, T. (2011). Jan Hus at Calvary: the text of an early fifteenth-century *Passio*. *Journal of Moravian History*, 11(Fall), 45–81.

Gaehde, J. (1981). The rise of Christian art. In G. Barraclough (Ed.), *The Christian world: a social and cultural history of Christianity* (pp. 61–74). London: Thames and Hudson.

Gamble, H. Y. (1995). *Books and readers in the early church: a history of early Christian texts*. New Haven, CT: Yale University Press.

Ganoczy, A. (2004). Calvin's life (D. Foxgrover & J. Schmitt, Trans.). In D. McKim (Ed.), *The Cambridge companion to John Calvin* (pp. 3–24). Cambridge: Cambridge University Press.

Gerhardsson, B. (2005). The secret of the transmission of the unwritten Jesus tradition. *New Testament Studies*, 51, 1–18.

Gero, S. (1977). Byzantine iconoclasm and the failure of a medieval reformation. In J. Gutman (Ed.), *The image and the word: confrontations in Judaism, Christianity and Islam* (pp. 49–62). Missoula, MT: Scholars Press.

Gimpel, J. (1983). *The cathedral builders*. Salisbury, UK: Michael Russell Publishing.

Goh, D. P. S. (2010). State and social Christianity in post-colonial Singapore. *Journal of Social Issues in Southeast Asia*, 25(1), 54–89.

Good, D. (1992). Early extracanonical writings. In C. Newsom & S. Ringe (Eds.), *The women's bible commentary* (pp. 383–396). London: SPCK.

Graham-Dixon, A. (1996). *A history of British art* [Television series]. London: BBC.

Greeley, A. (1972). *Unsecular man: the persistence of religion*. New York: Schocken.

Green, D. H. (1994). *Medieval literacy and reading: the primary reception of German literature 800–1300*. Cambridge: Cambridge University Press.

Grossman, M. (1970). Wittenberg printing, early sixteenth century. In C. S. Meyer (Ed.), *Sixteenth century essays and studies* (Vol. 1, pp. 53–74). Saint Louis, MO: Foundation for Reformation Research.

Hadden, J., & Cowan, D. (Eds.). (2000). *Religion on the internet: research prospects and promises.* Amsterdam: Elsevier Science.

Haines-Eitzen, K. (2000). *Guardians of letters: literacy, power, and the transmission of early Christian literature.* Oxford: Oxford University Press.

Halsall, P. (1996). The correspondence of St. Boniface. *Internet Medieval Sourcebook.* http://www.fordham.edu/halsall/basis/boniface-letters.asp

Hamilton, G. (2013). Charlemagne and the vision of a Christian empire. *Northwest Religious Liberty Association.* http://www.nrla.com/article/30/academic-resources/history-s-lessons/charlemagne-and-the-vision-of-a-christian-empire

Harker, R., Mahar, C., & Wilkes, C. (Eds.). (1990). *An introduction to the work of Pierre Bourdieu.* London: Macmillan.

Harnack, A. (1893). *Outlines of the history of dogma.* London: Hodder & Stoughton.

Harnack, A. (1902). *What is Christianity?* New York: Harper Torchbooks.

Harvey, J. (1998). *Listening to the text: oral patterning in Paul's letters.* Grand Rapids, MI: Baker Books.

Haskins, C. (1902). Robert Le Bourge and the beginnings of the inquisition in northern France. *American Historical Review, 17*(4), 831–852.

Hastings, A. (1999). 150–550. In A. Hastings (Ed.), *A world history of Christianity* (pp. 25–65). London: Cassell.

Hatch, E. (1957). *The influence of Greek ideas on Christianity.* New York: Harper and Brothers Publishers. (Original work published in 1889)

Heather, P. (1994). Literacy and power in the migration period. In A. Bowman & G. Woolf (Eds.), *Literacy and power in the ancient world* (pp. 177–197). Cambridge: Cambridge University Press.

Hempton, D. (2005). *Methodism: empire of the spirit.* New Haven, CT: Yale University Press.

Hendershot, H. (2004). *Shaking the world for Jesus: media and conservative Evangelical culture.* Chicago: University of Chicago Press.

Herbst, M. (2007). "The pernicious effects of novel reading": the Methodist Episcopal campaign against American fiction, 1865–1914. *Journal of Religion and Society, 9,* 1–15.

Herklots, H. G. G. (1994). Discovering the oldest New Testaments. *Christian History, 43*(13, 3), 34–37.

Higman, F. (1996). *Piety and the people: religious printing in French, 1511–1551.* Aldershot, UK: Scolar Press.

Higman, F. (2000). Music. In A. Pettegree (Ed.), *The Reformation world* (pp. 491–504). London: Routledge.

Hippolytus. (215). The Apostolic Tradition. Rome.

Hjarvard, S. (2008a). The mediatization of religion: a theory of the media as agents of religious change. In S. Hjarvard (Ed.), *The mediatization of religion: enchantment, media and popular culture* (pp. 9–26). Bristol: Intellect.

Hjarvard, S. (2008b). The mediatization of society: a theory of the media as agents of social and cultural change. *Nordicom Review, 29*(2), 105–134.

Hjarvard, S. (2011). The mediatisation of religion: theorising religion, media and social change. *Culture and Religion, 12*(2), 119–135.

Hobbins, D. (2009). *Authorship and publicity before print: Jean Gerson and the transformation of late medieval learning*. Philadelphia: University of Pennsylvania Press.

Hoover, S. (1988). *Mass media religion: the social sources of the electronic church*. Newbury Park, CA: Sage.

Hoover, S. (1990). Ten myths about religious broadcasting. In R. Abelman & S. Hoover (Eds.), *Religious television: controversies and conclusions* (pp. 23–39). Norwood, NJ: Ablex.

Hoover, S. (2013). *Sabbatical report from Brazil*. Unpublished report.

Hoover, S., & Venturelli, S. S. (1996). The category of the religious: the blindspot of contemporary media theory. *Critical Studies in Mass Communication, 13*(3), 251ff.

Horsfield, P. (1984). *Religious television: the American experience*. New York: Longman.

Horsfield, P. (1992). Is the dam of sexual assault breaking on the church? *Australian Ministry* (May), 10–13.

Horsfield, P. (2013). The ecology of writing and the shaping of early Christianity. In K. Lundby (Ed.), *Media across religion: from early antiquity to late modernity*. New York: Peter Lang.

Horsfield, P., & Asamoah-Gyadu, K. (2011). What is it about the book? Semantic and material dimensions in the mediation of the Word of God. *Studies in World Christianity, 17*(2), 175–193.

Hurley, N. (1970). *Theology through film*. New York: Harper & Row.

Huschke, G. (2014). Huss, John, Hussites. http://www.ccel.org/s/schaff/encyc/encyc05/htm/huschke_georg_philipp_eduard.htm

Ignatius. (107). Epistle to the Romans. *Christian Classics Ethereal Library*. http://www.ccel.org/ccel/schaff/anf01.v.v.html

Innis, H. A. (1950). *Empire and communications*. Toronto: University of Toronto Press.

Innis, H. A. (1951). *The bias of communication*. Toronto: University of Toronto Press.

Irenaeus of Lyons. (180). Against heresies. *Early Christian Writings*. http://www.earlychristianwritings.com/irenaeus.html

Is bigger always better? (2014). *U.S. Congregational Life Survey*. http://www.uscongregations.org/blog/2014/02/17/is-bigger-always-better/

Jameson, F. (1991). *Postmodernism, or the cultural logic of late capitalism*. London: Duke University Press.

Janes, D. (1998). *God and gold in late antiquity*. Cambridge: Cambridge University Press.

Jenkins, P. (2008). *The lost history of Christianity: the thousand-year golden age of the church in the Middle East, Africa, and Asia – and how it died*. Oxford: Lion.

Jensen, R. (2006). Towards a Christian material culture. In M. Mitchell & F. Young (Eds.), *The Cambridge history of Christianity* (Vol. 1: *Origins to Constantine*, pp. 568–585). Cambridge: Cambridge University Press.

Jerome. Letters of St. Jerome. http://www.newadvent.org/fathers/3001.htm

Johnston, T. (2000). The Reformation and popular culture. In A. Pettegree (Ed.), *The Reformation world* (pp. 545–560). London: Routledge.

Jones, W. (1977). Art and Christian piety: iconoclasm in medieval Europe. In J. Gutman (Ed.), *The image and the word: confrontations in Judaism, Christianity and Islam* (pp. 75–106). Missoula, MT: Scholars Press.

Kahle, R. (1971). *Popcorn and parable: a new look at the movies.* Minneapolis, MN: Augsburg Publishing House.

Kamen, H. (1985). *Inquisition and society in Spain.* Bloomington: Indiana University Press.

Kay, W. (2011). *Pentecostalism.* Oxford: Oxford University Press.

Kay, W., & Dyer, A. (Eds.). (2004). *Pentecostal and Charismatic studies.* London: SCM Press.

Keen, M. (1986). The influence of Wyclif. In A. Kenny (Ed.), *Wyclif in his times* (pp. 127–146). Oxford: Clarendon Press.

Keenan, M. *Child sexual abuse and the Catholic Church: gender, power and organizational culture.* Oxford: Oxford University Press.

Kernan, A. (1987). *Printing technology, letters and Samuel Johnson.* Princeton, NJ: Princeton University Press.

Kim, K. (2007). Ethereal Christianity: reading Korean mega-church websites. *Studies in World Christianity, 13*(3), 208–224.

Kimber Buell, D. (1999). *Making Christians: Clement of Alexandria and the rhetoric of legitimacy.* Princeton, NJ: Princeton University Press.

Kirby, D. (2013). *Fantasy and belief: alternative religions, popular narratives and digital cultures.* Cambridge: Acumen Publishing.

Knowles, A., & Penkett, P. (2004). *Augustine and his world.* Oxford: Lion.

Kosto, A. (2005). Laymen, clerics, and documentary practices in the early Middle Ages: the example of Catalonia. *Speculum, 80*(1), 44–74.

Kuhn, E.-M. (2007). Justice applied by the episcopal arbitrator: Augustine and the implementation of divine justice. *Ethics and Politics, 9*(2), 71–104.

Küng, H. (1994). *Christianity: the religious situation of our time.* London: SCM.

Küng, H. (2001). *Women in Christianity* (J. Bowden, Trans.). London: Continuum.

Lambert, F. (1994). *Pedlar in divinity: George Whitfield and the transatlantic revivals, 1737–1770.* Princeton, NJ: Princeton University Press.

Landow, G. (1992). *Hypertext: the convergence of contemporary critical theory and technology.* Baltimore: Johns Hopkins University Press.

Lane, T. (1994). The crown of English Bibles. *Christian History, 13*(3), 6–11.

Lavington, G. (1749). *The enthusiasm of Methodists and Papists compared* (2nd ed.). London: J & P Knapton.

Lawrence, C. H. (1984). *Medieval monasticism: forms of religious life in western Europe in the Middle Ages.* London: Longman.

Lehmann, D. (1996). *Struggle for the Spirit: religious transformation and popular culture in Brazil and Latin America.* Cambridge: Polity.

Lerner, R. E. (2010). Early bestseller. *The Times Literary Supplement,* (5571), 25. http://search.proquest.com/docview/234329212?accountid=13552

Levine, A.-J. (2006). Introduction. In A.-J. Levine, D. Allison, & J. D. Crossan (Eds.), *The historical Jesus in context* (pp. 1–39). Princeton, NJ: Princeton University Press.

Lewis, J. (2005). *Language wars: the role of media and culture in global and political violence*. London: Pluto Press.

Ling, T. (1968). *A history of religion east and west: an introduction and an interpretation*. London: Macmillan.

Linnemann, E. (1966). *Parables of Jesus: introduction and exposition*. London: SPCK.

Lloyd, S. (1995). The crusading movement, 1096–1274. In J. Riley-Smith (Ed.), *The Oxford illustrated history of the crusades* (pp. 34–65). Oxford: Oxford University Press.

Loos, M. (1974). *Dualist heresy in the Middle Ages* (Vol. 10). Prague: Springer.

Lotz-Heumann, U. (2013). Confessionalization. In A. Bamji, G. Janssen, & M. Laven (Eds.), *The Ashgate research companion to the Counter-Reformation* (pp. 33–54). Farnham, UK: Ashgate Publishing Ltd.

Loughlin, J. (1907). St. Ambrose. *New Advent*. New York: Robert Appleton Company. http://www.newadvent.org/cathen/01383c.htm

Loyn, H. R., & Percival, J. (1975). *The reign of Charlemagne: documents on Carolingian government and administration*. London: Edward Arnold.

Lundby, K. (1997). The web of collective representations. In S. Hoover & K. Lundby (Eds.), *Rethinking media, religion and culture* (pp. 146–164). Thousand Oaks, CA: Sage.

Luther, M. (1518). Letter to Pope Leo X, accompanying the "resolutions" to the XCV theses (C. M. Jacobs, Trans.). In M. McDermott (Ed.), *Works of Martin Luther with introductions and notes* (Vol. 1). Project Gutenberg EBook.

Luther, M. (1545). Preface to the complete edition of Luther's Latin works. *Modern history sourcebook*. New York: Fordham University. http://www.fordham.edu/Halsall/mod/1519luther-tower.asp

Luttikhuizen, H. (2005). The place of the sacred: Islamic and Christian visual cultures in medieval Spain. *Christian Scholar's Review, 34*(4), 463–485.

Lynch, G. (Ed.). (2007). *Between sacred and profane: research religion and popular culture*. London: I. B. Taurus.

MacCulloch, D. (2009). *A history of Christianity: the first three thousand years*. London: Penguin.

Maddocks, F. (2001). *Hildegard of Bingen: the woman of her age*. New York: Image Books/Doubleday.

Malone, M. (2001). *Women and Christianity* (Vol. 2: *The medieval period: AD 1,000–1,500*). Dublin: Columba Press.

Marsden, G. (Ed.). (1984). *Evangelicalism and modern America*. Grand Rapids, MI: W. B. Eerdmans.

Martin, D. (1969). *The religious and the secular*. London: Routledge and Kegan Paul.

Martin, H.-J. (1994). *The history and power of writing* (L. G. Cochrane, Trans.). Chicago: University of Chicago Press.

Marty, M. (1961). *The improper opinion: mass media and the Christian faith*. Philadelphia: Westminster Press.

Marty, M. (1989). The social context of the modern paradigm in theology: a church historian's view. In H. Küng & D. Tracy (Eds.), *Paradigm change in theology* (pp. 174–201). New York: Crossroad.

Marvin, C. (1988). *When old technologies were new: thinking about electric communication in the late nineteenth century*. Oxford: Oxford University Press.

Matthews, G. (2006). Post-medieval Augustianism. In E. Stump & N. Kretzmann (Eds.), *The Cambridge companion to Augustine* (Cambridge Companions Online ed., pp. 267–279). Cambridge: Cambridge University Press.

Maurer, S. (2009). A historical overview of American Christian Fundamentalism in the twentieth century. In S. Hoover & N. Kaneva (Eds.), *Fundamentalisms and the media* (pp. 54–72). London: Continuum.

Maxwell, D. (1998). "Delivered from the spirit of poverty"? Pentecostalism, prosperity and modernity in Zimbabwe. *Journal of Religion in Africa*, 28(3), 350–373.

McComb, M. (2004). *Setting the agenda: the mass media and public opinion.* Cambridge: Polity Press.

McDannell, C. (1995). *Material Christianity: religion and popular culture in America.* New Haven, CT: Yale University Press.

McKitterick, R. (1994). *Books, scribes and learning in the Frankish kingdoms, 6th–9th centuries.* Aldershot: Variorum.

McLoughlin, W. G. (1978). *Revivals, awakenings and reforms.* Chicago: University of Chicago Press.

McLuhan, M., & Fiore, Q. (1967). *The medium is the massage.* New York: Random House.

McLynn, N. (1994). *Ambrose of Milan: church and court in a Christian capital.* Berkeley: University of California Press.

Meeks, W. (1998). The martyrs. *From Jesus to Christ.* http://www.pbs.org/wgbh/pages/frontline/shows/religion/why/martyrs.html

Meeks, W. (2006). Social and ecclesial life of the earliest Christians. In M. Mitchell & F. Young (Eds.), *The Cambridge history of Christianity* (Vol. 1: *Origins to Constantine*, pp. 145–173). Cambridge: Cambridge University Press.

Mendels, D. (1999). *The media revolution of early Christianity: an essay on Eusebius's Ecclesiastical History.* Grand Rapids, MI: Wm. B. Eerdmans.

Methuen, C. (2000). Science and medicine. In A. Pettegree (Ed.), *The Reformation world* (pp. 521–534). London: Routledge.

Meyer, B. (1998). Commodities and the power of prayer: Pentecostalist attitudes towards consumption in contemporary Ghana. *Development and change*, 29, 751–776.

Meyer, B. (2006). *Religious sensations: why media, aesthetics and power matter in the study of contemporary religion.* Amsterdam: Vrije Universiteit.

Meyer, B. (2011). Mediation and immediacy: sensational forms, semiotic ideologies and the question of the medium. *Social Anthropology*, 19(1), 23–39.

Meyer, B. (2012). Material religion – how things matter. In D. Hourman & B. Meyer (Eds.), *Things: religion and the question of materiality.* New York: Fordham University Press.

Meyer, B., & Moors, A. (Eds.). (2006). *Religion, media and the public sphere.* Bloomington: Indiana University Press.

Micklethwait, J., & Wooldridge, A. (2009). *God is back: how the global revival of faith is changing the world.* New York: Penguin Press.

Miles, M. (1985). *Image as insight: visual understanding in western Christianity and secular culture.* Boston: Beacon Press.

Millard, A. (2000). *Reading and writing in the time of Jesus.* Sheffield: Sheffield Acaddemic Press.

Miller, P. C. (2009). *The corporeal imagination: signifying the holy in late ancient Christianity*. Philadelphia: University of Pennsylvania Press.

Miller, S. M. (1994). Mavericks and misfits. *Christian History, 13*(3), 18–21.

Mitchell, M. (2006). The emergence of the written record. In M. Mitchell & F. Young (Eds.), *The Cambridge history of Christianity* (Vol. 1: *Origins to Constantine*, pp. 177–194). Cambridge: Cambridge University Press.

Moltmann-Wendel, E. (1982). *The women around Jesus*. New York: Crossroad Publishing Company.

Moorehead, J. (1999). *Ambrose: church and society in the late Roman world*. London: Longman.

Morgan, D. (N.d.). *A forest of images: print culture, modernity and religion*. Unpublished manuscript.

Morgan, D. (1998). *Visual piety: a history and theory of popular religious images*. Berkeley: University of California Press.

Morgan, D. (2005). *The sacred gaze: religious visual culture in theory and practice*. Berkeley: University of California Press.

Morgan, D. (2008). *Key words in religion media and culture*. New York: Routledge.

Morgan, D. (2010a). The material culture of lived religion: visuality and embodiment. In J. Vakkari (Ed.), *Mind and matter: selected papers of Nordic Conference 2009* (pp. 14–31). Helsinki: Society of Art History.

Morgan, D. (2011). Mediation or mediatisation: the history of media in the study of culture and religion. *Culture and Religion, 12*(2), 137–152.

Morgan, D. (2014). Noah: story and medium. *The Revealer,* April 17, 2014. http://therevealer.org/archives/19252

Morgan, D. (Ed.). (2010b). *Religion and material culture: the matter of belief*. London: Routledge.

Moss, C. (2013). *The myth of persecution: how early Christianity invented a story of martyrdom*. New York: HarperCollins.

Munro, D. C. (1906). The speech of Pope Urban II at Clermont, 1095. *American Historical Review, 11*(2), 231–242.

Naphy, W. (2004). Calvin's Geneva. In D. McKim (Ed.), *The Cambridge companion to John Calvin* (pp. 25–37). Cambridge: Cambridge University Press.

Neill, S. (1966). *Colonialism and Christian missions*. London: Lutterworth Press.

Neill, S. (1986). *A history of Christian missions* (Rev. ed.). London: Penguin Books.

Nelson, T. (1992). *Literary machines 91.1: the report on, and of, Project Xanadu concerning word processing, electronic publishing, hypertext, thinkertoys, tomorrow's intellectual revolution, and certain other topics including knowledge, education and freedom*. Sausalito, CA: Mindful Press.

Niebuhr, H. R. (1951). *Christ and culture*. New York: Harper and Row.

Nolan, M. L., & Nolan, S. (1989). *Christian pilgrimage in modern western Europe*. Chapel Hill: University of North Carolina Press.

Norton, D. (2011). *The King James Bible: a short history from Tyndale to today*. Cambridge: Cambridge University Press.

O'Donnell, J. (2006). Augustine: his life and times. In E. Stump & N. Kretzmann (Eds.), *The Cambridge companion to Augustine* (Cambridge Companions Online ed., pp. 8–25). Cambridge: Cambridge University Press.

Ong, W. (1967). *The presence of the word; some prolegomena for cultural and religious history.* New Haven, CT: Yale University Press.

Ong, W. (1982). *Orality and literacy: the technologizing of the word.* London: Methuen.

Osborn, E. (1959). Teaching and writing in the first chapter of the Stromateis of Clement of Alexandria. *Journal of Theological Studies,* 10, 335–343.

Osiek, C., Macdonald, M., & Tulloch, J. (2006). *A woman's place: house churches in earliest Christianity.* Minneapolis, MN: Fortress Press.

Palacky, F. (1869). Documenta Magistri Johannis Hus vitam, doctrinam, causam. In F. Palacky (Ed.), *Constantiensi Concilio actam illustrantia.* Prague.

Palladius. (1985). Dialogues. In R. Meyer (Ed.), *Palladius: dialogue on the life of St. John Chrysostom.* New York: Newman Press.

Pallares-Burke, M. L. (2002). *The new history.* Cambridge: Polity Press.

Peters, E. (1988). *Inquisition.* New York: Free Press.

Pettegree, A. (2000). *Art.* In A. Pettegree (Ed.), *The Reformation world* (pp. 461–490). London: Routledge.

Pettegree, A. (2005). *Reformation and the culture of persuasion.* Cambridge: Cambridge University Press.

Pettegree, A. (2010). *The book in the Renaissance.* New Haven, CT: Yale University Press.

Pettegree, A. (2013). Catholic pamphleteering. In A. Bamji, G. Janssen, & M. Laven (Eds.), *The Ashgate research companion to the Counter-Reformation* (pp. 109–126). Farnham, UK: Ashgate Publishing Ltd.

Philip, T. V. (N.d.). The missionary impulse in the early Asian Christian tradition. *PTCA Bulletin,* 5–14.

Phillips, J. (2007). *The Second Crusade: extending the frontiers of Christendom.* New Haven, CT: Yale University Press.

Plate, S. B. (2014). *A history of religion in 5½ objects: bringing the spiritual to its senses.* Boston: Beacon Press.

Pohlman, M. E. (2011). *Broadcasting the faith: Protestant religious radio and theology in America, 1920–1950.* PhD dissertation, Southern Baptist Theological Seminary.

Pope Alexander VI. (1493). The Bull Inter Caetera. *Native Web: Resources for Indigenous Culture around the World.* http://www.nativeweb.org/pages/legal/indig-inter-caetera.html

Pope Nicholas V. (1455). The Bull Romanus Pontifex. *Native Web: Resources for Indigenous Culture around the World.* http://www.nativeweb.org//pages/legal/indig-romanus-pontifex.html

Possamai, A. (2003). Alternative spiritualities and the cultural logic of late capitalism. *Culture and Religion,* 4(1), 31–45.

Possamai, A. (2005). *In search of New Age spiritualities.* London: Ashgate.

Postman, N. (1987). *Amusing ourselves to death.* London: Methuen.

Potter, R. (1996). The auto da fé as medieval drama. In M. Twycross (Ed.), *Festive drama: papers from the Sixth Triennial Colloquium of the International Society for the Study of Medieval Theatre* (pp. 110–118). Cambridge: Boydell & Brewer.

Powell, M. (1998). *The Jesus debate: modern historians investigate the life of Christ.* Oxford: Lion.

Prescott, J. E. (1886). *Christian hymns and hymn writers: a course of lectures*. Cambridge: Deighton, Bell and Co.

Pusey, E. B. (1857). *The councils of the church from the Council of Jerusalem A.D. 51 to the Council of Constantinople A.D. 381*. Oxford: John Henry Parker.

Putnam, G. (1906). *The censorship of the Church of Rome and its influence upon the production and distribution of literature*. New York: G. P. Putnam's Sons.

Reuther, R. R. (1993). *Sexism and God-talk: toward a feminist theology*. Boston: Beacon Press.

Richards, E. R. (2004). *Paul and first-century letter writing: secretaries, composition and collection*. Downers Grove, IL: InterVarsity Press.

Riché, P. (1978). *Daily life in the world of Charlemagne* (J. A. McNamara, Trans.). Philadelphia: University of Pennsylvania Press.

Riley-Smith, J. (1986). *The First Crusade and the idea of crusading*. London: Continuum.

Riley-Smith, J. (1995a). The crusading movement and historians. In J. Riley-Smith (Ed.), *The Oxford illustrated history of the Crusades* (pp. 1–12). Oxford: Oxford University Press.

Riley-Smith, J. (Ed.). (1995b). *The Oxford illustrated history of the Crusades*. Oxford: Oxford University Press.

Roetzel, C. (1997). *Paul: the man and the myth*. Edinburgh: T & T Clark.

Rooney, J. (2011). Visual and cultural mutations of the miraculous image: the role of religious pareidolia in shrine formation. PhD dissertation, University of South Australia, Adelaide.

Rosenthal, M. (2007). *American Protestants and TV in the 1950s: responses to a new medium*. New York: Palgrave Macmillan.

Sawhney, H. (1996). Information superhighway: metaphors as midwives. *Media, Culture and Society, 18*, 291–314.

Sawicki, M. (1994). *Seeing the Lord: resurrection and early Christian practice*. Minneapolis, MN: Fortress.

Schaberg, J. (1992). Luke. In C. A. Newsom & R. Ringe (Eds.), *The women's bible commentary* (pp. 275–292). London: SPCK.

Schaff, P. (1893). *History of the Christian church: modern Christianity: The Swiss Reformation* (2 vols.). Edinburgh: T & T Clark.

Schaff, P. (1894). Ulphilas. In P. Schaff (Ed.), *A religious encyclopaedia or dictionary of biblical, historical, doctrinal, and practical theology* (3rd ed., Vol. 4, p. 2416). Toronto: Funk & Wagnalls Company.

Schaff, P. (Ed.). (1890). *Eusebius Pamphilus: the life of Constantine* (2nd ed., Vol. 1). Edinburgh: T & T Clark.

Schillebeeckx, E. (1989). *Jesus: an experiment in Christology*. New York: HarperCollins.

Schussler Fiorenza, E. (1983). *In memory of her: a feminist theological reconstruction of Christian origins*. London: SCM.

Schweizer, E. (1991). *A theological introduction to the New Testament* (O. C. Dean, Jr., Trans.). Nashville, TN: Abingdon Press.

Sconce, J. (2000). *Haunted media: electronic presence from telegraphy to television*. Durham, NC: Duke University Press.

Scott, J. C. (1990). *Domination and the arts of resistance: hidden transcripts*. New Haven, CT: Yale University Press.

Scribner, R. W. (1994). *For the sake of simple folk: popular propaganda for the German Reformation*. Oxford: Oxford University Press.

Seaton, J. (2005). *Carnage and the media: the making and breaking of news about violence*. London: Allen Lane.

Shlain, L. (1998). *The alphabet and the goddess: the conflict between word and image*. New York: Viking.

Smith, J. (1999). Islam and Christendom. In J. Esposito (Ed.), *The Oxford history of Islam* (pp. 305–346). Oxford: Oxford University Press.

Spender, D. (1995). *Nattering on the net: women, power and cyberspace*. Melbourne: Spinifex Press.

Stancliffe, D. (2008). *The Lion companion to church architecture*. Oxford: Lion Hudson plc.

Stark, R. (1996). *The rise of Christianity: a sociologist reconsiders history*. Princeton, NJ: Princeton University Press.

Ste. Croix, G. E. M. d. (1981). *The class struggle in the ancient Greek world*. London: Gerald Duckworth.

Stegemann, E., & Stegemann, W. (1995). *The Jesus Movement: a social history of its first century*. Minneapolis, MN: Fortress Press.

Stolow, J. (2005). Religion and/or media. *Theory, Culture and Society*, 22(4), 119–145.

Stolow, J. (2007). Electricity and seance practice in the case of spiritualism. In H. De Vries (Ed.), *Why religion?* (Vol. 1). New York: Fordham University Press.

Stolow, J. (Ed.). (2013). *Deus in machina: religion, technology, and the things in between*. New York: Fordham University Press.

Sumption, J. (1975). *Pilgrimage: an image of medieval religion*. London: Faber and Faber.

Sutton, M. (2007). *Aimee Semple McPherson and the resurrection of Christian America*. Cambridge, MA: Harvard University Press.

Swatos, W. (1999). Secularization theory: the course of a concept. *Sociology of Religion*, 60(3), 209–228.

Tabor, J. (2012). *Paul and Jesus: how the apostle transformed Christianity*. New York: Simon & Schuster.

Tadmor, N. (2010). *The social universe of the English Bible: scripture, society and culture in early modern England*. Cambridge: Cambridge University Press.

Tamez, E. (2007). *Struggles for power in early Christianity: a study of the First Letter to Timothy* (G. Kinsler, Trans.). Maryknoll, NY: Orbis Books.

Tapsell, K. (2014). *Potiphar's wife: the Vatican's secret and child abuse*. Adelaide, SA: ATF Press.

Taylor, C. (2007). *A secular age*. Cambridge, MA: Belknap Press of Harvard University Press.

Taylor, J. (1977). Progeny of programmers: evangelical religion and the television age. *The Christian Century*, 379–382.

Tertullian. (c. 197). Apologeticum. *New Advent*. http://www.newadvent.org/fathers/0301.htm

Tertullian. (203). The acts of Perpetua and Felicitas. *Early Christian Writings*. http://www.earlychristianwritings.com/actsperpetua.html

Theissen, G. (2003). *The New Testament* (J. Bowden, Trans.). London: T & T Clark.

Theissen, G. (2012). *Die Jesusbewegung. Sozialgeschichte einer revolution der werte.* Gütersloh, Germany: Gütersloher Verlagshaus.

Thompson, E. P. (1963). *The making of the English working class.* New York: Vintage Books.

Tillotson, D. (2006). The practice of writing in the Middle Ages. *Medieval Writing.* http://medievalwriting.50megs.com/literacy/writing.htm

Tomkins, S. (2005). *A short history of Christianity.* Oxford: Lion Hudson.

Tompkins, P. (1981). *The magic of obelisks.* New York: Harper & Row.

Toulmin, S. (1990). *Cosmopolis: the hidden agenda of modernity.* New York: Free Press.

Turner, V., & Turner, E. (1978). *Image and pilgrimage in Christian culture: anthropological perspectives.* New York: Columbia University Press.

Vallikatt, J. (2014). *Virtually religious: myth, ritual and community in World of Warcraft.* PhD dissertation, RMIT University, Melbourne.

van der Meer, F. (1961). *Augustine the bishop: the life and work of a father of the church.* London: Sheed and Ward.

Vatican, T. (2014). History of the Vatican Library. http://www.vatlib.it/home.php?pag=storia

von Campenhausen, H. (1960). *The fathers of the Latin church.* London: Adan & Charles Black.

Wagner, R. (2012). *Godwired: religion, ritual and virtual reality.* London: Routledge.

Walker, W. (1959). *History of the Christian Church.* Edinburgh: T & T Clark.

Wallis, J. (2009). *God's politics: why the right gets it wrong and the left doesn't get it.* San Francisco: Harper.

Ward, J. O. (2000). Alexandria and its medieval legacy: the book, the monk and the rose. In R. Macleod (Ed.), *The library of Alexandria: centre of learning in the ancient world* (pp. 163–179). London: I. B. Tauris.

Watson, N. (1994). "The philosopher should bathe and brush his teeth" – congruence between word and deed in Graeco-Roman philosophy and Paul's Letters to the Corinthians. *Australian Biblical Review, 42,* 1–16.

Weber, M. (1930). *The Protestant ethic and the spirit of capitalism* (Taylor and Francis e-library, 2005 ed.). London: Routledge.

Weber, M. (1968). *Economy and society: an outline of interpretive sociology* (Vol. 1). New York: Bedminster Press.

Wertheim, M. (1999). *The pearly gates of cyberspace: a history of space from Dante to the internet.* Sydney: Doubleday.

Wesley, J. (1933). Preface to a collection of hymns for use of the people called Methodists. In *The Methodist Hymn Book for use in Australasia and New Zealand* (pp. v–vi). London: Methodist Conference Office. (Original work published in 1779)

Wessel, S. (2008). *Leo the Great and the spiritual rebuilding of a universal Rome.* Leiden: Brill.

White, L. M. (2004). *From Jesus to Christianity: how four generations of visionaries and storytellers created the New Testament and Christian faith.* New York: Harper San Francisco.

Wiles, M. (2005). Church fathers. In J. Bowden (Ed.), *Christianity: the complete guide* (pp. 243–265). London: Continuum.

Willis, P., & Maarouf, M. (2010). The Islamic spirit of capitalism: Moroccan Islam and its transferable cultural schemas and values. *Journal of Religion and Popular Culture*, 22(3), 1–45.

Wilson, B. (2008). *How Jesus became Christian: the early Christians and the transformation of a Jewish teacher into the Son of God*. London: Phoenix.

Wood, I. (1981). The conversion of the barbarian peoples. In G. Barraclough (Ed.), *The Christian world* (pp. 85–98). London: Thames and Hudson.

Woodhead, L. (2004). *An introduction to Christianity*. Cambridge: Cambridge University Press.

Woodhead, L. (2014). *Christianity: a very short introduction* (2nd ed.). Oxford: Oxford University Press.

Wright, N. T. (2005). *Paul: fresh perspectives*. London: SPCK.

Wuthnow, R. (1993). *Christianity in the twenty-first century: reflections on the challenges ahead*. New York: Oxford University Press.

Yang, F. (2005). Lost in the market, saved at McDonald's: conversion to Christianity in urban China. *Journal for the Scientific Study of Religion*, 44(4), 423–441.

Index

From Jesus to the Internet, Peter Horsfield © 2015 John Wiley & Sons, Ltd. Published 2015 by John Wiley
& Sons, Ltd.